LAND, PIETY, PEOPLEHOOD

The Mennonite Experience in America, Volume 1

Land, Piety, Peoplehood

THE ESTABLISHMENT OF
MENNONITE COMMUNITIES IN AMERICA
1683-1790

Richard K. MacMaster

HERALD PRESS
Scottdale, Pennsylvania
Kitchener, Ontario
1985

Library of Congress Cataloging in Publication Data

MacMaster, Richard K. (Richard Kerwin), 1935-
Land, piety, peoplehood.

(The Mennonite experience in America; v. 1)
Bibliography: p.
Includes index.
1. Mennonites—United States—History. 2. Mennonites
—Doctrines. I. Title. II. Series.
BX8116.M46   vol. 1   289.7'73 s [289.7'73]   84-15790
ISBN 0-8361-1261-X (pbk.)

On the cover: **The Conestoga wagon, with distinctive
double ends and heavy wheels, originated before 1750 in
Mennonite settlements in the Connestoga Valley of
Lancaster County, Pa., and quickly became a common
sight.** (Jan Gleysteen collection)

LAND, PIETY, PEOPLEHOOD
Copyright © 1985 by Herald Press, Scottdale, Pa. 15683
    Published simultaneously in Canada by Herald Press,
    Kitchener, Ont. N2G 4M5
Library of Congress Catalog Card Number: 84-15790
International Standard Book Number: 0-8361-1261-X
Printed in the United States of America
Design by David Hiebert

90 89 88 87 86 85 10 9 8 7 6 5 4 3 2 1

FOR EVE

CONTENTS

SERIES INTRODUCTION

In 1683 when the story of the Mennonite experience in America began, there was no American nation. Mennonites, Amish, and other groups whose faiths descended from sixteenth-century Anabaptism dwelt then in many places: alpine communities in Switzerland, towns along the Rhine, the polders of Holland, Hutterian communities in Moravia, lands reclaimed along the Vistula. Other persons in 1683 whose descendants would later claim the name Mennonite lived in tribal villages in West Africa, on the estates of conquerors in Old Mexico, on the mesas of the Sangre de Cristo. In these three hundred years as America has become a pluralistic nation, the stories of these diverse peoples have converged to form the Mennonite experience in America.

Mennonites and their kinfolks, the Amish, came to the New World at different times, for different reasons, and spoke different languages and dialects. Many carried in their memories the pain of persecution. Their cultures and even their church patterns and practices were not one but many. Gradually, however, they discovered each other and sensed their kinship. Tentatively and cautiously they began to work together in common tasks and to share a common pilgrimage. Often they found each other in times of national crisis and war. Inescapably the Mennonite experience has been bound intimately with the encompassing life of this emerging nation.

As have many other American groups, Mennonites eventually began to ask who they were as a people. They searched for their "identity" and "mission." To this end they began to tell their stories, often in fragmented and provincial ways. More recently, however, they have become aware that these separate histories are one interwoven story, a story intricately bonded with national history. Among them have arisen historians, schooled in the scholarly disciplines, prepared to give an account of these people, recognizing not only achievements but also dilemmas and failures. They offer not so much a denominational history, from the records of conferences and institutions, as a history of a people in all its rich variety. For Mennonites history has always been a statement of faith—the tracing of the ways of God with his people. Further, it is the intention of this history that it be one of disciplined integrity so that both shadow and light may be seen in the portrait.

In four volumes, the *Mennonite Experience in America* series savors the meaning of three hundred years of Mennonite history in a new world. Yet its authors tell not only of Mennonites, but also of America. They invite readers to relive the human perplexities, occasionally the anguish, and at other times the joy of a people of paradox and promise. Mennonites once lived separated from their neighbors, sometimes painfully so, and yet never really separated. Thus this series is a call to a dialogue, an invitation to further research, criticism, and revision both of this and other histories. These volumes are an invitation to come read, learn tales never before told, and reflect on the story of the Mennonites through three centuries of emerging nationhood.

      Robert Kreider
      Chairperson, Editorial Committee
      The Mennnoite Experience in America
      Bethel College
      North Newton, Kansas
      February 1983

EDITOR'S FOREWORD

AD 1983 marks three hundred years of ongoing Mennonite settlement in North America, but the publication of Richard MacMaster's book is more than the celebration of a moment. In the last two or three decades writers of American history have looked more and more to people's religious beliefs, identities, and motivations as a way to explain economic or political behavior, family and neighborhood life, ethnicity, and other matters. That trend fits with another, that of looking at the U.S. nation and its history at least partly through the eyes of minorities and of the powerless. These trends open new opportunities for telling the stories of particular religious groups. The Mennonite Experience in America series tells its story within the setting of the American nation, and in turn suggests what its story tells about that nation.

Careful work on the American part of the Mennonite and Amish story lags behind some other Mennonite studies. Two generations ago a new burst of historical research brought a thorough reevaluation of sixteenth-century Anabaptism. Out of those and other new efforts came *The Mennonite Quarterly Review, The Mennonite Encyclopedia*, and various other publications and series that now enjoy broad international reputations. High quality research and writing especially about sixteenth-century Anabaptism continues to flow from both Mennonites and other writers and from both Mennonite and non-Mennonite colleges, universities, seminaries, and presses. Meanwhile, here and there, some excellent writings have come forth on Mennonites and Amish in America, also; yet, the New World part of the story has not matured along with the Anabaptist part.

Audiences have matured. Not only have American historians showed renewed interest in religious history, but many Mennonites themselves are ready for something more. With the tricentennial of Mennonite settlement in North America at hand, quite a few have said they need a new history. That history should neither dwell too much on development of church organization and institutions, nor stop with tales only of Mennonite faithfulness and heroism. Instead of presenting Mennonites primarily as a "denomination" it must treat them, both religiously and socially, as a people. It must tell how their communities took shape and changed and operated, and how they have related to their neighbors. It must examine patterns of Mennonite wealth and how wealth has related to social and religious outlook and behavior.

The new history must study, for example, whether Amish and Mennonite attitudes toward blacks, native Americans, and other specific groups have been typically American, or different. It must tell how Mennonites have acculturated, both to their immediate local surroundings and to national attitudes and beliefs. It must use sources honestly and with discernment, examining a wide range of questions, some of which come from within Mennonite experience, others of which come from the best of American history scholarship. And it must tell of inner dilemmas and failures as well as of Mennonite faithfulness and successes. Such is the task, a task with promise for readers interested in Mennonite history and those interested in national history.

The task is one not only for researchers, authors, and editors. Members of an Editorial Committee—Robert Kreider as chairman, Cornelius J. Dyck, Leonard Gross, Peter J. Klassen, John A. Lapp, Wesley Prieb, and Willard Swartley, plus the editor—have contributed many hours as the project's governing body, as have numerous persons with whom they have consulted all along the way. Other very helpful persons have given substantial, direct financial support: Paul and Barbara Detweiler, C. J. and Wilma Dyck, John E. Fretz, Merle and Phyllis Good, David Groh, Walton Hackman, Gerald and Gwen Hartzel, Dwight and Ellen Hartman, Albert and Leanna Keim, Robert and Lois Kreider, Horace Longacre, Michael Loss, Richard and Betty Pellman, Herbert Regier, John and Rebecca Rutt, Edward C. Snyder, Will Stoltz, Carolyn C. Wenger, and Lloyd Zeager.

Other persons have contributed through organizations, some of which have provided sizable grants: the Commission on Education of the General Conference Mennonite Church, the Schowalter Foundation, Mennonite Central Committee,

Mennonite Mutual Aid, Goodville Mutual Insurance Company, the Franconia Conference of the Mennonite Church, Mennonite Biblical Seminary, Mennonite Historical Society, Eastern Mennonite Associated Libraries and Archives, the two Centers for Mennonite Brethren Studies at Pacific and Tabor colleges, Lancaster Mennonite Historical Society, Illinois Mennonite Historical and Genealogical Society, Virginia Mennonite Conference, Iowa Mennonite Historical Society, and Mennonite Historians of Eastern Pennsylvania.

James Madison University and Goshen College have contributed directly by providing the author and the editor respectively with office space, plus various research, clerical, and other services and direct research funds. And the project is organized under the Institute of Mennonite Studies, affiliated with Associated Mennonite Biblical Seminaries at Elkhart, Indiana, with the Institute providing various financial and scholarly services. Without such fine support, the task could not go forward.

Richard MacMaster's book is a good beginning. One of MacMaster's specialties is to study public tax and land-ownership records and in so doing to reconstruct a community's spatial, economic, and social patterns. Thus he has been able to tell much about the shape of eighteenth-century Mennonite communities in southeastern Pennsylvania and down the routes of migration into Maryland and the Shenandoah Valley of Virginia. Also, MacMaster is an accomplished editor and interpreter of documents that indicate the relations between pacifists and government in the American revolution; and that expertise shapes the latter chapters of this book. Other sections deal richly with congregational and community life and especially tell how Mennonites, as part of a larger Pennsylvania-German community, shared with others a common dialect, much common history, and the religious language of continental Pietism.

MacMaster has not given the final word. He could not, in three hundred pages, nor is the last word this series' purpose. His volume, and the three others to come, will perform their task only if they stimulate more new questions, new investigations, and other interesting writing. But

MacMaster is offering both an inner and an outer history of Mennonite life in colonial and revolutionary America. He both tells the Mennonites' own story, and makes clear how the group interacted with larger national history and development.

Theron F. Schlabach, Editor
The Mennonite Experience in America
Goshen College
February 1983

AUTHOR'S PREFACE

All good scholarship is a cooperative venture, and Mennonite scholarship perhaps especially so. "Basic to the Anabaptist vision of the church was the insistence on the practice of true brotherhood," the leading historical theologian of the Mennonite Church in the twentieth century, Harold S. Bender, declared in his classic address on "The Anabaptist Vision." And, said he, Anabaptists meant "not merely the expression of pious sentiments, but the actual practice of sharing possessions to meet the needs of others." It is most appropriate, then, that the writing of this book on Mennonite history has been a community effort.

Many of my fellow scholars went far beyond mere words of encouragement, to share freely of their knowledge and their time. Theron F. Schlabach gave much more of himself to this book than normally expected of an editor, as he challenged interpretations, oversaw the checking of elusive footnotes, and served as the power behind the drone. Cornelius J. Dyck helped strengthen especially the first chapter with his insight and historical knowledge of pre-eighteenth-century European Mennonite history. From their expertise Donald F. Durnbaugh, Robert Kreider, Carolyn Charles Wenger, Grace Showalter, and Robert Ulle, after reading the entire manuscript, each suggested important changes for the final draft. In more than one way, Joseph Miller and John L. Ruth also provided brotherly aid.

The competence and enthusiasm of numerous librarians and archivists made the hours of research fruitful and profitable. At the Menno Simons Historical Library of Eastern Mennonite College Grace Showalter, Lois Bowman, and James O. Lehman put their resources freely at my disposal, even during vacations and other off hours. Carolyn Charles Wenger, Lois Ann Zook Mast, and other staff members welcomed and aided me at the Lancaster Mennonite Historical Society, Lancaster, Pennsylvania—where Noah H. Good also offered his enthusiasm for research and his translations of eighteenth-century manuscripts. Joseph Miller, at the Eastern Pennsylvania Mennonite Historical Library, housed at Christopher Dock High School near Lans-

15

dale, Pennsylvania, helped me find numerous pertinent manuscripts, while Leonard Gross and Elizabeth Horsch Bender gave many hours to translating documents from the Archives of the Mennonite Church at Goshen, Indiana. Leonard Gross was another who read my entire manuscript, and offered valuable suggestions.

Giving invaluable assistance to my research into Pennsylvania sources were staff members at the Archives Division of the Pennsylvania Historical and Museum Commission, the Historical Society of Pennsylvania, the Quaker Collection at Haverford College, the Schwenkfelder Library, and the respective Lancaster, York, Berks, and Bucks County Historical Societies. In Maryland it was the staffs of the Maryland Hall of Records, the Washington County Historical Society, and the Washington County Public Library, while in Virginia it was the staff especially of the Virginia State Library's Archives Division. Marcia Grames and Deborah Baker at James Madison University obtained for me copies of many necessary materials through interlibrary loan.

The Mennonite Experience in America history project supported me for a block of time, and covered research expenses; its donors, both institutional and personal, are therefore also a major part of the community that made this scholarship possible. Good friends have shared insights and encouragement at various stages along my way, especially Klaus Wust, Jack P. Greene, J. William Frost, George M. Smith, and Robert D. Mitchell.

Helpful in other ways were Marijke Kyler who translated materials from the Dutch, and my student assistant, Diane Weeks, who deciphered my scrawls and typed a part of the manuscript. Theron Schlabach's research assistant, Timothy A. Schmucker, did a great amount of work getting chapter notes in order, and did it very competently.

My wife, Eve Bowers MacMaster, and children Sam, Tom, and Sara, acquiesced in my working on the book during many of the hours that a husband and father employed only from eight to five would have been spending with them.

Richard K. MacMaster, Bridgewater, Virginia
November 1982

LAND, PIETY, PEOPLEHOOD

CHAPTER

1

ALIENS IN FERMENT

One day in the autumn of 1671 Jan Floh, a Mennonite businessman of Krefeld in northern Germany, traveling in southern Germany from Heidelberg to nearby Mannheim on the Rhine River, met about twenty men and women whom he recognized as members of his own faith. They had just come, they said, from Bern, Switzerland. To Floh they were a pitiful sight: "old people, fifty, sixty, seventy years of age, naked and destitute," not having had "a night's rest in their own houses for more than a year." They had left their country, they said, because of a severe edict against people who believed as they did. Other Mennonites also were trying to escape, but authorities were guarding the roads and passes. Already the authorities had put some members of the despised religion into prison, and shipped some off to Mediterranean ports for sale as galley slaves. The slaves would have to row in warships in harsh conditions until they died. Some Mennonites had been flogged and branded with red-hot irons; one preacher had died a few days after such a branding.[1]

Floh gave the haggard group some money, which they received gratefully.[2] In so doing Floh was practicing the principle of mutual aid, which had been strong among Mennonites' predecessors, the Anabaptists. Mennonites had taken their name from Menno Simons, an Anabaptist who had lived in the Netherlands in the sixteenth century when Anabaptism was young. By the time Floh met these refugees, Anabaptism, or "Mennonitism" as it gradually was called, was already about 150 years old. The chance meeting brought Floh face to face with his own history.

From the first days of their movement, Anabaptists had known persecution and martyrdom. The movement began in Zurich, Switzerland, in 1525, when two young university students named Conrad Grebel and Felix Mantz and others became impatient with Ulrich Zwingli, who was their teacher and friend as well as a popular preacher and Protestant reformer in that city. The students and their friends were impatient because they believed their teacher was moving too slowly with reform. From 1523 to early 1525 Zwingli and other leaders, with the encouragement of the Zurich city council, held three public "disputations," with debates lasting as long as three days at a time. At first Zwingli was contending with Catholics, but during the year 1524 he found himself disputing more and more with Grebel, Mantz, and their allies.

The central issues under contention were: the authority of Scripture, whether the mass and infant baptism were biblical, whether the church should require fasting and refraining from meat during Lent, and the authority of the pope. From the debates, Zurich's religious and civil leaders affirmed scriptural authority as supreme and no longer required fasting. But the city council did not abolish the mass because it was decided the people were not ready for that step. Regarding infant baptism, the authorities decreed in January 1525 to retain the practice, even though Zwingli himself had earlier questioned whether it was biblical. With that decision they ordered Grebel and Mantz to stop "disputing and agitating." People who were taking the position that Grebel and Mantz were advocating, and therefore refusing to baptize their infants, were allowed eight days to have the baptisms performed before being faced with severe penalties.[3]

Zwingli consented to this limited reformation plan, hence his young friends' impatience. Although earlier Grebel himself had considered using town politics to achieve stronger reform, now the students and their allies began to say that political authorities, that is "the state," or in this case the city council, had no right to interfere in religious affairs. They also insisted that infant baptism was not really baptism at all, since it occurred without the knowledge, the voluntary faith, and the commitment of the person being baptized. The issues were deeper than the proper method of baptism; the real issues at stake had to do with the nature of the believer's faith and of the church. Those who were becoming Anabaptists believed that baptism and membership were appropriate only for those who were old enough to (and actually did) give evidence of new birth. The church should not pretend to include entire populations. Faithful yielding and discipleship to Christ were the marks of the true church.[4]

Willing to be more radical than was Zwingli on such issues, the group around Grebel and Mantz took a bold step: on January 21, 1525, immediately after the Zurich authorities' decision on infant baptism, they baptized each other with "believers baptism" (as their understanding of the ordinance has come to be known). This led to their name, at first applied contemptuously as a nickname, *"Wiedertäufer,"* or in English, "Anabaptists," meaning "re-baptizers." The new group also began regular celebration of the Lord's Supper in place of the mass. Such defiance of established authority brought harsh decrees, promulgated by Zwingli and other civil and religious leaders. Soon Anabaptists were suffering persecution and, eventually, executions.[5]

Partly because of persecution and because Anabaptists were zealous in proclaiming their message, Anabaptism spread rapidly. In various places throughout Europe different movements and leaders emerged who carried the Anabaptist label because they too advocated rebaptism. These numerous groups varied in degree in their acceptance of the doctrines of the Zurich group. At the same time, in various parts of southern Germany peasants were deeply restless not only over religious grievances but over many social and economic injustices as well. Anabaptists frequently sided with the peasants, especially against the compulsory exaction of tithes. The peasants' discontent broke out in the historic Peasants' Revolt of 1525. Thereafter, Anabaptism, often with good reason, became identified in the minds of authorities and other people with the peasants' grievances and rebellion. And of course revolt over religious, social, and economic grievances became a political problem as well. Authorities deeply feared all the different strains of seething unrest and often lumped all protest movements together under the label "Anabaptist."[6]

Anabaptism was far more than simply a matter of completing or carrying to its logical conclusion the unfinished work of the Protestant Reformers such as Martin Luther and Ulrich Zwingli. Anabaptists in Moravia developed communities (eventually known as Hutterite) in which they shared their wealth both for production and in consumption, and thereby challenged traditional attitudes toward personal property.[7] Numerous Anabaptists also turned to violence. Some of the early ones in Switzerland and southern Germany did so, but those who carried violent means furthest were in the North. Many Anabaptists in the Netherlands were not pacifist, and in 1534 a local war broke out at the German city of Münster, near the Dutch border, as a group of chiliastic Anabaptists seized Münster by armed force and tried to turn it into a "New Jerusalem." Civil and religious authorities mustered an even stronger army and crushed the movement in 1535. Now more than ever the Münster episode convinced people all across Europe, both authorities and others, that Anabaptists were dangerous, seditious, and a threat to social order.[8]

Most Anabaptists were pacifists, however, particularily those whom later Mennonites have preferred to count as their spiritual forebears. Pacifist Anabaptists believed that Christians should be willing to suffer and die for their faith rather than inflict suffering and death on others. Already in 1524, Grebel, writing to Thomas Müntzer, a peasant revolutionist and advocate of armed force, insisted that "true Christian believers are sheep among wolves" and should never resort to violent means. The symbol of the true Christian life was to be the cross, not the sword. Thus in place of force and destruction Grebel called for what became a strong emphasis of Anabaptism, namely *Gelassenheit*, or yieldedness. This emphasis came partly from medieval mysticism, and partly from an ascetic dualism between the church and the world, a dualism that was a heritage of medieval monasticism.[9]

Because Anabaptism took its shape partly by retaining those elements from medieval Catholicism, it was not simply an extension of the Protestant Reformers' logic. Indeed, some scholars have insisted strongly that it is best to consider Anabaptism a third way, "neither Catholic nor Protestant."[10] In any case, out of the mix, the movement developed an ethical rather than a sacramental Christianity. Anabaptists believed fully in Luther's key doctrine, justification by faith, yet they emphasized far more strongly than he that faith without works is dead. For them justification by faith could not be separated from a life of *Nachfolge Christi*, that is, of following Christ in a life of discipleship. On the crucial questions of salvation and regeneration, the Protestant Reformers emphasized more the initial deliverance from the guilt of sin; Anabaptists emphasized more the new quality of life that followed.[11]

In 1527, in the Swiss-German border city of Schleitheim, a group of Anabaptist leaders met to find consensus on certain doctrinal points. In the end they formed a statement written primarily by Michael Sattler of Switzerland, a statement that became for Anabaptists a kind of early declaration of faith. In addition to making certain points about standards for church leadership and reaffirming Anabaptist views of baptism and the Lord's Supper, the group at Schleitheim declared: that Christians should simply speak the truth and refuse to swear oaths; that in order to redeem errant members the church ought to apply discipline based on Matthew 18; that Christians should separate "from the evil and from the wickedness which the devil planted in the world"; and that such separation meant certain patterns of personal and social behavior, from keeping away from drinking houses to refusal even to carry (and certainly refusal to use) weapons of force. Those Anabaptists at Schleitheim thought that God gave governments authority to use force against people who lived outside the perfection of Christ; but Christians, they insisted, should neither wield the sword nor accept governmental offices that might put them in a position of invoking armed force.[12]

Swiss and other political and religious authorities in sixteenth- and seventeenth-century Europe thought that they could not allow individuals and congregations to define their own faith and ethics, and to begin to treat the church as a separate peoplehood. Such a course, the authorities thought, would cause more strains than the social fabric could bear. Consequently, persecution of Anabaptists became common. Life imprisonment, or more often death—by burning, hanging, the sword, drowning, and torture—became the order of the day. While in Switzerland outright killing of Anabaptists ceased in the 1570s, executions continued elsewhere until early in the seventeenth century, for instance the beheading of two Hutterites in Austria as late as 1618. And Swiss authorities continued to imprison Anabaptists and Mennonites, and to banish them and sell them as galley slaves. Persecution rose and fell more or less in waves even into the eighteenth century, and under pressure many Anabaptists sought refuge in places such as Moravia, the Palatinate, Strassburg, the Netherlands, and eventually, for some, North America.[13]

In 1536 Menno Simons, a former Catholic priest from the Friesland area of northern Holland, began to gather, unify, and lead Anabaptists who had been scattered and discredited in the wake of the Münster revolt. In time, Holland and some surrounding cities such as Krefeld allowed more freedom. In the latter 1570s Prince William of Orange ruled the Netherlands, and when Dutch Calvinists threatened their Anabaptist neighbors in 1577 and 1578, he objected. The following year, in a political agreement known historically as the "Union of Utrecht," he and others extended what was for that day a broad measure of toleration. William became the protector of Dutch Mennonites, and they in turn gave him substantial financial contributions that aided him in military struggle against Spain and against Spanish occupation.[14]

The end of persecution allowed Mennonites to move into the mainstream of Dutch life. That happened just as Holland was entering an economic and cultural golden age. As a persecuted and underground movement, Anabaptism had drawn its members mostly from the working class. Now the children of the original members found new opportunities in business and the professions. Like the English

Quakers a century later, they were helped to prosperity by the religious virtues of thrift, simplicity, hard work, and mutual aid. Dutch Mennonites became prominent especially in shipbuilding, in herring fisheries, and in whaling on the coast of Greenland. Because of their pacifism they shied away from other overseas commerce, including the Dutch West India Company's American trade, since trade ships needed to be armed against pirates and privateers. Other Mennonites grew wealthy from textiles, so much so that in Krefeld and in many Dutch cities, Mennonites eventually controlled the linen and silk industries. Prosperous Mennonite shipowners and clothmakers were often patrons of art and literature. No longer content with earnest but unlettered preachers, the Dutch Mennonites then looked about for ministers with more learning, whom they often found among university-educated Mennonite physicians. Thus Mennonites in the North translated their prosperity into expressions of higher culture.[15]

Shortly before he died in 1638, Hans de Ries, a preacher among the Waterlanders (a progressive wing of Dutch Mennonites), observed how the poor and suffering church of his youth had become rich and socially accepted. Yet even Dutch Mennonites kept some memory of their heritage of suffering. Beginning in 1562 they published a martyr book which they subsequently republished in many editions, and which in 1615 became the basis for a new work which de Ries composed. The de Ries' book eventually became the core of a much larger one that would do much to shape Mennonite mentality, including that of North American Mennonites, for two centuries. That book, the *Martyrs Mirror*, was a collection of hundreds of martyr stories, compiled by a Dutch elder named Thieleman J. van Braght and published in 1660.[16]

European Anabaptists and Mennonites did not speak with one voice. Long before van Braght published his book, they divided into many currents. Each congregation was largely autonomous; from one region to another, geographic barriers and strong leaders brought differences in emphasis and practice. For instance, Menno Simons emphasized the ban more than Anabaptists in southern Germany and Switzerland—a practice of deliberately ostracizing, in one way or another, errant members whom the church was calling to repentance. Although to some modern people the ban might seem harsh, Mennonites who emphasized it saw it primarily as an instrument of love applied for the erring one's highest good. They took quite literally certain passages in Matthew 18 and 1 Corinthians 5. As Menno interpreted those texts, after loving confrontation first by two members and then by the congregation, a persistent wrongdoer was to be cut off not only from the Lord's Supper but from all fellowship with believers, even from immediate family.[17]

Among the Dutch, the progressive Waterlanders rejected Menno's teaching on this point and were therefore reluctant even to use the name Mennonite. Divisions also split congregations in Friesland (the Frisian) from others in Flanders and elsewhere (the Flemish) and led to further splits within each of these groups.[18] Such division troubled de Ries, among others, for Christian unity was almost a passion of the Waterlander pastor. Out of such concern he helped English religious exiles in the Netherlands and mediated Mennonite influence on the English Baptists. Desire for unity was one reason why in 1615 he began publishing his books of martyrs. Recovery of the Anabaptism that had flourished in the time of the martyrs was a common ground on which separated brethren might unite.[19]

Long before de Ries published his martyr books, Mennonites of Holland and northern Germany had largely lost contact with their co-religionists in Switzerland. But another version of the martyr stories, published by a Frisian preacher and rival of de Ries named Pieter Jansz Twisck, included accounts of some Swiss and south German martyrs.[20] Moreover a wave of persecution begun by Zurich authorities in 1639 drove refugees into Alsace, the Palatinate, and elsewhere down the Rhine from Switzerland.

Some of the suffering ones reached Holland and told of Zurich's various cruelties. Now more than ever the Mennonites of northern Europe became aware of the Swiss fellowship of martyrs. In 1645 they began to send material aid to their Swiss brothers and sisters and over the years they worked to persuade the authorities of church and state in Switzerland to stop the persecutions. In 1659 and 1660, after one such intercession, authorities in the Swiss canton of Bern granted a ten-year reprieve. But in 1670 they adopted new laws to force Mennonites to join the established church or leave.[21]

A leader among those who arranged help for the Swiss was Hans Vlamingh, an Amsterdam merchant and a deacon in an Amsterdam Mennonite congregation. Because of a sign near its meeting place, the congregation was known as "By the Lamb." As early as 1659 Vlamingh began to raise funds for relief and also wrote letters to Zurich and to Bern. In 1664 the Lamb congregation divided and Vlamingh joined a newly formed one labeled "the Sun." In contrast to the Lamb group, which was more preoccupied with practical discipleship in life, the Sun congregation put greater emphasis on doctrine. Yet both congregations eagerly joined in the work of aiding the refugees. Despite its preoccupation with doctrine, the Sun congregation, in which deacon Vlamingh, was still quite active, did more than its share.[22]

With Bern's new expulsion order in effect, after 1670 Dutch Mennonites under Vlamingh's and others' leadership again collected and distributed money, food, clothing, and tools to help resettle refugees who were fleeing in a steady stream from Bern to the more tolerant Palatinate. Sometimes they sought the good offices of the Dutch government to induce Swiss officials to improve the persecuted minority's situation. Helping in such efforts were representatives not only from the different Mennonite congregations in Amsterdam, but also from ones in Rotterdam, Haarlem, and other cities, as the problems of their Swiss co-religionists stimulated Dutch Mennonites to broaden their activities. The activities helped to create stronger ties and some unity among divided Dutch Mennonites, and between the Dutch and others. The Swiss were not the only ones toward whom the Dutch expressed solidarity. In the 1660s, for instance, they had assisted a Mennonite-related group in Poland which was in distress, and later their aid would extend to Pennsylvania, eastern Europe, and Russia. By the opening years of the eighteenth century they saw a need for their efforts to have stronger institutional form and be more organized. In 1710 they formally organized a Fund for

Foreign Needs, governed by a Commission for Foreign Needs, with headquarters in Amsterdam. As the century continued, the fund and the commission would give a great deal of help to various Mennonites, usually in family or larger groups, who were emigrating to North America.[23]

In addition to opening up vistas for service and practical cooperation, rediscovery of their persecuted Swiss brothers and sisters helped bring Dutch Mennonites back to their own roots. In the preface to his *Bloedig Tooneel (Bloody Theater)*, or *Martyrs Mirror*, van Braght reminded them of the persecution in their own history, and observed that while people "are more easily converted by good examples than by good teachers, yet here you have both."[24] Moreover, the Dutch soon were deeply influencing the congregations in Switzerland, Alsace, and the Palatinate with whom they were in contact, and whom they were helping. These more southerly Mennonites had their own martyrologies and a hymnbook with many martyr ballads, the *Ausbund*, which were direct links to early Anabaptists and their persecution. But van Braght's *Martyrs Mirror* became the "great martyr book" and informed the faith of Mennonites even in the South.[25]

Mennonites in the South adopted the Dutch custom of reading sermons and used the printed sermons and devotional reading of northern European Mennonites as their religious literature. For instance, they gave wide circulation to certain writings of Gerrit Roosen and Jacob Denner, leaders of a congregation at Altona near Hamburg in northern Germany. In the last decades of the seventeenth century, Swiss Mennonites in Alsace and the Palatinate also subscibed to the Dordrecht Confession of Faith, a statement that northern leaders had drawn up at Dordrecht in Holland in 1632. That confession probably never replaced the 1527 Schleitheim document as an accurate expression of the Swiss Anabaptists' fundamental understanding of their faith. However, it was the only such statement available in print and thus was the only one read widely by the Swiss in areas along the Rhine and later in America. The Dordrecht Confession spelled out the biblical and theological framework of Mennonite thought and offered specific detail on

Jan Luyken copper engraving of Anneken Hendriks, burned at Amsterdam in 1571. (From *Martyrs Mirror*)

both faith and practice, including the foot washing rite and the ban.[26]

Dutch and Swiss Anabaptists had agreed in principle on the need for church discipline, including some version of the ban. The nature of Christ's church was such that only those who actively sought to follow the rule of Christ found in Matthew 18 could be members. But none of the south German or Swiss Anabaptists or Mennonites had ever carried the ban idea as far as the Dutch who followed Menno Simons on the point. The southerners were not willing to separate a family from ordinary, everyday relationships with an errant spouse, parent, child, or neighbor. Their practice was simply not to allow the erring one to participate in communion, or the Lord's Supper.[27]

In the 1690s, Jakob Ammann, a preacher among the Swiss Mennonites, was disturbed by the lack of discipline in the churches of Alsace. He wanted greater simplicity in dress, the revival of the custom of men wearing long beards, and the foot washing rite made a part of every communion service. He believed that a stricter use of the ban, including social avoidance even if it interrupted family relations, would help Mennonites recover their fervor.[28] Many congregations recognized their own laxity and heard Ammann's call for discipline gladly, while others were not convinced. In Alsace, where Ammann eventually won most of his followers, the shunning or avoidance of members who had not responded to milder church discipline was practical. But in Switzerland, congregations seeking protection from official harassment had learned often to depend upon their connections with family members who had joined the Reformed Church. Earlier these family members and other friends—who sympathized with and protected the Anabaptists but did not join them—had been called *"Halbtäufer"* (Half-Anabaptists).[29] In Ammann's day most Swiss congregations were not ready to break social connections with such helpful people.

Division grew sharper. Between 1693 and 1701 church leaders made many attempts to bring the two parties together, including efforts to have Gerrit Roosen, the Altona preacher and writer, arbitrate the conflict. But the breach did not heal. Ammann's followers, then residing in the Alsace, the Palatinate, and Switzerland, became known as the *Ammannsch*, or Amish.[30] By the late twentieth century the Amish virtually all reside in North America, there being no congregations left in Europe.

While division and exclusion were the rule in the South, in Holland new trends of cooperation and unity were developing by the end of the seventeenth century. The Lamb congregation especially, originally Flemish, now brought together Frisians, High Germans, and Waterlanders.[31] Moreover, through efforts of a learned physician-pastor named Galenus Abrahamsz de Haan, the trends also brought Mennonites into close contact with a group known as Collegiants, who had separated from Holland's state church over disagreement with certain points of Calvinist theology. Although they never became an organized religious body, the Collegiants had turned to believers baptism, home meetings for Bible study and prayer, and an emphasis on benevolent work (often in cooperation with Mennonites).[32] Some Mennonites criticized the Lambists' and de Haan's affinity for them;[33] but the first Mennonite settlement in America grew out of the Mennonite-Collegiant circle in the Lamb congregation.

That settlement was the dream of a man named Pieter Cornelisz Plockhoy. By 1661 Plockhoy, who had lived with an experimental communal group in England, was an advocate of radical reform. By writing and circulating certain pamphlets, he had tried to get parliamentary support for such groups. Among his arguments he pointed to the Hutterites, the communal Anabaptists of Moravia. At this point Plockhoy became interested in some land the city of Amsterdam owned in Delaware. His vision was that poor people might go there and establish a community. They would share goods, meet military obligations by a special tax rather than by personal service, and have religious freedom, democratic government, and no slavery or slave trade. In April 1662 the Amsterdam City Council agreed to help "25 Mennonist families" to go. Fifteen months later Plockhoy, his family, and forty-one other persons arrived in the New World and established their colony at what is now the town of Lewes, by the Delaware River.[34]

But alas, entanglement in larger history, and war! In 1664 the English and the Dutch descended into one of their bloody conflicts for empire. English troops captured Holland's North American settlements and lands. They plundered Plockhoy's settlement, and it was "destroyed...to a naile." The new village disappeared (although apparently some Dutch-named persons declared allegiance to the British and stayed). Thirty-one years later Plockhoy himself, by then old and blind, appeared with his wife at a more permanent Mennonite settlement, Germantown in Pennsylvania, near Philadelphia. There with help from the Mennonite community the Plockhoys lived out their lives.[35]

Germantown was the scene of the first Mennonite settlement in America that became permanent. Rather than being a radical experiment, that colony grew out of Mennonites' following normal lines of trade, empire, and migra-

Site of short-lived 1663-64 Plockhoy settlement,

tion. Established in 1683, it also came to reflect the religious complexity of European Mennonitism, including a strong admixture of Quakerism.

For some time, Mennonites had followed Dutch movements to North America, where the center of the Dutch would-be empire was New Amsterdam (which the British captured in 1664 and renamed "New York"). Prior to 1683, or even 1663, there were Mennonites in New Amsterdam. In 1652 a certain Anna Smits ran afoul of the law by using what the authorities considered "slanderous and calumniating" language against a sermon preached by the officially approved Dutch Reformed minister; she was an Anabaptist. The following year church officials objected to letting a Lutheran minister settle and start a congregation in Dutch North America lest "the Mennonites, as well as the English Independents [Congregationalists], who are numerous here, might seek to introduce like public assemblies."

From 1659 to 1661 various official documents identified a certain shoemaker who owned land on New Amsterdam's Broad Street as "the Mennonite" to distinguish him from another man with the same name, Pieter Pieterzen.

near present-day Horekill, Delaware. (Jan Gleysteen collection)

Reformed Church authorities wrestled with the question of whether to allow Mennonites to take communion. One young Mennonite requested full membership, but left for the West Indies before the question of his baptism was resolved.[36] Apparently quite a few Mennonites at least attended Reformed services, and in the end allowed the Reformed faith to absorb them or their offspring. The Mennonites never did establish their own congregations, either in New Amsterdam or on Long Island, where apparently a few other Mennonites settled.[37]

Back in Europe meanwhile, in the early 1650s Prince Karl Ludwig, ruler of the Palatinate, began to rebuild his lands, which had been badly devastated in the Thirty Years' War of 1618-1648. It occurred to him that Mennonites might help in the reconstruction task, for Swiss Anabaptists had accumulated much experience developing marginal lands in Switzerland's rugged Jura Mountains, into which their refugee ancestors had fled. In 1664 he issued a decree of religious toleration, and in 1671 he explicitly invited Mennonites and gave further promises of civil and religious privilege. By those decrees, the law in Karl's territories gave Mennonites the right to worship. However, they were not to meet in groups of more than twenty families, or seek converts from outside their own ranks, or rebaptize members of other churches. They also had to pay a special annual tax of six gulden per family.

These restrictions limited Mennonite religious development in the Palatinate; often it was the same in other lands where Mennonites fled. Congregations remained small, with many preachers. For the most part, Mennonites stopped evangelizing. They also became politically cautious, and began to associate payment of special taxes with gratitude for tolerance and liberty. For despite the restrictions, the kind of limited toleration Karl Ludwig granted seemed generous. The Palatinate itself became a major refuge for displaced Swiss Mennonites.[38]

In the latter 1650s Quakers began to spread their message among Mennonites—in Holland, Krefeld, and areas further south along the Rhine as far as the Palatinate. One of the Quakers, William Ames, who had formerly (as a Baptist) espoused believers baptism, felt a special affinity for the descendants of Anabaptists and tried especially hard to convert them. By the 1660s and 1670s some small Quaker groups emerged, made up mainly of former Mennonites.[39]

In 1677 William Penn, the Quaker who would soon (in 1681) receive Pennsylvania and Delaware from English King Charles II as payment of a debt, visited Quaker meetings of Holland and Germany as he accompanied Quaker founder George Fox on a preaching tour. Already Fox had visited North America concluding that it might be a haven for Europe's despised religious minorities. Mennonites and Mennonites-turned-Quaker attended the meetings Fox and Penn held where presumably they heard something of Fox's ideas for North America, which Penn already shared. On the other hand, some Mennonites did not automatically warm to the Quakers' ideas. Probably because certain Mennonite preachers disputed the belief that Quakerism was a rebirth of the apostolic church, the Quakers found certain Mennonite preachers to be, in their opinion, "the most virulent and obstinate opposers of Truth in this land."[40] Moreover, by the 1670s and 1680s some Mennonites saw political reasons for keeping aloof from Quakers: the Quakers tried to make converts and refused to pay certain war-related taxes with a zeal that brought them renewed persecution in Krefeld and elsewhere. Many Mennonites by contrast cherished their hard-won toleration and preferred to be "the quiet in the land." So the Mennonites paid all taxes and all tithes to the state churches, and stayed clear of evangelism and political expression and whatever else might bring them trouble.[41]

Yet Quaker-Mennonite tensions were something of a family quarrel and some Mennonites continued to join with the Friends (as Quakers preferred to call themselves). Some even worshiped in both groups. So if William Penn would preach more than only Quakerism, if he would preach settlement on his new world lands, as he soon did, there were Mennonites at hand to listen. One who listened was Jacob Telner, a Mennonite merchant of Amsterdam who had joined a Quaker meeting in 1676 but continued to address Mennonites as brethren. In 1678 Telner traveled to North America where he visited Quakers in New York and New Jersey.

In 1681, based at Krefeld, Telner became "Penn's chief agent in the promotion of Quaker and Mennonite emigration from Krefeld and its neighborhood to the New World."[42] In 1683 Telner, still identified as an Amsterdam merchant, and two other Krefelders, Dirck Sipman and Jan Streypers, each purchased 5,000 acres north of Philadelphia in Pennsylvania for £500 English money. Soon thereafter Telner arranged for three other persons to buy 1,000 acres each: Govert Remke, Lenert Arents, and Jacob Isaacs van Bebber. Sipman, Remke and van Bebber were Mennonites. Then Telner and Benjamin Furly, a Quaker leader and a land agent at Rotterdam for William Penn, struck a deal with a Quaker merchant and shipowner at London named James Claypoole to transport some thirty-three emigrants to the Philadelphia port aboard the ship *Concord.* [43]

An example of those who would go was Herman Isaakz (or Isaacs) op den Graeff. In 1632 his grandfather had represented the Krefeld congregation to sign the Dordrecht Confession. Herman himself associated with the Quakers to the point that he was banished from Krefeld in 1680.

Artist's conception based on historical research of the ship *Concord* on which the first Germantown settlers arrived. (Art by Jan Gleysteen)

Another example was Jan Lensen, a Mennonite linen weaver from Krefeld. Jan Streypers, one of those who bought 5,000 acres, leased fifty of those acres to Lensen and extended an eight-year loan to help Lensen and his family go and establish themselves. In return Lensen promised to clear eight acres of the land and work for Streypers twelve days each year during the eight years. Streypers had a son, Leonard, who also emigrated, and who wanted to learn weaving. So the landlord contracted further to lend Lensen "a linen-weaving stool with 3 combs . . . and for this Jan Lensen shall teach my son Leonard in one year the art of weaving." The son, in turn, was obligated "to weave faithfully during the said year."[44]

The *Concord* sailed, with perhaps forty or fifty Krefelders aboard. On October 6, 1683, it anchored at Philadelphia and deposited fifty or more passengers from Germany onto American soil: the group from Krefeld, plus ten who accompanied Francis Daniel Pastorius, a Pietist and agent for a German syndicate known as the Frankfort Land Company, which was interested in Pennsylvania lands. Among the Krefelders, only Jan Lensen and his family were clearly Mennonite rather than Quaker.[45] Yet the group, that was established at Germantown, some six miles northwest of Philadelphia, contained the seed of the first ongoing Mennonite settlement in the new world.

The Krefelders were fortunate. On the Atlantic, Herman op den Graeff later informed European friends in a letter, they encountered no storms. In fact, the voyage had been easier than crossing from Rotterdam to London. Once they arrived at Germantown, each family received a three-acre lot in town and another forty acres nearby. Op den Graeff, at least, thought the distribution fair, especially since that left 6,000 more acres the group might divide later. Nor did it take long for the new immigrants to sense economic progress. "We already begin to spin flax," op den Graeff reported only four months after the *Concord's* arrival. "If any reputable spinsters who like to work desire to come here we should receive them all."[46]

Indeed the Krefelders had entered an expansive economy. Philadelphia offered "sufficient habitations," op den Graeff reported further, "as the city is being rapidly built

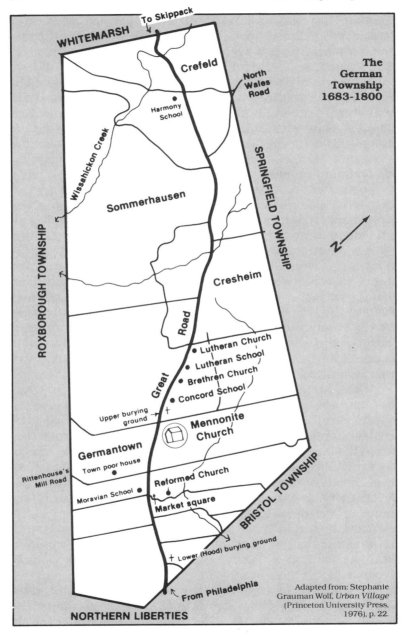

The
German
Township
1683-1800

Adapted from: Stephanie
Grauman Wolf, *Urban Village*
(Princeton University Press,
1976), p. 22.

up." By the close of 1685, when the first wavelet of immigration through Philadelphia subsided, ninety ships had delivered 8,000 immigrants there.

Many had arrived as indentured servants (that is, persons under contract to serve for designated lengths of time for only minimal compensation, persons whom the masters could buy and sell during the designated periods almost as slaves). One list of families arriving at Philadelphia between 1682 and 1687 records 192 indentured servants compared to only 89 free heads of families. In Bucks County, lying just north of Philadelphia and Germantown, 49 percent of adult males in 1687 were indentured. Such servants soon appeared in Germantown, although it is not clear in what proportions. What is clear is that Germantown settlers overwhelmingly belonged to the artisan and yeoman classes. As Daniel Francis Pastorius, a Pietist and a Germantown leader, reported in 1698, they were "for the most part tradespeople, such as cloth, fustian, and linen weavers, tailors, shoemakers, locksmiths, carpenters." Most were linen weavers.[47]

But if economic life progressed quickly for Germantown people with Mennonite connections, a stable religious life came more slowly. A specifically Mennonite congregation did not emerge until the little group of Mennonite-Quakers had felt pulled in several religious directions, and until more persons who were actually Mennonite had arrived and settled.

In 1684 five more Krefeld families arrived. The male heads of those families were Veit (David) Scherkes, Walter Siemens, Herman Daurss, Jacob Telner himself, and Isaac Jacobs van Bebber. They were all Quaker except van Bebber who, like his father Jacob Isaacs van Bebber, was Mennonite. Eventually more of the new immigrants who continued to arrive in Germantown came from the Palatinate than from Krefeld. And as time passed, more Mennonites than Quakers came.[48]

After Quakers converted some Mennonites beginning about 1657, Palatine rulers treated the Quakers as being merely a species of Mennonites. After all, the two groups held many beliefs in common, they attended one another's meetings, and family ties bound them together. But as the Quakers insisted on preaching publicly to all comers and on balking at special, military-related taxes, the authorities grew impatient. Moreover, the Quakers allowed women to preach, and a visit of two Quaker women preachers in 1678 was apparently, to the authorities, the last straw. From then until 1681 Palatine authorities harassed and banished Friends, especially at Kriegsheim and Alzey. The persecution helped stimulate emigration to Pennsylvania. Actual Quakers were few; Palatine Quakerism nearly ended with the emigration of five Kriegsheim families headed by Hans Peter Cassel, Gerhardt Hendricks, Peter Schumacher, Widow Sara Schumacher, and Heivert Papen.[49] But these last Quakers were kinfolk of Mennonites, and their departure stirred Mennonites to follow. So also did new devastation in the Rhinelands in 1683 and 1684, caused by armies of the French monarch Louis XIV.

What had been Mennonite-Quaker emigration from the Krefeld, the Palatinate, and elsewhere to Germantown by 1686 had become Mennonite emigration, although some Quakers of Mennonite background continued to emigrate from Holland and some Reformed and Lutherans arrived in Germantown as well. Between 1685 and 1690 Hendrick Bucholtz, Hans Peter Umstat, Jacob Isaacs van Bebber, Matthias Isaacs van Bebber, Willem Hosters, Arent Koester, Herman Koester, Paulus Koester, Jan van Lovenigh, Jan Neuss (or Neusz), Matthias Neusz, Dirck Sellen, Hendrick Sellen, Martin Sellen, Jacob Seimens, and Jan Streypers all arrived with their families from Krefeld. In 1688 Dirck Keyser, a Mennonite silk merchant from Amsterdam, brought his family to Germantown from New York. Willem Rittinghuysen, a Mennonite papermaker of Amsterdam, and his family, arrived a year or two later. Also, Morgan Edwards, Baptist historian, declared in 1770 that as early as 1692 some Mennonite families had come to Pennsylvania from New York. Movement from the former Dutch colony was apparently significant not only for Pennysylvania's commercial and social life in general, but also for its Mennonite beginnings.[50]

At first the only Germantown settlers to hold regular religious services were the Quakers, or Friends, meeting in homes and in a small building also used as the town hall. Many who had never been Friends in Europe attended with them. But in 1690 a Dutch Reformed minister who visited Germantown reported that of forty-four families there, only twenty-eight were Quaker. And opposition to Quakerism brought diverse elements together: Reformed, Lutherans, Catholics, and Mennonites, said the minister, "lovingly meet every Sunday, when a Mennist, Dirck Keyser, from Amsterdam, reads a sermon from a book by Iost Harmensen." There was even a Collegiant strain.[51]

Reading a sermon was traditional for Dutch Mennonites, and interpreters have often called Keyser's Sunday services the first Mennonite worship in America.[52] Although a Mennonite led these services, clearly the congregation was too varied to be classified as a Mennonite one.

Before a truly Mennonite congregation emerged, another set of events helped create a demand for it: a division among Pennsylvania Quakers around the teachings of a learned Scottish Quaker, George Keith. Keith had in fact traveled with Fox and Penn during their trip on the continent in 1677. In 1684 he arrived in America, and by then was preaching that Quakers were not sufficiently grounding their faith on the Bible and on the Christ of the New Testament. He also called Quakers to be more consistent against using force. Leading Friends were prominent in Pennsylvania's government, thus church authority and civil political power were much intertwined. Keith objected to that.

By the 1690s two opposing camps, one for and one against Keith, were forming among Pennsylvania Quakers—including those of Mennonite background.[53] In fact, a later, hostile interpreter of Keith thought he saw in Keith's doctrines the definite influence of Krefeld Mennonitism.[54] In any case, a family such as the op den Graeffs soon found itself divided: Herman op den Graeff and a spirited brother of his, Abraham, along with Jacob Isaacs van Bebber, supported Keith at the Friends' 1692 annual conference, or "Yearly Meeting." Their brother Dirk op den Graeff and Francis Daniel Pastorius and others opposed him. Eventually Keith took his case to the more prestigious Quaker leaders in En-

Portion of last page of the 1688 Germantown antislavery petition, with signatures "Gerret henderichs," "Derick up de graeff," "Francis Daniell Pastorius," and "Abraham up Den graeff." (William I. Hull, *William Penn and the Dutch Quaker Migration to Pennsylvania*)

gland. Failing to convince them, he returned to Philadelphia and led a breakaway Quaker group. The Philadelphia Yearly Meeting listed some 143 Quakers who temporarily went with Keith but who later left for other churches or for none at all. "In Germantown," declared the report, "Herman Opdegraff, Abraham Opdegraff and his wife, Cornelius Sidcot and wife, Jacob Isaac Vanbiber and his wife, Isaac Jacobs Vanbiber and his wife, Mathias Isaacs Vanbiber, Jan Doeden, and David Scherckjes" had been those involved with Keith but now "some goe to the Baptists and others keep to no Religious Society."[55]

While the Keithian controversy was taking shape (and soon would help stimulate the beginning of a Mennonite congregation), another issue somewhat divided Pennsylvania's Quakers. That issue was slavery. Like Plockhoy in his colony, three Quakers of Mennonite origin, plus the German Pietist Francis Daniel Pastorius, took a strong stand against both slavery and the slave trade.

At a meeting in Germantown in 1688 Garrett Hendricks, Dirk op den Graeff, Abraham op den Graeff, and Pastorius drafted and signed a most remarkable document. Already twenty-five years earlier, the reformer Plockhoy and his "25 Mennonist families" from Amsterdam had rejected human bondage for their colony on the Delaware. Now Henrdricks, the op den Graeffs, and Pastorius produced one of the earliest and clearest antislavery statements in American history—and indeed in the whole history of slavery's abolition in Western culture. Among other points the four argued that when Christians bought slaves they were buying stolen goods. Moreover, they were separating families. And "now tho' they are black we cannot conceive there is more liberty to have them slaves, as it is to have other white ones." In America people were "oppressed w :Sch are of black colour" much as "in Europe there are many oppressed for Conscience sacke." [56]

The signers addressed their protest to the regional "Monthly Meeting" of Quakers. Apparently seeing the issue's weight and potential for division, that meeting sent it on to the higher Quarterly Meeting. The higher body also judging the issue to be "of too great a weight for this meeting to determine" sent it still higher to the colonies' Yearly Meeting. But neither was the Yearly Meeting ready to handle so problematic a question. Indeed, nearly a century would pass before Pennsylvania's Quakers would come fully to grips with the issue. In 1688 the Yearly Meeting tabled the question, and there it rested.[57]

Was the protest in any sense a Mennonite expression? Obviously it was more immediately Quaker than Mennonite. Yet not only the op den Graeffs but also Hendricks were of Mennonite background. And reference to European religious persecution as a reason for sympathy with blacks in their oppression surely grew out of Mennonite as well as Quaker experience. It would seem also that British Quakers in the higher Meetings to whom the statement went were not as ready to take up antislavery as were Pastorius and the three signers of Mennonite and continental background. Moreover, apparently at least one of the signers, Abraham op den Graeff, later returned to Mennonitism, becoming a member of Mennonite congregation that emerged at Germantown.[58] According to tradition, in a very old Mennonite meetinghouse in Germantown there still stands a table upon which the protesters wrote their statement.[59] After some years Germantown did get a Mennonite meetinghouse. A permanent and definitely Mennonite congregation slowly emerged.

About 1694 a Lutheran preacher named Henry Bernard Koster arrived in Germantown. Koster strongly emphasized the person, nature, and work of Christ, and also biblicism. He soon found the home of Isaac Jacobs van Bebber open for his message. Van Bebber had been a Quaker, but before that a Mennonite, and since that a Keithian. Now a small congregation of another sort formed temporarily at his home. By 1699 a Baptist preacher, one William Davis (who hoped to win the group to his own message), described it as "a kinde of Society [who] did Break bread, Lay on hands, washed one anothers feet, and were about haveing a Comunity of goods." Actually by 1699 Koster had withdrawn and different leaders were pulling the congregation in various directions. "In a little time," according to Davis, "they disagreed, and broke in pieces."[60] One fragment would become the Germantown Mennonite congregation.

In 1698 a new contingent of Mennonites had arrived from Krefeld and had begun to meet with the group at van Bebber's house. After that it was not long until the Mennonites decided that they needed a preacher and some deacons. For preacher they chose the papermaker Willem Rittinghuysen (or Wilhelm Rittenhausen, or, in the anglicized version better known to history, William Rittenhouse). For their first deacon they decided upon Jan Neuss, a silversmith. The papermaker took up his new duties as the congregation's leader in 1699. That date is perhaps the best for marking the beginning of Mennonite church life in America.[61]

In 1690 Rittenhouse had built the first paper mill in England's American colonies, locating the structure along a creek near Germantown, and making use of scraps from the region's burgeoning textile industry. For some generations the papermaker's family would be prominent in colonial and revolutionary Pennsylvania's business, science, and politics. One great-grandson would be David Rittenhouse—astronomer, scientist in charge of producing armaments to fight the British in the American revolution (his Rittenhouse branch having by then departed from Mennonitism), and first director of the United States Mint. Some accounts have presented William Rittenhouse as having been the first Mennonite bishop in North America. He was not; he only read sermons to the congregation on Sundays, and did not baptize or conduct communion.[62] In fact, the congregation soon sought

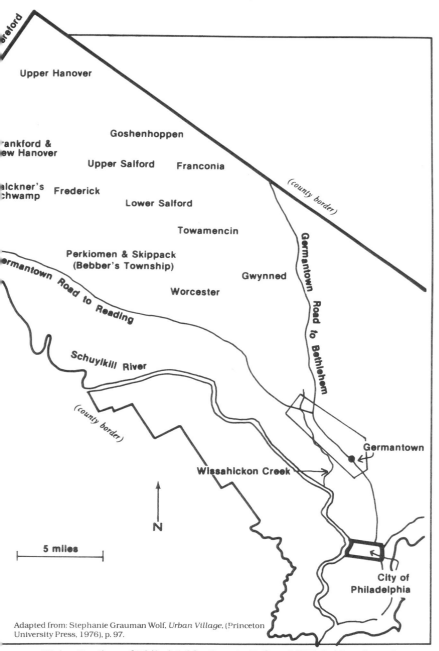

Upper Hanover

Goshenhoppen

ankford &
ew Hanover

Upper Salford   Franconia

alckner's
chwamp   Frederick

Lower Salford

Towamencin

Perkiomen & Skippack
(Bebber's Township)

Gwynned

ermantown Road to Reading   Worcester

Germantown Road to Bethlehem   (county border)

Schuylkill River

(county border)

Germantown

Wissahickon Creek

N

5 miles

City of
Philadelphia

Adapted from: Stephanie Grauman Wolf, *Urban Village*, (Princeton
University Press, 1976), p. 97.

**Major Portion of Philadelphia County Before 1785 (with selected town-
ship and other place names)**

more official leadership, especially after 1700, when some newcomers arrived from Dutch Mennonite congregations at Hamburg and nearby Altona in West Prussia. Among the newcomers were Cornelis Claessen and his two sons-in-law Claes Berends and Isaac van Sintern, plus Herman Karsdorp and Paul Roosen, all with their families. A spirit of strong congregational life existed at Hamburg and Altona, and these new arrivals brought that spirit with them.[63]

Before long, Berends wrote back to his home congregation to ask if the Hamburg-Altona people could send a bishop. In March of 1702 the leaders there replied that they could not. They instead urged the Germantown Mennonites to do as early Christians had done: call preachers from their own number.[64] The group chose Hans Neuss (not the same as the Jan Neuss earlier appointed) and Jacob Godschalk. Later, in 1708, after more Mennonites had arrived, they chose five deacons and overseers: Isaac van Sintern and Herman Karsdorp from Hamburg, Hendrick Kassel and Martin Kolb from Kriegsheim in the Palatinate, and Coenrad Jansen, a Hollander. At that time Godschalk assumed the duties of bishop. With him there to officiate, the congregation observed the Lord's Supper, the first Mennonite communion service in the New World. In 1708 the group also built the first known Mennonite meetinghouse in North America. The a log structure was placed on a Germantown lot some members had owned for about a decade.[65] With these developments, a full-fledged Mennonite congregation existed in America.

Thus, some Dutch Mennonite tradition took root in Pennsylvania soil. Educated but self-supporting ministers read sermons and then began to assume full pastoral roles. Among those early Germantown Mennonites there was a deep commitment to biblical nonresistance to the point that they refused to do jury duty or to hold offices in government which rested ultimately upon military or police power. At least members often cited such objections in order to ask for exemptions.[66]

Dutch Mennonitism also took root to some extent at a place called Skippack, in present-day Montgomery County, northwest of Philadelphia in a rural area some twenty miles

The first Germantown Mennonite meetinghouse was a log structure built in 1708. This 1770 stone structure replaced it and is the oldest Mennonite meetinghouse still in use in North America. On its premises are marks of the revolutionary war Battle of Germantown. (Jan Gleysteen collection)

beyond Germantown. There a Mennonite settlement developed on lands owned for a time by Matthias Isaacs van Bebber, brother of Isaac Jacobs van Bebber in whose home the congregation had earlier met. Matthias van Bebber bought some of that land from Dirck Sipman and Jan Streypers, the two who with Jacob Telner had originally purchased 5,000-acre tracts. Then in 1702 he purchased 6,166 additional acres from William Penn, making enough for a settlement at "Bebber's Township," as the Skippack area also was called. The new settlement quickly drew Germantown Mennonites to it. Already in 1702 Claes Jansen, Johannes Umstat, and Johannes Kuster established themselves there. They were young men whose parents had come from Holland or Krefeld in the 1680s. Others followed, attracted by favorable terms and by land agents of their own faith.[67]

Most settlers at Skippack were Mennonites, but not all. When others came, they and Mennonites often intermarried. The fact is that ever since Mennonites began their experience in America, they have not kept as much to themselves as some commentators on Mennonite history suggest. Germantown and Skippack Mennonites had emigrated from the same neighborhood in Europe as had most of their Quaker or Reformed or other neighbors. Already in Europe they had often had family ties with their neighbors, and now they formed more. Willem Dewees, an early Reformed settler in Skippack, married William Rittenhouse's daughter; Cornelis Dewees, his brother, was a brother-in-law of Mennonite settler Hermanus Kuster.[68] Sometimes a Dutch Reformed minister conducted Mennonite marriage ceremonies.[69] At Skippack the Reformed people as well as the Mennonites, had arrived from Holland and the lower reaches of the Rhine, and the settlement continued to mix the two groups. The case was similar with Mennonites and Quakers. Martin Kolb, one of the Skippack Mennonite pioneers, for instance, was grandson of a Quaker immigrant from Kriegsheim named Peter Schuhmacher; so Kolb was kin to many Quakers, or Friends.[70] How could Mennonites have built an isolated community on the Skippack even if they had tried?

As would often happen when daughter churches formed as settlement expanded in America, the Germantown group and the cluster at Skippack continued to think of themselves as one congregation. In fact the center of Mennonite community life in the New World gradually shifted from Germantown to the more rural, outlying settlement.

Up to 1707 most Germantown and Skippack Mennonites, including even those from the Palatinate, were of Dutch background. Then in 1707 a new group began to arrive: Palatine Mennonites whose ancestry was more Swiss than northern. According to Jacob Godschalk at first, "for a whole year they kept by themselves," hesitating to worship with their Dutch and north German co-religionists.[71] For instance, among the new arrivals were, Wynant and Anna Bouman. A Mennonite banker of Amsterdam named David Rutgers, fourth in a line of David Rutgerses and deacon in the Lamb congregation, had helped the Boumans emigrate by advancing them and their three children twenty-eight guilders for getting to London, and then letting his London agent pay out £8, 10s. in English money for each person's food and passage on the Atlantic voyage. Others were Jacob, Johannes, and Mr. and Mrs. Martin Kolb. For a time they did not join the Germantown congregation even though they had family ties to Mennonites at Hamburg and Kriegsheim, the origin of some of the earlier arrivals. Hans Graeff later settled at Groffdale in Lancaster County but lived in Germantown before 1710. He may not have come in the 1707 migration, but he too held aloof from the Germantown congregation.[72] It was not automatic that Mennonites would gather together as one people in the New World.

However, in 1708 at least some of the new arrivals from the Palatinate did join their northern European co-religionists in worship, bringing the congregation's total membership to thirty-three baptized persons. On May 9, 1708, newly designated bishop Godschalk baptized eleven persons, and two weeks later he administered the first Mennonite observance of the Lord's Supper in the New World. After that more newcomers arrived from Europe and some who had come earlier, or their children, now joined the congregation. By 1712 Germantown and Skippack had ninety-nine baptized Mennonite members.[73]

And so finally Mennonite communities and a Mennonite congregation were established in the New World. Although those members of the faith whose origins were Swiss were still suffering much greater persecution and civil disability, the first Mennonites to make the ocean passage were Dutch and north German. In Plockhoy's brief experiment the religious (or religio-social) motive was strong, but Mennonites had migrated to New Amsterdam even earlier merely by following the movements of trade and empire. In Germantown and Skippack, which were the first true Mennonite settlements, the religious motive may well have been at work. But if it was, it worked mainly through Mennonite contacts with the more ostracized Quakers. The motive of those who came truly as Mennonites, rather than as Mennonite-Quakers, was the desire to follow empire and trade.

CHAPTER

2

IMMIGRATION:
MOTIVES AND MUTUAL AID

By the second decade of the eighteenth century, significant Mennonite emigration from Holland and northern Germany had all but ended. Enough Mennonites had arrived from those regions to establish a definite Dutch and North German element among Mennonites in a few counties north of Philadelphia. But that ethnic element would never dominate New World Mennonite communities as a whole through the eighteenth and most of the nineteenth centuries. In Holland and northern Germany, Mennonites enjoyed much freedom and economic opportunity. So, after the first few had gone to America, not many others followed. Instead, emigration proceeded from farther south.

In the eighteenth century new waves (or at least ripples) moved northward out of Switzerland into regions along the German Rhine; and out of those Rhineland regions, especially the Palatinate, other ripples formed and moved to Pennsylvania. Mennonites arriving in America from areas along the Rhine were overwhelmingly Swiss in origin. Very soon Mennonite communities in the New World became overwhelmingly Swiss and South German. That condition lasted until well into the nineteenth century, indeed until the 1870s, when large numbers of Mennonites of mainly Dutch and North German ancestry immigrated from Russia and settled in the western prairie states and provinces of the U.S. and Canada. Even thereafter, Amish people everywhere, and the great majority of Mennonites east of Kansas, Nebraska, Minnesota, and Manitoba, could trace their roots back to Switzerland and southern Germany.

European Rhinelands

Historians of immigration debate whether the strongest motives for moving have been the pull of new lands or various difficulties (that is, pushes) that people were feeling in their old homelands. Were conditions in the New World really so promising, or were restrictions and lack of opportunity in native lands so hopeless? Mennonite immigration to Pennsylvania in the eighteenth century would seem at first glance to be a classic case of strong "push" factors. To be sure, Mennonites heard various glowing reports spread by "newlanders"—that is by people who returned from America and tried to persuade neighbors to sail back with them[1]— and they were exposed to the exaggerated accounts published by zealous land agents. Yet the Mennonite experience of persecution and flight had surely made them as a pilgrim people aware that they had no lasting home in the Palatinate or in the cities and towns of the German Rhine. In 1727 seven Mennonite pastors wrote a letter from Mannheim confessing their inability to stem the tide of emigration. "The land is so full of people and the distress so great that the poor people hardly know how to support themselves," they explained.[2] Making the same point again and again in letters to their coreligionists in Holland, church leaders in the Palatinate emphasized not so much the glories of the New World but the problems their people were having at home.

Members of the Dutch Mennonites' Commission for Foreign Needs took a different view. That was the commission formed in 1710 with headquarters in Amsterdam, to better organize Dutch Mennonites' longtime aid to Mennonites and others, often refugees, suffering persecution and other hardships in different countries. Commission officals suggested to the Palatine Mennonite pastors that the stronger motive was the lure of Pennsylvania.[3] Apparently Dutch Mennonites, who were no longer in a struggle just for a tolerable existence, had all but forgotten hard times. So they interpreted the emigration as a movement not to escape hardship but to enjoy better opportunities. But their brothers and sisters farther south had ample reason to feel pushed.

The new emigration had roots in renewed persecution

in Switzerland, particularly in Canton Bern, and in various difficulties that Swiss emigrants or their children encountered when they settled in the German Rhinelands. In January 1708 a Mennonite merchant of Deventer, Netherlands, reported to Dutch Mennonite leaders what his community had been learning through letters from Switzerland and from a visit of two Swiss Mennonites. Bernese authorities had issued new edicts for jailing or banishing Mennonites (or Mennonites and Amish) and for punishing others who came to their aid. Indirectly, the reports suggested that the cause of persecution was their continued evangelism. Members of the established Reformed Church were often attending nighttime meetings that Mennonites held secretly, the merchant reported. Even some who had no thought of leaving the established church came, because they sought release from "certain things that hold them in bondage" and wanted to be "better people." In one congregation, eighteen persons had recently left the established church to join the Mennonites.[4]

In fact, while they suffered through generations of official rejection the spiritual descendants of Anabaptists in Canton Bern had managed to continue an underground church life. This they often did with the collusion of friends and relatives who risked fines and arrest for their help. Very possibly one reason that official resentment increased in the first decade of the 1700s was that the authorities were also fighting a new religious movement, Pietism. Like Anabaptism, Pietism stimulated various unauthorized religious expressions and activities. In 1699 authorities exiled the Pietist pastor of the largest Reformed congregation in Bern, Samuel Guldin, and other ministers for holding unauthorized prayer and Bible study meetings. No doubt the new religious movement revived some interest in the Mennonites. Alarm about Pietism made new government action against Mennonites almost inevitable.

Almost no Mennonite ministers left their flocks in the new wave of persecution. They felt they had to stay with their congregations for the sake of "babes whose eyes are [only] beginning to open to the way of truth."[5] If the ministers were exiled, they often slipped back home and continued their work in secret. One who finally did leave but only after several returns was a Benedikt Brechbuhl (Brackbill). Eventually Brechbuhl became a noted founder and spiritual leader of the first Mennonite settlement in present-day Lancaster County, Pennsylvania, south of Lancaster City along the Pequea (pronounced Peck-way) Creek. He united with the Mennonites in the 1680s at an age suggesting he converted from the Reformed faith. In the 1690s he became a preacher. Authorities banished him twice, but he returned. In 1707-1708 he was at Deventer for a time, probably in exile, but later in 1708 was back at Eggiwil in Canton Bern. There he was arrested and exiled. Again he returned, and on January 12, 1709, he and his wife tried to conceal themselves from a search party whom authorities sent looking for him. He hid under a pile of hay, but then the searchers began to poke their swords into the stack and the swords began to graze him, so he emerged and surrendered. Officials arrested not only him but also two non-Mennonites for harboring him: a brother of his named Christian and a neighbor named Hans Haldiman. For some eighteen weeks Brechbuhl remained in prison in a "special hole," bound by chains. Then for a year he was sentenced to a workhouse to make cloth from four o'clock each morning until eight at night.[6]

Finally the authorities decided to ship Brechbuhl and other prisoners to what is now North Carolina. A group of enterprising businessmen had invested in Carolina land: including Johann Rudolph Ochs, a native of Bern who had become an engraver in the British Royal Mint, and various well-to-do citizens of Bern led especially by two promoters, Franz Ludwig Michel and Christoph von Graffenreid. Needing population, the schemers had contracted with officials to take Mennonites there. On March 18, 1710, they loaded Brechbuhl and fifty-six other prisoners on boats to travel down the Rhine to Rotterdam and embark for the New World. The Rhine trip meant passing through Holland, of course, and that alarmed William Penn. Perhaps confusing the Mennonites with a different group headed not for Carolina but for his own Pennsylvania (also under Michel's auspices), Penn feared the Dutch government would interfere. But interference was exactly what the Dutch Mennonites wanted.

They were just then in the process of organizing their Commission for Foreign Needs in response to the new persecutions in Switzerland. So they appointed Laurens Hendricks, Mennonite pastor at Niemegen, to meet the refugees once the group was inside Holland. With help from the Dutch government, Laurens arranged for the refugees to be set free. To him they seemed most strange: wearing "long and unshaven beards, disordered clothing," and "great shoes, which were heavily hammered with iron and large nails." But, he said, they were devout, being "very zealous to serve God with prayer and reading and in other ways." To the more sophisticated Dutch pastor they seemed "very innocent in all doings as lambs and doves."[7]

None of that group went directly to America; instead many sought to reunite with families scattered in Switzerland, Alsace, and the Palatinate. Brechbuhl spent some time in Holland and then settled his family in the Palatinate. He continued to travel up and down the Rhine regions and even to Denmark and Prussia to speak on behalf of his persecuted brothers and sisters in Canton Bern, sometimes even taking his plea to the highest royal officials. Dutch Mennonites and the Dutch government opened diplomatic channels to get Swiss Mennonites released to the Dutch Mennonites' charge. They were so successful that throughout 1710 and 1711 a Dutch consul in Bern was kept quite busy with details. From places as distant as Hesse, Denmark, and Prussian Lithuania the refugees received various invitations to settle. According to a report from Swiss ministers in 1710, many refused to leave "on their own volition," counting instead "on the mercy of God" to let them "remain in the land as long as they can." Yet some went.[8]

A few Mennonites and Amish who left Switzerland went to Holland or away from the Rhine areas. Most went to Alsace or the Palatinate. But even as they did, many of their coreligionists were moving out of those same regions and going to the New World. Mennonites in the Palatinate and other Rhine areas faced an ironic situation. About a half-century earlier, their parents had moved from Switzerland northward into German provinces, drawn by landlords who were willing to help arrange religious toleration in order to fill underpopulated lands. Rents had been low. But in the half-century the efforts of the Mennonites themselves had helped make the soil more valuable. So rents had risen. Also, taxes had gone up, especially for religious minorities subject to special fees. By the early eighteenth century unstable prices for farm labor and farm produce were adding to the burdens of heavy taxes. Also in certain years and certain places, there were crop failures, unusually harsh winters, and new wars.[9] So while the Swiss who were facing outright persecution might find the Rhine areas relatively attractive, Mennonites and Amish already there thought more and more of emigrating. (Incidentally, their experience of being used by landlords and officials in the latter seventeenth century resembled in many respects that of Scotch settlers in Northern Ireland, many of whom would also enter Pennsylvania and become neighbors of Mennonites there and down into the back-country valleys of Maryland and Virginia.)

In such a situation, of course, the difficulties of remaining in the the Rhine regions were all too real. Consider the case of Hans Stauffer. In the latter 1680s Swiss authorities had banished him and he had settled at Alsheim, near Worms in the northern part of the Palatinate very near the Rhine. He then had to pay heavy taxes and fees. In the year 1703, for example, Palatine officials exacted three gulden forty-five kreutzers from him at one time and four gulden sixteen kreutzers at another in order (as he recorded in an account book) to help pay for war with the French and "costs of summons in the second registration." Stauffer also paid two gulden directly to a military officer. In 1704 he paid an average of five gulden per month in wartime levies—plus additional sums to "the French quartermaster at Altzei," to "the French wagon service," and again to a military official. He made further payments in 1705 "on the new French contribution." Eleven different times, for three days each, military authorities billeted a cavalryman with him. On three other occasions Stauffer kept an army wagoner, and he paid for two men to transport oats to the army. Meanwhile in 1705 Stauffer's Mennonite congregation had to pay still further "contribution" as a group. For that, Stauffer recorded, "I gave both burgomasters eighteen guldens forty-five kreutzers as contribution toward the third registration." On November 9, 1709, with his wife and five children, Hans Stauffer departed for America.[10]

Difficulties like these could be abated temporarily. In 1713 the so-called Peace of Utrecht stopped the heavy military activity. In 1714 a Mannheim Mennonite named Jacob Schnebli praised God that "it is much better than it was a year ago because the taxes were very heavy" at that time. But just as suddenly, the problems could resume. In 1716 a new ruler, Karl Philip, severely restricted the right of Mennonites to buy Palatine land, and at the same time doubled the Mennonites' fee for military exemption. With the land restrictions, well-to-do Mennonites competed more and more with poorer ones for lands to rent.[11] Hence, one more "push" to emigrate.

By the time of Karl Philip's new decree, promoter Johann Rudolph Ochs and his associates were offering the harassed Mennonites a solution. As early as 1702 Ochs' associate Franz Ludwig Michel had been in Virginia laying groundwork for what he and his fellow-investors hoped would be a Swiss colony there. Over the next few years, Michel explored the valleys of the Shenandoah, Potomac, and Susquehanna Rivers for other promising sites. In 1710 he served as William Penn's agent for locating lands for the Swiss Mennonite pioneers who settled along Lancaster County's Pequea Creek. About that time, of course, Michel, Ochs, and their friends were promoting their Carolina venture, the one to which they hoped to send Benedikt Brechbuhl and those fifty-six other Bernese Mennonite refugees. Then, their colony in the Carolinas failing to materialize, the same promoters, ever persistent, turned again to the Potomac region and focused their efforts on a tract in Maryland just above present-day Washington, D.C.[12]

Once again the Ochs group invited Mennonites to settle, this time in a section "separated from Virginia and Pennsylvania by high mountains" and "about thirty miles from the sea." By 1714 and 1715 Ochs had prepared a German-language circular to communicate his appeal. By 1716 apparently many Mennonites in Switzerland and the

Palatinate were reading it. Ochs promised would-be settlers that in Maryland they would "enjoy freedom of conscience" and be able to "worship according to their conscience" in an environment that he described, in the exaggerated language typical of such advertisements, as an earthly paradise. In the words of early twentieth-century Mennonite historian C. Henry Smith, "this portrayal of the enticing riches of the land beyond the seas which were to be had almost for the asking no doubt sounded like a description of the promised land to the ears of the poverty-stricken Swiss refugees and the war-ridden Palatines, whose farms at best consisted of a few worn out acres for which they were forced to pay exorbitant rents and taxes."[13]

Apparently the efforts of Ochs and his associates were successful at least to a point, for quite a few Mennonites emigrated in the spring of 1717. A few started out without enough resources for the trip. Rotterdam church leaders reported in April that 300 Mennonites from the Palatinate were in their city awaiting passage, and that among them were four families without money for the journey. The Commission for Foreign Needs wrote to the preachers in the Palatinate to discourage further emigration, lest it put impossible demands on the Commission's limited resources. At the same time, Dutch Mennonites found ways as private individuals to help the four needy families and send them on their way. But in the end only a few needed such assistance—an indication that this 1717 migration had been carefully planned and financed.[14]

On the other hand, the 1717 Mennonite emigrants did not find new homes in Maryland or Virginia where Ochs and his associates were trying to direct them. Martin Kendig, one of the Pequea pioneers of 1710, had returned to Europe to recruit settlers for the Mennonite colony in present Lancaster County, Pennsylvania. Benedikt Brechbuhl and Hans Burckholder presided at a meeting of Mennonite leaders at Mannheim, and the leaders decided to favor emigration to Pennsylvania. Thereupon Brechbuhl and Burckholder led some sixty families to join the Pequea settlers. Other Mennonite emigrants of 1717 found new homes in the region between the Skippack and the Perkiomen, northwest of Philadelphia. The year 1717 brought one of the largest Mennonite migrations in the eighteenth century. On September 3, 1717 three ship captains reported to the Pennsylvania authorities that they had brought 363 persons from the Palatinate to Philadelphia.[15]

None of this large group of Mennonites went directly to the lands advertised by Johann Rudolph Ochs; his project, like many others, had to be abandoned. A few years later, however, several Mennonites who emigrated from the Kraichgau in Baden in 1717 moved to Virginia's Shenandoah Valley and took up land in a new settlement that Ochs and Jacob Stover had established there.[16] Promoters such as Ochs and Stover helped provide white settlers for the American frontier. But back in the Palatinate, emigration could practically decimate a particular Mennonite community. For instance, between 1697 and 1717 Mennonite population in the Alzey district in the far northern part of the Palatinate, some fifteen miles northeast of Worms, dropped from sixty-four to nineteen families.[17]

In their moving, Mennonites were part of a much larger transfer of German-speaking peoples emigrating to Pennsylvania and elsewhere. Some 5,000 immigrants from German-speaking countries arrived in Pennsylvania between 1683 and 1726. By 1726 an estimated 20,000 persons of German or Swiss-German descent lived in the colony. Five ships brought 1,198 Germans to Philadelphia in September and October of 1727. The number of immigrants dropped to fewer than half that number in the next years, but rose again to 2,095 in 1732. With many peaks and valleys in different years, German-speaking immigration rose overall until the number who arrived at the port of Philadelphia each year from 1749 to 1754 averaged 4,332. In these same years, other Germans came ashore in Nova Scotia, Maine, Boston, New York, the Maryland and Virginia ports on Chesapeake Bay, and the Carolinas and Georgia; but for those entries there are no exact figures. The years 1749 to 1754 brought peak numbers for the eighteenth century. Then the Seven Years' War of 1756-1763, concomitantly in the New World the French and Indian War changed circumstances, ushering in an unsettled, revolutionary era for America, and sharply reducing immigration for a time.[18]

On the whole, Mennonite migrations from Europe into Pennsylvania followed larger patterns of German migration, rather than the Mennonites' showing their own unique trends. To be sure, Mennonites made up a larger proportion of the total in the 1720s and 1730s than in later decades. A high proportion of arrivals in those earlier decades were Mennonites or members of somewhat similar minorities such as Dunkers and Schwenkfelders, who perhaps more than their "church" neighbors (that is, Lutheran, Reformed, and Catholic) were inclined to emigrate in congregational groups and extended families. But ships to America frequently carried no more than one or two Mennonite families as Mennonites traveled with neighbors of other faiths. And the overall pattern was that the years of greatest Mennonite emigration were peak years for Palatine emigration generally. Movements of people out of the region of Bonfeld, a village near Heidelberg, shows that the years of exodus—1709, 1717, and 1727—were years when even larger numbers of "church" people (in this case Lutherans) left. Of one hundred leaving in 1717, no more than perhaps thirty were Mennonite—ten adults and twenty children. About two thirds were Lutheran. One Mennonite, a bricklayer, had a child who had been baptized as a Lutheran. Most of the Bonfelders traceable in America settled outside of developing Mennonite communities, although four Mennonite families, those of Heinrich and Martin Funck and of Franz and John Heinrich Neff, did settle among other Mennonites in the vicinity of Lancaster.[19] In general, Mennonite migration followed the larger patterns of emigration from regions along the Rhine.

Mennonite emigration reflected the larger pattern with regard to age distribution. According to historian Marianne Wokeck, that distribution "was relatively more balanced in the 1730s, when both proportionally and absolutely more men over fifty immigrated, than in the 1740s, when few men in that age group arrived"; and it became very lopsided in the 1750s, when almost no male Germans over fifty immigrated into Philadelphia. Yet even for Mennonites, and even in the 1730s, the New World was a place primarily for young families starting adult life. A group of thirty-two Mennonites who arrived on the *Samuel* in 1732 with their passage paid at least in part by the Dutch Mennonites' Commission included one man of forty-seven with a much younger wife and their children; a widow of forty-six; a family headed by a man of thirty and his twenty-eight-year-old wife with their children; two other heads of families aged twenty-six and twenty-eight; and seven young men aged between twenty and twenty-four, four of them married. The age distribution was similar among other categories of *Samuel* passengers: both among those who were probably Mennonites but paid their own way, and among those known to have been of other faiths.[20]

Studying German immigration to the port of Philadelphia, Wokeck found that "the increase of younger men occurred noticeably in the early peak years of 1732 and 1738, when the most crowded ships transported disproportionally high numbers of twenty-year-old males." The youthful pattern and the decline in the number of men over fifty became even more typical in the 1740s, for in that decade the number of eighteen-year-olds increased significantly. That was due to a new conscription law in the Palatinate that did away with the traditional exemption for men engaged to be married, and practically allowed only the rich to buy out of the draft.[21]

Through all this—the seasonal ups and downs and the age distributions—Mennonite emigration followed general emigration patterns closely enough to make one conclusion seem quite clear: although some of the difficulties of staying in Europe came from special legislation and discrimination against Mennonites, many more came from economic conditions, wars, and other circumstances that troubled Mennonites' nonpacifist "church" neighbors about as much as it troubled Mennonites and other pacifists.

The action of the Commission for Foreign Needs to help those thirty-two Mennonites on board the *Samuel* was part of a larger Mennonite pattern. Since almost all German emigrants including Mennonites passed through Rotterdam, and since Dutch Mennonites were influential and well-off financially, the Commission was in an excellent position to furnish both advice and money to brothers and sisters from the southern regions along the Rhine. As the eighteenth century progressed, it operated what was virtually an emigration office. Many departing Mennonites could testify to the commitment of the Dutch to mutual aid within the larger Mennonite fellowship. Contributing also to emigrants' needs were congregations in Switzerland, in Alsace, in the Palatinate, in Krefeld, and in Pennsylvania.

Thanks largely to the Commission, the departures of Mennonites, Amish, and Schwenkfelders from Europe were exceptionally well organized and financed, compared to eighteenth-century-German emigration in general.[22] This was ironic, for Commission members tried again and again to discourage their Palatine brothers and sisters from going. Dutch Mennonite leaders regularly wrote to preachers in the Palatinate and elsewhere begging them to stem the outgoing tide. They tried to counteract the attraction of Pennsylvania by pointing to the hardships involved in starting anew in a wilderness and by warning that Penn's generous guarantees of religious liberty might one day come to an end. They emphasized the perils of the passage, sometimes with clippings and translations from Dutch newspapers telling stories of shipwrecks, of pirates and privateers, and of a case of 150 Palatines who sailed from Rotterdam in 1731 and did not reach land in the New World until twenty-four weeks later, after many had starved to death and the survivors had subsisted on rats and other vermin. The Commission members repeatedly asked preachers to refuse to grant emigrants church letters or certificates of membership.[23]

The Dutch Mennonites also tried to lessen the difficulties their brothers and sisters were facing in the Palatinate, for they promised to help the needy among Mennonites in that region if they did not leave. If too many Palatine Mennonites emigrated, the Dutch reasoned, the strain on the Commission's resources would be too great. Commission members even tried to dissuade the emigrants who could pay their own way on grounds that if too many prosperous Mennonites left, the poorer brothers and sisters who remained would have to find employment outside the Mennonite community. Moreover, the Dutch reasoned, if only the poorer Mennonites stayed, rulers who had extended toleration to Mennonites because they created economic wealth and paid extra taxes might rescind that toleration.[24]

To Dutch Mennonites' minds the Palatine motives for going seemed frivolous. "It would be a totally different matter if persecution existed in the Palatinate and these people in their need would have to leave their homes," some Amsterdam preachers advised in 1727. It seemed to the comfortable Dutch that Palatine Mennonites were anxious to risk a difficult and dangerous voyage "simply to have a change of air on the uncertainty that things would be better for them in Pennsylvania."[25]

Yet despite all their doubts, the Hollanders provided organization and financial assistance that was crucial for many who wished to emigrate. For instance, on May 19, 1727, a group led by preacher Hans Oberholtzer, and deacon Christian Moyer, arrived at Rotterdam after a voyage down the Rhine on four ships. They had come from Kriegsheim and neighboring villages in southern Germany near Mannheim, the center of earlier Mennonite migration to Pennsylvania. In November 1726 their pastors had written to the Commission saying that when spring came several families would begin the trip to Pennsylvania. Most had sufficient means, the pastors said, but a few would need help. Two families, eight persons altogether, lacked passage money. Oberholtzer and Moyer asked for help, and the Commission agreed.[26]

Some families in this group had come to the Palatinate from Canton Bern only a few years earlier. Ulrich Stauffer brought his family directly from Switzerland. Swiss records show that Christian Stauffer, guardian of his brother Ulrich's family, a Mennonite who had already left Bern, petitioned the authorities in March 1727 for permission for Ulrich's wife, Lucia Stauffer (born Ramseyer), and their six children to emigrate to Pennsylvania and to take with them their property of £1,900. The account book for 1727 of the Landvogt of Signau, Canton Bern, records that "Lucia Stauffer, wife of the Anabaptist Ulrich Stauffer, has emigrated to Pennsylvania with her children and has paid the emigration tax on 550 crowns." The Stauffers sailed in September 1727

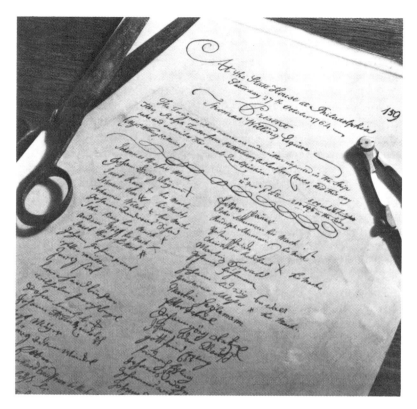

Ship lists with passenger signatures collected by port authorities are valuable records of Mennonite and Amish arrivals. This one from the _Hero_, Oct. 27, 1764. (Jan Gleysteen collection)

on the _James Goodwill_ with 166 other Palatines including about ten other Mennonite families.[27]

The majority of the Mennonites in the Oberholtzer-Moyer group sailed on the _Friendship_ and landed at Philadelphia on October 16, 1727. They made up more than half the passengers on this ship. If the Dutch were impressed with the perils of passage, they had a point: preacher Hans Oberholtzer and six other heads of families died on the Atlantic crossing and ten other men were too sick to sign the statement of allegiance when the _Friendship_ reached port. We do not know how many women and children died on shipboard. The Mennonites who survived the voyage joined their former neighbors from Kriegsheim and Alzey in the settlements between the Perkiomen and Skippack Creeks. A few years later Abraham Swartz, Andrew Swartz, Christian Moyer, and Valentine Kratz were trustees of the Salford meetinghouse (near present-day Harleysville, Pennsylvania); and other *Friendship* immigrants appeared on tax lists in the same neighborhood. Three or four went farther west to Lancaster and York counties. Several Reformed families on board the same ship settled in the Goshenhoppen area, a bit north of Salford on the Perkiomen Creek.[28]

The Commission came to the rescue of another forty-five persons who lacked funds to pay their own way. The forty-five, who made up ten families, were part of a larger group of 150 would-be immigrants who arrived in Holland in 1727. The foreign needs commission paid passages for all forty-five on a ship named *Molly.* Among those who received help were Michael Frantz, later a well-known preacher in the Conestoga Dunker congregation, Peter Good, Samuel Oberholtzer, Christian Holderman, Samuel Good, Rudolph Landis, Jacob Hochstetter (who died on board), Jacob Huber, Rudolph Boehm, and Martin Kindig. Other Mennonites, including Christian Wenger, Jacob and Samuel Baer, Hans Longenecker, Jacob and David Martin, Michael Schenck, Hans Funck, and others, sailed on the *Molly* at their own expense. Many of these Mennonites settled along Muddy Creek and the Conestoga in Brecknock, Cocalico, and Earl Townships in northeastern Lancaster County. Their Catholic, Lutheran, and Reformed fellow-passengers, by contrast, concentrated around Goshenhoppen and Falckner Swamp in present-day Berks and Montgomery counties.[29]

Mennonite immigrants came from one region one year, and from a different section in another year. In 1731 and 1732, for instance, some Mennonites, mostly young, left villages near Heidelberg for new homes in America. Hans Heinrich Martin may be typical of them. Martin was a thirty-year-old farm worker. He had leased some land from Nicholas Stumpf, a farmer in the Kraichgau region of Baden, near Heidelberg, and had farmed there in 1728, 1729, and 1730. As the result of "the great misfortune of a fire on my farm," his landlord wrote in 1731, Martin lost "his total harvest of

A label in German script on the lid of this chest in the restored 1719 Herr House near Willow Street, Pennsylvania, reads: "This chest belongs to Hans Marti Amwäg and Barbera [sic] Wisler and Anle Medi Amwäg and Maride [Marita] Amwäg. Written in the year 1737. (Courtesy Lancaster Mennonite Historical Society)

1729, as well as his hay and straw." After this disaster Martin tried to start over, but he "now wants to move to try his fortune elsewhere, with his pregnant wife and three small children." Stumpf testified that the Martins were "pious, honest, and virtuous, and living in peace with all." Martin had "behaved as a good servant", cared for "his land and goods as an experienced and able farmer, and has kept them in such a way that I would have liked to keep him longer."[30]

With economic ruin facing him at home, Heinrich Martin "got a good letter from his brothers in Pennsylvania," so good that the preachers in the Grumbach congregation where the Martins worshiped "could not keep him from this trip." Therefore Heinrich Kendig and Michel Kreibel, pastor and deacon, wrote a letter in the Martins' behalf to the Commission for Foreign Needs. They testified that "he is a brother and his wife a sister in our congregation of the so-called Mennonites" and that he was going to Pennsylvania "to seek his fortune by God's help." Durs (Theodore) Horsch with his wife and three children traveled with the Martins from Grumbach to Rotterdam, with similar testimonials from landlord and pastor.[31]

The good organization and financial assistance available to Mennonite emigrants did not mean that they necessarily crossed the ocean in large clusters, much less as entire congregations. Martin and Horsch were typical of Mennonite emigrants in that, assisted by their home congregation and anticipating help from Mennonites in Holland, they set out by themselves, not as part of a large emigrant group. Near the close of their journey to Holland the two young families were joined by Heinrich Kever (Geber) and his large family from Krefeld. The Commission for Foreign Needs gave each family some money. But, as Dirk van Beek of the Rotterdam Mennonite congregation reported to the Commission in Amsterdam, the money was far from enough. The three families could not find a ship ready to sail for America, van Beek wrote, "and may have to remain another two weeks, so that they are forced to spend the money which you gave them to help with the cost of their passage." They could neither go to Pennsylvania nor return to the Palatinate without additional help. The Dutch Mennonites found more money and eventually the Horsch family sailed on the *Snow Lowther,* a small craft in the tobacco trade. The Martins and Gebers joined a larger party of Mennonites on the *Britannia.* [32]

The Dutch were thorough in their efforts. The following year more Mennonites from the Martins' and Gebers' home district emigrated. In May 1732 the Commission for Foreign Needs addressed a circular letter to the congregations above Mannheim and Heidelberg in Baden (then included in Ober-Pfalz, the Upper Palatinate), responding to a letter sent them from Immelhausen advising "that again several families from the Palatinate are planning to come this way and go on to Pennsylvania." Several lists of this party in the Commission's archives illustrate the Dutch thoroughness. Commission officals noted that Christian Frantz from Haselhof had "assurance from Pennsylvania that his freight will be paid in money" for himself, his wife, and eleven children. Christian Huber from Durnen had the same "assurance from his friends and father in Pennsylvania." Samuel Brand, a young unmarried man from Boekschaft, was "able to pay his own travel costs," as were many others from their community. Hans Scherer's widow, traveling from Boekschaft with three children and her two daughters' husbands, Ulrich Burkholder and Jacob Good, had 255 guilders and would need some help. The cost of passage for a family of two adults and four children amounted to 300 guilders, so the Samuel and Martin Moyer families had sufficient for their voyage. Christian Martin and his wife and two children had only 100 guilders. Oswald Hostetter from Hasselbach, with his wife and four children, had 650 guilders which were more than adequate for their passage and a start in Pennsylvania. Christian Gehman with his wife and child and his brother Benedict, also from Hasselbach, had sufficient passage money; their neighbor Michael Dirstine had only thirty guilders, but "expects the rest from his friends" in America. Commission officials did not stop at organizing and financing the emigrants for the journey. They noted that Hans Witmer and his wife had no church letter and had been dismissed from their congregation. And they thought someone should induce him to pay a fine he had left unpaid upon leaving home.[33]

With such care for detail, the Dutch Mennonites arranged for seventy persons to sail for Pennsylvania on the *Samuel* and the *Plaisance* in 1732, along with several Mennonite families from the same communities who did not require the Commission's help. People of those groups seem to have settled in Pennsylvania with families from their own home congregations. The Gehmans, Dirstines, and Hostetters from Hasselbach went to Bucks County. Many of the emigrants from Boekschaft and Mocksheim went to Lancaster County, settling in Brecknock and Earl townships.[34]

Thus Mennonite emigration in these years was both organized and partly financed by the Commission for Foreign Needs. The emigrants left most frequently with a few others from the same congregation or at least the same district, but even in the more organized groups there were families who left their homes by themselves. Many traveled as extended families who included grandparents, parents, and brothers-in-law and sisters-in-law. But a large proportion were young fathers and mothers or single men and women. The Dutch Mennonite records indicate that such people were "going to Pennsylvania to better their fortune" or start over after some economic disaster. Some Palatine preachers cited the fear of renewed warfare in the Palatinate as a motive for people to leave, but that explanation often comes coupled with references to poverty, lack of land, and high taxes. C. Henry Smith, the first historian to study Mennonite immigration into Pennsylvania, observed that the movement, "although following its own course in a measure, yet was also influenced by the general movement, being heaviest when the total number of Palatine arrivals was highest, and lightest when the general movement was at a low ebb."[35]

The Commission for Foreign Needs helped Amish emigrants as well as Mennonite. Benevolent activity in the latter 1600s, before the formal organization of the Commission, had brought divided Dutch Mennonites together for such practical purposes; now, in the same spirit, it ignored the lines created by the Reist-Ammann quarrel of the 1690s. At least it aided some Amish enough to make one *Reistisch* (that is, Mennonite, as compared to Amish) pastor in the Palatinate jealous. In 1742 the pastor, Hans Burkholder of a congregation at Gerolsheim near Frankenthal, remarked that he had heard of an emigrating Amish congregation who had received letters from the Commission encouraging them to come ahead, and telling them that the Dutch "would see that they landed safely." Burkholder thought it strange that Commission officals encouraged the Amish but discouraged their fellow-Mennonites.[36]

If the Dutch really were partial to the Amish, neither that fact nor their reasons are clear. But from the outset Amish migration differed somewhat from that of Mennonites who had refused to follow Jacob Ammann. In Switzerland itself the Amish congregations were quicker to leave. That was because, compared to Reist's followers, the Amish developed a more separated and exclusive understanding of church. Amish congregations did not have many of the kind of people earlier known as "Half-Anabaptists," that is, people who outwardly conformed to the state church but who sympathized and were in close contact with Mennonites or Amish. Such people created ties to the local communities. Neither did the Amish have as many Reformed Church Pietists attending their gatherings. The *Reistisch* thought that to leave the Half-Anabaptists and the Pietist fellow-travelers would be to abandon babes in the faith, or "little ones who were just opening their eyes."[37] The Amish left more easily, because they had drawn clearer boundaries and had cut ties more cleanly with family and friends in the established church. As for Amish who later left for America not from Switzerland but from the Palatinate or Alsace, they too seem to have been better able to finance their own emigration than were many of the *Reistisch.* Apparently those Amish emigrants to whom Burkholder referred, whom the Dutch helped in 1742, needed only some direction and guidance. This appears to have been the pattern with most eighteenth-century Amish emigrants. Again, the reason may well have been a more close-knit group structure.[38]

Amish families may have come to Pennsylvania as early as the 1720s and early 1730s, for shiplists of those years include names that some researchers have presumed to be Amish. However, identity of those names is not positive, and it may be that no Amish arrived until 1736. Whatever the truth, in that year Amishmen Melchior Detweiler and Hans Sieber, both in their thirties, arrived with their families, perhaps as advance agents for a larger Amish group who then crossed the Atlantic in 1737. The first two families traveled on the *Princess Augusta,* a ship that carried passengers from Switzerland and Alsace as well as from the Palatinate. By 1744 the Detweilers had settled on Northkill Creek at the foot of the Blue Mountains in northwest Berks County, Pennsylvania. In 1737 Sieber and an Amishman named Jacob Beiler, who had immigrated scarcely two months earlier, jointly patented land, 184 acres for each, on Irish Creek in what was then Bern Township in Berks County. The Irish Creek location became the center of a second early Amish community.[39]

Amish immigration began in earnest on October 8, 1737, with the arrival of the *Charming Nancy,* a ship that had at least nineteen Amish families on board. The *Charming Nancy* was evidently an unhealthful ship, for during the voyage Hans Jacob Kauffman, keeping a diary in the margins of an almanac, recorded the deaths of twenty-two children and two adults among the Amish passengers alone. Jacob Beiler, Jacob Mast, Christian Miller, Christian Hershberger, Christian Berkey, Hans Zimmerman, Henry Stehly, and Ulrich Spicher with their families were among the *Charming Nancy* passengers who survived, found new homes, and became neighbors along Irish Creek. Berkey and Zimmerman also purchased land before the end of 1737. Others in the group settled along the Northkill.[40]

The ability of Sieber and Beiler each to purchase 184-acre tracts so soon after crossing the ocean suggests that some Amish immigrants had managed to collect sufficient capital for the journey and for a start in the New World. Amish settlers in both the Irish Creek and the later Northkill settlements obtained title to land within a few years of their arrival, nearly all of them within ten years of immigrating. Joint purchases of land were fairly common in eighteenth-century Amish settlements. Perhaps such willingness to work together and pool resources goes far to explain why the Amish managed to finance their own emigration.

In keeping with a sense of close-knit group life, some Amish quite naturally established themselves where other Amish had settled ahead of them. Hans Burkholder, in the letter questioning Dutch policy in 1742, referred to twelve Amish families who crossed the Atlantic together on the *Francis and Elizabeth* and landed at Philadelphia on September 21, 1742. Johannes Gnage, brothers Moritz, Christian, and Johannes Zug, Johannes Gerber, Jacob Gut, Heinrich and Christian Miller, Christian Yoder, Sr., Christian Yoder, Jr., and Jacob Yoder all joined the Amish communities in upper Berks County. Jacob Kurtz was the only one in this group who chose to settle in Lancaster County. Two years later, in 1744, others brought their families to the Amish settlements on Irish Creek and the Northkill: brothers Hans and Stephen Kurtz, Christian and Jacob

Koenig and Christian's son Samuel, Yost Yoder, Michael Stucky, and Johannes Schneider. When the first Amish bishop in America, Jacob Hertzler, arrived on the *Saint Andrew*, he also bought land at Northkill. That was in 1749. Landing a few days after the Hertzlers were some Amish families who crossed on the *Phoenix* and settled among members of their faith who were already in Berks County.[41]

Yet by no means did all Amish follow that pattern. Most Amish who arrived in 1749 went to areas where Amish were few. Preacher Abraham Kurtz and Christian Schowalter, from the same Amish congregation in the Palatinate, both settled in Lancaster County's Earl Township; so also did Amishmen Jacob Seiler, John Rupp, and others. An Amish preacher named Abraham Drachsel (Troxell) led a group to settle in the Lebanon Valley. Perhaps Amish were already following a pattern that a scholar named James Landing noticed in later Amish migrations westward to states such as Ohio and Indiana: small nuclei of Amish, often with kinship ties, scattering into new areas, then other Amish gradually filling in the spaces between to create the larger, heavily-Amish communities known today.[42] Apparently, once the Amish landed in the New World the enticements that pulled immigrants to America, such as price and availability of land, were strong enough to prevent them from all settling together despite the strength of Amish group life.

In contrast to the largely self-financed Amish, quite a few *Reistisch* Mennonite emigrants depended on the Dutch Mennonites or others outside their own congregations for finances as well as other help. They received help despite the bias of the Dutch against emigration. In the first group who left when the outflow of Mennonites of Swiss origin began about 1707, only Wynant Bouman asked for such help. In 1709 emigration coming from Hesse and the Palatinate and passing through England swelled to some 13,500 in a single year. Among those thousands were some sixty Mennonites, some of them very poor. In April 1709 some Rotterdam Mennonites informed other Dutch leaders that "nine or ten families," all Mennonites, had recently "arrived here from the Palatinate . . . from Worms and Frankenthal." They had testimonials from their congregations, and were headed for

Pennsylvania. But they were "poor people," with "hardly any means to feed themselves, even less the money necessary for being shipped from here to England and from thence to make the great journey"; and in America, "they will need money to get settled."[43].

Apparently someone helped that group, for records indicate that they passed through London. Moreover, later in the same month English Quakers in the London Yearly Meeting took note of needy Palatine refugees passing through their country's ports, including "about Sixty Persons that have been lately obliged to leave their Native Country the Palatinate on Account of General Poverty and Missery (and are now here) being by Religion them called Minists." At the moment, the Quakers understood, "charitable persons" were meeting the sixty persons' needs. Later, in July, the Yearly Meeting accepted a bill of £48 for Mennonites' passage and freight to Pennsylvania.[44]

In August of 1709 Jacob Telner, then temporarily in London, informed Dutch Mennonites that English Quakers had already helped eight Mennonite families, and that he thought the Dutch might help six other families "of our brethren, namely High German Mennonites," who wanted to go to Pennsylvania. It is not clear who those families were, although historian Martin H. Brackbill has shown convincingly that they probably were not Lancaster County's first Mennonite settlers, as some have thought. Family heads among the first settlers were Martin Kendig, Martin Oberholtzer, Jacob Miller, Martin Maili, Christian Herr, and Hans Herr, who, with their families, were in London on June 24, 1710. From that city they wrote to the Dutch Mennonites and referred to having been delayed there more than ten weeks, straining their finances. Apparently they had appealed earlier to the Dutch for emergency help, for they thanked the Dutch for a contribution that had evidently reached them in London.[45]

Apparently at least in that case the Dutch only lent rather than gave the money. Even while it helped various emigrants, the Commission continued to advise against emigration. Perhaps partly for those reasons many of the emigrants depended on mutual aid from the congregations they left or to which they went. And when they did, whether they received the help from Europe or from the New World, usually they were to make repayment by contributing to the poor fund of whatever congregation they joined in America.

While mutual aid appears more strongly among the Amish, it existed among both Amish and Mennonite. In the alms book of the Mennonite congregation at Skippack someone later noted that one Abraham Groff had repaid £2 advanced him on October 6, 1742. The advance had been "to pay for his freight or passage over the sea . . . but with the understanding said Groff was to repay it when able." Groff had been a passenger on the *Francis and Elizabeth,* a ship that had transported both some Mennonites and some Amish.[46] In an Amish congregation, farther west in the Conestoga-Pequea region, one Abraham Kurtz received payment of £13 in April and May of 1777. That was from a man named Samuel Schenck, whose Amish brothers had helped in 1774 by paying a Mr. Robert Ritchie for money advanced to Schenck for passage on the *Union.* [47] In other words, fellow church members had rescued Schenck from being sold as a redemptioner, a kind of indentured servant who otherwise would not have been a free man until he had worked a specified time to pay the passage money.

Back in Switzerland, in March 1754, the steward of the bishop of Basel complained that peasants in his district had little cash because a group of Anabaptists who had recently left had drained the community of money by first collecting all debts owed to them. If he was referring to a group of Swiss Mennonites who emigrated that year from the Sonnenberg region, which indeed fell within the bishop's district, some members of the group nevertheless were poor and unable to finance their passage. Consequently, both their home congregation and their new one in Lancaster County to which they headed provided aid that reached across the Atlantic. The ministers of the Sonnenberg congregation agreed to advance 740 kronen to help "several poor ones" among "several of our people" who "have decided to travel to America." The steward reported that there were twenty-six persons who paid an emigration tax; among them were Hans Schwarz, Jost Schonauer, Isaac Neuenschwander, Niclaus Moser,

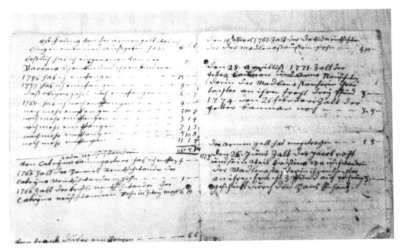

These pages from the almsbook of the Bowmansville Mennonite congregation in Lancaster County, Pennsylvania, show the record of passage payments from Barbara Schenk and her children, Catharine Neuschwander, Francis Diller (left page), Magdalena Stauffer, Peter Bauman, Jacob Roth, and Christina Newswenger (right page) from 1756 to 1773. (Courtesy Lancaster Mennonite Historical Society)

Magdalena Stauffer, Ulrich Neukommet, and Babi Burckhalter who were all "people from the mountains near Corgemont, most of them very poor." Also among them were Abraham Brechbuhler and his family and Ulrich Leichti and his family, who were "very poor Anabaptists," so poor they "could hardly pay their rent." On the other hand it appears that most of the groups managed to pay their own way. One member, Ulrich Engel of Sonceboz, was so wealthy that of £100 which the twenty-six emigrants paid, Engel paid £67.[48]

The Sonnenberg congregation put Engel in charge of an agreement that those who received help would repay in America, as they became able. So Hans Burkholder, Jost Schonauwer, Barbara Schanck, Catdrina Baumgardner, and Madlena Neuwenschwander formally agreed that when they arrived "in America in Benzelvania [sic]," when "by the blessing of God they or their (families) can accomplish it," they would "secure and pay...with the condition that this...shall be for the poor there." The immigrants did not forget their obligation. In America deacon Joseph Wenger, who arrived in the same party, kept careful account of poor funds. Between 1756 and 1766, Barbara Shenk and her children paid £66, 5s., 10d. in small installments. From "Catherine Baumgartner or Newswander" Wenger received £4; other sums came from her sons John and Christian Newschwander of Earl Township, and from Frantz Diller of Brecknock, another passenger on the *Phoenix*, the ship on which the group traveled. As late as 1774 the children of Madeline Stauffer paid small installments "towards her passage expense." Her son David Neuschwander, "Peter Bowman and Anna Neuschwander the daughter of Madeline Stauffer," and "Jacob Roth and his wife Christina Neuschwander the daughter of Madeline Stauffer" are listed in Deacon Wenger's records. In a separate undated document, Nicholas Tschantz, Peter Burkholder, Ulli Burkholder, and Joseph Wenger agreed "that nothing is to be required from Hans Burkolter for the passage money for his wife paid by us."[49]

The emigrants didn't forget others with similar needs later on. Christian Aeschliman arrived at Philadelphia on October 29, 1770, on the ship *Sally*. Deacon Joseph Wenger and Nicholas Tschantz, Mennonite farmers in Brecknock Township in Berks County, borrowed money from other members of their Mennonite congregation to help Aeschliman in his need. Wenger's account of the poor money in the Bowmansville Mennonite congregation records their effort at mutual aid: "November 18 1770 Jacob Good loaned to Nicholas Tschantz 2 pounds 10 shillings which was used to pay passage for Christian Eshelman. On Novr. 18 I Joseph Wenger have handed over to Nicholas Tschantz money which I have borrowed from Old Jacob Sensenig which shall be used to pay Christian Eshelman's passage 12 pounds. Nicholas Tschantz has received from John Ulli Reist money for the Poor Fund the sum of 13 pounds. Novr. 18 1770 I Joseph Wenger have handed over to Nicholas Tschantz from the Poor Fund the sum of 8 pounds." These Swiss Mennonites in Brecknock and Earl Townships evidently contributed £22, 10s. to bring a needy brother to America. It is possible that Christian Eshelman was Deacon Christian Aeschelman, a man who signed the agreement with the *Phoenix* immigrants in 1754—or at least a member of his family. If so, the mutual aid went full circle.[50]

The story of Amish and Mennonite emigration to America in the eighteenth century is a chronicle of mutual aid and assistance, a chronicle of transatlantic peoplehood. With the Commission for Foreign Needs plus local congregations in Holland, western Germany, Switzerland, and America providing the aid, Mennonites and Amish who crossed the Atlantic were better organized and better financed than many of their neighbors who crossed with them. New World Mennonites and Amish made America all the more attractive by preventing the newly arriving brothers from falling into indentured servitude. They did so even more by providing communities into which their brothers and sisters could enter.

Improved financing and organization is not the whole story of mutual aid. The aid was both result and symbol of a deeper reality. Swiss and Palatine immigrants went to Holland in full knowledge that a community awaited them there, a community to which they belonged and on whose resources they could draw. Dutch Mennonites may have resisted the implications of this theory of the church as an extended family; at least in some of their letters to the Palatinate, they seemed to. Yet for all the problems, the way Mennonites and Amish dealt with needy emigrants and immigrants is a tribute to success in building a community that extended beyond national, linguistic, and cultural frontiers.

The families who stepped ashore at Philadelphia and at other Atlantic ports had emigrated for a variety of reasons. Virginia Mennonites declared in 1785 that their "forefathers and Predessors came from a far Country to America to Seek Religious Liberty."[51] Such a statement is often heard, and emphasizes the attractions pulling Mennonites to America. It also emphasizes religious rather than economic motives. But in fact, economics was also very important to the men and women who sought "to better their fortunes in Pennsylvania."[52] And much of the economic motive was not the attraction of America but the difficult conditions that pushed Mennonites, Amish, and others out of lands along the German Rhine.

Mennonite and Amish identity and sense of community did not proceed solely from their heritage of persecution for the faith. In the eighteenth century harsh laws or outright persecution were by no means the major motives for crossing to America. Heavy taxes and bad economic conditions were more likely reasons. Yet even as they moved for largely economic reasons, the emigrants retained a strong instinct of community. The vast amount of mutual aid surrounding the emigration was a practical expression of that instinct. And the aid served to reinforce both the "pushes" and the "pulls."

CHAPTER

3

THE LAND BASE OF COMMUNITY

Once Mennonite and Amish immigrants entered America, the "pulls" took over. It seems that from the outset those pulls were largely economic rather than being an attraction to some clear vision of how to shape a religious community. Availability of land and enticements that land agents offered were prime shapers of Mennonites' settlement patterns. Mennonites were often in a better position than others to buy land in or near neighborhoods where other families of their faith already lived. Therefore, in many cases, young Mennonites just getting established or Mennonites recently from Europe could help expand existing settlements or buy land not previously held by Mennonite people. Some of the neighborhoods of course began to fill up, and some of the families moved on or immigrated directly from Europe to new places where the process might start anew. But whether in older or newer locations, neighborhoods emerged with enough concentrations of Mennonite people on the land to form Mennonite communities.

Mennonites always continued to live among neighbors of other faiths; their settlements were not isolated, exclusive enclaves. Yet in key communities of southeastern Pennsylvania in the eighteenth century, Mennonite families tended to form a stable or an increasing proportion of the inhabitants, rather than being displaced by people of other faiths or ethnic groups. Mutual aid, a sense of community, and no doubt much hard work helped them get, develop, and keep land in their own neighborhoods. Such economic and social influences did not necessarily work against the pur-

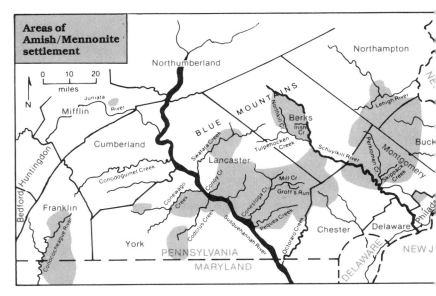

Southeastern Pennsylvania, about 1780. (Adapted from James Lemon, *The Best Poor Man's Country*)

suit of religious vision or the building of religious community; certain kinds of religious community need specific geographical location and some comfortable amount of wealth as prerequisites. On the other hand, by 1770 at least one Mennonite preacher thought his people's pursuit of wealth was interfering with their religious vision. Whether or not he was right, economics did much to determine settlement patterns, and land was the base for other aspects of community.

In 1710 most of the land of eastern Pennsylvania was still unmarked wilderness without fences or boundary lines except on paper in the Land Office in Philadelphia. But already much of it was in the hands of speculators, chiefly merchants in Philadelphia or London. Serving as a speculator for northern European Mennonites, and attracting some of them to Skippack, was Matthias Jacobs van Bebber. Meanwhile non-Mennonites, under similar but different enticement, were clustering farther north at Falckner's Swamp and Goshenhoppen. Lands farther west were also increasingly important. In 1710 Samuel Guldin, the Pietistic Reformed minister banished from Switzerland, reported from Pennsylvania that "for more than forty miles [from Philadelphia] everything has been taken up." Land, he said, "is very expensive, so that one hundred acres of uncultivated land cost eighteen pounds sterling or more, if it is near the city."[1]

So the Mennonites of Swiss-origin often settled farther out. In 1710 Penn's agents sold some of them acreage in what was then Chester (later Lancaster) County, along the Pequea Creek, six to eight miles south of where the city of Lancaster would be founded twenty years later. More families arrived in the next half-dozen years with names such as Brenneman, Brubaker, Baer, and Hershey. Their coming touched off a flurry in the Penn family's land offices. In November 1717 officials granted a blanket warrant to Hans Herr and Martin Kendig, members of that original group to whom the Dutch Commission had granted a loan because of the delay in London. The warrant provided for surveying 5,000 acres along the Pequea or the Conestoga or their branches, and dividing the land into plots of various sizes. The officials said they wished to accommodate persons "lately arrived in the Province" who were Herr's and Kendig's "relatives, friends or acquaintances"—if the two Mennonites could certify that the arrivals were "honest, conscientious people."[2] In effect the officials were giving the Pequea Mennonite colony a blanket land option and letting Herr and Kendig be their intermediaries for settling Mennonites. In that option lay the beginnings of quite a few present-day Lancaster-area Mennonite communities.

The Penn family had a carefully worked out system for putting settlers on their lands. A warrant was a formal authority from the Penns, their commissioners, or the governor. It directed the surveyor-general to survey a tract for the land buyer on certain terms. The surveyor-general then filed the warrant and issued an order to a deputy surveyor of that county to make the actual survey. After that official had done so, and had run boundary lines, he returned a draft on the tract to the Land Office in Philadelphia. Then the land could be patented or titled.

More common, actually, were various informal agreements. On taking out a warrant the buyer was supposed to pay purchase money but often did not need to. Sometimes the buyer instead paid quitrents to the Penn family as proprietors. Quitrents were a kind of holdover from feudal dues; in Pennsylvania they were to be an annual payment of one-shilling for every hundred acres.

William Penn died in 1718, an event that for fourteen years thereafter actually favored the Pequea Mennonites. Confusion about his estate caused officals to close the Land Office. With that office closed, speculators were unable to take out warrants on the more desirable lands and the Mennonites enjoyed fourteen years of grace before they had to put down any payment. Finally in 1732 the Land Office sharply dunned the respected Kendig and Herr for money owed on land warranted in 1717.[3]

The fourteen-year breathing spell gave settlers time to accumulate capital they needed to pay for the land. Some settlers and their heirs held land under warrants for nearly fifty years. But by mid-century this form of land tenure had all but disappeared in heavily Mennonite townships. In one such township, the present East and West Earl townships northeast of Lancaster, only 18 percent of the land was held by warrant alone in 1759. This contrasted with the less-desirable land in Elizabeth Township, two dozen miles to the north of Lancaster City, where 89 percent of the land was held under warrant alone in the same year.[4] In some other areas, the land warrant system worked very much to the advantage of land speculators. In Lancaster County it helped actual Mennonite settlers.

The Penn family itself speculated in land near that first Swiss Mennonite settlement, along the Pequea. Shortly before his death in 1718, William Penn had a tract of 16,000 acres surveyed. The tract, named "Conestoga Manor," lay between the Susquehanna River and the Conestoga Creek, somewhat west of the Pequea settlement. The Penns held such manors off the land market ostensibly as estates for their own use. Actually they were allowing the land to appreciate in value as settlers brought neighboring acres under cultivation. Conestoga and Susquehanna Indians lived within Conestoga Manor and fur traders had established trading posts close to Indian towns. The region was a large level, well-watered and uncultivated section. It very soon caught the eyes of Scotch-Irish people, most of them Presbyterians. Time and again a squatter or squatter family built a cabin and cleared an acre or two only to have the Proprietors' agents serve notice of eviction and burn the cabin. The Scotch-Irish were pushed north and west onto speculative lands held by one James Logan, an important politician in the province. There they found Christian Brenneman and a few other Mennonites established since 1720 at a former Indian trading post at the mouth of Conoy Creek.[5] Other Germans including some Mennonites soon came and in the long run won the land competition. In 1759 in this supposedly Scotch-Irish stronghold persons with German surnames made up 35 percent of the tax list; in 1782 they made up 62 percent.[6]

Eventually the Penns opened Conestoga Manor, and Mennonites did even better there. At first, land speculators sold exclusively to Mennonites. This they did because the best Lancaster County land was rising in price beyond what Scotch-Irish settlers could pay.[7]

The warrant the Penns issued to Herr and Kendig in 1717 and Mennonites' ability to purchase land in nearby Conestoga Manor resulted in Mennonites having vast control over the shaping of their own Lancaster-area communities. Hardly any policy could have done more to shape the history of the Mennonite people in their eastern Pennsylvania heartland. Of course there were also other historic developments. Not the least of these was emergence quite early of apparently vital congregational life in the original Pequea colony. The center of colony life came to be a very modest stone house built in 1719 by Christian Herr, a minister. The building served both as the Herr family home and as a meeting house (a house that in the 1980s is still standing, expertly restored). One of the colony's leaders was none other than Benedikt Brechbuhl, the harassed Swiss minister who had done so much to promote emigration, and then in 1717 had himself emigrated to the Pequea. The Pequea congregation set a pattern: a Mennonite community

The Herr House southeast of present-day
Lancaster, Pa. Built in 1719 by Christian
Herr, it served as both home and meetinghouse. Now restored. Inset: Door of Herr
house in 1969, before the house's restoration.
The inscription above it reads: "17 CHHR 19",
for "Christian Herr, 1719". (Jan Gleysteen
collection)

and congregation resting solidly on a land base. The warrant did much to set that pattern.

As land agents, Herr and Kendig were to a large degree responsible for growth of Mennonite settlement in Lancaster County. The growth was orderly and rapid. It was the work of various people of differing occupations, not just farmers. That group leaving Bonfeld in 1717, for instance, included not only a Mennonite bricklayer, but also a Mennonite miller and two Mennonite physicians.[8] Indeed Mennonite settlements commonly included millers, weavers, and other tradesmen. Yet access to land was the key to community development. Herr and Kendig's remarkable system let newcomers acquire land on long-term credit. It favored the development of Swiss Mennonite enclaves within the expanding settlements on the Pequea and the Conestoga.

Those enclaves were usually on the area's best land. Non-Mennonites came as well, but in regions near Lancaster prosperous farming came to be identified with Mennonitism. In 1741, noting that some Mennonites owned as much as 1,000 acres each, Reverend William Wappeler, Lancaster's first Catholic pastor, declared that "the Mennonites are wealthiest among the Germans." A Presbyterian pastor in Philadelphia named Jedidiah Andrews, commenting on the Pequea Mennonites in 1730, similarly remarked that Mennonites were "many of them wealthy men, having got the best land in the Province." Andrews, however, also saw Mennonites as traders, and not just as landownders; for he noted that although they lived sixty or seventy miles out of Philadelphia, they came "frequently to Town with their waggons, laden with skins (which belong to the Indian traders), butter, flour etc."[9]

Finally, Andrews was aware of the persecution which Mennonites had suffered, of their nonresistance, and of their not really living exclusively to themselves. They, he said, "tho' called Palatines, because they come lastly from that country, are mostly Switzers, being drove from the Canton of Bern, for they are Baptists, and won't fight or swear. They don't shave their heads"... and: "There are many Lutherans, and some Reformed, mixed among 'em."[10] Andrews was correct in noting that Mennonites mixed with neighbors of other faiths.

But Mennonite prosperity enabled the group's members to pay high prices, and often made it difficult for others to buy the best farms.

Those who found it hard to compete with Mennonites for land may well have included the Amish. Early Amish immigrants did not settle much near Mennonites either at Skippack or in Lancaster County, but instead chose locations along the Northkill and Irish Creeks in present-day Berks County, in the Lebanon Valley north of Lancaster County, and elsewhere. That was the pattern, despite the way the Amish managed to finance their immigration. Eventually some Amish farmers did gain a foothold in Lancaster County by leasing lands until they could raise purchase money (as some did also in Berks County). And there was that group of Palatine Amish who settled in Earl Township in Lancaster County with Abraham Kurtz, who arrived in 1749 as a preacher. But Amish (and some Mennonite) immigrants who arrived later in the eighteenth century often found the price of land too high in older settlements. In some cases, they bought and farmed inferior land, often on the frontier of the colony, until they were able to buy better land elsewhere.[11]

By the time that numerous Amish settlers arrived in Pennsylvania (about 1737 to 1752), there were no large grants of land left in the eastern counties for incoming settlers. Since the Amish often arrived with some capital, quite a few were able to buy land already partly cleared and improved by previous owners, owners who sometimes held the land only by warrant. But for some reason the Amish seem to have preferred patented land, so that they obtained patents very soon.[12]

In 1754 in Bern Township, Berks County, the Amish comprised at least thirty-six out of 168 persons assessed to pay taxes. The farms they held were on rolling land around Scull Hill and Irish Creek, or in another district at the foot of the Blue Mountains between present-day Shartlesville and Hamburg. Soils in those two districts were light and thin compared to soils in the Chester, Conestoga, and Pequea Valleys.[13]

Prices for land in Bern Township were low enough that within a few years the Amish settlers acquired extensive acreages. Those who arrived after the first several years generally managed to buy next to other Amish settlers already there. Hans Gnage, who immigrated in 1742, joined with Christian Beiler in purchasing 147 acres in Bern Township in 1747. His property touched the farms of Christian Beiler, Conrad Reif, Jacob Kauffman, Jacob Stutzman, and Christian Stutzman. Two miles farther west, in January 1750, only four months after landing at Philadelphia, bishop Jacob Hertzler purchased 190 acres near present-day Hamburg. His property was bounded by the farms of Isaac Kauffman, Jacob Yoder, Benedict Lehman, and Christian Yoder, all Amish. In 1752 Ulrich Speicher, who had come on the *Charming Nancy* in 1737, purchased 193 1/2 acres near Bernsville adjoining the farms of Christian Stehly, Christian Hershberger, Johannes Lantz, Jacob Mast, and preacher Jacob Kauffman.[14]

The Irish Creek settlement drew Kauffmans, Lehmans, Millers, Zimmermans, Masts, Hershbergers, Burkis and Speichers from the 1737 immigration, as well as Christian Yoder and Mortiz and Christian Zug of the 1742 group. Most of the 1742 immigrants went farther toward the frontier, choosing land in the Northkill settlement at the foot of the Blue Mountains. Melchoir Detweiler owned land there as early as 1744. Many of the Northkill Amish settlers owned substantial acreages.[15]

Soon after coming to America a few Amish families were able to acquire the comparatively high-priced farmland of the Conestoga Valley. In 1748 Jacob Kurtz, a brother of the Abraham who managed to buy in Earl Township, purchased 175 acres on the north bank of the Conestoga in Manheim Township in Lancaster County. Christian Schowalter of Earl Township seems to have financed his land by allowing a Philadelphia merchant named Joseph Sims to hold a mortgage on it, contracted in 1750. In 1754 Christian Rupp, who came on the *Restauration* in 1747, and his brother John Rupp, who arrived with Abraham Kurtz, Christian Schowalter, and Jacob Seiler in 1749, jointly purchased 298 acres in Earl Township. Jacob Seiler took title to eighty acres in 1750. The Earl Township Amish, including Christian Schmucker, originally a poor tenant farmer, purchased some

of the best land in the township.[16] They were exceptions to
the general pattern of settlement on the poorer soils of
northwestern Berks County.

But Earl Township was more Mennonite than Amish.
The formation of Mennonite settlements there in communities that became known as Groffdale and Weaverland
illustrates how Mennonites often turned the warrant system
to their advantage, or otherwise acquired land. By the end of
1710 Hans Graeff, who had immigrated several years earlier,
had obtained a warrant for 1,000 acres on the upper reaches
of the Pequea in present Paradise Township. A survey in
October 1716 returned 1,060 acres for "Hance Groff." Graeff
sold this land in July 1717 to Abraham Dubois who took out
a patent and paid £100 due the land office. An adjacent 120-
acre tract eventually went to Graeff's eldest son Jacob along
with other land. In 1715 Hans Graeff obtained a warrant for
an additional 300 acres, which he and his wife, Susannah,
sold to Jacob Souder in 1719.[17]

In 1716 some runaway horses led Hans Graeff to the
stream later known as Groff's Run; he followed it from its
source to the Conestoga and recognized that land of high
quality lay along it. So he obtained a warrant for 1,419 acres
on both sides of Groff's Run and in the spring of 1717 settled
on the north bank near the head of the stream. Graeff did not
actually take title to this tract until 1737, when he paid £141
and 18 shillings for it. In 1738 he deeded 419 acres in the
northwest corner of his property in tracts of 200 and 219
acres to his sons Marks and Samuel, and another 260 acres
in the southeast corner to his son Peter. Before the father
died in 1746, he divided the remainder of the Groffdale tract
in 200-acre parcels to sons Daniel, Hans, and David. By that
year daughter Fronica, wife of a preacher named Henry
Landis, received ninety-four acres in her own name. Hans
Graeff was thus able to provide seven children with farms
averaging 188.6 acres of some of the best land in Lancaster
County. Even more remarkable, at one time or another he
had possessed a total of 3,990 acres on little more than
handshakes![18]

The land system administered by Herr and Kendig
made large contiguous grants possible so that Mennonites

Adapted from Samuel Wenger, et al. eds., *The Wenger Book: A Foundation Book of American Wengers* (Lancaster, Pa.: Pennsylvania German Heritage History, Inc.. 1978). pp. 162-163.

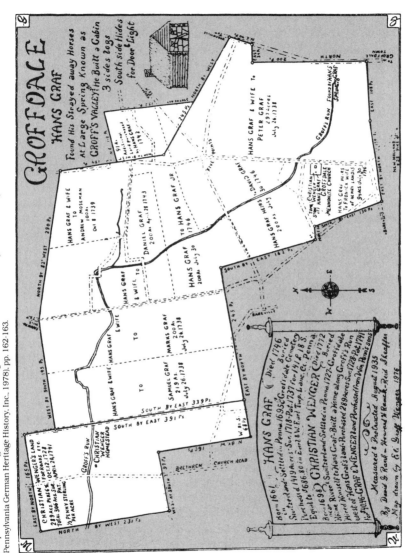

One of the early Lancaster County, Pennsylvania, Mennonite settlements.

could swarm and start new colonies nearby. Hans Rudolph
Nagele and other Mennonite settlers took up large tracts adjacent to the Groffdale patent soon after Graeff settled there.
Nagele was a preacher and in the early days the Groffdale
Mennonites probably met at his house for worship. Graeff
built a grist mill on Groff's Run to serve the growing community. And he gave his name to the Groffdale community.[19]

Before the end of 1721, another Mennonite named
Henry Weber (Weaver) had explored the country eastward
from Graeff's settlement and applied for 3,000 acres of land
westward from a block of grants north of the Conestoga held
by Welsh people. In the spring of 1723 Weber and two of his
brothers, Jacob and George, moved to the rich bottom lands
between what is now Blue Ball and the Conestoga. Their settlement drew other Mennonites to what became known as
Weaverland.[20]

After 1727 there was another large immigration of
Mennonites coming mainly from the Palatinate. Land grants
surrounding Groffdale and Weaverland were still available.
Christian Wenger, for instance, landed in Philadelphia in
September 1727 and by 1728 had a survey warrant, or order,
for 291 acres adjoining the Groffdale tract. Through such
warrants he and others obtained farms, expanding the
recently established Mennonite communities.[21]

A few years after Christian Wenger obtained his warrant for land near Groffdale, Michael Bachman, a Mennonite
who immigrated in 1717, was on his way to becoming one of
the major landowners in the Conestoga Manor area—and
indeed in all of Lancaster County. In 1735 Bachman bought
1,500 acres in Conestoga Manor and immediately resold a
large part of it to other Mennonites at £60 per hundred
acres. That was four times the going price for land in neighboring Hempfield Township in the same year. By 1738, in
Conestoga Manor between Bachman's tract and a tract of
3,000 acres along the Susquehanna reserved for the Penn
family, Andrew Kauffman, Jacob Hostetter, John Herr, Abraham Herr, Jr., Michael Bachman, Michael Shank, John
Shank, Christian Martin, Michael Myer, Jacob Brubaker,
Samuel Oberholtzer, Henry Kilheffer, and Rudy Herr bought
3,278 acres in tracts ranging from 150 to 664 acres at

equally high prices. Most or all of these persons were probably Mennonite.[22]

In that area in 1757, persons with Mennonite surnames made up forty-two of the seventy-five taxpayers in Conestoga Township. That they were comparatively wealthly is clear: they comprised twelve of fourteen persons paying ten shillings or more in taxes and thirty of thirty-five paying five shillings or more. They included forty-one of fifty-six persons who paid three shillings or more in taxes. Only one taxpayer from the presumed Mennonite group paid less than three shillings. Persons presumably non-Mennonite made up eighteen of the nineteen who paid less than three shillings and twenty-nine of the forty who paid less than five shillings.[23]

A tax assessment of Earl Township in 1756 illustrates well the success of the Graeffs, Weavers, Carpenters, Sensenys, Summys, Wengers, and other Mennonite families in obtaining land to build the Groffdale and Weaverland communities. There were eighty Mennonite taxpayers. Although comprising only a third of the township total of 242 taxpayers, they owned half the assessed land: 10,133 of 20,443 acres. The average Mennonite holding was 126.6 acres compared to an average of 86.9 acres for all the Earl Township taxpayers. More than half the general population (125 persons), but only 20 percent of the Mennonites (16 persons), owned fewer than 100 acres. Only two Mennonites owned fewer than fifty, although 35 percent of the general population owned less than that amount. Earl Township included thirty-five landless men, in most cases tenant farmers; but only one Mennonite rented a farm. Those statistics do not include Amish. There were at least three Amish families in Earl Township, each assessed for 100 acres, and Christian Schmucker, "a poor man," was an Amish tenant farmer. The average for non-Mennonite German settlers was eighty-three acres. They comprised slightly more than half the Earl settlers (129 of 242). Two much smaller ethnic groups, each including thirteen taxpayers, were also represented in Earl Township: the Welsh owned 121.6 acres on the average, comparing closely to the Mennonites; and the Scotch-Irish, poorest of the lot, averaged only 65.7 acres. The remaining three taxpayers had English surnames.[24]

Acreage figures do not correlate absolutely with wealth. The quality of the soil could have made 100 acres far more valuable as a farm than 300 acres of rocky hillside; and a four-acre subsistence farm was obviously not the equivalent of a millsite of four acres. The assessment figures make clear, however, that the average Mennonite holding amounted to what eighteenth-century people considered a substantial farm. Only twenty-one Earl landowners were assessed for 200 or more acres; sixteen of them were Mennonites. At the other end of the scale, more than a third of the Earl taxpayers owned too little land to earn an adequate living by eighteenth-century farming methods, but that was the case with only two Mennonites.[25] From other sources we know that Mennonites owned much of the best farmland and the most valuable mills. If we take property values and soil quality into consideration, we must adjust the 1756 statistics of Mennonites as substantial landowners even farther upward.

On the other hand, at least part of the reason why Earl Township Mennonites averaged out as relatively wealthy, apparently, was that less wealthy Mennonites lived in other townships, outside of the heart of the Mennonite settlement. Land in nearby Brecknock Township was considerably less valuable, and farms generally smaller. Mennonites were only about one-seventh of that township's population. But that seventh seems to have been slightly less prosperous than the township's average. Where the average farm size was 83.6 acres, Mennonite farms averaged only 83.3.[26]

A very painstaking assessment of Earl Township in 1780 put land values at from £3 to £20 per acre. The assessors assigned top values to very small tracts, evidently on the basis of improvements on them. The officials generally rated farmland between £6 and £9 per acre, and put 176 of the 271 separate tracts into that category. Of all tracts, they assessed 214 of the 271 as being worth from £5 to £10 per acre. Only fifty-six of the tracts included land worth £10 or more. The average for Earl Township farms in 1780 was 137.8 acres, worth £8 per acre.[27]

Mennonites still owned more than their share of the

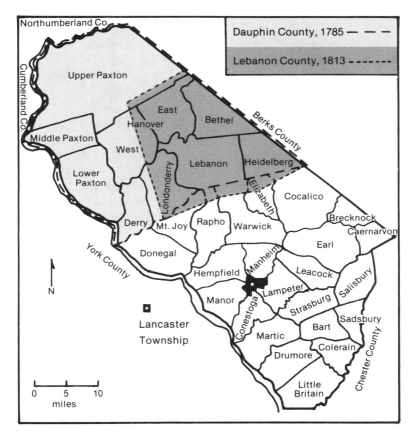

Lancaster County, Pennsylvania, about 1780. (Adapted from James Lemon, *The Best Poor Man's Country*)

township's best farmland. Almost without exception their farms' per-acre values were in the upper half of the range. Of those tracts worth £10 or more per acre, Mennonites owned thirty-six out of fifty-six, or 64 percent, even though they were only 40 percent of the township's landowners. Of 113 landowners known or presumed to have been Mennonite, only nine owned land worth less than £8 per acre.[28]

Moreover, of eight Earl Township taxpayers whose total land holdings were worth £3,000 or more, seven were Mennonites. Michael Wenger, John Graff, and "Fat" John Carpenter each owned 250 acres worth £12 per acre. Christian Carpenter had 300 acres worth £11 each. Henry Weaver had land worth only £9 per acre, but he had 315 acres of it plus a gristmill, a sawmill, and a hempmill. Christian Rooth owned 310 acres of £9 land plus a gristmill. Widow Mary Witmer had a gristmill and 300 acres of £10 land.[29]

Earl taxpayers with property worth from £3,000 included seventeen Mennonites, two Amish, two Lutherans, two Anglicans, two Reformed, and two unidentified persons. Mennonites thus comprised twenty-four of the thirty-eight largest taxpayers. These Mennonite farmers owned an average of 243 acres worth an average of £10 per acre. The two Amish farmers in this category each owned 160 acres of £12 an acre land.

Quite a number of Mennonites held land scattered over several townships rather than in a single large grant, making their holdings perhaps even more impressive. Michael Bachman who came to Pennsylvania in 1717 owned over 3,000 acres on separate farms in Manor, Manheim, Warwick, and Cocalico and on the frontier in Lebanon and Derry townships. He left substantial farms to each of his children, sons and daughters alike. His son Peter received the 441-acre homestead farm near Neffsville, Christian a 244-acre farm in the Manor, and John and Michael 323 and 233 acres respectively in what is now Lebanon County. Daughters and sons-in-law were not forgotten; each unmarried daughter and each married one with her husband inherited a farm of at least 240 acres. Bachman valued the land in Warwick, Manheim, Lebanon, and Manor townships in 1755 at £1 an acre. He considered the homeplace in Manheim worth £1, 10s. an acre and a 200-acre tract on Middle Creek only 7s., 6d. an acre (i.e. only £0.375 since of course 20 shillings equals £1, and 12 pence equals 1 shilling). Even at this conservative price, Bachman's real estate alone amounted to £5,069.[31]

Extensive acreage did not translate into large-scale farming. Lancaster pioneers relied on their own families' labor, with perhaps a few indentured servants or redemptioners, and the technology and farming methods available to them did not permit them to put more than a fraction of their land into production. Researcher James T. Lemon has

TABLE 3 - 1

COMPARATIVE WEALTH
1780 Assessment, Earl Township
Lancaster County, Pennsylvania

Assessed Valuation	All	Amish	Mennonite	Other
£100—499	54	1	8	45
500—999	78	1	13	64
1,000—1,499	64	2	14	48
1,500—1,999	44	1	16	27
2,000—2,499	21	2	12	7
2,500—2,999	9	0	5	4
Over 3,000	8	0	7	1
Totals	278	7	75	196
Under £500	54	1	8	45
Under 1,000	132	2	21	109
Under 1,500	196	4	35	157
Under 2,000	240	5	51	184
Under 2,500	261	7	63	191
Under 3,000	270	7	68	195
Totals	278	7	75	196

concluded from tax assessments in eighteenth-century Lancaster and Chester counties that farmers rarely had more than thirty-five acres in crops; the rest of their land lay fallow or in woodland. A typical 125-acre farm had eight or ten acres in wheat, two to four acres in rye, and perhaps as much as six acres in corn. Farmers raised some oats, buckwheat, flax and hemp. Orchards averaged 100-150 trees. Some acres provided summer pasture or forage and hay for the winter.[32]

Wheat farmers considered a yield of forty bushels an acre exceptional enough to deserve comment in the newspapers. The more usual yield was in the six to eight bushel range, with fifteen bushels per acre typical for some limestone soils.[33]

Wills made by Mennonite farmers in the eighteenth century often included detailed instructions for the widow's support. Since the son who inherited the homeplace had to supply everything from the produce of his farm, these wills give us a glimpse of the diversified farming on the Lancaster plain. In 1755 Michael Bachman, "aged but in good health," directed that when he died and his wife became a widow their son should provide her each year with fifteen bushels of wheat, four bushels of malt to make her beer, two barrels of cider, three gallons of rye or apple liquor, 100 pounds of pork, fifty pounds of beef, apples to eat and dry, and as much hackled hemp as she could spin. Abraham Herr, a much younger man in 1755, wanted his widow to have ten bushels of wheat, three of rye, three of barley, twenty of oats, a hogshead of cider, and a half-barrel of liquor. She was also to get "a fet hocke of waight of 150 pounds" to provide pork for her table. Meanwhile, she was to "bring up the children in fear of God and teach them in reding and writting."[34]

Barbara Kindig in Conestoga Township was to have "use of the plant and capatch garden" and a cow, in addition to twelve bushels of good wheat each year, three of rye, three of barley, 100 pounds of pork, two barrels of cider, twenty-five pounds of flax, five pounds of wool. Jacob Weaver inherited 250 acres in Lampeter Township on the express provision that he provide John Weaver's widow each year with fifteen bushels of wheat, two bushels of malt for beer, two barrels of cider, 100 pounds of pork, fifty pounds of beef, a sufficient quantity of hemp and flax, six pounds of wool, firewood, two gallons of rum, and two gallons of "beech or apple liquor." Benjamin Hershey's plantation in Hempfield Township was to provide for his father Andrew Hershey's widow and daughter. Each year he was to give them thirty bushels of good wheat and "as much Indian corn," and also two fat hogs. He was to send them "cyder as much as they have occasion for drink or as much malt for beer, which they chuse best" and "apples for the winter and to dryet." They were to have three-fourths of an acre of flax, two cows, and three sheep. Andrew Hershey directed his son to let them live "in the new house which I build in my orchard."[35]

Clearly, Lancaster Mennonites were engaged in diversified farming, with an emphasis on grain. When we analyze twelve Lancaster County wills from 1734 to 1769, wills that can be identified as Mennonite from bequests to the poor of Mennonite congregations or from other evidence, we find that each of the farms mentioned raised wheat. The average bequest was fourteen bushels.[36]

Half of the wills mentioned rye, with an average allowance of five bushels, and two others provided rye liquor; so at least eight of twelve farms grew rye. Only three of the twelve wills considered cornmeal or Indian meal essential. But corn was commonly raised for silage if not for human consumption. Half the wills provided barley or malt, nearly always with the added explanation, "to make her beer." Only one will mentioned oats. Each of these wills specified pork, reducing the amount if provision was also made for beef. The widow generally received a fat hog, which meant a hog weighing 120-150 pounds and valued at twenty shillings. Flax and, less frequently, hemp appeared in nearly all the wills studied, with a half acre field of flax the most common provision. Only half the wills mentioned wool or sheep. Apples, whether for drying or as cider, figured in all the wills. John Kegay's widow was to have four apple trees of her choice. One will mentioned peach brandy. Separate mention of a garden or "plant garden" and a "cabbage garden" was common. A third of the wills made provision for firewood and one specified that the widow was to have "the stove room."[37]

These careful listings "of commodities and money to be supplied to widows" struck historian James T. Lemon as a reflection of "the degree of insecurity around old age" that surprisingly "occurred amongst Mennonites." The thoroughness with which Mennonite landowners provided for the necessities of their widows suggested to Lemon a weakening community structure. Mennonite fathers often kept no less detailed accounts with their sons and sons-in-law of every farm implement, animal, or sum of money advanced in the father's lifetime. Such accounts survive in old account books and in wills that expressed the testator's desire that each family member have his or her fair share and no more.[38] Actually such provision may have reflected concern for the community as well as the family.

Wheat was the cash crop of these Lancaster County farms. The 1756 assessment of Earl Township indicated that the farmers grew an average of 6.59 acres. Some of the wheat they made into beer, partly for home use and partly for sale. The mills that formed an important part of every rural neighborhood in eighteenth-century Pennsylvania ground some wheat into flour. The family consumed part of the flour in the household baking, but heavy-laden "Conestoga" wagons carried barrels of flour to Philadelphia, some of it to be shipped to the West Indies.[39] Mennonite farmers contributed substantially to Pennsylvania's reputation as the granary of the English colonies.

In counties east of Lancaster, Mennonites who settled along the Schuykill, the Perkiomen, and the Skippack rarely acquired huge tracts of land as found among Lancaster Mennonite landholdings.[40] The pattern Hans Herr and Martin Kendig established was unique to the Pequea colony. Elsewhere Mennonites had to buy land from speculators or from earlier settlers. In 1719-1739 land prices in Skippack and Lower Salford townships varied between three shillings and £1 an acre depending on the quality of the land, with five or six shillings the average. This compared favorably with land prices on the Lancaster plain (the highest prices in Pennsylvania), which averaged ten shillings per acre in the 1730s and more than doubled in the 1740s to between £1 and £1, 10s. an acre.[41] The cost of land alone was probably not enough to deter Mennonites from acquiring acreage for future development. The Philadelphia and London merchants who held warrants for undeveloped land were anxious to sell for cash or on short-term credit. They were not interested in tying up salable land with long-term credits, so they made land available in marketable quantities to whoever wished to buy it. Mennonite newcomers and sons of earlier settlers had to compete for land on an open market.[42]

The only extensive grant of land to a Mennonite in eastern Pennsylvania was that tract of 6,166 acres patented by Matthias Van Bebber in 1702. No other township at such a distance from Philadelphia was settled as early as Bebber's. Many of Bebber's first buyers were Mennonites, but none of them bought on a large scale. The average Mennonite holding indicated in a 1734 tax assessment of Perkiomen and

Skippack Township, as Bebber's Township was officially called, was only 106 acres. The largest property holder was not a Mennonite but Henry Pawling, an English Quaker who owned 1,200 acres or about 20 percent of the township. The nineteen other non-Mennonites held an average of 161 acres. The overall township average was 146.[43] So the farms of the first Mennonite settlers in Skippack were considerably smaller than the area's average.

An assessment of Perkiomen and Skippack made in 1756 showed little change in the next generation. If 1,000 acres then owned by Solomon Dubois is included, there were sixty-one landowners, holding an average of 159 acres. Without the Dubois tract, the average was 145.3. By 1756 Skippack farmers had cleared 3,618 acres of a total 9,705, or slightly more than a third of their land. The average farmer had 59.3 acres in cultivation, 14.1 of them in wheat. Altogether wheat grew on 864 acres in the Skippack settlement. The 1756 harvest was apparently between 5,000 and 7,000 bushels. The range of individual farm sizes was considerable, acreages ranging from 10 to 1,000, but only four persons owned fewer than 50 and only six persons owned more than 250 acres. Of 51 landowners owning between 20 and 250 acres, 41 owned farms in the 50-150 acre range.[44] The picture that emerges is of a community where nearly every farm was large enough to provide an adequate livelihood, with wheat as the cash crop, but without much of the extensive landholding that occurred among Lancaster County Mennonites.

Exactly who was a Mennonite at Skippack in 1756 is uncertain; there is clear evidence for only a very few. But even after one allows for a considerable margin for error, the Skippack Mennonites appear to have been in the middle range of landowners. One Mennonite owned 280 acres. Nobody presumed to have been Mennonite owned more than that or fewer than fifty. Approximately eighteen Mennonites and twenty-three non-Mennonites owned 151-250 acres. Mennonite, Lutheran, and Reformed adherents owned adjacent farms of similar size. No obvious distinction is evident among them. Two young Mennonite farmers leased land from their fathers. Three other Mennonites were among the eleven Skippack landowners who rented parts of their farms to others for yearly sums ranging from £2 to 22, obviously depending on the quantity and quality of the Land. The average was £6, 10s.[45]

In eastern Pennsylvania both Mennonite and Amish settlers increased their productivity by expanding the labor force. In Skippack in 1756 about half the landowners, thirty of sixty-one, owned indentured servants. In 1752 Mennonite Jacob Clemens and his brother John, of Lower Salford Township in present-day Montgomery County, jointly purchased such a laborer. The following year also, according to Jacob, the two brothers "freed a carpenter from the ship and each of us paid one half of his freight, and we must furnish him with clothing as long as he works for us. He belongs to each of us in equal shares." The brothers hired the man out to work for wages in the neighborhood. Meanwhile John Clemens kept a free hired man, evidently a fellow-Mennonite, and kept account when he purchased small articles of clothing for his employee, carefully charging the costs against the man's £10 annual wage. It may have been just as cheap to keep the free man as an indentured one: in 1750-1755 a hired man's annual wage averaged only about two thirds the initial cost of an indentured servant, and under the terms of indenture the master himself had to pay for the servant's clothing and the like. But indentured servitude continued to be a source of labor. By 1771-1772, the first years for which there are complete records, to get an indentured servant cost an initial capital outlay of £25. Eighteenth-century purchase records indicate that many Mennonite and Amish farmers traveled to Philadelphia and purchased servants, particularly German or Scotch-Irish redemptioners.[46]

Nevertheless, probably no more than six or seven of those thirty Skippack farmers who owned indentured servants in 1756 were Mennonite. The majority of Mennonites along the Skippack relied on their own sons or on seasonally hired labor.

Slavery existed in Pennsylvania and in 1756 three Skippack farmers owned a total of five slaves, probably (judging by the slaves' ages) a family of parents and three children scattered in the three separate households. None of those three slaveholders were Mennonites. There are other tax lists from southeastern Pennsylvania in the latter eighteenth century which suggest that in several very rare cases a Mennonite here or there owned a slave. And according to local traditions one at Skippack, a certain Samuel Pennypacker, owned one in the 1780s. At least a century later a knowledgeable amateur historian also named Samuel Pennypacker told of his earlier namesake who "was a member of the Mennonite Church ... and every Sunday ... attended its services in the old meeting house upon the Skippack," and who also owned a black known as "Schwartz Piet" (Black Pete). The later Pennypacker observed quite plausibly that probably the memory of "Schwartz Piet" lasted a whole century precisely because his case was so rare. In fact Mennonite opposition to slavery was well known in the eighteenth century, so that opponents of slavery sometimes pointed to Mennonites as good examples.

The noted Quaker itinerant John Woolman told the story of a Mennonite in York County who spent the night in an open field rather than be the guest of a slaveholder, the Mennonite telling the slaveholder forthrightly that he did not want hospitality that his host would never offer to a poor, powerless slave. A modern historian, Alan Tully, has found that such slavery as existed in southeastern Pennsylvania was more a matter of conspicuous consumption than of economics; and another Quaker preacher, John Hunt, held up to his people the example of Lancaster Mennonites who rejected "superfluities" such as colored ribbons on bonnets—and slaveholding. Hunt went on to tell of a Lancaster County Mennonite who had in fact broken his church's rule by buying a black servant. According to Hunt's account the Mennonite then had a dream that he was trying to climb a ladder but his slave kept pulling him down. Consequently, when he awoke he went to the courthouse and liberated the bondsman.[47]

Whatever Mennonites' sources of labor, settlers in Perkiomen and Skippack Townships followed many different occupations, often in addition to farming. Of seventy-nine persons whose occupations appeared on the townships' tax lists for 1756, forty-three were farmers. Yet nearly half of those persons were not solely farmers. In every rural Pennsylvania township at this time, most of the people got the major part of their incomes from farming. Yet quite a few pursued other occupations, usually depending on the farmer and serving one or more needs of farm families. Throughout the region, nonagricultural occupations were increasing by mid-century—an indication, according to historian Duane Ball, of growing prosperity. Whereas earlier farmers, as pioneers, had been jacks-of-all-trades, by mid-century southeastern Pennsylvania's economic development (fueled by an agricultural boom) allowed craftsmen and artisans to thrive by following trades in more specialized fashion. A farmer's younger son who stood to inherit little or no land and who could not afford to buy a farm when he married could begin as a blacksmith or a wagonmaker, prosper in his trade, and perhaps buy the farm he earlier could not afford. Because the nonagricultural work force grew substantially, Ball concluded, a sizeable increase in population could and did occur without "decrease in land holdings or farm size." The Perkiomen and Skippack data agree with Ball. In 1756 there were thirty-six taxpayers in the two townships who were not mainly in agriculture. They included ten weavers, a fuller, and a blue dyer; four millers; two tanners; three cordwainers and a "shoomacker"; two blacksmiths; a locksmith; four "maisners" (masons); four "jabers" (day laborers); a tailor; an innkeeper; and a schoolmaster.[48]

Mennonites were prominent in the crafts. Among early Mennonite settlers not only those from Krefeld but also many from the Palatinate had worked in Europe's textile trades. Now, in 1756 in Perkiomen and Skippack Townships, Mennonites monopolized the cloth industry, providing the community with nine of ten weavers, the man who ran the fulling mill to bleach the cloth, and the dyer. Mennonites also owned the only two tanneries in the Skippack-Perkiomen region; and a Mennonite worked with leather as one of the cordwainers. Another founded one of the gristmills, and the locksmith was of Mennonite background.[49] There seems to be no record of Mennonites in other trades.

Nearly all Mennonites who were in trades also farmed or at least owned farmland. In 1756 Valentine Hunsicker, a

Names of the House-keepers.	Their Trades or Occupations.	Number of Children under 21 Years.	Names of Inmates, who are married.	Names of single Men, Servants, or Sojourner
Peter Pannabacker	miller 44	8		
Henrey Baringer 10	farmer	1		
Abraham Sealer	miller 56	5		
Richard Jacobs	farmer 40	7		
Michel Zigler junir	taner 18	3		
William Zigler 18	weaver	2		
Jacob Kreater 22	weaver	7		
Elizabeth Kolb 12		6		Jacob Ritzel
Dilman Kolb 18	farmer	3		michel Oberly
Henrey Kolb 18	farmer	5		andrew horsh
Jeane Kolb 24	weaver	5		frederick Opper
John Frit 18	farmer	3		John pannebacker
George Clauser 10	maisner	1		Joseph Spyll
Adam Godwals 18	farmer	6		vallentin Phile
Joseph Datwiller 20	te	4		Robbert Jacobs
				Jacob van Jose
John Barrens 10	massier	3	30	Amotevanf
Henrey Datwiller 16	farmer	3		George Zisler
Abraham optegrave 18	te	6		Adam van Jose
Edward optegrave 18	farmer	2		Peter van Jose
John Butterweck 16	sailer	2		Adam Painter
Barbara Smith 18		3		Peter hotten ba
Jacob misenhimer 12	Jaber	5		Daniel Ryler
John Cugh 10	farmer	2		Georg Shut
Nichole Selzer 12	farmer	4		Philip milli
				Abraham
John Ryler 22	farmer	5		
Philip ens 10	Shoomacker			
Adam Seer 10	Jaber	2		
Deeter Sealeker 24	inkeeper	1		
Henrey Slighter 10	Cordwinder	5		
William Johnson 10	Jaber			

Perkiomen/Skippack tax list, 1756. (Historical Society of Pennsylvania) weaver, owned 225 acres with 100 of them cleared and twenty acres in wheat. Isaac Kolb, another Skippack weaver, owned 220 acres and was farming eighty of them, twenty of those eighty in wheat. Farms of Mennonite tradesmen were usually well above average in size. Henry Cassel, also a weaver, was one of the few exceptions, owning only sixty acres with twenty under cultivation, eight of them in wheat. Three Mennonite artisans appear to have been landless, but it seems clear that one, a weaver, was living on his son's 125-acre farm and that another may have lived on his father's land.[50]

The Mennonite purchasers of Skippack land shared only one of the advantages enjoyed by their brethren on the Pequea and the Conestoga. In 1735 James Steel, a land agent for the Proprietors and a speculator in his own right, complained to Michael Ziegler, prominent Mennonite at Skippack, that for thirty years none of the community's Mennonites had paid quitrents. Steel had written in 1733 to Henry Pannebaker, a land surveyor and speculator, asking him to collect the quitrents due the Proprietors at the rate of one shilling sterling for every 1,000 acreas contained in the tract confirmed to Matthias Van Bebber. In 1735, in Quaker style, he informed Ziegler that "I desire thee to speak with the inhabitants of Bebbers Township" telling them that quitrents "must be forthwith paid." The best way, he thought, was for the people themselves to decide how they should apportion the payments and then pay them to Ziegler or someone else whom they might choose, who would then pass the money along to the Proprietors.[51] Ziegler later became a minister, then an elder (or bishop); so Steel's approach illustrated a frequent pattern, that of economic and church leadership going hand in hand. Steel's approach was also a softer one than the Proprietors sometimes used. The Penns actually threatened to repossess lands held by Schwenkfelders, another pacifist group whose members were not paying quitrents.[52]

As Mennonite settlers moved up the Skippack into adjacent Lower Salford Township, they found much of the land there held on warrant by Steel and a partner named David Powell, of Philadelphia, and by Dirck Jansen of Germantown.

In Lower Salford itself Mennonites of Skippack made the first purchases of land. That was in 1718, and such purchases continued at a steady rate for the next decade. In some cases, sellers allowed fairly long credits. Andrew Lederach purchased 132 acres from Powell in 1718, but did not receive full title until 1735. Henry Ruth held 220 acres of Powell's land from 1718 to 1728 before getting a clear title. Purchases in Lower Salford were somewhat larger than in Bebber's Township. Fifteen Mennonites whose holdings were assessed in 1734 and whose names appeared on a 1738 list of the Salford Mennonite meetinghouse's trustees held an average of 213.5 acres, almost exactly double the average Skippack acreage.[53]

Warrants to speculators barely kept pace with the advancing frontier. Two warrants for 1,000 acres each in Franconia Township, close by Skippack and Salford, were located and surveyed for Philadelphia merchants in 1708. James Dickinson of Cumberland, England, and Thomas Wilson of King's County, Ireland, obtained warrants for Franconia Township land in 1714. By 1723 sales to Mennonite and other settlers were in full swing.[54]

The pattern of land ownership along the Skippack made it impossible for Mennonites to block out large tracts like those at Groffdale and Weaverland. The smaller tracts obtained by Mennonites in this area were often too small for further subdivision. Grain farming in the eighteenth century was not labor-intensive, and farms of sixty to seventy-five acres were considered too small to support a family.[55]

Only a few Mennonite landowners in the Skippack settlement thus had the luxury of dividing their homesteads among their offspring; in most cases a half or a third of the homeplace would not have been a viable unit. In 1718 Gerhart Clemens, who already owned land in Bebber's Township, bought 300 acres in Lower Salford from David Powell, and in 1726 he erected the first gristmill in the township. In 1734, by purchase and by warrants on unclaimed land, Clemens was able to get title to 690 acres. In the two townships he owned a total of 824 acres. So in 1738 he gave farms of 136 and 151 acres to his sons Jacob and John, and in 1741, 260 acres to son Abraham. And he did so without appreciably reducing his own property. By separate purchases over a period of twelve years, Dielman Kolb acquired 532 acres in Lower Salford. In 1733 the Kolbs exchanged half of this land within the family. Kolb's son-in-law, Andrew Ziegler, purchased the original tract back with a small addition.

In 1767 Ziegler had a resurvey made of the new total of 554 acres for the purpose of dividing the tract among his sons. The three sons of Ziegler each received a 184.6-acre share, the same size as the farms provided by Hans Graeff of Groffdale for his sons. On the other hand, when Heinrich Funck, a Mennonite bishop who owned 201 acres and a mill in Salford, wanted to provide adequate acreage for his sons, he had to buy 166 acres a few miles east in Bucks County. For the great majority, the family property sufficed for only one or at most two sons. The common pattern of early Mennonite wills in the Skippack settlements was for one son to buy the family farm from the estate, thus providing money for bequests to the other children.[56]

In the 1720s, since Mennonite pioneers east of Lancaster County could not generally subdivide their farms, and since land in the older settlements was already high-priced, Mennonites began to disperse over a very wide area in what are now Bucks, Northampton, Lehigh, and Berks counties. That the price of land was a factor is clear from the experience of Michael Ziegler. In 1718, Ziegler bought 100 acres in Bebber's Township for £25, although he did not get full title until 1734. In 1722 Gerhart Clemens sold him an additional fifty acres and in 1727 he purchased 100 acres in Lower Salford for £100. Thus at the end of nine years the price he paid for land was four times what he paid at the outset. Ziegler's next purchase was in 1728 in Goshenhoppen, about fifteen miles further up Perkiomen Creek, where he acquired 450 acres. That gave Michael Ziegler 700 acres, an adequate patrimony for his sons. But the Ziegler family had to scatter from Skippack to Goshenhoppen.[57]

The pattern of land purchases by Mennonites in the Perkiomen valley shows influence of Mennonite land agents. Gerhart Clemens, who left the Palatinate as a poor linen weaver in 1709, became not only a large landowner in his own right but acted as seller for speculators. A notebook kept by Clemens records a trip to Maryland in 1713 to confer with Matthias Jacobs van Bebber, and tells of advances of large sums of cash by a family named Sprögel who held title to Frankfort Company lands in Falckner's Swamp and Goshenhoppen. As agent for David and Samuel Powell, Clemens sold land in what would later be Hereford Township in Berks County. Two buyers were his nephews Daniel Stauffer in 1720, and Daniel's brother Jacob in 1724. They were sons of Hans Stauffer, the immigrant. Soon after the Stauffer family came from the Palatinate in 1710, they had settled on the Schuylkill in Chester County. Later the father located them on land near Valley Forge. After 1729 other Mennonites from Chester County and newcomers from Europe moved to the Manatawny region of Berks County. There they joined the Zieglers and others who had moved up the Perkiomen to Goshenhoppen, and established a strong Mennonite congregation at present-day Bally, at the north edge of the Bucks, Berks, and Montgomery County Mennonite community.[58]

Eighteenth-century settlers used the name "Goshenhoppen" (or "Goschenhoppen") rather loosely to designate the entire region drained by the Perkiomen Creek. Sometimes they limited the region's boundaries more strictly to New Hanover Township in Philadelphia (later Montgomery) County and adjacent Hereford Township (later Hereford and Washington townships and the Borough of Bally) in Berks County. For our purposes, Goshenhoppen will comprise these two neighboring townships. The Frankfort Land Company, a German group, originally held title to large tracts in Falckner Swamp and Goshenhoppen. In 1708 John Henry Sprögel acquired title in his own name to 12,000 acres in Goshenhoppen and sold this land to Thomas Tresse, a Philadelphia ironmonger. In 1746 the Tresse heirs gave deeds to the actual settlers in New Hanover Township.[59] Uncertainty about title may actually have made land in neighboring Hereford Township more attractive.

All the large landowners in Hereford and New Hanover, whether Mennonite, Lutheran, Reformed, Schwenkfelder, or

Catholic, acquired their lands between 1725 and 1745. They nearly all settled in Goshenhoppen between 1717 and 1733. The Jesuit priest at the Catholic Church in Hereford Township was the only latecomer, purchasing his land from Mennonite owners in 1755.[60] Mennonites in Goshenhoppen all acquired their land in the years of the first settlement. They were typically named Bechtel, Stauffer, Latshaw, Bower, Gehman, Strom, Bauman, Hiestand, Ziegler, or Beidler, and took up their lands in the 1720s and 1730s. The community remained relatively stable thereafter. Some newcomers and sons who did not inherit their fathers' farms sought land for themselves in adjacent Northampton and Bucks counties.[61]

In Goshenhoppen, Mennonites followed many of the same occupations as at Skippack, but did not dominate any one trade. In 1767 half the weavers in Hereford Township were Mennonite, but Schwenkfelders, Lutherans, Reformed, and Catholics also followed this occupation. Among Goshenhoppen Mennonites there were also wagoners, tanners, and millers. One of the five shoemakers in the community was a Mennonite, but apparently there were no Mennonites in the iron industry or among the blacksmiths, potters, carpenters, joiners, masons, and tavern keepers. By 1779 Goshenhoppen Mennonites were exclusively farmers, tanners, and weavers.[62]

In 1768 sixteen Mennonites owned land in Hereford Township. The township taxed two other Mennonites; one, although a son of a landowner, was landless. No large landowner or speculator occupied extensive lands in the township, so the range of landholdings represents actual farms. The largest single landowner in the whole Goshenhoppen community was the Catholic priest, with 400 acres; a Lutheran farmer ranked second, with 300 acres; and a Schwenkfelder was a close third, with 290 acres. But in Hereford Township, Mennonites' average acreage was somewhat higher than the township's average: 151.1 acres compared to 126.5. Moreover, although in 1768 Mennonites comprised only 25 percent of the taxpayers in Hereford Township, eight of them were among the twenty largest taxpayers and only one was among the thirty-five lowest. Fifteen

Mennonites were in the upper half of the tax assessment and only three in the lower half.[63]

In New Hanover Township, there were apparently only nine Mennonites among eighty-four landowners taxed in 1769. John Moyer was taxed for a gristmill located on land belonging to Abraham Moyer. The average acreage for the eight Mennonite landholdings was 158.75, just a bit above the township average of 150.6 acres. Landholdings in New Hanover ranged from 22 to 520 acres. Michael Ziegler paid taxes on 74 acres; other Mennonite farms were between 136 and 200 acres.[64]

Although the few Mennonite farms in New Hanover Township were not much larger than the average, the entire Goshenhoppen community in 1768-1769 exhibited a common southeastern Pennsylvania pattern: Mennonites, on the average, being among the larger landholders. Mennonites generally sought places where land of reasonably good quality was available in quantity, of course at reasonable prices. As land in developed settlements became less accessible and more expensive, the Mennonites did not always merely fill the gaps in established settlements or expand them; they also began new settlements. Except perhaps in the case of Herr and Kendig's arrangement (a notable exception, to be sure), they enjoyed no special social or political connections that gave them advantage over their Lutheran and Reformed neighbors for acquiring land. They did, however, have more money.

According to geographer Lemon in his study of southeastern counties in eighteenth-century Pennsylvania, Quakers in south-central Chester County and Mennonites in Lancaster County were the most affluent of southeastern Pennsylvania's rural residents. Their wealth, he thought, came from hard work, mutual aid, and other such factors, not simply from occupying the best limestone soils, for in many cases they did not have the best land. He found that "they produced more wheat than others, owned more horses . . . and probably were more inclined to try new techniques to improve yields." In what is now Montgomery County, Mennonites and Schwenkfelders enjoyed a local reputation as the best farmers. And indeed they did succeed well at farm-

ing, even where they lived on red shale soils that were inferior to limestone ones. A correspondent writing in 1787 in a
Germantown newspaper scolded farmers in general for not
using fertilizers and other agricultural improvements, but
held up Mennonites and Schwenkfelders as examples who
did better.[65]

The broad acres of Mennonites and their skill and advanced practices in farming translated into substantial
wealth by local community and eighteenth-century standards. Not all their leaders were sure such wealth was good
for them. That Mennonite preacher who spoke in 1770
against Mennonites' pursuit of wealth thought that too
many members of his church were showing "pride and
vanity" by displaying "all manners of fashions," as they
dressed "in all kinds of costly clothing" and lived
"splendidly."[66] No doubt some did live more fashionably and
splendidly than the ideal upheld by their preachers; but from
a different perspective. In 1770, Baptist historian Morgan
Edwards reported that Mennonites, "like the Tunkers, use
great plainness of speech and dress."[67] Moreover, the Mennonite preacher failed to notice that land and a certain
amount of wealth also formed a base for religious community. Some of those communities are still strong to this
day, economically, religiously, and otherwise.

CHAPTER
4

LAND AND COMMUNITY ON THE FRONTIERS

As the frontier of white settlement moved south and west from eastern Pennsylvania in the eighteenth century, a certain number of Mennonites followed. Theirs was a search for good land at low prices. Often they soon established new congregations, yet it was land that had drawn them rather than a specific aim to establish some model of religious community. The quest for land had more than one motive. It seems quite clear that some Mennonites who were fairly wealthy went to new areas to speculate and perhaps to invest like modern capitalists. Others who were relatively poor, and therefore unable to afford land in older communities, were merely seeking their own pieces of ground. And then there was a third motive: desire for enough acreage so that sons and daughters (or sons-in-law) might have viable farms even after parents divided their estates. Behind that third motive was a strong family bond.

For eighteenth-century Mennonites and Amish in North America the family was the most basic of social units. So the social motive of family maintenance, like the economic motives of land and profit, was apparently more directly important in Mennonite migration to the frontier than was any clear religious motive. Mennonites and Amish who moved were generally more self-conscious about getting property and getting their families established than they were about establishing church or religious community. On the other hand, in their view there was hardly any reason to separate such motives, or to view them as competing. They were quite traditional people with a holistic approach to life.

**Eighteenth-century migration
from Pennsylvania
to Maryland and Virginia.**

Juniata Ri

B L I

•Bedford

Rocky Sprir

Chamb

PENNSYLVANIA

Conococheague River

Leiters

Potomac River

Hagerstown

Beaver C

Potomac

A P P A L A C H I A N   M O U N T A I N S

S H E N A N D O A H   M O U N T A I N S

SHENANDOAH MOUNTAIN

Shenandoah River

B L U E   R I D G E   M O U N T A I N S

MOUNTAINS

•Strasburg

Woodstock

Edinburg

North Fork

MASSANUTTEN MTN.

South Fork

Forestville

New Market

Luray

Brock's Gap

Linvill

Harrisonburg

VIRGINIA

N

•Staunton

Charlottsville

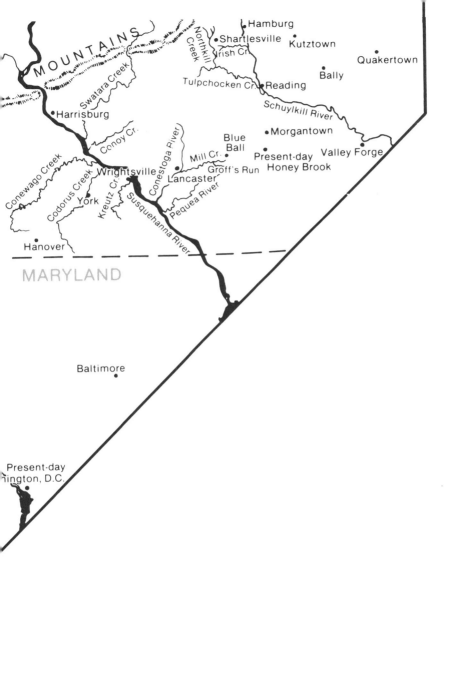

For them, land and family were not only ends in themselves but were also bases of the religious community. Even if economic and social motives were more direct and explicit than religious ones, those motives did not necessarily compete with motives of faith.

Whatever the motives—economic, sociological, or religious—within a few years of the first settlements near Lancaster the quest for land carried some Mennonites across the Susquehanna River into what would eventually become York County. Before long, in the 1730s, it carried others southward into the Monocacy and the Conococheague valleys in western Maryland and on down into the Shenandoah Valley of back-country Virginia. At that time land was still available at reasonable prices back in Lancaster County along the Pequea and the Conestoga, but not in large quantities; so pioneers pushed on. Eventually, especially from the mid-1750s to the mid-1760s, or roughly the time of the French and Indian War, Indians bent on retaliation drove some settlers back and discouraged others from going. Yet land prices in the older communities were rising, and in the 1760s and 1770s new waves of Mennonite and Amish people migrated to frontiers. In 1773 Andrew Ziegler and others at Skippack wrote of Mennonite congregations at "Quitophila, Great and Little Schwattara [in Lebanon and Dauphin counties], Tolphokin [in western Berks County], and on the other side of the river Susquehana by Yorktown, Great and Little Conewago, Mannakesie, to Verginia, Meriland, Schanatore [Shenandoah], and further to Carolina, where are many and large congregations."[1]

Both within given counties and overall, Mennonites' usual pattern was to choose land in several different places rather than to cluster tightly together. This was true in places as far apart as Lebanon County in Pennsylvania, Washington County in Maryland, and Shenandoah County in Virginia. Just as Mennonites had been part of larger migrations as they crossed the Atlantic, they now moved to new frontiers and settled there right alongside English, Scotch-Irish, and non-Mennonite Germans. Their pattern does not suggest much desire for separatism.

Land prices made such migration most attractive. In the 1730s when farmland in Lancaster County was selling generally from 10 to 15 shillings per acre, Lancaster County Mennonites bought acreage in Virginia at prices from 1 to 4 shillings. A decade later Lancaster County land values had about doubled to about 25 to 30 s.; but a settler could purchase even somewhat improved land in Mennonite settlements in Virginia's Shenandoah Valley for 4, 3, or even 2 s. per acre.[2] In that situation some long-established settlers in the older communities sold out at profitable prices and moved on. And newly arriving Mennonites from Europe often decided they could not afford the older settlements' prices, and also went to the frontiers.

Mennonites were concerned about quantity as well as price. In new regions, especially in Virginia, tracts of 1,000, 5,000, or even 10,000 acres were available long after they were out of the question in southeastern Pennsylvania. In the frontier regions the economic motive of speculation and the family one of providing farms for sons and daughters easily mixed: a reasonably small capital investment could put one in the land market as a speculator and still provide adequate patrimony for the next generation. Transactions of several Lancaster Mennonite investors in Virginia followed this mixed pattern.[3]

The Penn family and other large-scale land speculators manipulated land sales in ways that directed the flow of settlers to one region or another. Earlier the generous terms offered Mennonites through Herr and Kendig had in fact served Penn family interests by getting settlers onto land which Maryland also claimed. Now once more in the 1730s, Pennsylvania authorities promoted settlement west of the Susquehanna in order to preempt land claimed by Maryland's proprietor Lord Baltimore. For that land and for tracts in other places, land sellers employed agents in older Pennsylvania communities to recruit settlers. Since many immigrants were illiterate, at least in English, the agents often did not publish advertisements but relied on personal contacts, leaving only a minimal record of their activities.[4]

In the 1730s Lancaster-area Mennonites considered the claims of these rival agents. Some agents offered lands across the Susquehanna in present-day York County, others in the more distant Shenandoah country. Mennonite migration to those two regions was somewhat linked,—and not only in time. Pennsylvania authorities had promised Indians that they would preserve the Susquehanna's western shore as Indian hunting ground and never sell land beyond the river. As late as 1729 they chased out squatters who settled there and burned their cabins. But Lord Baltimore insisted that trans-Susquehanna land as far north as the fortieth parallel (about the latitude of Lancaster and York) belonged to Maryland. So in 1731 one of Baltimore's agents, Thomas Cressap, moved in where the Penns had chased squatters out. Soon he was in a dispute with Lancaster County neighbors across the river, including Martin Kendig, who wanted to pasture horses on the Susquehanna's west bank. Kendig was also promoting new settlement in the Shenandoah Valley of Virginia. Indeed he had assembled horses to carry settlers and their goods down the valley. The settlers had chosen Shenandoah partly because Pennsylvania authorities had temporarily closed York County to settlement.[5]

In the Shenandoah Valley a man named Jacob Stover was planning a new settlement. Stover may have been reared Mennonite, as his name was a variation of "Stauffer." He had been born in Switzerland. In 1741, on his deathbed, he had a Presbyterian minister baptize him, which he probably would not have done had he been baptized as an infant.[6] Whatever his religious upbringing, in 1730 he and several associates asked the Virginia House of Burgesses for permission to establish a German-speaking Swiss colony on the South Fork of the Shenandoah River. In response the group got a patent for 5,000 acres near present-day Luray and attracted about a hundred people to settle. Stover's associates in seeking permission to settle had surnames common among Lancaster County Mennonites: Herr, Funk, Kindig, Souder. Few of the signers were among those who joined the settlement, however.[7]

Stover, who had lived in the colonies for at least twenty years, returned to Europe to recruit other settlers and also to work with British officials (in cooperation with the well-known Johann Rudolph Ochs of London, who had earlier helped promote emigration of Mennonites and others to British lands in America). He was seeking permission for another colony in western Virginia.[8] At one point he induced a hundred settlers to cross the Atlantic in the company of a Lutheran minister, but once in America that group decided to settle in New York rather than on Stover's lands. Creating further troubles, some other Virginia speculators challenged Stover's Virginia land title. But when that happened, in 1733 some of Stover's settlers, including Mennonites Abraham Strickler, John Roads (or Hans Rood), and Michael Kauffman, pleaded with the House of Burgesses to consider the title good. They had purchased their land from Stover in good faith "about four years past," the petitioners said, and they had paid the promoter "upwards of four hundred pounts" (about 1 s. per acre). They had "run the hazard of their lives & estates" to come more than 200 miles from Pennsylvania "when there was very few inhabitants in them parts of Shenando, & they frequently visited by Indians." Now they had "nine Plantations, fifty one people, old & young" and "expect to have two more familys to seat on the sd. land this spring."[9]

While that settlement, known as Massanutten, was beginning, other Mennonites began to settle near present Strasburg in Virginia, on the Shenandoah River's North Fork. In 1735 Jacob Funk of Lancaster County bought 2,030 acres there, and soon some relatives and neighbors joined him. One of them, Henry Funk, of the Lancaster (not the Franconia) Funks, built a mill on Town Creek by 1739, assisted by a cousin also named Jacob who was a carpenter and joiner. That cousin later joined the Ephrata Cloister community back in Lancaster County. Henry remained a Mennonite and opened his home as a meeting place for a small Mennonite congregation that developed in Jacob Funk's settlement.[10]

Some Mennonites only speculated in Virginia land, while others found new homes there. Several early owners of the Massanutten land never left Lancaster County but resold to Mennonites who actually went. Others, among them John Brubaker of Hempfield Township and Joseph Steinman (Steman) of Manor Township, bought tracts and then passed them on to sons and daughters or their spouses. Thus Brubaker's son Abraham migrated to Virginia in 1735 and Steinman's son-in-law, Peter Ruffner, went in 1739. Some, including Ruffner, settled and then sold considerable tracts to other Germans coming from Pennsylvania.[11]

Among such Germans, Mennonites were numerous, both in the "Massanutten" (present Luray area) settlement and in the "Shenandoah" (present Strasburg area) one. A Moravian who visited Massanutten in 1748 observed of settlers there that "most of them are Mennisten" with a few Lutheran and Reformed people among them.[12] If land is what drew the settlers to Virginia, they nevertheless established congregations when they got there. To worship, the Massanutten group at first met in one another's homes. An early preacher was Martin Kauffman, who died in 1749. A house known as "the White House" that his son built around 1760 served as a place for worship; and various investigators, among them Harry A. Brunk, foremost of Virginia Mennonites' historians, have believed that a nearby log meetinghouse later used by Baptists was originally Mennonite. Other Massanutten preachers were John Roads, whom Indians killed in a massacre of his family in 1764, and Jacob Strickler, who died in 1784. In the Shenandoah settlement farther north, one pastor was evidently Martin Funck, with the congregation meeting at Henry Funk's mill. A 1758 letter to Holland says that Funck, an elder as well as a minister, was "by occupation a miller," and that at one point, evidently also in an Indian raid, he was "compelled to flee and leave all he had behind."[13]

In the Roads massacre Indians (actually led by a white) killed father, mother, and three sons on the site, plus a son and two daughters whom they took captive; another daughter managed to escape with her baby sister, and another son, also taken captive, was released after three years.[14] It was probably the worst massacre any Mennonites ever suffered. The family apparently made no attempt to fire back, and indeed in Mennonite history generally there is little evidence of self-conscious Mennonite hostility or contempt for Indians. Yet the Virginia story illustrates that Mennonites were sometimes very near the front edge when

Monument near Luray, Va., with inscription: "Memorial to Rev. John Roads (Mennonist) his wife and six children, massacred here by Indians Aug. 1761. Buried on river bank N.E. Emigrated from Zurich, Switzerland 1728. Came to Virginia two years later." Inset: Homestead near Luray, Va., of Roads family killed by White-led Indians during French and Indian War. (Jan Gleysteen collection)

whites moved in on Indian lands; and of course land-grabbing, rather than personal hostility, was the ultimate source of Indian anger. How close nonresistant Mennonites were to a land-grabbing process based on force and violence is even clearer in events on the west bank of the Susquehanna in Pennsylvania.

About 1733 Pennsylvania authorities decided that in order to fend off the claims of Maryland's Lord Baltimore they would issue licenses for settlement west of the Susquehanna River. Despite earlier promises by the Penns that the area should be Indian hunting ground, some Mennonites did not hesitate to move in. So migration from older Mennonite settlements began to turn away from Virginia and to follow what, geographically, was a more normal course: westward along Kreutz and across Codorus Creeks, past what would later be York and Hanover, and down the Monocacy Valley into Maryland. Unfortunately Germans and Scotch-Irish and others who took up the licenses, known as "Blunston licenses" for the man who issued them, soon ran into conflict with other whites whom Baltimore had sent to settle there.[15]

In 1736 Thomas Penn confirmed land titles growing out of the Blunston licenses; about one fourth of the title holders were Mennonites. Several were recent immigrants from a region in southern Germany around Mannheim in the Palatinate. Coming over from 1727 to 1733, most of these German immigrants had first settled along the east side of the river. But as soon as it seemed legal they had quickly crossed the river and moved onto the new lands. Most of them settled along Kreutz and Codorus Creeks in Manchester and Hellam townships.[16]

Leader and public spokesman for these Mennonite settlers was one Michael Danner (or Tanner). Upon immigrating in 1727, Danner had actually crossed the Susquehanna and squatted illegally. He had lost his land when authorities had turned squatters out, but in 1734 he returned, taking up 200 acres in the Kreutz Creek valley under a Blunston license. A dozen or so other Mennonites, including Nicholas Bieri, Henry Strickler, Peter Welde, and Nicholas Bucher, got land nearby in the same way and settled with their families.

Since the Blunston licenses did not amount to clear title, many of the settlers decided to accept Maryland's claim to jurisdiction and accept its titles. Of that decision they soon repented. So they petitioned both Lancaster County authorities and the Pennsylvania government in September 1736[17] to consider them Pennsylvania subjects after all. Among other points they complained that Maryland authorities had told the settlers "that we were worse than Negroes" in the sense of not being real citizens, "for that we had no Master, nor were under the protection of any Laws."

In that same month a force of gun-toting Marylanders invaded. The blustering group, a posse of armed citizens led by a sheriff, marched on Kreutz Creek and demanded that the Germans once more acknowledge Maryland's rule. The settlers fled to a plantation known as Wright's (present-day Wrightsville) where they encountered a Lancaster County sheriff coming in with a posse of his own. At that point a resolute Danner decided to become a peacemaker, requested safe conduct, and went back to the Marylanders. When he did, colonial records tell us, he found them "plundering the Dutch people's houses, by taking out at the Windows Cloth & what they Could meet with, under the pretence of publick Dues" (that is, of collecting taxes). The Marylanders also threatened to burn the Germans' houses, "but did not after Michel Tanner had talked with them."[18]

Danner managed to get oral assurance that Maryland would not collect taxes until the Germans "were better able to pay." But the Marylanders refused to put their promise in writing, and in fact, the dispute grew even more violent around the nonresistant Mennonites and others during the winter of 1736-1737. While Danner and two men named Conrad Strickler (a Mennonite) and Jacob Welshover were burying a neighbor's child, the Maryland sheriff seized them and carried them off to Annapolis and jail. Nicholas Bieri soon found himself also in prison.[19] Just how the men got out of jail is unclear. But the experience does not seem to have taught them to be more careful, or more hesitant as a nonresistant people to go after economic resources whose possession rested very directly on violence. By 1738 Danner, with some other Mennonites, and others, had moved on farther to a place near present-day Hanover, Pennsylvania where Irish Catholics from Maryland were claiming a vaguely defined right to settle. Disputes over rival Pennsylvania and Maryland titles erupted, and did not die down until the latter 1740s even though Great Britain, as sovereign, imposed a Pennsylvania-Maryland boundary line in 1739. In 1749 Danner, whatever the general Mennonite attitude toward political office, became one of the commissioners of newly organized York County.[20]

Thus by the end of the 1740s Mennonites were among German settlers who formed a wide arc through present-day York County. Some were already pushing down into Maryland. A Moravian named Leonard Schnell left record of staying overnight in 1743 with a Mennonite named Abraham Mueller in what is now Frederick County, Maryland. He may be the Abram Miller who is known to have paid taxes on 300 acres in Frederick County ten years later. That same year, 1753, a Jacob Rohr (Rohrer), who is known to have been Mennonite, owned 767 acres in Maryland, probably in present-day Washington County. Morgan Edwards, a Baptist who commented on Mennonites in 1770, understood that a Mennonite congregation had begun in Maryland about 1743, and had "since greatly increased in number and wealth."[21]

There were close links among the newer Mennonite settlements west of the Susquehanna, in western Maryland, and down the Shenandoah Valley in Virginia. Frontier communities were staging grounds for new out-migrations, and Mennonites in those places migrated more often than did those in older, populous Mennonite settlements. Thus migrants to Maryland and Virginia (and a few even down into the Carolinas) were more likely to have come from fringe areas of southeastern Pennsylvania Mennonitism, areas such as Whitehall Township in Northampton County, Brecknock Township on the Lancaster-Berks County border, Donegal Township in Lancaster County, and Paxton Township in Dauphin County, than from the Mennonite heartlands around Lancaster or Skippack. Frontier Mennonites then maintained ties not only among frontier settlements but back to southeastern Pennsylvania, especially the com-

Interior and exterior of Mill Creek Mennonite meetinghouse near Hamburg, Page County, Va. (Massanutten settlement), dating from ca. 1740. (Jan Gleysteen collection)

"White House" near Hamburg in Page County, Va. (Massanutten settlement), built in 1760 by minister Martin Kauffman, Jr., and used by his congregation of Mennnoist-Baptists from about 1770. (Jan Gleysteen collection)

munities from which they had come. Thus when Virginia Mennonites fled from Indian assaults in the 1750s, they were likely to return to settlements west of Lancaster City. Later, after 1760, Virginia Mennonites perceived a new menace: revivalistic preachers. And when they did they sought counsel from ministers back in the same area.[22]

Some of the settlers in new communities soon accumulated much more property than they could ever have hoped for back in older settlements. According to records of Augusta County, Virginia, Mennonite Abraham Strickler of the Massanutten settlement left more than £200 worth of personal property in 1746 in addition to extensive real estate. According to a modern historian of that area, he "was a rich man for the time and country." Martin Kauffman, the Mennonite minister, who died in the same community in 1749, left almost as much personal property. Of sixty-five persons who died in that decade and had their estates inventoried in the county's records, those two Mennonites were among only six persons with that much personal property. Fifty of the sixty-five left less than £100 worth each.[23]

Among Mennonites of the next generation in Virginia, some of whom can be identified through Mennonite petitions to the Virginia Assembly, there were also persons of considerable wealth. Upon dying in 1770 one John Stickley, of Cedar Run in northern Shenandoah County, left an estate worth £1,576. Jacob Strickler of Massanutten, who died in 1784, left £1,045 worth of personal property alone. Henry Funk of Funk's Mill, who died in 1784 near Strasburg, left £434 worth of personal property, 1,155 acres in one location with mills, 294 acres with another mill, and still another 179 acres in the Strasburg area. In addition he ostensibly owned 2,000 acres "on the Western Waters." Back in Pennsylvania on the west side of the Susquehanna, it was possible also to do quite well. Nicholas Bieri died in 1762 and left £60 in cash, £600 in accounts owed to him, and a farm worth £400.[24]

Most persons like these had probably gone to the frontier not out of economic necessity but more in a capitalist spirit of speculating and investing. With that, they mixed the hope to establish sons and daughters and their families on land. But there were others who went more out of relative poverty, those who could not afford farms of viable size in older communities with rising land prices. Farms in southeastern Pennsylvania averaged about 125 acres; farms with fewer than 75 acres were considered too small to adequately support a family. Historical geographer Lemon concluded that moving because of relative poverty began sooner and more often among church Germans than among Mennonites and other more wealthy sectarians. Yet he was sure that Mennonites sometimes moved from the same motive, at least by the 1780s when some of them moved to Upper Canada (present day Ontario). Of course the desire to establish sons and daughters on the land mixed with this motive as well as with the more capitalistic, speculative one.[25]

Those Amish who settled in the 1730s to 1750s far up the Schuylkill Valley in Berks County, along Irish Creek, in the Northkill region, etc., are very good examples of having moved to fringe areas in order to afford viable-sized farms. But, since the soils in those areas were thinner, they seem to have found a new reason to move on to new frontiers: soil depletion.[26] A traditional explanation for Amish movement away from Northkill and Irish Creek was Indian raids of 1755 to 1758. And indeed there were serious incidents, especially that which the family of Amishman Jacob Hochstetler, an immigrant of 1736, suffered in September 1757.

One morning before dawn the Hochstetler family's dog was agitated, and the family arose to find eight or ten Indians on the attack. One son briefly opened a door of the house only to receive a shot in the leg. The Indians then set fire to the house. The family survived the fire for a time by going to the cellar, but finally had to come out. Thereupon the attackers fell on the family and killed the mother, one son, and one daughter, and took the father and two sons prisoner. Through it all the father had insisted that his sons must not shoot back, which they wanted to do—the surviving one later insisting that they probably could have frightened the Indians away. On the other hand, in this case the Indians may have been angry not merely over the whites' taking their lands, but because of a more personal affront. Some evidence suggests that a few years earlier Mrs. Hochstetler had rather rudely turned away some Indian beggars, so that the Indians now wanted vengeance especially on her.[27]

Tragic as that experience was for the Northkill Amish community, that incident and other frightening encounters with Indians probably do not explain why Amish families began to move on. The Indians' raids may have been one motive, but not many Amish moved away until 1761, and by that time the Indians were no longer much of a menace. As late as 1785 the Northkill community remained the strongest Amish settlement in America. In 1767 Bern Township had thirty-one Amish taxpayers, assessed for an average of 99.9 acres each; in 1784 there were still twenty-eight Amish landowners, averaging 121 acres. In most cases when Amish farmers did leave, they sold to other Amish.[28]

Some who moved found land in Berks County's Tulpehocken Township some five to ten miles west of the heart of the Northkill community. Others went to northern Lancaster County's Bethel Township in what is now Lebanon County, a region where Indian raids had been far worse than at Northkill. In 1750 Abraham Drachsel (Troxell), an immigrant Amish preacher who had arrived on the *Pheonix* only a year before, settled a mile north of what is now the town of Lebanon. Soon other Amish also settled there, some of them new immigrants and some from the Northkill. One who did, for instance, was Hans Gnage. By the time he died in 1772 he had prospered as a farmer and miller, and owned 240 acres and a gristmill.[29]

By 1770 three other major Amish movements were in full swing: one to the east end of the Conestoga Valley (around present-day Morgantown); one to the Chester Valley (near present-day Elverson and Honey Brook); and the third one far west to Brothers Valley in Bedford (now Somerset) County. In each case, Amish moved in search of good land. The more successful among them, by moving, were able to buy not only for themselves but for their children. In the 1760s Abraham Kurtz, the Earl Township Amishman, bought 204 acres in Berks County's Cumru Township for a son; in the same decade he bought two tracts totaling 440 acres in Lancaster County's Salisbury Township. The latter purchases marked the beginning of Amish settlement along the Lancaster-Chester County line near Honey Brook and Elverson. In the 1760s also Christian Kurtz, a son of Abraham, bought land a bit farther north in Lancaster County's Caernarvon Township in the Conestoga Valley. According to the Caernarvon Township assessor in 1779, Christian Kurtz and several nearby Amish families named Yoder were on "good land."[30]

Amish were not the only ones to take poorer, fringe-area lands until they could raise capital for better farms. In 1750 a group of Mennonites named Basler and Showalter (Jacob Showalter and five of his sons) arrived on the *Brotherhood* and took up land in Northhampton County, along the Lehigh River in Whitehall Township. In 1755 Ulrich Showalter witnessed an Indian raid from the roof of his house there, yet most of those Mennonites continued to farm along the Lehigh. Indeed others joined them, and by 1770 the congregation there felt established enough to build a meetinghouse. Within a few years, however, some of them sold their lands and moved to better soils in Chester and

Lancaster counties and in Virginia.³¹ Meanwhile Swiss Mennonites arriving in 1754 on the *Phoenix* mostly found they could not afford land in the Lancaster-area heartlands, and so purchased poorer tracts in Brecknock Township or remained landless for several years. In time, however, some did manage to buy better farms in the Earl Township neighborhood.³²

As long as Indian troubles lasted, not many Mennonites moved as far out in Pennsylvania as the present Cumberland, Adams and Franklin counties; settlers there were mostly Scotch-Irish. But once those troubles abated, about 1763-1764, a new wave of Mennonite migration began and continued in the latter 1760s and the 1770s. Not all early Cumberland County deeds remain, but John Stoner (probably a Mennonite) was the only German settler now known to have been in Antrim Township of Cumberland (now in Franklin) County in 1758; by 1762 there were at least eight Germans in the township, among them the names Hege, Gingrich, Hoover, Stoner, and Snobery. There the German influx seems to have begun somewhat earlier, to be sure. But apparently not a single German lived in the same county's Letterkenny Township as late as 1762. Then a Mennonite from Lancaster County named Martin Wenger pioneered there, and in 1771 was taxed for 180 acres (35 of them cleared), and for two horses, two cows, and two sheep. By 1775 several other families named Huber, Groff, and Shirk had moved down from Lancaster County, and there was a congregation that worshiped at John Huber's house near Rocky Spring.³³

Those counties in Pennsylvania and others across the border in Maryland made up a region known as Conococheague. Although Mennonites had come as early as the 1740s, there were not many of them until the wave in the 1760s and 1770s. Even as early as 1770 Morgan Edwards, the Baptist commentator, reported that there were some 400 Mennonite families in the region, with 800 or more baptized members. Ministers' names, he reported, were Henry Funk, John Riffle (Reiff), Isaiah Hawser, Samuel Beightley, and Tillman Wesenbach. Just how accurate Edwards' statistics were is not clear; yet clearly the Mennonites were becoming numerous. A 1776 list of "Dunkers and Menonists," who were fined in a district of Frederick (now Washington) County in Maryland for not drilling with the revolutionary militia, named fifty-five adult Dunker and Mennonite males in that township alone, bearing such surnames as Avey, Newcomer, Hoover (Huber), Bowman, Root, Stover, Shoop, Funk, Byerly, Coogle, Lesher, Miller, Bachley (Bechtel), Pifer, Good, Rohrer, Road (Rhodes), Vulgamet (Wolgemuth), Weldy, Houser, Bomberger, Hess, Garber, Studebaker, Coughinour, Thomas, Broombaugh, Gansinger, Shank, Lidey, Postalor, Washabaugh, Huffer, Herr, and Calglesser.[34] The common Mennonite names in the list were those found far more often in the Lancaster area than farther east in the region of the present-day Franconia Conference.

Some of the Mennonites first settled as tenants on a 10,688-acre manor, the Manor of Conococheague, laid out south of present-day Hagerstown along the Potomac River and owned by Maryland's proprietor Lord Baltimore. One, Peter Settee (Zetty) had bought 200 acres in Lancaster County's Donegal Township in 1760 but then for some reason had moved to 105 acres he did not own on the manor. There his family lived in a log house, thirty feet by twenty-four, with a shingled roof; the barn, also of logs but with a roof of overlapping split boards, was only twenty by ten feet. By 1783 he had planted an orchard of twenty trees, but cleared only seventeen acres for farming and pasture. Among other tenants with comparable holdings were ones named Jacob Houser, Christopher Brunk, and Jacob Brunk. The two Brunks (whose Mennonite identity is not absolutely certain) had come from different sides of the Susquehanna River in Pennsylvania. Within a few years they and Settee bought land in Virginia.[35] Meanwhile, by 1783 both Jacob Houser and Jacob Brunk had bought some of the Conococheague Manor land, Brunk 159 acres and Houser 100. Other Mennonites lived in the region of the manor. Several owned mills in addition to farms, and at least two were distillers.[36]

Somewhat to the east of that community along the Potomac was a settlement known as Beaver Creek. There a Mennonite preacher named Isaac Houser was one of the community's wealthiest men, owning 753 acres valued at £507 (only about seventy of the acres cleared, however). Only a Jacob Hess owned more taxable wealth. Although Hess had only 261 acres he owned more cattle and horses, and, most of all, a mill. Also, even though he appeared on the 1776 list of Dunkers and Mennonites, he owned an adult male slave.[37] If indeed he was a Mennonite, his being a Mennonite slaveholder was a very rare case.

Another Mennonite community developed a bit to the north in Maryland, around present Leitersburg. Among those who settled there was Christian Newcomer, who sold a Lancaster County farm in 1775, moved there, and in 1783 was assessed for 276 acres worth £328; eventually, under the impact of Methodistic revivalism, Newcomer would join the United Brethren movement and become one of its leading itinerant preachers and a bishop so important that some have referred to him as the "Saint Paul" of the United Brethren church. A brother of Newcomer named Henry also moved there; by 1783 he owned 266 acres and a mill (and in 1781 had been exposed for trying to help organize a group of Tories to fight against the American revolution). Others in that community who apparently were Mennonite included Hershbergers, Hoovers, Stauffers, and Shanks. One, Jacob Shank, was so poor that the assessor valued his farm of fifty acres (only fifteen of them cleared) at only £25. The area was so frontier-like that of nearly 40,000 acres in the total tract, more than 31,000 were still wooded in 1783. Still another Mennonite community developed around Hagerstown and Maugansville. There, too, a Mennonite preacher was one of the district's wealthiest men in 1783: Samuel Bechtel, Sr., with 381 acres worth £778, a gristmill, and a still. His total taxable worth was £1,369. Another distiller was a settler named Christian Rohrer, while a Jacob Rohrer was a brewer.[38]

Thus in the 1760s Mennonites in Maryland settled in four different communities. Whether each cluster organized as a separate congregation is unclear, but the locations of different preachers' homes suggest that each did. However, land prices and soil depletion, rather than the specific motive of planting new congregations and religious communities, still appear quite clearly to have been what stimulated Mennonites to move.

To quite an extent, once again the Mennonites were moving right along with other German-speaking people. To be sure their patterns of movement may not have been exactly the same as those of their neighbors. Geographer Lemon has stated that in Lancaster County in the 1770s, the least turnover of land to entirely new owners was in the strongly Mennonite townships of Lancaster County.[39] That apparently was not directly due to owners being Mennonite, but was rather because the most prosperous farmers were least inclined to migrate out. Yet Lemon also demonstrated that between 1772 and 1782 roughly half of the adult males in Lancaster County disappeared from tax rolls. Even after allowing for death and natural succession of the next generation to property, he concluded that nearly 30 percent got up and moved during those years. The fact was that by the 1760s and 1770s it was becoming very difficult to get land in older Mennonite communities; and after 1780 the crunch was serious. So by the 1780s Mennonites were moving out in ever greater numbers, even from previously fairly stable communities. Consider Brecknock Township. From 1772 to 1782 it had the lowest out-migration rate of any in Lancaster County.[40] But during the next ten years, members of the small Mennonite community there scattered to such places as Cumberland County in Pennsylvania and more distantly to Rockingham County (Harrisonburg area) in Virginia and the Niagara Peninsula of present-day Ontario.[41]

In Brecknock and adjacent parts of Earl Township into which that particular Mennonite community spread, some Mennonite families had been established since the 1730s. In 1771, their average acreage was 108. Others who came directly from Switzerland in 1754 and 1755 had settled there. In 1771, the average acreage of these families was only ninety-five. That average conceals a wide inequality among those 1754-1755 immigrants, however, for some of the Swiss who arrived with resources became well established. For instance, by 1771 Francis Diller, who had arrived on the *Phoenix* in 1754, owned 300 acres and paid more taxes than did 90 percent of his neighbors; he also was the community's first distiller. And Ulrich Burkholder, who arrived in 1755 and was a preacher and blacksmith as well as a farmer, owned 100 acres and paid at least average taxes. But others were poor: in 1771 Daniel Gehman, Christian Swartz, and Joseph Wenger, all part of the 1754 group, each owned fewer than fifty acres.[42]

Mutual aid from a congregations's alms fund might have helped a family already poor in Switzerland to get across the ocean, but it did not extend to getting a family really well-established in America. The children of widow Katharine Baumgartner Neuenschwander paid money to the Bowmansville poor fund for some years to repay passage money advanced in 1754. By 1776 sons John and Isaac had moved on to western Maryland. Son Christian, still landless in Earl Township in 1771, later moved across the line into Brecknock Township—then in 1784 left for Rockingham County, Virginia, still landless. Peter Burkholder, brother of preachers Ulrich and Christian, also remained landless and in 1780 appealed that he was too poor to pay a fine for not serving in the militia. In the 1780s he, too, moved to Rockingham County in Virginia. He and Christian Neuenschwander were both men in their thirties, with families, when they moved. One of the small children who went along was Peter Burkholder, Jr. (1783-1846), who in manhood became a prominent Virginia bishop and author of a notable confession of faith and other writings.[43]

It was not only the poorer Mennonites, however, who left Brecknock and the adjacent part of Earl Township near the end of the century. In 1790 Francis Diller's son Abraham, who had inherited the 300 acres and two stills, relocated near Newville in Cumberland County. In 1795 Jacob Good, Jr., who owned at least 300 acres in Brecknock Township, moved to Virginia.[44] He had married a second time and very probably moved in order to provide land for his second family. So while poorer Mennonites seemed to have viewed the frontier as an opportunity just to get initially established, the frontier attracted some more wealthy people as well. Some of those apparently went to increase their fortunes in more or less capitalistic fashion, while for a man such as Good the prime motive may well have been the family.

Capitalistic speculation, in contrast to merely wanting to get oneself or one's family established, was apparently a fairly strong motivation. Often those who moved to one frontier area later sold out and moved on. In fact, it seems that newer communities soon had higher rates of out-migration than did older ones. In 1768, for instance, one Abraham Bieri bought a farm in Shrewsbury Township in York County from fellow-Mennonite Abraham Weldi, who apparently then moved on to Frederick County, Maryland. Sixteen years later Bieri sold the York County farm and moved to Rockingham County, Virginia.[45] Moreover, of seventy-two "Members of the Menonist Church" who signed a petition to the Virginia Assembly in 1785 (asking for exemption from militia fines), at least sixteen had lived in York County, Pennsylvania, and at least ten in western Maryland during the previous twenty years.[46] Surely almost all of them previously had migrated to those places.

In the treks to Virginia, later arrivals often did not settle in the Massanutten and Shenandoah communities established in the 1730s. There were of course the exceptions that "prove the rule." In 1763 Mennonite Jacob Reiff of Lancaster County's Hempfield Township bought 627 acres in the vicinity of Henry Funk's mill in the Shenandoah community, mortgaging it to a brother-in-law back in Lancaster County apparently to raise the purchase money. Later he bought 300 acres more; and another brother-in-law, George Westerberger, moved to the area, and in fact became one of those who signed the 1785 petition.[47] But others clustered in new places. In the 1750s Mennonite Jacob Gochenour and Jacob Stauffer (or Stover), who probably was a Mennonite, bought land in the vicinity of present-day Woodstock, more or less half way between the two original settlements. Gochenour died in 1771 and by that time he had a number of neighbors who were Mennonites, including Ulrich Kessler, Benjamin Layman (Lehman), Christian Andrich, Abraham Beydler, and Isaac and Jacob Kauffman.[48]

By 1780 the community also included a Mennonite John Heisi and three brothers who had moved from Lancaster County's Manheim Township: Tobias, Daniel, and Martin Meili. In 1778 a sister of the Meilis with her husband,

Matthias Huber, also from Lancaster County, joined her brothers in Virginia; but in the 1780s the Hubers moved westward to Rutherford County, Tennesee. Meanwhile another Meili brother-in-law, David Bechtel, moved west in Pennsylvania, across the mountains, to Bedford County.[49]

In the 1760s and 1770s still other Mennonites began to establish settlements in Virginia near present-day Edinburg, New Market, Forestville, Quicksburg, and elsewhere. John Henry Neff, a physician, was the pioneer here, taking up 400 acres on Holman's Creek in 1750.[50] A few went from what is now the Franconia Conference region, but most came from that arc that stretched from Lancaster and across York counties and down into western Maryland—an arc of which the whole Shenandoah Valley was really just a geographical extension. Rockingham County with Harrisonburg as its seat would eventually, of course, become site of one of the more permanent and populous of Mennonite communities, or really site of several of them. Already in 1785 twenty-three of seventy-two Virginia Mennonites who petitioned for militia-fine exemption lived in Rockingham County, as compared to only eleven in the old Massanutten settlement and ten in the "Shenandoah" one. A number of others lived in newer settlements fairly near Rockingham County. The signers from Rockingham County mostly lived in the northern part of the county, along Linville Creek or in Brock's Gap northwest of present Harrisonburg.[51]

Tax assessments of 1787 and 1788 reveal that the Linville Creek and Brock's Gap settlers had chosen land considered to be good. The average holding in the district was 249 acres, and the average value 7 s. per acre. Mennonite farms were not much larger—an average of 257.4 acres—but they averaged 9s., 6d. per acre in value, and few Mennonites had land assessed at less than 9 s.[52] At about the same time, in adjacent Shenandoah County, a lawsuit in 1786 resulted in careful records concerning 146 tracts of land there. The tracts averaged 200 acres each, with twenty to twenty-five percent of the land under cultivation. On them were 155 log dwellings, averaging 16' x 20' and one-and-one-half stories. Early Shenandoah Valley historians commented on German settlers' excellent barns; ninety-three of the 146 tracts had barns, ranging in size from 18' x 22' to 30' x 70', and a third having thatched roofs. Half of the tracts had apple orchards, averaging 74.6 trees each.[53]

Among the owners of the 146 tracts were fifteen Mennonites who had signed the 1785 petition for exemption from militia fines. In contrast to the 200-acre overall average, the average tract held by those Mennonites was 238.1 acres, with individual acreages ranging from 400 to seventy-two. The Mennonites all lived in log houses that were, with only one exception, considerably larger than the average. One Mennonite house, Abraham Beydler's, measured 20' x 54', and the average was 26' x 30'. Moreover, the Mennonite houses commonly had cellars and stone chimneys. Mennonite barns also were large by local standards. Jacob Gochenour, for instance, had a "new long barn 60' x 28'" as well as a "new log springhouse inderpinned in stone." Abraham Smuts (Smoots) owned a barn, a stable, a leather drying house, a bark mill, nine tanning vats, and a "very old mill unfit for use, dam broke." Mennonite farmers averaged three horses and five head of cattle each, although Abraham Beydler and Christian Grove (a decendent of Lancaster County, Pennsylvania, Groffs) each had nineteen head. Two Mennonite farmers had tenants on parts of their lands. Oddly, Mennonite orchards were smaller than others, averaging only fifty trees each.[54]

While most of the first Mennonites to settle in Rockingham County and across the line in Shenandoah County were from the Lancaster-to-Maryland arc, in the 1780s two new streams began to bring Mennonites. One stream was from Pennsylvania's Bucks and Northampton counties, in the present Franconia district. The other was young people coming from the old Massanutten and Shenandoah Mennonite communities farther north in Virginia's Shenandoah Valley. For instance in 1786 Henry Funk, Jr., preacher-son of the prominent Franconia elder Heinrich Funck, arrived. In the next year Henry Brumbach moved from the Massanutten settlement to a spot four miles west of Harrisonburg. In fact Brumbach was old enough already to have owned considerable land in the Massanutten region, but he moved nevertheless. Some other Mennonites from the Massanutten

settlement moved much farther. Jacob Baer migrated down
the Valley to Rockbridge County in 1788. In the same year
some of the Coffmans, a family who was descended from the
pioneer Kauffmans of Massanutten and who in later history
would produce some strong leaders of Mennonites, moved to
Greenbrier County in what is now eastern West Virginia. A
Ruffner family moved to a valley known as Kanawha near
present-day Charleston, West Virginia.[55]

And so Mennonites were scattering as part of the larger
American frontier process. Some of the churches they established showed promise but would eventually die out—the
fate, for instance, of the old Massanutten settlement itself. It
seems that some Mennonites isolated themselves too much.
The Coffmans who moved to Greenbriar County apparently
tried to meet and worship as Mennonites, but never really established a congregation. A few kept their Mennonitism for
decades, often returning to the Shenandoah Valley for marriage partners or even to live. But most of that wing of Coffmans drifted away from Mennonitism, many becoming
Methodists.[56] Yet in other places within that Lancaster-to-
Maryland arc, or in Virginia's Shenandoah Valley, the settlers did establish lasting congregations. Even if they did not
go precisely with some vision of a new Mennonite religious
community, they were so much people of the faith that rees-
tablishing fellowship and worship was about as natural as
building themselves houses.

Eighteenth-century Mennonites probably would not
have wanted to sort and separate their motives as much as
twentieth-century analysts want to do. They lived life as a
whole, and did not make much attempt to distinguish
between the religious, the social, and the economic spheres.
Nevertheless in retrospect it seems clear enough that what
lured migrating Mennonites was, overwhelmingly, land.
Sometimes eighteenth-century Mennonites even let the land
quest pull them into situations that now seem to have been
inconsistent with a nonresistant faith—situations in which
they got caught in the violence of competing land claims or of
Indian-white relations. The lure of land was evidently very
strong. Was the strongest part of it the opportunity to speculate and make profits from investments in modern, capi-

talistic fashion? Or was it a somewhat older, more tribalistic motive of wanting soil on which to establish extended families and clans? That question is harder to answer than is the one of whether religious community or land was the main motive. The more speculative, capitalistic motive, and the more family-and tribal-oriented one, were very much mixed.

CHAPTER

5

------◆------

"LIKE FISH IN WATER"

"You can hardly imagine how many denominations you will find here when you attend a big gathering like that at Abram Heydrich's or Abraham Jaeckel's funeral," wrote a Goshenhoppen resident to friends in Europe in 1768. Yet the writer, Schwenkfelder leader Christopher Schultz of Hereford Township in Berks County, assured his correspondents that "we are always at peace with each other." To despise others for their religions would have seemed foolish at Goshenhoppen. "Everybody speaks his mind freely. A Mennonite preacher is my next neighbor and I could not wish for a better one. On the other side I have a big Catholic church," and "the present Jesuit Father ... confides more in me than in those who come to him for confession. ... Next to them the Lutherans and Reformed have their congregations," the Reformed being "the most numerous here." "We are all going to and fro like fish in water."[1]

Goshenhoppen was not as densely Mennonite as were some eighteenth-century settlements in eastern Pennsylvania such as Skippack or Pequea or Earl Township. Yet Schultz's vivid picture of how Pennsylvania's German "church" and meetinghouse peoples lived and moved among each other was a good one even for more densely Mennonite communities. As Mennonites nurtured their children and worshiped in America, they were not in isolation.

A few historians, most notably Dietmar Rothermund, have used language that suggests the eastern counties of colonial Pennsylvania became quite a prototype of what later would be a live-and-let-live pattern among churches in the

United States as it became a nation. That pattern would be one of "denominationalism." There might be competition among denominations but in Rothermund's words it was "competitive coexistence" that included "practical tolerance." As denominationalism has developed, the denominations have learned to look on each other—at least on most Protestant groups—as legitimate branches of the larger Christian church and of American Christianity.[2] Yet the first authors to write colonial American religious history have often been denominational historians who have emphasized differences rather than cooperation and mutual acceptance.

In the spirit of emphasizing differences, many who have written specifically about colonial Pennsylvania have assumed or argued that the German sectarians who settled there were quite isolated from the colony's social and political currents. They have often contrasted the "sects," or "meetinghouse people"—especially Dunkers, Mennonites, and sometimes Schwenkfelders—with the "church" Germans, mainly Lutheran and Reformed and sometimes including Catholic. Their language sometimes implies a very high wall of separation between the meetinghouse people and the church Germans. One such overwrought interpretation in a recent college textbook says that the sectarians were like " 'Protestant monks and nuns' with their quaint habits," while church Germans "dressed and, outside their homes, spoke as Americans." The church people, moreover, "entered politics" and "became merchants, and the numerous skilled craftsmen among them added much to Pennsylvania's prosperity. They rejected pacifism."[3]

Some Mennonite and closely related writers have put forward some version of this isolationist interpretation. Historian Martin Schrag has written that between the sixteenth and the eighteenth centuries Mennonites did not even maintain a status quo, but chose greater and greater isolation as they moved from Switzerland and elsewhere to the New World. Schrag said that to do this, they made farming "a sacred occupation involving a minimum of economic integration with the larger society." Hand in hand with the isolationist interpretation is a suggestion that Mennonite religious and cultural patterns became fixed, with faith and life remaining the same from generation to generation. Mennonite historian J. C. Wenger has said that throughout the eighteenth century "no significant changes were made and no one intended to make any."[4]

Such statements point to much that is true, yet they beg scrutiny. Historical geographer James T. Lemon, studying eighteenth-century tax records of Lancaster and Chester counties, has concluded that among the population at large two thirds of taxable heads of households were farmers. Moreover, among artisans and laborers who made up most of the other third, "many . . . tilled some land and pastured some cows." The fact is, Mennonite patterns were not greatly different. In addition to or instead of farming, a goodly number of Mennonites were of course also tradesmen. A 1773 letter of Mennonites to Europe commented on Mennonite occupations and mentioned only two that the church actively discouraged: officeholding, "because force is used therein," and innkeeping, "because it leads to a great number of irregularities." The letter also commented that no American Mennonites were engaged in ocean shipping.[5] Of course Mennonites also avoided the military. But with those few exceptions, the occupational pattern of Mennonites in colonial Pennsylvania scarcely differed from the patterns of Scotch-Irish Presbyterians or of German Lutherans.

Nor was language as great a barrier as some have thought. Well into the nineteenth century a German could live, work, and travel from New Jersey to South Carolina using his own language. Moreover, eighteenth-century Mennonites knew at least as much English as did their German "church" neighbors. Skippack elder Andrew Ziegler and other Mennonites wrote a somewhat "Dutchy" English; but virtually all Pennsylvania Germans did that. The only bilingual *Fraktur* surviving from the eighteenth century are pieces produced not primarily by "church" Germans but by (or sometimes for) Mennonite and Schwenkfelder school pupils in Franconia and nearby Salford townships. In 1770 Mennonite parents in Lancaster County's Strasburg Township advertised for a schoolmaster qualified to teach English. And there were many Mennonites among residents of Earl Township who signed a petition in 1785 saying they were "desirous to have their children instructed in the English language," and English-speaking children instructed in German as well, "because both languages appear to us in this country essential to the man of business and for almost every profession and calling."[6]

Since eighteenth-century Mennonites left few documents, historians have been tempted to read back into the 1700s the cultural patterns of the most conservative and separatist nineteenth- and twentieth-century Amish and Mennonites. Some Amish and Mennonites themselves are tempted to do the same, because it implies that their spiritual ancestors and perhaps they themselves have "kept the faith." Such isolation, lack of change, and consequent "faithfulness" may indeed have been the case. But to say so requires evidence, not merely convenient assumptions. And the burden of proof must be on those who make such assertions, for it seems unlikely that a subgroup could remain so uninfluenced and so unchanged in societies as dynamic as those in North America. If Amish and Mennonites did not change from the Swiss mountains to the valleys of Pennsylvania, Maryland, and Virginia, then they did not interact with the New World environment.—an unlikely possibility.

Perhaps Mennonites did not always live quite as tolerantly toward their non-Mennonite neighbors as Schultz's image of "fish in water" suggested. In the 1740s they rebuffed ecumenical efforts of one set of neighbors, the Moravians. The Moravians were essentially a group of radical Pietists from Lutheran churches who even in Europe had begun to cluster in Pietistic fellowships, especially at "Herrnhut," the estate of their most prominent leader, a count named Nickolaus von Zinzendorf.[7] Some European Mennonite leaders liked what they saw of the Moravians. A prominent preacher in an Amsterdam congregation, Johannes Deknatel, formally united with the new group in 1738 even while continuing to be a Mennonite.[8] Late in 1741 Zinzendorf himself arrived in Pennsylvania to visit. One of his purposes was to help get a Moravian community established at Bethlehem (at the northeastern edge of Mennonite settlements) to do mission work among red Indians and white set-

The

Chriſtian

CONFESSION

Of the Faith of the harmleſs
Chriſtians, in the *Ne-
therlands,* known by
the name of

MENNONISTS.

A M S T E R D A M.
Printed, and Re-printed and Sold by
Andrew Bradford in *Philadelphia,*
in the Year, 1727.

**Title page and last page of first American printing (1727) of the Men-
nonite Dordrecht Confession of Faith, 1632.** (Courtesy Mennonite Historical Library, Goshen College)

tlers. On New Year's Day in 1742 he held the first of a series
of interfaith synods, this one at Germantown. The first meeting was in the home of a certain Theobold Endt, who had
married a Mennonite. Its purpose was unity and cooperation
among the Pennsylvania Germans' various churches and
sects. But apparently no Mennonite attended.[9]

Shortly thereafter Zinzendorf traveled to Skippack where a Mennonite leader named Martin Kolb received him cordially. Moreover some Mennonites did participate in a second synod in mid-January held at Falckner Swamp in the home of a Schwenkfelder, and also in a third one in the Oley Valley in Berks County, in the home of a certain Johannes De Turck, a Moravian who had been reared Mennonite. But thereafter, for some reason, both Schwenkfelders and Mennonites withdrew from the discussions. About that time Mennonites in America began to publish some books, and various historians, most notably John Joseph Stoudt, have suggested that they did so to reestablish their separate identity in the face of the Moravian effort to meld groups together.[10]

Whatever their motives, in the 1740s Mennonites in America did begin printing. Up to then their only American publication had been an English version of the Dordrecht Confession of Faith, reprinted in 1727 in Philadelphia from an English translation produced in Holland. Now in the very year of Zinzendorf's synods, 1742, Pennsylvania Mennonites put to press a new edition of their ancient hymnal, the *Ausbund*, with some martyr stories added as an appendix. Later in the 1740s a new press operated by radical, Seventh-Day German Baptists living communally at Ephrata, Pennsylvania, in Lancaster County, printed *Die Ernsthafte Christenpflicht* (Earnest Christian Duty), a prayerbook that Mennonites in the Palatinate had compiled and published in 1739, and *Güldene Aepffel in Silbern Schalen* (Golden Apples in Silver Vessels), a Swiss-Mennonite devotional book.[11]

Meanwhile, also in the year of Zinzendorf's synods, 1742, Skippack-area Mennonites decided that they needed a German version of another venerable book that was key to Mennonite faith and outlook, the *Martyrs Mirror*. First they wrote to Mennonites in Holland asking them to please translate that ancient work from the Dutch and send over a supply, but the Hollanders declined. So the Pennsylvania Mennonites undertook the sizable project themselves. To do the translating they engaged Peter Miller, a learned man who was a member of the Seventh-Day German Baptists' monastic community at Ephrata. To print the manuscript they contracted with the Ephrata community and its press. Either because they did not trust the Ephrata group with their precious book, or out of economic prudence, they carefully stipulated that they did not necessarily have to buy the printed books. The work was so massive that Miller and the Ephrata people took three years at it. By 1748-1749 they produced 1,300 copies, each copy running to 1,512 pages, making the new book the largest one printed in America up to that time. In the end the Mennonites were quite happy with Miller's translation (although they refused to buy some copies bound with a frontispiece depicting Christ being baptized by immersion).[12]

Perhaps the printing of those basic Mennonite books was itself a sectarian act. But the Mennonites had in mind mainly a positive effort to teach what they believed, especially to their youth. In a second letter to Dutch Mennonites they spoke of wanting the *Martyrs Mirror* in German "to make every preparation for steadfast constancy in our faith" in the face of what seemed to be ever stronger war talk in America. This, they said, was necessary particularly because in their communities many young men were coming to adulthood. That same sort of positive purpose also permeated another Mennonite book of the 1740s, a small one printed on the Sauer press at Germantown in 1744, entitled *Ein Spiegel der Tauffe, mit Geist mit Wasser und mit Blut* (A Mirror of Baptism, of the Spirit, with Water, and with Blood). Its author was Heinrich Funck.[13]

Funck immigrated to America in 1717 and became a prominent miller, landowner, and progenitor of various Funks later important to Mennonite history. He was also a very influential elder in the Franconia congregation, a congregation in the very heartland of what was becoming a Mennonite conference region. In the 1740s he provided much of the initiative for getting both the *Ausbund* and the *Martyrs Mirror* printed. In the meantime he penned his book on baptism—the first book known to have been published by an American Mennonite author. The main thrust of Funck's *Mirror of Baptism* was to set forth a Mennonite understanding of becoming a Christian and following Christ—even to the point of suffering (hence, baptism . . . with blood).[14]

Der
Blutige Schau-Platz
oder
Martyrer
Spiegel der Tauffs-Gesinten
oder
Wehrlosen-Christen,

Jesu ihres Seligmachers willen
getödtet worden, von Christi Zeit an
biß Jahr 1660.

Aus gen Chronicken, Nachrichten und Zeugnüssen gesamm- her Sprach heraus gegeben

V. BRAGHT.

übersetzt und zum erstenmal ans Licht gebracht.

und
hofft

EPHRATA in Pensylvanien,
Drucks und Verlags der Bruderschafft.   Anno MDCCXLVIII.

Title page of 1748 *Martyrs Mirror*. Inset: A page on the press at Ephrata Cloister, Ephrata, Pa., where it was printed. (Jan Gleysteen collection)

Funck's main thrust was positive, yet he also openly disagreed with points of his neighbors' creeds. Running through his book were very strong assumptions and assertions that the proper mode was to baptize only adults who had personally repented, and to do it by sprinkling or pouring. Thus Funck took strong positions on issues that have sharply divided Christians in North America. In a later and larger book published only posthumously (in 1763), Funck was more conciliatory. In that book's preface Funck said that Christians should not divide over mere "difference of understanding and form in the matter of things ceremonial." Clearly alluding to the different churches, he wrote of God making his tabernacles out of many different kinds of material to be fitted together harmoniously.[15] But Funck's first book was quite partisan. Moravians as well as Lutherans and Reformed could clearly have read it partly as a rebuke; for like those other two churches, Moravians had never broken with the practice of infant baptism. A group who could take it as an even sharper rebuke were the Dunkers. The Dunkers had broken with infant baptism but they rejected sprinkling and pouring, insisting strongly on immersion as the proper baptismal mode.

The Dunkers, or "German Baptists" (later, Church of the Brethren), were religiously and in geographical origin close cousins of the Mennonites. Not only did they accept adult baptism but, as Church of the Brethren historian Donald Durnbaugh has pointed out, their first minister, Alexander Mack, had also accepted much from Anabaptism. They drew heavily on seventeenth-century Pietism but also looked to sixteenth-century Anabaptism for a restitutionist view of the church and a strong emphasis on obedience and discipleship.[16] If Mennonites felt the need to set boundaries, it was against Dunkers as much as against anyone, for with them they had a family quarrel.

In their first generation in America the Dunkers were aggressive evangelists and proselytizers. After arriving in Germantown in 1719 they soon had a kind of revival going in that community, a revival of which several former Mennonites became the "first fruits."[17] In the 1720s Dunker missionaries worked in the Skippack and Franconia commu-

nities. A 1724 meeting of the Dunker movement near Ephrata, north of Lancaster, took place at the home of a Mennonite minister, Rudolph Nagele. In that area in 1725 the
Dunkers began more formally a congregation, the Conestoga,
when a new leader, Conrad Beissel, met with a group in
another Mennonite home and baptized seven persons:
Nagele and his wife; the host John Landes and his wife;
another Mennonite couple; and one other person. Later
those former Mennonites went with Beissel when, about
1728, he separated from other Pennsylvania Dunkers to
form the communal Seventh-Day German Baptist community at Ephrata.[18] Among Dunkers who did not separate,
an early and prominent pastor was Michael Frantz, who in
1727 had arrived in Pennsylvania as a Mennonite, with help
from the Dutch Mennonites' Commission for Foreign Needs.
And so it went. Quite a few Mennonites in the 1720s and
1730s were won over by the Dunkers' more aggressively
experiential and Pietistic form of Christianity. Mennonite
converts probably made up no more than 10 percent of the
early Dunker members in America, but they included some
prominent leaders.[19]

By the 1740s the Dunkers were largely past their first
missionary phase, a phase that drew members also from Lutheran and Reformed backgrounds. But the special relation
with Mennonites continued. Records of the Mennonite and
the Church of the Brethren congregations at Germantown,
for instance, indicate that families such as the Keysers and
the Knorrs moved back and forth between the two groups
quite frequently.[20] In what is now York County at the
western edge of early Mennonite settlement, Dunkers began
their first congregation in 1738 in the midst of Mennonites
living near Hanover. Apparently former Mennonites were
among the first members and within a few years three sons
and a son-in-law of Michael Danner, the Mennonite pioneer
in that area, became Dunkers. One of the sons, Jacob, became a prominent Dunker preacher who organized congregations in Pennsylvania, Maryland, and Virginia. Both he
and a brother, Henry, wrote hymns. One congregation that
he organized, the Codorus in York County, included Nicholas
Bucher, a former Mennonite whom the Commission for

Foreign Needs had helped with passage in 1727, and some Brillharts whose father Samuel had identified himself as a Mennonite when he immigrated in 1737.[21] Family ties may have been at least as important as doctrine in the various crossings back and forth between Mennonite and Dunker. If a congregation of one or the other group suffered poor leadership for a time, or took to quarreling about some local issue, familiar faces of aunts and uncles in the other's nearby meetinghouse surely made transition easier.

Thus Mennonites were sometimes partisan, but also often friendly and open across the lines of religious division. They continued firmly to reject Moravian attempts to bring Pennsylvania Germans all under one religious roof. A list that a later Moravian leader has drawn up of "persons attached to the Brethren" (that is to the Moravians) in 1748-1754 identified only two from Lancaster County that had formerly been Mennonites, plus a half dozen or so from Skippack and elsewhere. Yet a Moravian missionary named George Hantsch, who made special efforts in the summer of 1748 to work among Lancaster County Mennonites, reported very warm receptions in the homes he visited. Mennonite preacher Benjamin Hershey interrupted the cutting of his grain for several hours for friendly conversation. Preacher Christian Martin and his family in Manor Township made Hantsch feel "genuinely welcome," Martin being "a dear man and quite emotional and concerned for his soul." Preacher Christian Good in Brecknock Township "was quite friendly to us, and quite satisfied with us over the conversation we had on the Dear Savior." Hantsch's remarks are consistent with much other evidence of warmth between Moravians and Mennonites at about that time.[22]

Mennonites in eighteenth-century Pennsylvania seem generally to have accepted a religious pluralism like that which historians of the nineteenth-century United States have labeled "denominationalism." The tabernacle imagery that Heinrich Funck invoked in his 1763 preface very much suggested that outlook. To be sure, Funck implied that there were limits to tolerance for other groups, for he went on to say that the material in the tabernacle all had to be good stuff.[23] But that, too, was like nineteenth-century United

States "denominationalism": few Protestants in the nineteenth century would expand their circle enough to include, say, the "Mormons." Within certain ranges there was mutual acceptance. And in the eighteenth century Mennonites pretty much shared such a pattern of acceptance. Indeed, in one sense they were hardly "sectarian"; for to some religious historians, to be sectarians is by definition to reject the logic of denominationalism and to refuse to accept other churches as legitimate.[24]

If eighteenth-century Mennonites had wanted isolation they might have pursued it far more deliberately. Instead, after emigrating from Europe right alongside many "church" people, they settled and lived side by side with the peoples of various faiths. Although Lemon in his studies of southeastern Pennsylvania counties concluded that Mennonites, Quakers, and other sectarians developed especially strong group discipline and mutual aid, in fact Mennonites could have tried even harder to reproduce the closeness of European villages or even to create communitarian colonies such as the Moravians attempted at Bethlehem and the Seventh-Day German Baptists achieved at Ephrata. The Moravians and the Ephrata group may not have tried to be separatist so much as to create communities of a certain quality; but Mennonites could have worked for such tight communities as separatist devices. They did not.[25]

Instead Mennonites (and Amish) very quickly accepted the American pattern of open communities, made up largely of individual farmsteads. A few of them chose to live in Pennsylvania's cities and towns. Social historian Laura L. Becker has described the ethnic mix in Reading in 1772-1773 by pointing out that "the blocks on either side of Penn Square held six German Lutherans, seven German Reformed, four English Anglicans, four English Quakers, one German Catholic, and one German Mennonite," with their families. Since they thus lived among each other, Becker concluded, they must have "mingled frequently, at least on an informal basis." Historian Stephanie Wolf, studying eighteenth-century Germantown, found that Mennonites never were more than 15 percent of Germantown's population, and also that, judging by how often they bequeathed money to the poor of their own congregation, they must have kept a strong Mennonite-group consciousness. Yet she too found the Mennonites to have lived scattered among people of other faiths.[26] Thus, the Mennonites of southeastern Pennsylvania did not choose to live in isolation.

Moreover, even in their churches and their schools— the very realms of life having more directly to do with nurture, worship, and the shaping of attitude and belief—Mennonites did not attempt nearly as much isolation as they might have. To organize and support elementary education for their children, Pennsylvania Germans, including Mennonites, worked through their churches. Yet they hardly ever tried to run schools along strictly denominational lines or to make them parochial in the modern sense. Mennonite school trustees, operating a school in or alongside their meetinghouse, might well hire a Reformed or Lutheran schoolmaster and gather pupils from both Mennonite and non-Mennonite homes. Or a Mennonite schoolmaster might teach as many children of church Germans as of Mennonites or other meetinghouse people.

In Germantown, in 1759, some Mennonites joined with neighbors to create a school which they designated as "free to all denominations whatsoever without any regard to Name or Sect of People." Like other eighteenth-century schools, this one charged tuition. To keep that from becoming a hardship, in 1763 Mennonite Nicholaus Rittenhouse joined with Christopher Sauer, the Germantown printer with German Baptist connections, and with John George Alsentz, pastor of the Reformed church, to be a committee for reducing fees for the poor. And in 1775 Mennonites again joined with others to establish a second union school in Germantown.[27]

Nor was such cooperation a pattern only among the more urbanized Mennonites such as the Rittenhouse family. In 1748 the Reverend Henry Melchoir Muhlenberg, noted paster of southeastern Pennsylvania's Lutherans, wrote of a schoolhouse at Matecha, near Goshenhoppen, that one of his deacons had built with Mennonites' help. Not far away in Lower Salford Township in what is now Montgomery County, in 1758, a majority of local school trustees receiving title to school land were Mennonites, but others were Dunkers, Lutherans, and Reformed. In 1771 the Lower Salford Mennonites built a new meetinghouse with a schoolroom and the community school then moved into the Mennonites' building. The case was similar in Earl Township of Lancaster County. In 1765 when a local school there received title to land at least seven of twelve trustees were Mennonite, yet the deed said the school was for "residents of the said Township and the neighborhood adjacent of whatever denomination soever." In 1775 a group of Earl Township residents taking title to another school plot included Amish and Mennonite— one of the few cases in which Amish and Mennonites shared a meetinghouse or a schoolhouse.[28] In these cooperative schools, and even when a school was tied (as many were) more directly to a Mennonite congregation, the school was more a bridge than a barrier between different religious groups.

Schoolmasters often moved from one parochial school to another without much concern for sectarian or denominational boundaries. John Conrad Wirtz, for instance, was the first Reformed Church schoolmaster at Goshenhoppen in the 1730s but afterwards Mennonites at Conestoga hired him. Lancaster County Mennonites employed such non-Mennonite schoolmasters as John Christian Strenge, a Lutheran. Strenge taught in Hempfield Township in Lancaster County, probably in present-day East Petersburg in a log building used as a schoolhouse and meetinghouse.[29]

In Bucks County, beginning in 1779, John Adam Eyer, a Lutheran *Schuldiener* (schoolmaster), taught at the Perkasie Mennonite school in Hilltown Township and at neighboring Deep Run Mennonite school in Bedminster Township. Eyer's roll book has many surnames long familiar in the Bucks County Mennonite community as well as others long associated with Lutheran and Reformed parishes. Boys and girls from Mennonite families probably were in the majority, but children from Lutheran and Reformed families may have made up a third to a half of their classmates. After teaching at Deep Run and Perkasie for eight years, Eyer taught for shorter terms in other Mennonite communities, including Vincent Township in Chester County and Strasburg Township in Lancaster County.[30]

Conversely, Mennonite schoolmasters taught students of other denominational backgrounds. Surely the most famous of all colonial Pennsylvania schoolmasters was Christopher Dock, a man whom scholars now strongly believe to have been a Mennonite. Dock immigrated from Germany apparently in 1718 and began to teach school at Skippack and also, during some summers, in the Mennonite meetinghouse at Germantown. Whether Dock taught in the meetinghouse or in a separate structure at Skippack is unclear, although beginning with 1747 the Mennonite congregation's almsbook makes some references to a separate school building. For a time, from 1728 to 1738, he quit and farmed full time (except perhaps teaching briefly at Germantown); then, returning to the classroom, he divided his schedule between Skippack and Salford. A deed to the Lower Salford congregation makes clear that a building erected in 1738 was intended "for a meeting house and a school house." After twenty-six years of teaching in schools related to Mennonite congregations, Dock wrote in 1750 that "in my experience in this country I have had, at my school, children of various religious denominations, so that I could not teach them the same catechism."[31] Very likely other schoolmasters had similar experiences.

Dock was evidently a most gifted teacher, one who was thoughtful about his techniques. As early as 1750 Christopher Sauer I, the famed Germantown printer, invited the Skippack schoolmaster to offer an account of his methods to the public, and asked Mennonite preacher Dielman Kolb to help persuade him. The modest schoolmaster wrote the account, but then declined to let it be published. In 1764 he did allow Sauer to print, in Sauer's *Geistliches Magazien* another school document he composed: *Hundert nothige Sitten-Regeln für Kinder* (A Hundred Necessary Rules of Conduct for Children). It was not until 1770 after Dock's death that the more important account appeared publicly, entitled *Schul-Ordnung* (School-Management or School-Regulation), printed by Christopher Sauer II, the older printer's son.[32]

In *Schul-Ordnung*, Dock described teaching methods that have seemed quite progressive even to twentieth-

Skippack schoolmaster Christopher Dock (1698?-1771) as painted by Oliver Wendell Schenk. (Reproduction from Jan Gleysteen collection)

century educators. The essay indicates a school with very young students. To induce them to learn their ABCs Dock used a system of rewards such as giving a child a penny or two fried eggs. As the little ones advanced enough to begin reading the New Testament, Dock had "good Testament readers" from among older students help them. Reading matter also included newspapers and letters. For practice in letter-writing Dock had pupils in one of his schools write to some in his other school. Christopher Sauer II, in an introduction to *Schul-Ordnung,* indicated that he was impressed not merely with Dock's scholastic achievement but also with his ability "to instruct children in letters and religion" by loving interest and example.[33]

Mennonite schools resembled Lutheran, Reformed, and Schwenkfelder ones in both curriculum and in a kind of common piety. Often the only books used were ABC books and the New Testament, with the pupils copying out their own penmanship examples, arithmetic and singing booklets. The ABC books were intended as primers for the reading and spelling classes and contained edifying verses, prayers, hymns and scripture passages. The Reformed pioneer clergyman Michael Schlatter had 1,000 copies of an ABC book printed for distribution in 1753, and Christopher Sauer issued a *Hochdeutsches Reformirtes ABC und Namenbuch* in 1766. This book was used across denominational boundaries. Mennonites and Lutherans did not publish their own ABC books until the turn of the nineteenth century.[34]

Mennonites made extensive use of a rhyming ABC verse beginning:

> Witt du bald ein doctor werden, ohne grosse Muh
> Kanst du alle Kunst auf erden, das dirs fahlet nie
> Das heist Viel in wenig Stunden,
> in dein ABC gefunden. . . .

which meant (freely translated):

> To be a scholar, very quickly, in an easy way,
> For the knowledge that, though earthly, will not
> quickly fade,
> You will get your knowledge faster,
> If your ABCs you master.

Copies of this little verse survive in many places. The second verse cultivated morality even more directly:

A is for All things, which we must leave.
  Bosheit (evil) starts with B.
C is for the Cross, we take up with joy,
  Demuth (humility) comes with D.
E points to Eternal Life,
  F begins our joy *(Freude)*,
And *Gedult* (patience) comes with G.

In the verses was also a hint that the doctor, the learned man, might be on the wrong path. In any case, the rhymes pointed not just to the alphabet, but to holy living. Christopher Dock composed an even more elaborate set of moralizing ABC verses.[35]

For some Mennonites it may have been enough if their children learned the three R's plus proper morality and religion. Abraham Herr of the Pequea Community, making a will in 1755, enjoined heirs to "bring up the children in fear of God and teach them in reding and writting." But some others wanted more advanced instruction. Those Germantown schools taught both English and German, and even more. In 1760 the trustees proposed "reading, writing and learning of languages and useful arts and sciences," including perhaps Latin, Greek, and Hebrew. On the other hand, Mennonite and Dunker trustees of the school that opened in Germantown in 1775 decided that English alone should be the language of instruction. Apparently acculturation did not necessarily bring a broader educational outlook.[36]

Mennonite rural schools also taught English. A deed issued in 1739 for the Methacton meetinghouse property in Worcester Township of present-day Montgomery County expressly called for classes in English as well as in German. A group of *fraktur Vorschriften* made by (or partly for) Mennonite pupils in Salford and Franconia townships in Philadelphia (Montgomery) County between 1760 and 1771 all contain English passages, ranging in content from a fair translation of a German hymn and Scripture selections to folk proverbs. These *Vorschriften* may have come from

Christopher Dock's school, but this is by no means certain. In 1772 Mennonite Jacob Carpenter made provision in his will for a schoolhouse at the end of his lane in Lampeter Township, where one John Eastwood kept school. A Mennonite whose name had been anglicized from Zimmermann to Carpenter was probably not very isolated from the larger community's life; and presumably a schoolmaster with the English or anglicized name Eastwood taught at least some classes in English. Finally, in 1770 John Brackbill and other Mennonites of Lancaster County's Strasburg Township advertised for a schoolmaster qualified to teach English, Latin, and bookkeeping to replace another who had taught those subjects.[37]

That Mennonites felt a need for such practical subjects (for legal documents, etc., even some Latin was practical) suggests one reason why they did not choose to isolate themselves very sharply from the larger life of the colony. To do so would not have been very practical. But another reason lay more in the religious realm, in the very nature of their faith. In the eighteenth century practically all Pennsylvania Germans (except perhaps the Catholics) more or less shared a common religious idiom. Virtually all Lutheran and Reformed congregations in America were not high church or very ceremonial but instead were imbued with a low-church Pietism. Sects such as the Moravians and the Dunkers owed their existence quite largely to similar Pietism, all from a Pietistic movement that emerged on the continent of Europe in the latter seventeenth century. Schwenkfelders, with a strong tradition of spiritualism, felt an affinity for and adopted much of the same outlook. And Mennonites, who emphasized personal and practical faith more than doctrine and ceremony, also felt strong affinity.[38] When a pietism of somewhat different and more anglicized tone would emerge in the form of American revivalism, Mennonites would gradually resist.[39] But to quite an extent colonial Mennonites were ready to share with their fellow Pennsylvania Germans a common religious mood and language. Therefore one influence that helped Mennonites move easily among their neighbors, "to and fro like fish in water," was the common idiom of European-derived Pietism.

CHAPTER

6

<hr>

THE INNER RELIGIOUS LIFE: MENNONITES AND PIETISM

"I must look to Jesus alone if I will go the way to life. He is the way and also the light. Whoever follows Him does not err at all." Thus wrote Gertraut Alderfer, eleven-year-old child of a Mennonite family in Lower Salford Township between Franconia and Skippack, in 1787. She wrote it as she prepared a manuscript of *Fraktur*, or *Vorschrift*, a kind of manuscript that in many Pennsylvania German schoolrooms had become an art form. It was a form already moving from folk art to a stylized and somewhat formal art, with decorations made up of likenesses of birds and flowers and various intricate lines and bright (though seldom brilliant) colors. Gertraut Alderfer's *Vorschrift* captured in a few lines a vast body of Anabaptist-derived Mennonite teaching on discipleship, obedience, and yieldedness to God's will. Continued she: "To all those who truly want to be children of God here on earth, who come to the Father all devout as children by this way, the Father receives them all as heirs, if they avoid evil desires and give themselves completely to the truth."[1]

A group of *Vorschriften* made at the same school and in neighboring Franconia Township a generation before Gertraut Alderfer composed her handiwork also suggests much about the way eighteenth-century Mennonites understood the Christian life. In a 1765 *Vorschrift* Martin Detwiler, apparently a Franconia school pupil, anticipated death and the judgment which awaited the sinner. Another such pupil, Christian Stauffer, wove together the theme of judgment with another theme, suffering. "Rule me," he lettered, "according to Thy suffering, do not leave me in sin." "I plead

Typically pietistic Fraktur, found in a copy of the *Ausbund,* probably done by or for a schoolgirl. Inscription means: "With each new day more time doth pass, and who knows which will be the last/ This nice song-book belongs to Ana Stauffer/ And is given her by her father for the honor of God on the 24th of March, 1793. Guide me dear Savior, lead me into Your Kingdom, Hallelujah." (Jan Gleysteen collection)

from the bottom of my heart that Thou wilt forgive me all my sins which I have committed in my entire life and would also preserve me to this day in Thy protection from my manifold sepulchre." In 1766 a youngster named Huppert Cassel alluded to persecution and suffering, but pointed even more strongly to separation from the world's evil. "If in singleness of purpose we ... incline completely to the way of Christ,

casting out all falsity," he printed, "we are soon despised."
For the young Cassel the Christian life meant "separating
himself from the false unto God." "What God has not commanded, should not be called good."[2]

Themes such as separation and suffering clearly
echoed longtime Anabaptist emphases. Indeed, the language
especially of the young Cassel's *Vorschrift* was very much like
that of the oldest Anabaptist confession of faith, the
confession made at Schleitheim in southern Germany in
1527.[3] But such *Vorschrift* had other themes that did not
especially hark back to Anabaptism. Stauffer and Cassel
wrote bilingually, and Stauffer included in English somewhat lighter moralisms such as, "Down with vice and serve
the living god with fear"; or, "Evil communication Corrupts
good meaners [*sic*]." Cassel, writing at about Christmas-
time, included in fair English a rendering of the seasonal
hymn, "How Brightly Shines the Morning Star."[4]

These other themes sounded much more like the
Pietism that various Germans, whether Lutheran, Reformed,
Moravian, Dunker, or Mennonite, had brought or were accepting from the European continent. Pietism very much
permeated a 1775 Lancaster County *Vorschrift* made by a
Manor Township schoolmaster for pupil Anna Karlisen
(Charles). "I am a poor child of man, sick at heart and blind of
eye," the precious *fraktur* letters stated. "I stand in great debt
and fear both hell and death. I should be Christ's little lamb,
pure and pious in faith and love; but, alas, I failed in that and
am a child of darkness.... I will go to the Good Shepherd
and admit to him my guilt. Lord Jesus, oh, have mercy, have
mercy upon me." Especially in its emphasis on the tender,
sweet shepherd Jesus, in contrast to the Jesus who leads the
Christian through bitter suffering, that *Vorschrift* had a
definite tone of Pietism.[5]

Such Mennonite *Vorschriften* pose what is a broad and
fundamental problem in understanding Mennonite religious
life in eighteenth-century America. Anabaptism and Pietism
had enough in common or became so inextricably mingled
that it is easy to attach the label "Anabaptist" to some religious perceptions that found wide acceptance among
Pietistic "church" Germans; Conversely, one can too easily
treat as Pietistic accretions some perceptions that were very

authentic to Mennonite faith. After studying the hymns of schoolmaster Christopher Dock, German hymnologist Ada Kadelbach has observed that while "his writings and hymns are in no sense incongruent with Mennonite doctrine . . . they show a definite stamp of pietism which affected nearly all of the Protestant groups in Pennsylvania in the eighteenth century."[6]

Surely a Mennonite and a Lutheran Pietist would each have agreed with Huppert Cassel's *fraktur* statement that to "incline completely to the way of Christ" meant necessarily to be despised. But did "separating himself from the false unto God" have the same meaning for the Mennonite as for the Lutheran Pietist? Dietmar Rothermund, a historian who wrote from a generally secular and impartial perspective, has observed that in colonial Pennsylvania "the churches, unlike the sects, had never committed themselves to an imitation of Christ on all seven days of the week"; hence they had no difficulty separating religious and secular concerns. Rothermund made a valid distinction. Yet he probably did not quite take into account how Pietistic were the "church" Germans in Pennsylvania.[7] And somewhat like Anabaptism, Pietism strongly emphasized everyday holy living.

Moreover, in practice, for eighteenth-century Mennonites the attempt to live obediently did not bring such sharp and dramatic confrontation with evil as it had for earlier Anabaptists. In Protestant Europe as well as in America, the eighteenth century was a time of transition from the Reformation-era understanding of religion as a public duty in a unitary society to an understanding of religion more as a private matter for citizens in increasingly secularized and pluralistic societies. The older notion of unitary society, and with it the idea that rulers should enforce correct belief upon individuals, still prevailed in some places. Hence the occasional persecutions of Mennonites especially in Canton Bern. Schwenkfelders also still suffered some persecution, particularly in Austrian Silesia. But in the Netherlands, in Great Britain, and in many German states, the situation had changed or was changing. And of all places where Mennonites lived, Pennsylvania carried the change the farthest.

Fraktur design in a songbook to indicate that Eleanor Ruth of Vincent School, Chester County, Pa., owned it. Dated 1800. Ruth was a common Mennonite surname. (Jan Gleysteen collection)

Anabaptist and early Mennonite understandings of yieldedness and discipleship had taken their shape very much from outright persecution or the constant threat of it. To a large extent waves of persecution had helped Anabaptists solve the difficult problem of indecisive or indifferent members, the problem of church discipline. Leaders could enforce their congregations' understandings of obedience in the form of the church's rules and regulations, or *Ordnung,* because the less zealous who might not accept such discipline constantly drifted back into the state churches. It is true that at the time of the Reist-Ammann division the *Reistisch* Mennonites were inclined to allow those not fully committed to continue to associate with Mennonite congregations.[8] About 1700 Hans Reist initiated a prayer into Mennonite devotional literature for such half way people, and in 1739 the prayer found its way into the book *Die Ernsthafte Christenpflicht* (Earnest Christian Duty), which American Mennonites reprinted in 1745 and frequently thereafter from its earlier German edition. The prayer was on behalf of "good-hearted people who love us and do good unto us and prove mercy with food and drink, house and shelter, but who have little strength to come into the obedience of God."[9] Nevertheless the specter of persecution and suffering had helped keep alive the ideas of a voluntary church and deliberate personal choice of one's faith, in contrast to a church made up of persons who had been reared in the faith never having to make a very clear decision.

In new and more tolerant American circumstances the central concern of eighteenth-century American Mennonite religious life was how to preserve the fervor and commitment of that suffering church of martyrs and refugees. To some extent Mennonites worked at the task by emphasizing responsibility toward one another through mutual aid. Alms books, wherein congregations kept record of their poor funds (or deacon's funds) were much more important to Mennonites than were registers of baptisms, marriages, and funerals. Indeed, since they viewed such ceremonies as symbols rather than as sacraments, Mennonites did not keep registers of the latter kind while a fair collection of eighteenth- and nineteenth-century alms books survive to this day.[10] Hans Tschantz, Lancaster-area Mennonite bishop who was active especially from the 1740s to the 1770s, declared in a sermon that taking spiritual and material responsibility for fellow-members "was made as a law and whoever does not care for his brother's needs comes to an awful end."[11]

The alms books recorded much more than aid to immigrants coming from Europe. The Skippack congregation's book, for instance, listed such items as money spent for hauling a poor man's effects to a certain house, and for maintaining him there; money loaned to a man from Carolina (perhaps an immigrant who had entered North America there); the cost of a pound of sugar for a certain Maria van Fossen; and purchase of supplies for the communion service.[12] Alms books mingled expenditures for keeping up church property, for communion supplies, for operation of schools, and for aid to members. Such mixing suggests that

Mennonites did not see one kind of expenditure as particularly more religious than another. Nor did Mennonites stop their charity with their congregations' alms funds: in various communities, Mennonites served regularly as public overseers of the poor.[13] But the alms books strongly suggest that Mennonite congregations took care of their own widows, orphans, and poor.

No doubt such practice of congregational mutual aid helped to keep Mennonite congregations vital as Mennonites began to prosper in America. Historian Frederick B. Tolles has demonstrated very well that in the case of Pennsylvania's Quakers, growing wealth subjected the fellowship to the strains of class and interest-group divisions. At the same time the Quakers more and more became a group made up of "birthright membership." According to Tolles and others who have refined and expanded his analyses, most notably scholars Jack D. Marietta and Kenneth L. Carroll, the Quakers then had to make a deliberate effort to reverse a trend away from their own sectarian emphasis, a trend toward becoming merely another American "denomination" rather than a sect. For Mennonites, the experience of the Schwenkfelders was even closer. A small group of persecuted families from a single rural neighborhood in Silesia, the main body of Schwenkfelders migrated with Mennonite help to southeastern Pennsylvania in 1734. There, inroads of Pietism tended to blur any clear theological identity based on the writings of their sixteenth-century spiritualist founder, Caspar Schwenkfeld. But strong organization, adaptable institutions, and commitment to mutual aid seem to have sustained them.[14] Very probably, in a similar way, mutual aid helped to sustain the lives of Mennonite and Amish congregations.

No doubt also among both Mennonites and Amish, as with the Schwenkfelders, a simplicity of church structure helped congregational vitality. Historian Martin E. Lodge has concluded that in Pennsylvania the sects such as "Mennonites and Schwenkfelders, were, in general, more successful than the churches in establishing their religious institutions." He found that with Dutch Mennonites the sects' immigration "was better planned, organized, and financed" than that of the church peoples. Even more important in Lodge's judgment, "sectarian institutions were better adapted to the primitive conditions of the New World than were church institutions." As soon as a group of Amish or Mennonite families settled in a place, a congregation could quickly take shape. In contrast to their Lutheran or Reformed neighbors, such settlers did not have to wait for trained clergy to arrive, or wait until they could pay a preacher a salary. Instead they chose leaders directly from their own ranks, and the preachers earned their own livings. Lodge concluded that this gave the sects an advantage for getting healthy congregational life underway.[15]

But mutual aid and simple, adaptable structure do not tell the whole story of how Mennonites worked to keep congregations vital in the easy going, tolerant American situation. Another pattern was movement in the direction of Pietism. In the seventeenth and early eighteenth centuries, Pietism had emerged in various Protestant regions of Europe. It was a religious renewal movement, centered in some Dutch universities and later in Germany in the University of Halle (founded largely by one of its most prominent leaders, Philipp Jakob Spener, with another August Hermann Francke, serving as a popular professor) and at an advanced school at Herborn. Somehow, probably because Pietists emphasized mission and America seemed like a mission field, it happened that the strongest of early pastors among "church" Germans in Pennsylvania were from such schools: Heinrich Melchoir Muhlenberg, a very able and influential early shepherd of the Lutherans; and Samuel Guldin and Michael Schlatter, similarly influential for the Reformed. Thus, not only Moravians and Dunkers, but prominent leaders of the main German denominations also, helped bring continental Pietism to communities where Mennonites settled.[16]

As a religious renewal movement, Pietism was concerned above all with personal conversion, religious experience, Bible study in small fellowships, and devotional life. To some degree it affected church structure and organization, for Pietists produced a variety of benevolent and missionary activities.[17] It also spawned some new groups such as the Moravians and the Dunkers.[18] But for the most part, Pietism offered little outright challenge to existing authorities and structures, either church or state. It did not have Anabaptism's overtones of political dissent, or of fracturing the supposedly unified Christian society. Instead, Pietism was more narrowly "religious." Pietists objected to what they saw as a deterioration of Protestantism in the years elapsed since the Reformation, especially to a kind of scholasticism in the Lutheran and Reformed churches that they said overemphasized arid and rigid doctrine and relied too much on ceremony. Rather than directly challenging political patterns of either church or state, they were largely content to form unofficial fellowships within existing churches. So they were not subjected to the persecutions that Anabaptists suffered.[19]

Because persecution and suffering did not shape Pietism as they had shaped Anabaptism, often Pietists gave somewhat different content to certain emphases. Like Anabaptists they emphasized *Gelassenheit* (yieldedness), but they tended to limit it much more to a quietistic resignation of one's spirit to Christ in the course of repentance and enjoyment of salvation. Among Anabaptists it had carried more the very practical meaning of willingness to suffer, bodily. For Anabaptists had found the idea of martyrdom bearable only if they could surrender self very literally, and accept it joyously as God's will. Likewise, the idea of devotion to Jesus: to Anabaptists the concept implied following the "bitter Christ," the Jesus who led through hardship and suffering. To Pietists devotion was more likely to mean the soul's finding rest and comfort with Jesus the gentle shepherd—the embrace of the "sweet Jesus." Yet, despite such differences, Pietism had much in common with Anabaptism, with its emphases on renewal, on making faith personal, on going directly to Scripture rather than searching for God's message through a maze of formal theology, and on warm, mutually supporting fellowship.[20]

Moreover, as Mennonites in North America began to live comfortably and to feel no persecution, they clearly had trouble keeping a sense of the suffering that had earlier been so central to their faith. So now Pietism, often using the same words but without so much connotation of suffering, seemed more and more a natural language for Mennonites and for bolstering Mennonite religious vitality.

In Pennsylvania, political authorities scarcely paid any attention to whether a young man was baptized by an Amish bishop or confirmed by a Lutheran minister. Neither carried notable penalties or legal reward. The Amish, the Mennonite, the Lutheran, and the Reformed pastor faced tasks that were very much the same. A Lutheran such as the Rev. Friedrich Schultz of New Goshenhoppen worked with his teenaged confirmands to teach them Bible and catechism, and in 1753 sadly entered into his church book that "so far all of these are in need of one thing--John 3:3" (i.e., the new birth).[21] The Goshenhoppen Mennonite pastor had young people in his congregation who would be expected in time to be baptized and accepted into the church with about the same kind of emphasis. Both pastors were nurturing faith of young people born within the Christian family. They might bring some different emphases to their task, but the task and much of what they taught were similar.

The danger was very real that full membership in the church, whether by baptism or confirmation, would become merely a rite of passage for those who were accepting what the Quakers came to call "birthright membership." In 1770 the Baptist minister Morgan Edwards observed that "touching the subject of baptism the Mennonists still retain their integrity by administering the ordinance to none but those who profess faith and repentance and make vows of subjection to the Gospel of Christ, which keeps up the distinction between the world and the church." But Edwards had heard that "the parents sometimes insist on their children being baptized before they will consent to their marriage." He thought that the policy of such parents was a mistake, for children might "be forced to a thing which should be a matter of personal choice following conviction and calls of conscience." Edwards apparently had little or no direct contact with Mennonites, and most probably received his information from Christopher Sauer II, Dunker printer at Germantown; but his evidence at least suggests how Mennonites' neighbors in Pennsylvania perceived them.[22]

It would thus be a mistake to see Pietism too simply as an alien influence that seeped into the Mennonite community. It did seep in, especially through books and hymnals compiled by members of other denominations. But it might have appeared even without those outside sources. Mennonite historian Robert Friedmann has deplored its coming; he thought that Pietism lessened Mennonites' older Anabaptist sense of conflict with the world and changed their outlook from one of conquering and bringing the world under Christ's lordship to a search mainly for inner peace and godliness. In *Mennonite Piety Through the Centuries* Friedmann developed those themes at book length.[23] But the changes that Friedmann noted occurred equally among Mennonites who were quite far removed from the Pietism of Lutheran and Reformed churches. With or without Pietist influence Mennonites interpreted discipleship more and more in terms of adhering to their own group's discipline and practices, and less and less in the language of spreading the rule of the Lord in the world. So it is practically impossible to say clearly what came as the influence of the Pietistic movement, and what was simply a gradual change in the Amish and Mennonite peoples' own piety.

With the threat of persecution gone, transmitting faith became more and more a matter of nurturing young people raised within the congregations. So Mennonites in America increasingly felt a need for catechisms. For that they often used writings of a Pietistic Mennonite named Gerrit Roosen of the Hamburg-Altona area of West Prussia, particularly a 1727 book entitled *Christliches Gemütsgespräch von dem geistlichen und seligmachended Glauben* (Heartfelt Christian Conversation Concerning Faith that is Spiritual and Brings Blessing)—a title loaded with Pietistic phraseology. At first they imported Roosen's book from Europe, but in 1769, in Lancaster County, they made the first of several editions printed in America by the end of the century.[24] Eighteenth-century inventory and estate sales often listed a "Menonist Catechism,"[25] which was probably Roosen's book. Also, some time before 1750 the Skippack schoolmaster Christopher Dock prepared another catechism in the form of questions with answers from the Bible.[26]

An element in the Roosen and the Dock catechisms was traditional Mennonite teaching on nonresistance and suffering. For instance Dock asked in his Question 43 "whether on this road to life we may expect crosses and troubles." The next nine questions provided scriptural comment on "troubles and persecution" as part of the Christian life, and led to an exhortation on loving enemies. Roosen dealt with nonresistance and suffering but in the context of the relationship between the Christian and the state. If the government rejected nonresistant Christians' humble petitions, he exhorted, "then we should have rather to suffer everything that God would permit to be done unto us than to yield obedience in violation of our conscience and act contrary to the commandments of God."[27]

Actually, Roosen dealt with suffering only briefly. For both writers, the main issues were otherwise. Dock was concerned with faith, repentance, and holy living. Roosen was more theological, more concerned with the categories of orthodox Protestant thought. Of the two, Dock was the more engaging. His theology conveyed a warmhearted evangelicalism, for he was interested primarily in bringing the children entrusted to his care to the personal faith in Christ that leads to holy living. He adapted his approach to fit the American situation. In America, he noted, schools did not "stand upon such pillars as the common man cannot well overthrow" (meaning, apparently, that schools did not rest, as they did in Germany, on the pillars of the state and its official church). Instead, "children of various religious denominations" attended school together and could not be catechized in the tenets of any one particular faith by the authority of the schoolmaster. So Dock left the instilling of particular denominational concerns to the parents. He himself taught generally acceptable and Pietistic hymns and psalms to the children, and made them familiar with the New Testament. He encouraged students to find passages which illustrated qualities such as justice and injustice and humility and vanity, or which revealed themes in salvation history. Then the children were "to ask questions and have them answered by another quotation, so that one impresses the other, explains, and amplifies it."[28]

Dock was easily intertwining Mennonitism and Pietism. His method of explaining Scripture by other Scripture was very characteristic of Mennonite preaching and of a Mennonite writer such as Heinrich Funck. His emphasis on finding that which he could teach to children from all denominations fit what was very much an aim of Pietists: to find the common ground on which all Christians could come together (as Count von Zinzendorf had of course tried to do with his synods). Dock himself composed a number of hymns that well illustrate Mennonites' absorption of continental Pietism. In quite Pietistic fashion the hymns urged persons to yield to Christ's invitation, repent, and avoid evil; and they presented separation from the world specifically as shunning personal sin. But Dock's Pietism did not become an extremely inward religion. "True saving faith must include everything which abets life and a holy walk," he wrote, and Christ wanted a faith that expressed itself in "active love."[29]

Throughout the eighteenth century, Mennonites (although not the Amish) in America were shifting largely from Anabaptist to Protestant, often Pietist, hymns. To be sure they reprinted the *Ausbund* in 1742 and continued to use it throughout the century, with its sixteenth-century Anabaptist songs that told stories of suffering or expressed reactions to it. The Amish continued to use the *Ausbund* well into the nineteenth century; Old Order Amish still use it. But by the latter decades of the eighteenth century the Mennonite congregation at Groffdale in Lancaster County, for instance, was also using a Reformed hymnbook entitled *Neuvermehrt- und vollstandiges Gesangbuch,* known more commonly as "Lobwasser's *Gesangbuch.*" Martin Mellinger, who settled in present-day East Lampeter Township of Lancaster County in 1773, later reported that by the end of the century Lancaster-area Mennonites "had all sorts of hymnbooks, the old Swiss songbooks and Reformed hymbooks." One book popular among Mennonites, as it was among various denominations, was a psalter the Dunkers published in 1744, entitled *Das Kleine Davidische Psalterspiel.* Thirteen "Psalter and Hymn Books" listed in 1778 in the estate of a preacher of the Hammer Creek congregation, John Baer of Cocalico Township in Lancaster County, were probably copies of that Dunker book. In the latter part of the century, at least some Mennonites in the Franconia region were also using the *Psalterspiel* and the Lobwasser book, plus also a Lutheran publication known as the *Marburger Gesangbuch.* Outside of church, Mennonites of that region also liked to sing from various melody books used in singing schools.[30]

The shift from ancient Anabaptist hymns to a different hymnody, generally Pietistic and heavily borrowed from the Reformed tradition, was so great that right after the turn of the century Mennonites both in the Lancaster area and in the Franconia region published new collections. When they did, the Lancaster book, entitled significantly *Ein Unpartheyisches Gesangbuch* (A Nondenominational Hymnal) (1804),[31] included some sixty-three *Ausbund* hymns. But those were still only 17 percent of the new hymnbook's total.[32] The Franconia offering, *Die Kleine Geistliche Harfe der Kinder Zions,* published in 1803, included only two.[33]

The fact was, already by the middle years of the eighteenth century, colonial Mennonites were mingling Anabaptist and Pietistic hymns. The shift was not difficult, for it was easy to use terms such as suffering, obedience, and humility in ways that only gradually took on more Pietistic and less Anabaptist content. If that was true for hymns it was true also for books which Mennonites read and published.

In a letter sent to Krefeld in 1773, Skippack elder Andrew Ziegler and some colleagues described what Mennonites were reading in Pennsylvania: "In the first place, we recognize the Holy Scriptures, especially the Evangelists, for our chief rule. Besides, we have the writings of Menno Simons, in German and Dutch; also the *Martyrs Mirror,* of T. J. van Braght, in the German language which has been printed here in folio ... the [Dordrecht] Confession of Faith in the German, Dutch and English languages, and many other books which our old preachers have published and left behind for us, as Joost Hendricks, Willem Wynands, Jacob Denner and many others."[34]

The Dutch and north-German influence was understandably strongest in the Mennonite congregations which had developed from Germantown and Skippack. Such infuence came especially from the Hamburg-Altona Mennonite community, for Wynands and Denner were both pastors in that congregation. European Mennonite sermons, catechisms, and devotional reading generally came from communities that by the eighteenth century enjoyed both toleration and wealth. Hamburg-Altona Mennonites, for instance, were among the most secure and affluent of all. Persecution and a suffering church had little practical meaning in these Mennonite communities and the appeal of Pietism was its practical application of the gospel to the daily life of the ordinary Christian. Gerhard Roosen's catechism, a book of sermons by Jacob Denner, and other Mennonite writings from Hamburg-Altona tended to blur the line between Anabaptism and Pietism. *Ersthafte Christenflicht,* the European Mennonite prayerbook republished in America several times in the eighteenth century, is a striking example of such blending. It drew from a Swiss Anabaptist source, but also from the spiritualist Caspar Schwenkfeld and from Johannes Arndt, a Lutheran who is sometimes known as "the father of German Pietism."[35]

A development that helped American Mennonite communities accept such books was the fact that European Mennonites were widely accepting some Pietistic devotional writings by Gerhard Tersteegen. Tersteegen, a very influential Reformed Pietist, had many friends and correspondents among Mennonites both in northern Germany and in the Palatinate. He is known to have preached in the Mennonite meetinghouse in Krefeld. In America many Mennonite homes had a prayerbook he compiled, entitled *Geistliches Blumengärtlein* (Little Spiritual Flower-Garden). That was true not only in the Mennonite heartlands of Pennsylvania but also in Virginia's Shenandoah Valley, among the more frontier Mennonites. Virginia settlers had Tersteegen's work and one by Johannes Arndt entitled *Paradies-Gärtlein* (Little Garden of Paradise); Roosen's "catechism"; the sermon book by Jacob Denner; and a seventeenth-century Pietistic version of biblical history, Jan Philipsz Schabaelje's *Die Wandelende Seele* (The Wandering Soul), a book read very widely by Mennonites in the eighteenth and nineteenth centuries.[36]

Among Schwenkfelders in America there was dispute about how to accept Pietistic writings: Christopher Schultz of Goshenhoppen wanted the writings of their spiritualist founder, Caspar Schwenkfeld, to be normative, while a less traditional group wanted various newer, Pietistic works to carry equal weight. Schultz lost the dispute, and works of Tersteegen and Arndt took their places right alongside those of Schwenkfeld.[37] Among eighteenth-century Mennonites the outcome was similar, evidently without even much dispute. Pietistic writings became almost as important to Mennonites as were the writings of Menno Simons, if not equally so.

Whereas a few Reformed and Lutheran pastors among the Pennsylvania Germans had libraries reaching two hundred volumes or more, Amish and Mennonite preachers generally possessed at most only a very few books in addition to the Bible.[38] Very probably, therefore, the few books they owned were crucially important to their thought. The writings of the one original author among eighteenth-century American Mennonites, Heinrich Funck, contain a little bit of church history probably taken from *Martyrs Mirror*, but otherwise reflect a person whose whole stock of literary ideas and allusions came from the Bible.[39] Although Funck was prosperous enough that he easily could have collected a library if he had so chosen,[40] he was very nearly "a man of one book." The inventory made in 1778 of Lancaster County preacher John Baer's estate included, in addition to hymnbooks, four German Bibles; one English one; six New Testaments; "A Book of Martyrs"; a work described as "Delineation of the First Christians," by a radically Pietist German named Gottfried Arnold; one of Jacob Denner's books; and "sundry" others.[41] We do not know how many were in the "sundry" category, but they were probably few enough that we may assume the few mentioned indicate what Baer mainly read and probably what he preached.

As in the case of Funck, the Bible itself formed the thought of Mennonite preachers far more than did any other book. It was not exactly that the preachers used the Bible for proof texts to create a tightly rationalized theology. Instead, their main method was to tell the story of salvation history. This they did by using one scriptural passage to illuminate another, remarkably like Christopher Dock said he used passages to teach his students. If Funck's sermons were like his books, as they probably were, his sermons made much use of allegory. Dwelling especially on Old Testament law and worship, Funck used a method of seeing numerous and subtle "figures," and then seeing further in those figures elaborate meanings to explain the salvation work of Christ, the proper response of the Christian, the ultimate fate of the godly and the ungodly, etc. Extant Mennonite sermons from both the Franconia and the Lancaster regions are also, like Funck's books, intricately woven chains of Scripture references.[42] At least in the few sermons that have been preserved (perhaps the better ones) the preachers were remarkably skilled at staying with a theme, generally that of salvation history, through a great number of scriptural passages. The method was to repeat the central biblical message, not to build philosophical and theological systems with proof texts to rationalize them.

Hans Tschantz, a Mennonite preacher and bishop in Lancaster County, left a notebook of sermons for use at communion, foot washing, baptism, ordination, and marriages. Tschantz died in 1776; his notebook contained personal records from between 1743 and 1764, so the sermons probably belong to those years. Each sermon is a web of Scripture passages. Unless Tschantz added comments not recorded, his own words were merely connecting phrases and transitions. He invariably quoted at length, often whole chapters, rather than an isolated verse or two. The linking reference is embedded in the original context. Surely those who heard Tschantz preach regularly, if they listened, became familiar with large portions of Scripture and with important biblical themes.[43]

They also absorbed biblical exposition with ultimately an Anabaptist emphasis on obedience. Tschantz moved inexorably to predetermined conclusions by the way he chose his passages. A sermon on "the New Birth," for example, has as its primary texts John 3 and Romans 6. Tschantz began

with Genesis and the human fall. Expanding the Genesis account, he added, evangelistically and by way of transition:
"He has given them knowledge to see the works of the Lord
and had established a heritage and declared a covenant with
them. He opened their eyes and they have seen the glory of
the Lord and have heard Him with their own ears. He said to
them: Get right with your neighbor and your God." In the
fullness of time, God sent a redeemer. "He asks obedience of
all men but if man from youth grows up in the fear of the
Lord and walks accordingly, he will be saved. But often the
man lives in unrighteousness. He walks in wickedness and
he will have his inheritance with the lost. Therefore man
must believe the Word and must be born again if he wants to
be saved."[44]

That uncharacteristically long transition set the theme
that Tschantz then pursued: that the new birth leads to
walking in newness of life. Tschantz quoted the first Epistle
of John in entire chapters, leading up to: "For this is the love
of God, that we keep His commandments." This passage led
Tschantz to Matthew's Gospel for passages about fruit-bear-
ing and sowing in righteousness. Then he returned to the
original context in Hosea, and to Galatians and Paul's remarks about sowing in righteousness. Along the way,
Tschantz quoted extensively from Matthew, John, and
Romans—all to develop his theme that the new birth makes
itself evident in obedience.[45]

Like Funck, Tschantz thought easily in terms of figures
and signs and allegory. Through signs and imagery he
explained the church. In retelling the story of the lame man
whom Peter and John encountered at the temple (Acts 3),
Tschantz broke off at Peter's words, "Look on us." Look on
us, the church, he said, in effect. "Christ and His apostles
have gathered a people out of all nations. O Lord of Lords, out
of all trees thou has chosen the vineyard. Out of all the lands
of the earth hast thou chosen, and out of all the flowers hast
thou chosen me. Out of all the depths thou hast filled a brook
and out of all the cities that were built hast thou sanctified
Zion and out of all the fowls thou hast chosen the dove and
out of all livestock thou hast chosen a lamb and out of nations the people in which thou hast pleasure. And as we will

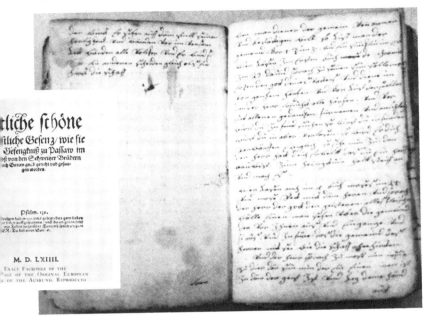

The crudely handmade Hans Tschantz sermon booklet, written in German script, here notes that when one wants to ordain ministers one reads 1 Timothy 3 to the congregation. (Courtesy Lancaster Mennonite Historical Society) **Inset: Title page of the first American printing of the *Ausbund*, 1742.** (Courtesy Mennonite Historical Library, Goshen College)

be this people and this church that God has chosen, to hear the glad sound of His voice on that great day will be a great reward, as written in Song of Solomon 2:1-14."[46]

Around this rhapsody on the church, Tschantz developed themes of faithfulness and humble obedience. The Scriptures portrayed the church as "a spiritual body," he said. "Unholiness has no place in her." Christ would not recognize as his church those who "do not break from their unrighteousness and become born anew (1 Corinthians 5:5).... Therefore we should walk humbly in this time of grace and live a Christian life the way Peter says" (in 1 Peter 2:1-12).[47]

Mennonite sermons and writings used language which

made a very sharp distinction between the ungodly and the godly, and emphasized that the godly would suffer, because their righteousness was so contrary to the evil world. Such language was very reminiscent of the early Swiss and South German Anabaptists' statement at Schleitheim, in 1527. One modern scholar, Beulah Hostetler, has argued that the principles set forth at Schleitheim amounted to a powerful set of core values, or informal "charter," that even in eighteenth- and nineteeth-century America was still at the center of Mennonite group life, particularly in the Franconia region. Consistent with Hostetler's analysis, eighteenth-century Mennonite sermons and writings emphasized that the Christian should bear suffering with humility and yieldedness.

A 1782 sermon of a Franconia-area Mennonite minister named Christian Holdeman developed the theme "the children of God and the children of men." Moving through numerous Old and New Testament passages, Holdeman concluded that "true Christians seek to walk in the ways and follow the footsteps of Jesus which are love, joy, peace, long suffering, gentleness, goodness, faith, meekness, compassion; patient in suffering, not seeking to avenge themselves, not proud, but lowly, humble; not avaricious, not seeking honor or high places or offices in the world but rather seek after God; and yield themselves willingly under the banner of the cross of Christ. They give to Caesar the things that are Caesar's and to God the things which are God's. They do not exalt themselves against the word of God, but bear all with meekness & patience."[48]

In 1770 an anonymous Mennonite preacher from somewhere in eastern Pennsylvania organized his remarks very much around the idea of humility, and then spoke specifically of humility's affect on how Christians lived. This was the preacher and the sermon who emphasized that pursuit of wealth was interfering with Mennonites' religious vision. By accepting poverty and lowliness, and by disregarding mockery and derision, the preacher said, Jesus "has left us a clear example of how we are to follow him." But "we wicked human beings—world-loving, greedy for honor, proud, disobedient—do not want to know the lowly, meek, despised, and narrow way of Jesus, nor to walk in it." Instead we say, "It is not meant to be taken so exactly." We make "many excuses for ourselves and say Joseph also had a coat of many colors, and Job was also rich, and Solomon, too."[49]

Or, the preacher continued, people said that "Samuel made use of the sword." With such excuses, "they make so many covers for their sins to their own destruction and walk right past the path set by Christ's command and say it cannot be obeyed." Christ said clearly, "If you love me, keep my commandments." But we do not keep the commandments when "we daily live like the rich man and clothe ourselves in purple and costly linen, with all kinds of forbidden ornamental decorations, with cutting the hair and curling the hair and so many other things."[50]

Nor was the anonymous preacher preoccupied with mere clothing. He was sorry that the aim of too many parents was to see their children be "industrious and strive to become rich and highly respected in this world." Parents should instead rejoice when their chidren "strive to get rich in eternity, and regard themselves in truth lowly, poor and unimportant in this world." In the mind of this preacher, humility was not merely a spiritual attitude but a very practical matter. Yes, it was the Christian's spiritual response to Jesus, but it also meant, in daily practice, a nonresistant and plain style of life, a life not given to seeking wealth, status, and power.[51]

The fact was, actual suffering was farther and farther removed from the Amish and Mennonite peoples' actual experience. As that happened, the humility theme seems to have subtly begun to replace the theme of suffering as an organizing idea for Mennonite and Amish theology and self-perception.[52] The paradox of a theology of suffering for a people who were prospering was very evident in the case of Heinrich Funck. So also was a beginning of groping toward the humility theme as a way out of the paradox.

Heinrich Funck was hardly a sufferer. He had wealth, he had able and promising children, and, within the frame of his own Franconia-area community, he enjoyed prominence as a religious and a cultural as well as an economic leader.[53] Nevertheless, in his first book (1744), under the heading of "baptism with blood," he dwelt at length on how the Christian must be ready to follow Christ in suffering. In one sense, because he used the language of suffering, he stood squarely (as historian Robert Friedmann has emphasized) in the ancient Anabaptist tradition. Yet in another sense he was not, for he scarcely made any practical application of suffering to real life but instead wrote almost entirely in spiritual terms.[54] In that sense he was perhaps more like a Pietist than an Anabaptist. Even most Pietists might have spiritualized less radically, and found more practical applications, than did Funck.

In a second and larger book, published posthumously in 1763, Funck finally faced up to the paradox of a prosperous, comfortable people retaining a theology of suffering. To be sure, he did so in scarcely more than a couple of pages in a 300-page book. In fact in the book as a whole there was very little that really spoke to questions and dilemmas of everyday life, or to the tangible conditions of human existence. Instead *Eine Restitution* (A Restitution), as the book was called, was mainly an elaborate construction to show how a multitude of details in the Old Testament prefigured the work of Christ in the New. It also elaborated on the final fates of saints and sinners according to the book of Revelation and other Scriptures. Except on a very few pages, Funck kept his discussion entirely in a spiritual realm rather than moving on to applications for Christians' ethical questions, their style of life, their political or economic or social attitudes and behavior, or any other questions of practical discipleship.[55]

Instead of being such a practical book, *Eine Restitution* was a book to probe the mysteries of a reality beyond what is apparent. As such it is a book scarcely comprehensible to a modern person attuned to material reality, to science, and to modern ways of social, political, economic, and ethical analysis. And being devoted to probing spiritual mysteries, the book poses another paradox and a question: how could a practical man of affairs write in a manner so completely detached from everyday life issues? After all, Funck was a leader in his community, and a man of means; did his theology not speak to the ethical and relational questions he surely faced every day in his own and his community's life?

Was it influence from Pietism that kept Funck's discussion confined to the spiritual realm? Probably not. True, Pietists often used highly spiritualized language, yet Funck did not dwell on some of the Pietists' favorite themes, such as the *Busskampf* (the struggle of the soul to yield itself in repentance), or *Gottseligkeit* (the blessedness of resting with God through Christ). More likely the explanation is that Funck made few practical applications of his spiritual understandings because he never really solved that first paradox: how to maintain a Christian life and ethic built on the concept of suffering when suffering was no longer the fact. He never got his theology and the facts of his life quite together. Perhaps that is why he himself never published his book.

What few practical applications Funck made in *Eine Restitution*, however, were revealing. In an elaborate and very lengthy discussion, he presented the jubilee theme of the Old Testament as a figure of sinners' release from spiritual bondage through the work of Christ. For the most part he gave the theme that spiritual meaning rather than seeing a message for justice in the world's economic and social relationships. Yet he wrote not only of a spiritual relationship with Christ, but also of a quality of fellowship within the church. "All believers should live in this restored, gracious, hallowed year of release as one body," Funck declared; and while he clearly meant also a spiritual fellowship, he continued: "so that everyone may be supplied according to individual needs, as regards food and raiment." For in the church of the New Testament, members had given as every man had need. "Men were appointed to supply the needs of the poor and the widows," so that bodily needs were met.[56] Of course a non-Anabaptist Pietist could have written what Funck wrote, for Pietists also emphasized warm fellowship and charitable works. Yet Funck's language was revealing because it showed that when he did get practical, he was still in touch with Anabaptist themes such as a closely knit believers church and mutual aid. At another point he also defended the idea of a disciplined church. He even advocated discipline in serious cases for wrong doctrine, as well as for "sensual indulgence" or fashionable dress.[57]

About the only other case where Funck made some practical application in *Eine Restitution* was when he took up the question of suffering. But his discussion there was especially revealing, because it signaled the impending Mennonite shift that would more or less put humility in the central place occupied up to then by suffering. Why, he asked, were nonresistant people no longer suffering? He suggested that maybe it was because God was now keeping rulers from persecuting defenseless Christians. But he thought the more likely explanation was that nonresistant people themselves were no longer willing to have their blood shed in a kind of keeping of the Passover feast. How did nonresistant people now avoid suffering? "The following means are used: Christian humility is disregarded. The ways of the world are adopted in a life of pride and ambition for wordly honor and wealth in order to be like the world, and thereby avoid being despised by the world."[58]

In that non-suffering spirit, Funck continued, nonresistant Christians were trying to get rich and to curry the favor of the powerful. In a clear reference to political deals Mennonites had made in Europe, Funck deplored "contributions ... to kings, princes, dukes and nobles great and small" until the rulers of course would not allow anyone to injure their "well-fed 'milch cows'." Then Funck turned quite obviously to Pennsylvania politics. "There are also some nonresistant churches who make an effort to elect officials or magistrates according to their own wishes and ideas," he wrote sadly, "and some even seek these offices themselves and serve in them in order that they may assure not only those in our own time, but also our children, exemption from the feast of affliction as kept by Jesus." In order once more to keep the feast of suffering, "a man must make amendment within, in faith in Jesus, in love, in hope, in trust in God, in humility, in truth, in righteousness, in patience; in short, do the works of righteousness by keeping the commands of Jesus Christ," that God's Spirit might come and live within; "for by the Spirit of God man is prepared for the spiritual passover."[59]

Thus Funck showed himself aware that there was a

problem of maintaining a suffering theology and a suffering approach to life when suffering was no longer the fact. And he suggested that the way out of the paradox was to emphasize humility. In the decades that followed, other Mennonites would take up that solution and emphasize humility more than suffering.[60] But Mennonite thought and practice would not develop quite as Funck had advocated. Funck assumed that humility would merely be the vehicle for a return to a Christian life in which suffering would once again come and be the mark of faithfulness. What actually happened was more in the vein of that anonymous 1770 sermon. Instead of a return of suffering, humility itself more and more became the mark of faithfulness and took suffering's central place in the Mennonite understanding of the Christian life. By century's end the new formula would find strong expression in another major early American Mennonite writing, a small-book-length piece entitled *Nützliche und Erbauliche Anrede an die Jugend* (Useful and Edifying Address to the Young), by a Lancaster County minister named Christian Burkholder. By 1804 twenty-seven Mennonite ministers would endorse Burkholder's statement and for decades in the nineteenth century it would be among the most official of Mennonites' statements of faith.[61]

Robert Friedmann, in his book on Mennonite piety, sharply criticized Burkholder's *Address* because he thought it showed how far Mennonites had moved away from Anabaptist principles in favor of Pietism. It is quite true that Burkholder emphasized certain themes dear to Pietists, such as repentance, new birth, and inner spiritual transformation. But these themes by no means conflicted with Anabaptism, and Friedmann rested his case elsewhere. His point was that Burkholder had given up the ancient Anabaptist emphasis on confronting the world and accepting suffering.[62]

It is true that in Burkholder the humility idea was far more central than was any emphasis on suffering. But nobody should consider Burkholder's writing to be only Pietism. Burkholder and other Mennonites who followed him in the next six or seven decades were able to relate humility far more practically to Mennonite and Amish life and ethics than Heinrich Funck had been able to do with the increasingly hypothetical suffering theme. Moreover, they did not at all reduce humility mainly to an attitude necessary for a highly spiritualized repentance, as some Pietists were more inclined to do. Instead they applied humility very practically to life and ethics. With that emphasis, Mennonite and Amish teaching and (to a degree) practice in the early nineteenth century stood quite in contrast to the mood and the behavior of the proud, ambitious, expanding young nation that was the new United States of America.[63] Indeed the humility theme probably kept Mennonites in the United States much more in confrontation with their world than trying artificially to maintain the language of suffering could have done. As for Pietistic influence, such influence did indeed continue in Burkholder and those who followed. But it may well have helped at least as much as it hindered keeping the Anabaptist-Mennonite-Amish faith renewed and vital.

Burkholder and those who followed belong to the nineteenth-century story. Before Burkholder wrote (in 1792), Mennonites, Amish, and other nonresistant people did once more "suffer" to some degree in the French and Indian and revolutionary wars.[64] Yet, interestingly, that new experience of "suffering" was not enough to restore suffering rather than humility to the central place in Mennonite perceptions of the Christian life.

These were some developments in Mennonites' inner religious life. More tangible developments came in their meetinghouses, in observances of ordinances, and in other ceremonies.

CHAPTER
7

MEETINGHOUSE AND CONGREGATIONAL LIFE

If schools and a common language of Pietism brought Mennonites and their various Pennsylvania German neighbors together, in some cases their more formal congregational life also involved cooperation. Among the Germans as among others in colonial America, different religious groups often shared the same church building. To be sure in 1748 there were apparently only about twelve such union or "community" church buildings (gemeinschaftliche Kirchen) in the German communities of Pennsylvania. These were mainly in Berks and Lehigh counties. At that time fewer than one in five of Pennsylvania's Lutheran and Reformed congregations used such buildings. Often church leaders thought that the different denominations would get along better, would walk more in "the way of love," if each kept a respectful distance from others. Yet by 1776 (probably due to frontier expansions) nearly 45 percent of Lutheran and Reformed congregations in Pennsylvania were meeting in union buildings. So also were many in New Jersey, Maryland, and Virginia.[1]

As Mennonites and Amish formed congregations, they often met in private homes. The Amish seem to have done so almost always. In the 1770s one Amish congregation built a stone meetinghouse in Chester County and thereafter met in it until the congregation eventually died out about the 1830s.[2] But that stone meetinghouse was very much the exception; virtually all Amish continued to worship right in their dwelling houses. Apparently they did so not out of hardship but because they preferred that pattern. Some Mennonites, in Lancaster County and elsewhere in Pennsylvania and in Maryland and Virginia, met in homes also apparently by choice. In 1740 John Herr, a Mennonite preacher in the Willow Street-Strasburg district south of Lancaster, built a dwelling house with a large meeting room in the second story. The Strasburg congregation worshiped there regularly until 1804, even though its people were part of a prosperous community and surely could have afforded a building. Much the same was true of a congregation several miles west at Willow Street which met until 1849 in the home which Christian Herr had built in 1719. Other Lancaster-area congregations rotated their meetings among different members' houses.[3]

Other Mennonites of Lancaster County elected to build meetinghouses. Apparently the first group of them who officially bought land for that purpose was the "Hernley" or "Rapho" congregation, in the northwestern part of the county. In 1745, at least, officials issued a warrant to John Leman, Rudy Behme, and Jacob Lighter for twenty-eight acres—'for the use," a "meetinghouse patent" said, "of the Society of Mennonists, living in Rapho Township." But meetinghouses existed much earlier on undeeded land. In 1750 a deed for an acre in Hempfield Township assigned the land to John Jacob Brubaker and Ulrich Roadt (Rhodes) in their capacity as elders and trustees for the "Society of Mennonists" there. In fact, a meetinghouse already stood on the plot.[4] In the 1750s and 1760s several of the long-established congregations of Lancaster County built meetinghouses, the Groffdale congregation, for instance, constructing its first one in 1755. The Weaverland congregation first took a deed for land in 1766, and a date stone indicates that a stone structure which may have been the congregation's first building dated from that year.[5]

Farther east, in the Franconia region, congregations were much quicker to build. Often at first they erected log structures, but many congregations eventually replaced those buildings with more permanent stone ones. In some places Mennonites erected houses for worship before other denominations did. Lutheran pastor Henry Melchior Muhlenberg wrote in 1743 that there was a Mennonite meetinghouse in the vicinity of Providence, Pennsylvania, "but there has never been a Lutheran church."[6] Not particularly considering their buildings to be sacred, Mennonites often used the same facilities during the week for schools. Or a congregation built a school first and used it for a time as a meetinghouse, or perhaps built two buildings at the same time.

Usually when Mennonites began to use meetinghouses they built their own. But in some cases they too shared union buildings. Indeed, they did so often enough to suggest that even in the strictly religious realm they were not trying to isolate themselves. The deeds to several eighteenth-century Mennonite meetinghouses contain provisions much like those of the *gemeinschaftliche Kirchen*, or community church buildings.

Sometimes the union arrangement worked without a formal deed. At Goshenhoppen, about the late 1720s a land speculator set aside a plot for the Lutherans, the Reformed, and the Mennonites to use. For decades all three groups worshiped there in a common log building (presumably meeting at different times, which was convenient, since in those days a given congregation did not meet every Sunday). Then in 1749 the larger tract that included the plot was sold, and officials recorded that the "Calvinists [Reformed] and Mennonists Congregations" purchased the plot jointly. A deed was issued "for the use of Churches, Meeting House, School House, and Burying Ground." However it was not until 1796 that the two religious groups got clear title to their joint land. By that time they had decided they wanted separate houses of worship, and a new deed gave four acres to the Reformed congregation for a church building and a cemetery. For their meetinghouse and burial ground the Mennonites received two acres "and the buildings thereon erected." The two congregations continued to share another part of the property for a common school. The deed expressly forbade either group from using its church or meetinghouse property for an exclusive parochial school.[7]

Nearby in Hereford Township a Mennonite meetinghouse built about 1732 stood on land never deeded to the congregation and in 1747 the owner sold the land to the local

Catholic priest. Now, technically, a Catholic Father owned the Mennonite meetinghouse. Yet apparently for some eight years thereafter the Mennonite congregation continued to meet in the building. In 1755 it bought the structure and an acre of ground on which it stood for £2, 10s and received a deed saying the land "shall always and forever be used as a meeting house and burial ground." Meantime Mennonites helped the Catholics build themselves a chapel on the property. Whether they did it for pay or out of neighborliness is not clear. But clearly there was quite a friendly spirit of cooperation and coexistence in the Goshenhoppen community.[8]

On the western edge of Pennsylvania's established Mennonite communities, in York County's Manheim Township, in 1761, Michael Danner requested a warrant for some six acres (the site of Bair's Hanover Mennonite meetinghouse). He wanted it "for the use of the Menoist Congregation." Thirteen years later a group of trustees received clear title to the property, and one trustee was a man appointed to represent the Lutherans and the Reformed. The document said that those groups had a right to conduct funerals in the building and to bury their dead in the cemetery. Many years later, a person involved in a court case concerning the property testified that the only religious services the Lutherans and the Reformed ever held there had been funerals. Other Mennonites in or near Lancaster County, especially some near the fringes of the Lancaster-area Mennonite community, were also involved in the use of union meetinghouses. For instance, in Berks County's Brecknock Township, adjacent to Lancaster County, the first Lutheran congregation, founded in 1767, obtained land for its original church house from a Mennonite named Christian Bowman and then constructed a log building that Reformed and Mennonites as well as the Lutherans used.[9]

On the northeastern rim of Pennsylvania's Mennonite settlements, in Lower Saucon township of Northampton County, eighteenth-century Mennonites shared a meetinghouse and schoolhouse with Dunkers. Two neighbors named Kram and Rothrock, perhaps one of them Dunker and one Mennonite, provided the land. Apparently the building was not considered to be exclusively for Mennonite and Dunker use. When a deed was finally issued in 1802, long after Kram and Rothrock had given the land, it specified ownership by "the Menoist and Baptice Societice for to Build a house thereon for Keeping School and Public worship therein and also for a graveyard for the said Societice." But it added: "and other Neighbours which will chose to Burying their Deat (which Diet a Christian Death,) therein and to hold a Burial Sermon in the Said School house."[10]

Eighteenth-century Mennonites could easily use the same building for school as for worship because for them the building was utilitarian, not a sacred symbol or monument. The style was typically very much like Quaker ones of the day and region: low and humble, rectangular, unadorned, and with little space wasted. Often it had separate entrances for men and women. Inside, its furniture was most simple. Two backless benches have survived at Skippack, reputedly from the eighteenth century. Men and women sat on benches in different sections of the house—women usually in the center, men on shorter benches in outer sections between the outside walls and two aisles that led in from the doors. Front benches often were at right angles to the other benches, creating what eventually came to be called "amen" corners. The walls had pegs where men hung their hats. One or two plate iron stoves, with as many as five or ten plates each, heated the house.[11]

It is not entirely clear whether in the typical meetinghouse ordained men spoke across a table or a pulpit. Christian Funk, a Franconia-area elder who was a son of bishop Heinrich Funck and became controversial because of how he responded to the American revolution, wrote both of standing at the pulpit (*Lehrstuhl*) and of preaching at the table (*Tisch*). Sometimes preachers, bishops, and deacons were said to have sat on a *Lehrstuhl* or a *Predigerstuhl*; and, for instance, the *Predigerstuhl* used before 1771 in the Methacton meetinghouse in what is now Montgomery County was a raised seat with a wide desk. Seat and desk both extended roughly half the length of the wall. The pulpit had no special, elevated section; each minister simply stood and talked from where he sat. Other congregations used simple tables. The one the Hereford Mennonites in Berks County used was small and low. Whether on pulpit or table, there was typically a large Bible open for the preachers' use.[12]

At the doors, typically, were offering boxes handy to receive money from people as they entered or departed. Congregations did not, of course, pay their ministers, nor were there denominational programs and institutions. Instead, the money went into the deacon's fund, or poor fund. A surviving alms box from the Deep Run congregation in Bucks County is dated 1766, the year the meetinghouse was built. At the Hernley meetinghouse in Lancaster County a wall cupboard dated 1787, with handmade lock and hinges, probably housed the congregation's *Ausbund* hymnals and possibly the pewter communion cup[13]

In the 1766 Weaverland meetinghouse the congregation sat on backless benches made of two-inch oaken planks a foot wide. There was a long pine table around which song leaders sat on three sides, with a long bench for the ministers along a side wall. The preacher who addressed the congregation stood at the head of this table. According to Lancaster historian Martin G. Weaver this pattern reflected the earlier arrangements for worship in farmhouses when the people "had few singing books, and fewer Bibles, and it was necessary to gather the singers and instructors around the large dinner tables of the homes."[14]

These eighteenth-century Mennonite meetinghouses actually were symbols: they captured well their congregations' assumptions that the church was the gathered people and not the outward structures and that Christians were to be practical, humble, and direct. But Mennonites were not self-conscious about their symbols, so they found little occasion to refer to their buildings in writing or to discuss them self-consciously. Deeds usually referred to the meetinghouses in only the most general terms. A paper drawn up to solicit money for constructing one in 1803, for the Stony Brook congregation in York County, tells only a little. The congregation wanted a house, wrote four men named Martin Huber, Henry Strickler, Henry Kindig, and Abraham Hertzler, for its "general and exclusive use . . . for the definite purpose of proclaiming the Word of God, and especially for the recon-

Exterior and interior of Delp Mennonite meetinghouse, near Harleysville and Franconia, Montgomery County, Pa. Note the "long pulpit." (Jan Gleysteen collection)

ciling of people to God through Jesus Christ, and for the adoration of God through His Spirit in the way of repentance and faith, which is to be proclaimed in it, and at the same time, it is to serve as a common school."[15] That 1803 statement may be more evangelistic in tone than one written earlier would have been. Yet there is nothing in it that directly conflicts with what earlier generations believed.

Many of the eighteenth-century deeds specified that people of all faiths might use the building for funerals, and also that they might bury their dead in the meetinghouse ground. Whether or not held in Mennonite meetinghouses, funerals (as Christopher Schultz indicated in connection with his image of "fish in water") brought neighbors together from every religious persuasion. All the preachers of the neighborhood took part and paid close attention to what the other groups' ministers said. A neighboring Mennonite pastor named Martin Kolb conducted the funeral of John Philip Boehm, a noted, pioneer pastor of the Reformed Church in America, who lived in Lower Saucon Township of Northampton County and died in 1749.[16]

Weddings took place in homes. In 1780 a British soldier detained in the Lancaster area by American patriots happened onto a Mennonite wedding. As he recounted the story he arrived at the house "just as the ceremony began." In a large room "nearly 50 people were seated at two long tables." At the head of the tables two old men prayed by turns in German, apparently extemporaneously. The couple entered, and thereupon the two men "gave them good advice as to their future behaviour," then "asked if they were willing to live together." When the couple assented, "their hands were join'd and the affair was finished."[17]

Finished, that is, except for feasting, visiting, playing, and more feasting. At noon, continued the observer, "the tables were immediately spread and we had an excellent German repast (where everything was boiled and roasted to rags)." With the food came "plenty of cyder, toddy and beer." After that feast "the whole company adjourn'd to an extensive lawn where the young men and women play'd at various games till 4 o'clock," when the call came for dinner. "This meal was a profusion of soups, meats, pies, &c.", and was enough, thought the British military man, "for a Regt. of soldiers." The bride, "who was remarkably pretty," served as hostess. After that feast the people departed "without ceremony," except that a plate went round the table "in which every person puts what they think proper," as reward "to the cooks for their trouble. These people are of a sect call'd Mennonite."[18]

The Briton gathered that these Mennonites, like Quakers, thought it "unlawful to fight, or pay [war] taxes, and they never wear buckles or metal buttons. There are numbers of these people in this part of the country who are rich farmers." This particular wedding had actually been "esteem'd a very poor one—they sometimes have 500 guests."[19]

If marriage was an occasion for celebration and feasting, it was nevertheless a serious matter. Pennsylvania Germans, whether church or meetinghouse people, encouraged their young people to marry within the particular group, yet many did cross the lines to marry. Indeed with all sharing the common outlook of Pietism, marriage came to be about the only reason people did cross the lines. Otherwise, at least after the early aggressive evangelism of the Dunkers and the Moravians in the 1720s, 1730s, and 1740s had waned, church membership was largely a question of adopting the religion of one's parents and family. Mennonites apparently tried as hard as any group to keep marriage within the faith. Nowadays sociologists would take such efforts at "endogamy" as the surest sign that colonial Mennonites were an ethnic group; and many congregations did indeed resemble extended families.

Of course Mennonite leaders of the time saw the matter in religious, not sociological, terms. At century's end, elder Christian Burkholder cited God's command to Old Testament Israelites to marry within their own tribes;[20] and earlier, in that 1773 letter to European Mennonites, elder Andrew Ziegler and his colleagues said that when a person married a non-Mennonite, that person, "whether Brother or Sister, is notified to withdraw from the fellowship, the brotherly council, the kiss of peace, and the Lord's Supper, until they have made expiation to the community."[21] Such censure applied of course only to church members. Probably in many cases those from Mennonite or Amish homes who crossed the lines did so before they were church members. In any case there were enough marriages to persons from other groups, either church or sect, to make many ties between the webs of Mennonite families and similar webs within non-Mennonite congregations. One historian, Theodore Tappert, has even suggested that family ties across the religious lines helped to put pressure on ministers to tone down any emphases on theological differences between the groups.[22]

As did other churches of the time, the Mennonites "published the banns." That is, they announced publicly that a couple intended to wed, making the announcement far enough ahead of time so that anybody in the community could object who thought there was reason to do so.[23] To eighteenth-century people marriage was far less a romantic and personal affair than it is in the twentieth. It shaped the ongoing church and community, and so quite naturally church and community were to have a voice in the matter. Mennonites in the eighteenth century perhaps did not treat the marriage rite as an ordinance quite as some of their spiritual descendants have done in the twentieth. The Mennonite ordinances were not, strictly speaking, "sacraments" since Mennonites saw them only as symbols and not as actual purveyors of grace. Their ordinances were baptism and communion, or the Lord's supper.[24] Very closely related to those were: the rite of foot washing, observed in some congregations as a literal command from Jesus' example and words in John 13; and the ban, that is, discipline of errant members according to Matthew 18 and 1 Corinthians 5 and 6.

About the 1770s Martin Boehm, a Lancaster-area Mennonite elder who eventually left the Mennonites and helped to found the United Brethren in Christ denomination, seemed to his fellow elders not to be taking the ordinances seriously enough. Boehm was influenced by America's emerging new religious style, revivalism; for by the 1770s revivalism was beginning to affect the Pennsylvania German communities as it had penetrated the Congregational, Episcopal, and especially the Presbyterian communions some thirty to forty years earlier.[25] Somehow in the course of his revivalistic preaching, Boehm left an impression of speaking lightly of ordinances. So in 1781 or 1782 his brethren stated their view of what ordinances were about.

The Lancaster ministers were careful not to make the ordinances more than symbolic, yet they said that as symbols ordinances were too important to belittle. "The ordinances," they said, "which are commanded us in the gospel, are only types and guides of true, spiritual life." Death to sin through faith and repentance, the spiritual baptism, had to precede baptism with water. The communion or Lord's Supper ceremony represented "the communion of believers"; for even as wheat "from many grains through the heat of fire is made into one bread," so "by the power of the fire of the love of God" members were made into the one body of Christ. In other words according to those Lancaster ministers of the 1780s, individuals blended into the corporate. Communion, then, represented not merely a mystical relationship with Christ but the practical ideal of his followers living together in "the unity of the Spirit, in the bonds of peace." As for the foot washing rite, it represented "humility founded upon Christ, because by his power he has washed our souls." Overall, the Lancaster Mennonite leaders viewed ordinances as symbols of grace already transmitted and, not least, as means to strengthen the fellowship of believers.[26]

Paul the apostle had of course advised that before communion the Christian should engage in some self-examination (1 Corinthians 10:1-26; 11:17-34). The Lancaster ministers interpreted this to the effect that one was answerable not only to one's own conscience, but also to the church. In Mennonite practice a congregational counsel meeting held just before communion was a special time for the self-examination. Hans Tschantz, the Lancaster-area Mennonite elder, designated Matthew 18 and 1 Corinthians 5 as passages from which to preach counsel-meeting sermons.[27] In using those texts Tschantz was probably typical of eighteenth-century Mennonite practice; conservative Amish have specified those passages for their counsel meetings *(Ordnungsgemeinde)* right down to the twentieth century.[28]

Those passages speak of how to deal with persistent sin, and, as eighteenth-century Mennonites and Amish interpreted them, they gave guidance on how to apply the ban as an instrument of church discipline and a means of redeeming the errant. However, since their division in Europe in the 1690s, Mennonites and Amish had interpreted the ban differently. Almost all Mennonites no longer held to Menno Simons' strict interpretation; instead they were inclined merely to ban the person from full participation in formal church life, especially from communion. The Amish believed in cutting the person off also from certain ordinary social relationships, particularly from eating at table with church members, and, in case the spouse was still a member in good standing, also from sexual relations. In either group, the person might ultimately be expelled if he or she refused to listen to the congregation's counsel.[29] Yet, at its deepest, the counsel meeting's purpose was still a positive one. Since the Lord's Supper was to symbolize unity in the congregation, the counsel meeting was occasion for members to repair any ruptures in that unity, and to testify that they were at peace not only spiritually with God but also in a very practical sense at peace with persons around them.

The counsel meeting's exact form varied from congregation to congregation. Moreover, it could be an occasion for setting limits to the power of an ordained leader. In the congregations of the Franconia district, in the 1770s, the ordained men had a custom of meeting and conferring before the full congregations met. In 1777, when the conflict was brewing around elder (or bishop) Christian Funk concerning his response to the American revolution, Funk observed custom and invited his fellow-ministers to such a meeting. As usual he suggested that the congregations' regular time for communion was approaching, which meant also the time for seeing "whether we were at peace." Ordinarily the ministers would have gathered, declared that they themselves were indeed at peace with God and their fellows, and then proceeded to set the dates for counsel meetings and communion services. But this time, according to a later account by Funk, the ministers decided to change procedure.

Instead of ordained brethren questioning members about spiritual unity and peace, "private members should interrogate."[30]

Defending himself many years later, Funk said he found the procedure strange. Were not "ministers and shepherds ... appointed for the purpose of giving counsel, help, and comfort to troubled members"? In some of the Franconia-area congregations, therefore, Funk followed usual practice. But in others two ordained men, Christian Moyer and Henry Rosenberger, arranged for laymen to do the questioning and to encourage members to "state what they had against their ministers." Apparently members did accuse Funk.[31] A cynic might see the procedural change as mere political maneuver. But if it was that, it also had its positive sides. The altered procedure demonstrated that ordinary members could have direct voice in congregational government, a voice they could raise against a leader who was not listening to his people. Moreover the procedure seemed to resolve the conflict for the moment. Time would prove the result to be only temporary; but at the time, Funk went to each man and woman who complained of him, and made peace with each in turn. When "the whole congregation was again in peace," the group was able to commemorate the Lord's supper.[32]

As for the ceremony itself, the 1773 letter of Skippack ministers to friends in Europe apparently reflected the custom among Bucks, Montgomery, and Philadelphia County Mennonites: Among European Mennonites, the letter asked, did the preachers break and distribute the bread? And did members receive it "all sitting at one table"?[33] Apparently also, Franconia Mennonites observed the communion rite only once a year and associated it with the Passover tradition, while their coreligionists in the Lancaster region observed communion twice yearly. When Hans Tschantz of the Lancaster region preached communion sermons he emphasized not only the passion and death of Jesus the suffering servant, but spoke also from passages in 1 Corinthians 10 and 11, passages that emphasized congregational self-examination and unity.[34]

In Tschantz's day and place the foot washing ceremony

probably occurred somewhat separately from communion; at least Tschantz seems to have offered a separate meditation for it.[35] The evidence suggests that in the Franconia region only three eighteenth-century congregations—Germantown, Skippack, and Methacton—observed this ceremony, while those in Tschantz's region around Lancaster almost all did so.[36] A few congregations let it lapse in the late 1700s and early 1800s. Yet sentiment for the practice remained so strong that in the early 1800s it was performed for a time even in some United Brethren and Methodist churches who had many members of Mennonite background.[37]

The 1773 letter to Europe asked whether European Mennonites chose their preachers "out of the congregation" and "whether the whole congregation takes part in it."[38] In America, clearly, Mennonites did choose their leaders out of the congregation. Morgan Edwards, the Baptist historian, wrote in 1770 that Mennonites chose their ministers "by balloting; and when two or more are nominated they leave it to the decision of the lot which shall be the man." Then, he said, they put the man in office "by the laying on of hands of the presbytery attended with fasting and prayer." Hans Tschantz's texts for occasions of ordination—Proverbs 16:33; Acts 1:15-26; and Acts 6:1-8—indicate that at least around Lancaster at mid-century the congregations overwhelmingly made the choice by lot. Presumably the only reason to cite the Proverbs passage was to defend the lot, and the first one from Acts recalled a strong New Testament precedent for the lot's use. Prescribing 1 Timothy 3, Tschantz also indicated a process of examining potential candidates for the lot.[39] The Timothy chapter emphasizes that bishops and deacons should be chosen from those who are sober, blameless, monogamous, and, in the case of the bishop, skillful at teaching.

Also, 1 Timothy 3 emphasizes that bishops and deacons are not to be greedy for money. But the passage also calls for people who can manage their own households well. In practice, eighteenth-century Mennonite and Amish congregations expected all of their ministers to be self-supporting. Morgan Edwards reported in 1770 that Mennonites did not pay their preachers, "nor do their ministers assert their right to a livelyhood from the Gospel." Not paying their ministers, congregations seem generally to have chosen prosperous men to lead them. According to an Earl Township assessment of 1769, Peter Shirk, a Weaverland preacher, paid taxes on 200 acres and an oil mill. Deacon Michael Witmer owned 300 acres and a mill. Henry Weaver, later a deacon, owned 150 acres. Groffdale preachers Christian Burkholder and Henry Martin each owned 140 acres, valued quite highly at £9 and £11 an acre.[40] Virtually every Mennonite congregation had similarly well-off ministers. Even if their ministers never uttered a word in favor of thrift and hard work, eighteenth-century Mennonites heard such virtues preached. After all, eighteenth-century Mennonites were largely pre-modern, and traditional people do not differentiate roles and turn them into specialties as do modern ones. So leadership in one area of life such as economics easily spilled into another area such as religion.[41]

From a study of eighteenth-century Germantown, historian Stephanie Grauman Wolf has concluded that the churches of that town "played a very small role" in the community's overall life. The people found their leaders among their merchants and craftsmen, not among the pastors and preachers either of the "church" Germans or of the meetinghouse groups. Wolf thought that one reason for that pattern was Mennonites' practice of linking distant congregations, especially the link between Germantown and Skippack. And she thought that "since community leadership did not come from the church, the tendency to secularization was intensified."[42] A superficial reading of Wolf might give the impression, then, of a case in which Mennonites, instead of providing leadership to the secular community, instead did their bit to bequeath to America a secular social order.

It seems true that in Germantown the locus of community debate shifted from church house and meetinghouse to the tavern. Perhaps the major reason for that shift was religious diversity: no one church was dominant. If a secularizing trend was important, as Wolf suggested, Germantown seems to have been a special case among German-speaking communities. Where Wolf estimated that in Germantown in 1773 only 55 percent of the taxpayers belonged to any church, historian Laura L. Becker has found that in the same year, in the town of Reading in Pennsylvania's Berks County, 90 percent of taxpayers were members of one church congregation or another. In the 1770s religious affiliation in rural Pennsylvania neighborhoods, such as Goshenhoppen on the Berks-Montgomery county border and Earl Township in Lancaster County, ran closer to the Reading figure than to the Germantown one.

Moreover, even in Germantown, a man such as John Keyser, listed in a 1771 tax assessment as a cordwainer (leather worker), was a leader both in the Mennonite congregation and in the community as a businessman and a township office holder. Jacob Knorr, listed in 1771 as a joiner, kept the congregation's records in the 1770s and 1780s and was ordained as a minister apparently sometime in the 1770s; he served as well as a member of a local school board, as a township official, and in business. A preacher named Jacob Funk, after moving to the Germantown congregation in 1774, was also a community leader.[43] If these Mennonite leaders made some of their local community decisions outside the context of the meetinghouse, that pattern may have reflected the fact that the Mennonites did not identify their congregation only with Germantown; their congregation included Skippack, with the ministers serving at more than one meetinghouse, and the pattern may have reflected that fact more than it indicated a secularizing trend.

Outside of Germantown, in predominantly rural communities, quite a few self-supporting Mennonite preachers doubled as local-community leaders. As generally successful farmers, millers, weavers, or blacksmiths, they had their communities' respect in secular as well as religious matters. Thus it was that in 1735 William Penn's land agent James Steel looked to preacher Michael Ziegler to collect overdue quitrents in Skippack and Perkiomen townships. During the French and Indian War, Michael Ziegler, with Andrew Ziegler his son who was a bishop, and Preacher Dielman Kolb, Andrew's father-in-law, along with other Mennonite leaders joined with prominent Quakers to negotiate peace with Indians.[44] Unlike virtually all of their European predecessors, Mennonites in America did not find themselves ostracized from local-community leadership by persecution or the terms of their toleration. Mennonites voted. Some held local political offices. Moving from meetinghouse to tavern they sometimes selected tickets for upcoming elections, as they did, for instance, in the establishment of a tavern owner named Matthias Slough, near Lancaster, in 1768.[45]

Mennonites' local political participation was clearest in Lancaster County. The existence of a recognizably Mennonite vote there, and the way in which Mennonite leaders thrashed out lists of acceptable candidates, suggest tension between the traditional sense of community among Mennonites and the individualism that permeated the American colonies. On the other hand, Mennonite life was not entirely a matter of community, or of communal outlook. Mennonites might decide more or less to give common support to local political slates; but in their own church life they sometimes polarized around individual leaders, such as Christian Funk, or Jacob Funk, or Jacob Knorr.

If Mennonites chose leaders somewhat on the basis of their economic prosperity, they also believed in humility; and a congregation might allow the lot to fall on a person who considered himself unworthy of the position. At least that is the way Martin Boehm later described his own case when in 1756 his congregation south of Lancaster, Byerland, ordained him to preach. The congregation used the lot. (The usual means was to have each candidate choose a book, with one of the books containing a hidden slip of paper). Boehm, by his own later account, took his book "with trembling, saying inwardly, Lord not me. I am too poor." But his book had the paper; and since he believed the lot fell by divine appointment, he did not (as a few candidates have done in Mennonite history) feel free to refuse.[46]

Most congregations had a number of ministers and at least in Byerland's case that pattern allowed a period for the new minister to prepare himself before preaching. Apparently the normal Sunday service included a long sermon by the elder, Jacob Hostetter, followed by a shorter exhortation by a younger preacher and a testimony from each of the other ministers on "the bench." So for two years Boehm did not really preach, but only gave testimony. Meanwhile he immersed himself privately in the Scriptures, taking care to memorize some for the day when he would preach. Eventually Boehm moved up to giving an exhortation; later of course he became an elder in his own right.[47]

Exactly how ordained men shared other congregational leadership is less clear. The elder, or full-minister (*Voller* or *Völliger Diener*) clearly held a more powerful office than did other preachers and deacons. Not only did he carry a major role in worship, he also had to be present for baptism and for communion. He directed the other preachers, set preaching schedules, and took a lead both in settling congregational problems and generally in religious nurture of congregations. Nevertheless, he did not do all of that exactly as a superior in the hierarchical sense; he did it more as first among colleagues.

When they used the German language, eighteenth-century Mennonites and Amish seldom if ever used the German word *"Bischof"*. Later, in the nineteenth century when they began to use more English, they would adopt the similar English word, "bishop." And even in 1770 the English-speaking Baptist historian Morgan Edwards reported that Mennonites called "their ordained ministers bishops," a term he thought to be unique among non-Anglican Protestants in America. Yet he said that other men shared the Mennonite congregations' leadership. "The brothers," he said, "are allowed to speak in the church by way of exhortation or expounding, but are not permitted to preach publicly till they obtain license from the church. These they call preachers, helps, exhorters."[48] Whatever the labels, the Christian Funk case makes clear that preachers could at times make independent decisions and impose their will against an elder's wishes.

The relationship between elder and ministers quite clearly was not simply that of local pastors with the elder as overseer. As in Germany, Mennonite practice was to group several congregations into a district even if the congregations were some distance from each other. In 1773 Andrew Ziegler was elder for the three Franconia-district congregations who practiced foot washing, with three preachers also serving. But apparently Ziegler himself and at least one of the ministers lived outside the immediate area of those congregations.[49] Nor does the pattern seem to have been that of several congregations under separate ministers who served in turn under Ziegler as overseer. Instead, the members apparently thought of Mennonites throughout the district as being in a single congregation even if there were three separate meeting places. So the ministers and the elders served in all the locations, helping with worship, communion, etc. In that dispute surrounding Christian Funk, Ziegler's authority even extended to the north out of his immediate district, to Goshenhoppen and the Hereford congregation.

Having a whole body of ministers serving as a body of pastors in a district rather than separately in small congregations was a pattern in the Lancaster area as well. For instance, from 1733, when the first Mennonite minister arrived in the Hammer Creek district, until the building of the first Hammer Creek Mennonite meetinghouse sometime between 1800 and 1819, members in that district met in various homes, all served more or less by the district's entire group of ministers.[50] The pattern, then, was one of corporate pastorship, even if the "congregation" of the district met in fragments in several locations.

Compared to that of the elders, the authority of preachers remained more limited. The preachers were primarily teachers and exhorters, and so were often called "ministers of the word." In 1768 Henry Funk the younger, brother of Christian and of course another son of the late Heinrich Funck, was ordained to the ministry in a large district of Bucks and Northampton counties. Henry Funk was only a preacher, not an elder. So, as a fellow-Mennonite of his day said, he was not "authorized, according to the Rules of that ["Menonist"] Society, to baptize, or to administer the Lord's Supper." Nor as it turned out was his right to preach necessarily permanent. He, somewhat like his brother, was a controversial person; and at the time of the American revolution some of his fellow-Mennonites told authorities that he "was too absolute, and ... wanted the whole Society to be subject to him," and also that "he was a horse swapper."

Therefore, they said, he was "forbad, and not permitted, to preach any more among them."[51] Whether or not the accusations against Henry Funk were fair, his case, like his brother's, illustrated that Mennonites could effectively check the power of leaders who did not function according to a congregational consensus.

A third office (in addition to those of elder and of preacher) was that of deacon. One clear task for deacons was the one designated in the New Testament, administering poor funds and property of the congregations. What further responsibilities they held as ordained men is less clear. From 1756 to 1783 Christian Moyer was in charge of the alms fund in the Franconia congregation, yet his name did not appear on a 1773 list of the congregation's ordained men. On the other hand he was one of the ministers who met with Christian Funk in that difficult year of establishing peace before communion. And that year he conducted the counsel meeting at Plains meetinghouse not far from Franconia.[52]

Whatever the deacon's full functions, Mennonites did not assign deacons to merely a low-status position just because they dealt first of all with material matters. For their deacons the Amish preferred the term "minister to the poor" *(Armen Diener);* but Mennonites, following a practice that apparently began in Switzerland, often accorded them the honored term "elder" and referred to them as *Altester* or *Eltiste Diener."* [53] In 1771 ministers at Skippack, putting deacon Johannes Kassel in charge of their poor fund, referred to him as *"Eltesten Diener."*[54]

In addition to the local group of ministers with its three somewhat unequal and yet not hierarchical offices, more or less permanent conferences emerged about 1740—one in the Franconia district and another in the Lancaster area. The conferences dealt with controversial issues, and worked to resolve conflicts that arose among ministers, within congregations, or wherever. In the revolutionary era, Lancaster-area Mennonite bishops and preachers met to discuss such issues as military service and the oath of allegiance demanded by patriots, and also to deal with the impact of revivalism, particularly in the case of Martin Boehm. Because they and their Franconia-district counterparts did not leave

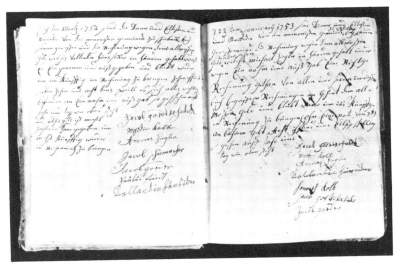

Pages from the Skippack almsbook, 1752-1753. (Courtesy Mennonite Library and Archives of Eastern Pennsylvania)

precise minutes, or any record at all on lesser matters, the exact manner in which conferences evolved remains obscure.

An unfortunate quarrel within the Germantown congregation in the early 1790s suggests how the Franconia Conference worked to resolve conflict. The exact nature of the quarrel remains unclear, except that the disputing parties all belonged to one extended family. One family member, possibly a non-Mennonite, said that if the congregation did not resolve the matter speedily he would "hand the thing over to the court." Normally the older bishop in the Skippack and Germantown congregations, Andrew Ziegler, would have intervened but he (the elder of two ordained Andrew Zieglers) was in his mid-80s. Because of his age, he declined to do so. So another Skippack bishop named Henry Hunsicker, who was scarcely forty, wrote to one of the disputing parties to suggest that if the quarreling brothers themselves could not make peace the Skippack-Germantown ministers would have to take counsel with their fellow ministers. Quoting Jesus' words, "Blessed are the pecemakers, for they shall be called the children of God," Hunsicker suggested that the wider group of ministers, in effect apparently meaning the Franconia Conference, would have to impose a decision.[55]

The dispute wore on for some months, with Hunsicker and Ziegler sending two of their brethren as peacemakers to Germantown before they were ready to involve the wider circle of ministers, that is, the conference. When the two could not bring peace, and the congregation expressed itself unwilling to attend services any more with two of the quarreling preachers, the wider group of ministers finally met. Even then they were unable really to reconcile the parties. So finally they resolved the matter less than happily by finally silencing one minister, Jacob Funk, "because he refused to admit error."[56] But the whole affair suggested that by the 1790s the conference held considerable authority. It had gotten power to approve or disapprove whatever settlement a congregation might make in such a case; and it had power to impose a settlement if the parties themselves or the congregation did not resolve the matter satisfactorily.

There was in Mennonites' pattern of organization very little sense of higher and lower officialdom; instead, authority remained much like the humble, close-to-earth architecture of their meetinghouses. The various consultations among ministers in the eighteenth century, and even the conferences, did not develop to the point of clearly being another layer of hierarchical control. Lines of responsibility and power were free-flowing, more horizontal than vertical. Authority was more traditional than modern; that is, it had a certain tribal quality about it in contrast to modern organization with its highly defined and specialized offices and roles. In certain ways, such as farming practices, Mennonites were as modern as anyone. And they were part of an economy and an empire that were on the road to modernization. But in their own group life, Mennonites remained more traditional.[57]

Those traditional forms of authority and social relations probably helped to establish the pattern of Mennonites' moving freely among their neighbors and more or less cooperating with people of other faiths. Mennonites had little overall denominational structure, so no central institutions or offices compelled their attention or promoted a denominational self-consciousness. Of course, that meant also that congregations did not have the advantage of central resources to help them develop vision, arbitrate local conflicts, and provide aids to worship and nurture. Nor did they have the machinery to mobilize people and resources for tasks such as mission, or even for ministering to those of their own people who scattered onto the frontiers. The traditional pattern had its weaknesses as well as its strengths. But it probably did help Mennonites move among their Pennsylvania German neighbors peacefully, as all went "to and fro like fish in water."

Schools, a common language of Pietism, and even certain patterns in more formal church life all helped that pattern of easy mixing. But then came the day when Mennonites had more or less to make a hard choice: Were they a part of the emerging North American world, as they lived comfortably in their communities at the end of the colonial period? Or were they, finally, a people apart? The immediate reason they had to make the choice was war: first the French and Indian War, then, far more importantly, the American revolution. The long-term reason was the new character which nation-states were beginning to take in the modern world. The patriots of the American revolution would put pressure on Mennonites and other nonresistant people to become part of their cause, for they were modernizers who were trying to get people to take on identity as national citizens in contrast to older identities based on village, clan, or faith. Would Mennonites give their loyalties first of all to that modern, emerging kind of nation-state,[58] or could they find a way to live comfortably in America with their own more traditional identity?

CHAPTER

8

———————◆————————

PATHS TO RENEWAL

In the middle years of the eighteenth century the spirit of renewal quickened the churches of America. Its story, the story of the so-called Great Awakening among the various Protestant denominations, is a familiar one.[1] The awakening movement had its most dramatic impact in revival preaching among Presbyterians and Congregationalists in the 1740s and in the work of Baptist and Methodist evangelists in the 1770s. In the second half of the century the movement spread and stirred virtually all religious groups, reaching even to the Mennonites and the Amish. New-style preaching in a revivalistic idiom, some of it by former Mennonites such as Martin Boehm of Lancaster County and Martin Kauffman of Virginia, gave rise to new groups, especially the United Brethren in Christ, the River Brethren (Brethren in Christ), and the "Menno-Baptists," who flourished in certain Amish and Mennonite communities and drew many members from Amish and Mennonite congregations. These groups came about as renewal caused division. But renewal did not demand division. Other preachers, most notably Christian Burkholder, stayed Mennonite and offered renewal from within the Mennonite community.

Strong emphasis on personal conversion, leading to a highly experiential kind of faith and personal commitment to Jesus Christ, was the common ground on which evangelists of the Great Awakening met. Old boundaries of denominational loyalties, fidelity to traditional ways, and even the categories of theological orthodoxy seemed less and less significant. The qualities sought in a minister came to be not his theological training or proper ordination by a bishop or a synod as much as his own inner conviction and his call for an intensely personal religious experience. Two preachers of Mennonite and Reformed background could embrace as brothers and then find some churches of their own denominations closed to them. A movement initiated by highly educated graduates of European universities welcomed unlearned and even illiterate preachers when those preachers had a sense of divine call.

Emphasis on conversion and personal experience not only displaced educational and denominational standards as tests of a true minister of Christ; it also gave a secondary role to all other forms of Christian life and nurture. Baptism and the Lord's Supper seemed less important. This was odd, for the experiential quest that dominated the Great Awakening had originated in the infrequent but thoroughly harrowing communion time of Presbyterian churches, with its searching inquiry into the security of personal election.[2]

The strength of the Great Awakening was its rediscovery of the truth that the disciples of Christ must be gathered anew in each generation by the conversion of men and women. Christian commitment cannot be inherited. Exposure to the church's teachings from one's youth may be helpful, of course. So also are the ordinances, preaching, Bible study, theological training, and other means of Christian nurture. But revivalists saw that such devices could also be empty human forms, devoid of meaning.

"Pietism's cornerstone was the doctrine of rebirth," Reformed Church historian James Tanis has observed.[3] The need to be born again in a personal encounter with Christ marked the preaching of Pietism in its many different forms. A study by Brethren in Christ historian Martin Schrag entitled "The Impact of Pietism Upon Early American Mennonites" has identified "the *centrality* of the *crisis new birth* and the need of a subsequent life of verbal witness and personal holiness" as the message that "transcended denominational values or structures."[4] At least for groups of Anabaptist background, this historic development brought a subtle shift in emphasis. The shift was from rebirth as merely the essential first step in a life of discipleship (as

Anabaptists had understood the point) to rebirth as a central personal experience which transformed and gave meaning to the rest of life and personal existence.

Also changed, even for some Pietists, was the understanding of the church and its nature. Earlier Pietists such as the Dunkers had sought to restore primitive Christianity. Now, Schrag has said at least in reference to the United Brethren, "a denomination came into being not primarily to actualize the New Testament church." The new denomination represented instead a corporate effort "to realize personal edification and a base for evangelism." In other words, rather than emphasizing the restored Christian community, the revivalists saw the church more and more as a means for restored individuals to work and fellowship together for common but still essentially individualistic goals.[5]

In recent years scholars have given some attention to how the Great Awakening (or Awakenings) of the eighteenth century affected German settlers in Pennsylvania, Maryland, and Virginia. One of them, Martin Lodge, has suggested that the sects, particularly the Mennonites and the Schwenkfelders, had stronger congregations than did Lutheran and Reformed people, because their church organizations were better suited to the New World. A certain concept of ministry enabled Mennonites to organize a congregation and draw leaders from within it rather than having to depend as church people did on a pastor set apart from the ordinary layman by education, calling, and ordination.[6] An inference might be that Mennonites and Schwenkfelders were therefore less susceptible to the religious decay of the time, and thus to the Great Awakening preachers' revivalistic message.

Lodge interpreted the Great Awakening in the Middle Colonies as a solution to a crisis of leadership and faith in both English- and German-speaking churches (churches as contrasted to sects). The crisis, in essence, was one of members' not knowing what to believe amid much diversity and lack of pastoral guidance. But he thought that revivalist (or "New Light") preachers, when they insisted on a regenerate and committed Christian ministry, provided only part of the solution. The other part lay in the fact that "their interpretation of conversion as an emotional experience provided the layman with an experimental [experiential] basis for religious belief." Crisis conversion gave certainty. "And when the New Birth was wedded to a specific set of doctrines ... these doctrines, too, were empirically reaffirmed." In this way, Lodge believed, the Great Awakening solved the layman's crisis of faith.[7]

In a 1976 article on the religious awakening among the Germans, John B. Frantz offered a kind of reversed, mirror image of Lodge's basic thesis. He thought the successful organization of Reformed and Lutheran synods and congregations in the 1750s marked the triumph of Lutheran and Reformed confessional Pietism over the sectarian Pietism of the Dunkers and the ecumenical Pietism of the Moravians. In Frantz's view the synodical churches had solved their own problem by absorbing Pietism. The Mennonite relation to this religious ferment was entirely negative: "Of the many sects that had settled in the Middle Colonies, only the exclusive Mennonites and Amish, who did not join in the Awakening, survived by maintaining their separation from the world."[8]

But two major articles by historians Martin Schrag and Sem Sutter, also published in 1976, detailed quite an impact of the Great Awakening on many Mennonite and Amish congregations in the decades after 1750.[9] Apparently the same Mennonite institutions that survived the evangelistic campaigns of Moravians and Dunkers in the middle decades of the eighteenth century somehow left the church exposed to Baptist and Methodist revivals, and (especially in the 1780s and 1790s) to the preaching of the River Brethren and of the United Brethren. It now seems that Mennonite institutions made members quite open to the evangelical awakening of the late eighteenth century. Far from standing wholly apart, Amish and Mennonite settlers had already absorbed much of the emphasis of Pietism. In the process, Anabaptist terms and the reality behind them took on shades of meaning common to Pietist usage. When in the last decades of the century new varieties of revivalism appeared which used lay preachers and very informal styles, Mennonite tradition offered less resistance than it had toward earlier strains. The Mennonite response was in contrast to that of the Lutherans and the Reformed. The synodical churches' better-established denominational leadership and institutions worked as barriers against such lay preachers and informality.

The revival movement made its impact on Mennonites and Amish through a rather long period of transition, for it often did so without causing immediate or complete breaks from the two groups' traditions. Most surviving accounts of the revivalists have come down from past observers or chroniclers with denominational loyalties. This inclined them to speak mostly of the opposite: of dramatic conversions, sharp breaks, and total, decisive rejection of "dead" traditions. Interpretations received by the second and third generation of revivalists whose fathers and mothers had left Mennonite and Amish churches have suggested a process deceptively clear and simple. Such interpretations say that Mennonite or Amish people, like members of other "unawakened" churches, labored under a cold, dead formalism—a religion of works—and that conversion and the new birth were strange to them. For instance, there was a certain John Neidig who was a Mennonite pastor in Dauphin County, Pennsylvania. After he experienced a conversion, he took up United Brethren revivalism. More than one hundred years later, in 1894, his son recorded the story. John Neidig's "new experience," the son wrote, "gave him a message which he in turn preached to his church, that they might be born again and have a change of heart in order to please God and get to heaven at last." But members of Neidig's Mennonite church "would not receive his new doctrine, as they called it, so in the course of time they shut the church door against him, and cast him over the fence, as they called it."[10] Thus the son recounted events in a way that had become typical: he told of the transition from Mennonite preacher to United Brethren evangelist as a single dramatic event, and presented Mennonites as resisting all change.

Evidence from the time tells of a rather different pattern. Mennonites understood perfectly well what was meant by new birth and conversion. Lancaster County Mennonite pastor Christian Burkholder, writing in 1792 (about the same year that Neidig's father left the Mennonite Church), insisted that the new birth was necessary for salvation. It is true that in his tract Burkholder downplayed the testimony of personal experience and insisted that the only true evidence of conversion is a changed life. But his tract was warmly evangelical and clearly he accepted the essential doctrine of the new birth.[11] The fact is, Mennonites were vitally concerned about such matters as repentance, faith, grace, the new birth, and discipleship.[12] Pietism and Anabaptism had some rather different emphases, but to a degree they were talking the same language or at least using the same words. This shared vocabulary was a bridge not only to European-style Pietism but to American revivalism of the late eighteenth century. This was why in the 1770s, 1780s, and 1790s some Mennonites heard revival preachers so readily.

According to an account based on reminiscences of Martin Boehm, that Lancaster County Mennonite preacher who became a founder of the revivalistic United Brethren, German-speaking Mennonites felt the influence of the best-known preachers of the English-speaking Great Awakening movement. Boehm recounted that "some converts of the eminent George Whitefield had reached New Virginia" (as the Shenandoah Valley was then called) "and commenced preaching a present salvation." Moreover, said Boehm, "under other New Light ministers' preaching some members of the Mennonite families became seriously affected."[13]

One of Whitefield's many converts in Massachusetts was Shubael Stearns, who organized a "Separate" or "New Light" Congregational Church eventually known as Separate Baptists. The Separates put great emphasis on a converted ministry rather than an educated one, and on plain dress and simple living. In 1754 Stearns and his congregation left New England and moved to Frederick County in "New Virginia." According to Wesley Gewehr, a historian of the Great Awakening in Virginia, every member of the congregation was an evangelist. "Springing as it did from the Great Awakening, the Separate Baptist movement everywhere had in it the fire and fervour of the Whitefield revival." But unlike Whitefield, these stepsons of the Puritans were not Calvinists. They preached free grace and salvation available to all who would accept. They rejected all formal creeds and made the Bible the only standard for their teaching. Stearns and his followers spent hardly more than a year in the Shenandoah Valley and then in 1755 moved on to North Carolina. But in that year they began a revival movement that would spread throughout the Old Dominion.[14]

It was in Virginia that Mennonites first got involved in the eighteenth-century evangelical renewal that we call the Great Awakening. Individuals whom Boehm named as influenced by the revival lived north of Strasburg, in present-day Frederick County near the Shenandoah County border. As a young preacher in Pennsylvania Boehm heard of the Shenandoah Valley's New Light preachers and determined to visit them. Many Mennonite settlers in Virginia had fled from Indian raids back to the Lancaster area in 1758, and had taken back reports of a revival. Time and place coincide with the revival begun by the Separate Baptists.

Martin Boehm had personal experience of the central message of Whitefield, Stearns, and other New Light evangelists. His church called him to the ministry in 1756. From statements he wrote many years afterward, Boehm evidently had already come under deep influence from Pietism. He had serious questions about his own salvation and only reluctantly accepted the call to preach. Then about 1758, according to that later account, he had a remarkable experience while plowing:

> I felt and saw myself a poor sinner. I was lost. My agony became great. I . . . kneeled down at each end of the furrow, to pray. The word *lost, lost, verloren,* went every round with me. Midway in the field I could go no further, but sank behind the plow, crying, Lord, save, I am lost!—and again the thought or voice said, "I am come to seek and to save that which is lost.!" In a moment a stream of joy was poured over me.

Boehm said that he left the field and, praising the Lord, told his wife of his new joy.[15]

The following Sunday after "the elder brother preached," Boehm told the congregation about his experience. The response of the Byerland Mennonites was to encourage him to speak "of our fall and lost condition, and of repentence." Thereafter, he continued in his new way of preaching.[16]

In 1761, evidently even as he preached that way, the Mennonites ordained him to be a bishop. It was in that same year that he went to see for himself what was happening in "New Virginia." He recalled half a century later how well and how scripturally Mennonite people there were able to give an account of what God had done for them.[17] Boehm's stay in Virginia was a second notable turning point in his life, following his earlier crisis conversion. His son Henry Boehm later remembered that the Shenandoah Valley was "the region my father visited in 1761, where he obtained new light, which he scattered with holy zeal."[18]

Boehm returned from Virginia an evangelist, but still a Mennonite one. He had "found many gracious souls who could give rashionel, and scripturel account of their experience and acceptance with God," he recalled in 1811. "Now I was much encouraged to seek the same blessing, in a greater degree." The last phrase is significant. Even in old age, Boehm did not see his trip to Virginia as a break with his past, but rather as an enhancement of it. Apparently in 1761 he was confident that the spiritual power of the revival could be appropriated into the life of a Lancaster County Mennonite congregation. "On my return, very large congregations colected not only on the sabath, but also on weekdays," he later wrote. This "was very displeasing to some of my Brethren in the Ministry" but "my heart was now inlarged. . . . I could not confine my labors to Jew only—but also to greek as fer as my situation & ability would admit." Thus Boehm soon took his message beyond his Byerland community and beyond the Mennonite brotherhood. Boehm further recalled that "about this time I set up reguler Family worship in my house in which (through grace) I have persevered to the present."[19]

Martin Boehm's account is typical as a Pietist autobiography: Presbyterian, Reformed, and Lutheran Pietists and revivalists recounted their experiences in similar words. Family prayer and weekday meetings—for Bible study, prayer, and preaching—were innovations that marked the triumph of Pietism and revivalism in local churches of every denomination. Reformed Church Pietist Philip William Otterbein, for instance, introduced weekday meetings into his parishes in Pennsylvania and Maryland in the 1760s.[20]

When Boehm the Mennonite began these new practices and new style of preaching, mainly west of Lancaster City in the Mennonite communities of Lancaster County's Conestoga, Manor, Hempfield, and Donegal townships, some of his fellow Mennonite ministers criticized him. Not all did, but by Boehm's later recollection "some of the [Mennonite] Meeting houses were shut against me."[21] Twenty years after Boehm returned from New Virginia with his enthusiastic message, his fellow bishops silenced and excommunicated him. Why the break? Were Mennonites so unable to accept the revivalistic message? Was the language of conversion and the new birth so foreign to Mennonites?

Even in Boehm's own later account of the break there is no hint that the Mennonite ministers objected to the main content of Boehm's preaching, that is, to experiential religion. Nowhere did even Boehm himself suggest that conversion and the new birth were strange ideas either to himself at the outset, to his fellow Mennonites, or to the Mennonite bishops who took action against him.[22] The fact is, for two decades Boehm's fellow bishops allowed him to continue preaching. During that time he invited revivalist ministers from Virginia also to preach, and preached in unusual settings: "big meetings" *(grosse Versammlungen)* in barns and the like. At one meeting in 1767 in the barn of a Mennonite named Isaac Long a bit northeast of Lancaster, Philip William Otterbein, who was a Pietist-revivalist in his own Reformed circles, heard Boehm preach. Feeling their spirits at one the two men embraced exclaiming: "Wir sind Brüder!"—We are brothers![23] Otterbein and Boehm later became the United Brethren movement's most prominent founders and early leaders. Church historians have presented that moment of embrace as an important event in the beginning of the Church of the United Brethren in Christ.[23]

But even for some thirteen or fourteen years after that event, Boehm continued to preach as a Mennonite. Fellow ministers who were uneasy evidently entreated with him as a brother, not as a heretic. This went on so long that when the Mennonite leaders made the break they noted that "some of

The Isaac Long barn, scene of the Otterbein-Boehm "Great Meeting" in 1767. (From Alfred L. Shoemaker, *The Pennsylvania Barn)*

those aged laborers who were not satisfied with him have since passed away." So for years after his visit to Virginia, and after the event in Isaac Long's barn, Mennonite authorities allowed Boehm to function as a bishop and evangelist in their own church.[24]

The experiences of Christian Newcomer also show that many Mennonites and Amish found the revivalistic emphases on conversion, the new birth, and experiential religion quite congenial. Born in 1749 in Lancaster County's Leacock Township, Newcomer became a carpenter and then in 1771 took over his father's farm. About that time he was baptized in the Groffdale Mennonite congregation. A nearby Reformed congregation's records tell of a marriage of "Christian Neukommer, Mennonite, to Elizabeth Baer, daughter of Reformed parishioner Andrew Baer," in 1772. In 1775 Newcomer and his family resettled in Washington County, Maryland. There they eventually joined the United Brethren movement, and Newcomer also became one of the movement's most important early itinerant preachers and bishops.[25]

In Maryland Newcomer was disappointed that few of his neighbors seemed ready to talk about experiential religion. But then he met George Adam Geeting, a schoolmaster, member of the Reformed Church, and associate of Otterbein. Newcomer found Reformed Pietists in western Maryland quite open to his message. However when he visited his wife's Reformed family in Lancaster County, "the work of grace appeared to them a strange work," he said, "and the language of Canaan as foreign as if it were Chinese or Hottentot."[26]

What of the Mennonite response? By his own later account, Newcomer, while still a Mennonite at Groffdale, spoke with his pastor (presumably Christian Burkholder) about "what some would call the Methodist doctrine" of entire sanctification. He found the pastor quite open to the subject. A few years later on a visit back to Groffdale he spoke on a Sunday morning in the Mennonite meeting and told of a new birth experience much like Martin Boehm's. The Mennonites reacted by inviting him to preach in Lancaster Conference churches during his stay.[27]

Mennonites understood and appreciated what Newcomer was saying. In a daily journal that he began in 1795 the Mennonite-turned-United-Brethren itinerant preacher often recorded warm welcomes among Mennonites. For instance, he told of a visit in October 1796 to "an uncle of mine a preacher of the Menonist Society on Linville Creek in Rockingham County, Virginia," and of his uncle's preaching "with considerable liberty from Psalm 34 v. 15." Henry Boehm also, son of Martin, recorded how a Mennonite had given "a powerful exhortation" when he, his father, Newcomer, and the famous Methodist bishop Francis Asbury were on a preaching tour of the Shenandoah Valley in 1800. Many of the places where Newcomer stopped regularly to preach in Virginia were homes of men who signed a 1785 petition as Mennonites—men named Grove, Miley, Funkhouser, Stickley, and Strickler, for instance.[28]

Nor was it only in Virginia that Mennonites gave

Newcomer such warm reception. In May of 1797 he held a long conversation with a Mennonite minister named David Sneider, living along the Conodoguinet Creek of Pennsylvania's Cumberland County, who received him "with gladness." On his next visit there, in February 1798, Sneider asked him to preach at the Mennonite meetinghouse. In May 1797 Newcomer's reception was equally warm as he "lodged with a preacher of the Menonists on the Schuylkill" farther east, probably in Berks County. In the same year, at a meeting near Millersville in Lancaster County, a Mennonite preacher "rose and gave testimony to the [revivalistic] doctrine advanced." Newcomer also mentioned meetings in Lancaster County in 1798 "at an Omish brother's house" and in 1799, near New Holland in Lancaster County, at "Knegis's, an Omish man."[29]

Far to the west in the Casselman Valley in southern Somerset County, Pennsylvania, around the time of the American revolution, some Amish and Mennonite families settled. There, in October 1799, Newcomer, on one of his visits, preached to Mennonites at the home of John Zook. According to Newcomer "the word spoken was accompanied with power; tears run [*sic*] plentifully and some cried aloud for mercy." Then "a Mennonite preacher named Gundy" asked him to stay the night, and "our souls immediately flowed together in love."[30] (By 1808 a Joseph Gunty and a Peter Fahrney, two of the first Mennonite preachers in the Casselman Valley, had become United Brethren preachers.[31])

Mennonites and Amish people were open to revivalistic preaching because they found nothing strange in talk of conversion and new birth—but also because their ways of organizing church offered few barriers. Moreover, congregations on the fringes of the Mennonite world very often welcomed almost any traveler with a sermon to give; endorsement by one member was enough to open the congregation's doors. Newcomer mentioned cases of Reformed congregations closed to him, but unlike Boehm, he mentioned no such cases among Mennonites.

Family connections also opened doors, and joined one area's positive response to River Brethren or United Brethren preachers with another. In Franklin County, Pennsylvania, in Washington County, Maryland, and in Frederick and Shenandoah counties, Virginia, Newcomer preached in homes whose families were all near relatives of Dr. Peter Senseny, another former Mennonite turned United Brethren preacher. On both sides of the Susquehanna River he preached at homes of Herrs and Hersheys who all were part of the extended family of United Brethren preacher John Hershey (also formerly Mennonite). Senseny and Hershey were both associates of Martin Boehm before 1785; apparently family networks spread the news of Boehm's revivalism.[32]

The nature of the listeners' particular community also seems to have influenced how Mennonites responded to the revivalists. A few families in long-established congregations such as Byerland or Mellinger in Lancaster County joined with Methodists or United Brethren, but the revivals had far less impact in such Mennonite communities than they had in frontier Mennonite settlements. Some small congregations on the frontiers just disappeared from the Mennonite map, their members absorbed into revivalistic groups. For instance, in Lebanon County, Pennsylvania, Mennonite pastors Caspar Shirk and Felix Light went to the United Brethren. With them apparently went most members of the so-called Shirk and Kauffman (later Dohner) congregations, along with the meetinghouses, burial grounds, and all. One such meetinghouse, Houser's in Washington County, Maryland, went full circle: long ago it passed to the United Brethren, but in 1966 the Mount Lena Mennonite congregation returned to its site. Other congregations, for instance in Dauphin County, Pennsylvania, and in Shenandoah County, Virginia, just disappeared without a trace.[33]

Aside from such disappearances, revivals' impact upon Mennonites was strongest in communities where Mennonites were relatively few, yet had been settled for a generation or two. Revivalism caught up Mennonites in these places more than in newer Mennonite settlements with recent or continuing arrivals from old communities. Thus, in Virginia, in Rockingham and Augusta counties the pattern was much like in old settlements back near Lancaster, whereas in present Page and Shenandoah counties the impact was strong. Apparently late settlers in Rockingham and Augusta counties were reinjecting a sense of Mennonite peoplehood from the older communities. In counties such as Page and Shenandoah a generation or two had been enough time to lose that sense, so that Mennonites were more prepared to march to new religious tunes right along with the people around them.

Yet, the question remains: why did the Christian Newcomers and the Felix Lights finally move out of the Mennonite community's embrace? The case of Mennonites influenced by the Separate Baptist movement in Virginia offers one answer: some of the very teachings which Mennonites considered primary in the New Testament, revivalists might consider at best secondary. In 1770 John Koontz, a German-speaking Baptist evangelist of church background, began preaching among Page Valley Mennonites. Soon he converted Mennonite Martin Kauffman, who then took up revivalistic preaching. In time four or five Mennonite ministers journeyed from Pennsylvania and tried to convince Koontz that Christians should not take part in war, hold slaves, or take oaths. Koontz said Baptists did not consider such points important; on them, each member had liberty. The visitors then left Koontz and in the words of the pro-revival historian Semple "held meetings in the neighborhood two days, striving publicly and privately against the revival that was then happily progressing."[34]

Were the visitors really striving against revival? Or were they resisting the Baptist view that while Scripture spoke plainly on, say, form of baptism, it was not plain concerning nonresistance, slavery, and oaths? About 1775 some in the recently formed Mill Creek Baptist Church, including Martin Kauffman, wanted their church to take a stand in favor of those "Mennonite" points. The congregation split, sixty or seventy members leaving and ordaining Kauffman as their preacher. According to Semple the group also held to the idea that saints once saved remained saved, and even embraced universalism—that is, a belief that ultimately all persons would be saved.[35]

From time to time the new group appealed for reinstatement with the Baptists, but the reunion did not happen. In

1793 the group petitioned the Virginia legislature to exempt
its members from bearing arms. A Baptist Association
minute of 1809, commenting on yet another attempt at
reunion, noted that this "Menonist Baptist Church" had
separated "because they would keep no slaves, swear no
oaths, nor bear arms in defence of their country."[36] So in
some revivalist circles it apparently was difficult to reconcile
revivalists' priorities with some teachings that Mennonites
thought were clear in the New Testament. Kauffman and his
followers apparently thought it both possible and necessary
to fuse such Mennonite understandings with revivalism. But
some revivalists apparently resisted, and in some cases new
priorities took revivalist-minded Mennonites out of the Mennonite Church.

The case of Martin Boehm is more central and instruc-
tive, although there is much about his story that remains obscure. Only late in his life (in 1811, before his death in 1812)
did Boehm himself recount his version at length. At least
only that late version survives in writing. As for the key document giving the Mennonite side of Boehm's case, it has been
lost; and although copied apparently with care, it comes
down only as reproduced in a much later publication.[37] Yet
such evidence clearly indicates that Mennonites and Mennonite leaders did not especially reject Boehm's emphasis on
conversion and new birth, and that they allowed him to
preach in his new style for those twenty years. Meetings such
as that in Isaac Long's barn and Boehm's embrace of Otterbein still were during Boehm's Mennonite phase, and do not
particularly belong to the story of break between him and the
Mennonites. The break occurred when Boehm began to
fellowship intensively with Methodists.

Methodist circuit riders began visiting Lancaster
County about the winter of 1780-1781. Benjamin Abbott, a
Methodist itinerant from New Jersey, has told of preaching
early in 1781 at Boehm's, by then an established Methodist
preaching place. On that occasion the meeting lasted
through a day and into the night. As it progressed, people fell
with loud groans in convulsions on the floor. Several song
leaders in succession stepped forward to begin a hymn, but,
according to Abbott, each fell and lay as if dead, slain by the

Spirit. Boehm declared: "I have never seen the Lord work in this way before."[38]

Boehm's expulsion from the Mennonites was, as nearly as the sources reveal, sometime no earlier than 1781 or even perhaps 1782 or 1783. When they took their action the Mennonites, according to their statement, did not specifically reject the groanings and convulsions. They did take issue, fairly or unfairly, with certain alleged and perhaps ill-advised statements of Boehm, e.g., that Satan is a benefit to humans and that light proceeds from darkness. These objections may reveal Mennonite distrust of revivalists' new language and preaching style; yet in no explicit way did the Lancaster Conference authorities reject revivalism or key revivalist emphases. Instead, their main charges suggest that they were concerned most with preserving a certain ideal of church. They wanted a disciplined Christian community, committed to certain literal and pacifist understandings of the teachings of Jesus.[39]

Essentially, the primary charges against Boehm were two. No doubt referring to Boehm's new, intensified fellowship with Methodists, the Lancaster Conference Mennonite leaders observed that "he had a great deal to do with forming a union and associating with" professing Christians who "walk in the broad way, practicing warfare, and the swearing of oaths . . . in direct opposition to the truths of the Gospel." Then they leveled two other complaints saying in sum that Boehm had been careless about how he dealt with and accepted people whom the church had put under discipline, and indeed that he himself had not responded well to the church's admonitions. Whatever unspoken dissatisfactions may have underlain it, this was the central case as the Mennonite leaders put it.[40] By the lights of modern evangelical interdenominationalism, ecumenicism, or easygoing American tolerance, their notions may appear simply parochial or legalistic. But an explanation more suited to those Mennonites' own outlook was that they saw Boehm breaking with the disciplined, close-fellowshiping kind of Christian community, and believed he was encouraging others to do the same. They could accept revivalism's central emphases, and, to an extent, revivalism's style and even some loose

Martin Boehm   **Philip William Otterbein**

fellowship with non-Mennonite revivalists. But when Boehm
began to find his primary fellowship outside of his own
church, to undermine discipline, and to show indifference
about core Mennonite understandings of Scripture, they had
to act.

Apparently even some who were quite revivalist or at
least thoroughly Pietist saw the issues much as did the
Lancaster Mennonite leaders. Boehm preached regularly in
Donegal Township in northwestern Lancaster County along
the Susquehanna River. About 1780 a group in that area, at
least some of them Mennonite, began their own fellowship
and drew up a Confession of Faith. Their location won them
the nickname "River Brethren"; the communion they started
is now the "Brethren in Christ." In recent years careful historians within the group have concluded that those early
River Brethren sought to integrate the Pietist emphasis of
the deeply felt crisis new-birth experience with the
Anabaptist-Mennonite understanding of the church and the
relationship of the church to the world. Martin Schrag,
Brethren in Christ historian, has dated the Confession as

first written sometime between 1779 and 1782—just at the time of Boehm's excommunication. Evidence strongly suggests that the River Brethren were a group initially influenced by Boehm.[41] Perhaps the Mennonites' action against Boehm induced them to reconsider the drift of their new religious commitments, particularly a drift toward new understandings of how church and world relate.

In any case, unlike the United Brethren who became essentially a German-speaking version of Methodism, the River Brethren took European-derived Pietism and aspects of American revivalism, and put them into an Anabaptist-Mennonite framework.[42] So much were they like Mennonites on certain issues that during the American revolution apparently not one served with the militia or pledged allegiance to the revolutionary governments. Like most Mennonites they nevertheless believed they must pay wartime taxes; indeed, early versions of their Confession specifically required faithful payment of taxes, including *Schutzgeld*, or protection money. On one point they may have been even a bit closer to Menno Simons than were their Mennonite neighbors: they emphasized the ban, or deliberate ostracization of offender members until they repented, perhaps rather more strongly. Such emphasis on the ban meant, of course, that they still believed in a close-knit, disciplined church.[43]

Thus, although in their own way the River Brethren were Pietists and revivalists, they agreed with the Mennonites who censured Boehm when the issue was the key one of the nature of the church. To them as to Mennonites, the new birth found its meaning in discipleship and obedience more than in the initial conversion experience. And they saw discipline not as legalism but as evidence of something positive, a bond of love. Members were "bound through love to watch out for each other," said their Confession, so "we consider it necessary and decided that nobody in important affairs should do anything without brotherly advice, such as marry, or change his dwelling, buy land, or whatever important." No words could have rejected individualism more clearly. And the words stand in contrast to most late eighteenth-century revivalism, whose preoccupation with personal experience produced very strong tendencies toward individualism. Schrag has emphasized how sharply this part of early River Brethren thought was different from some other forms of Pietism and particularly from the United Brethren outlook. On that point he found the River Brethren Confession to have been a close parallel to an Amish church discipline of 1779.[44]

Despite all of that, late eighteenth-century Mennonite faith was by no means totally at odds with Pietism, or with Pietism's American version, revivalism. Boehm, in an account of his conversion, said that "a new creation appeared to rise up before me, and around me. Now Scripture, before mysterious, and like a dead letter to me, was plain of interpretation, was all spirit, all life *(alles Geist und Leben)*. . . . It seemed as if I awoke to new life, new thoughts, new faith, new love." That language had much in common with some language in the historic Mennonite statement that Christian Burkholder wrote, *Useful and Edifying Address to Youth on True Repentance and Saving Faith in Jesus Christ.* Burkholder strongly endorsed the need for the new birth. To be sure, his intent was quite clearly to reply to revivalists at some points, and for that reason he made humility a central theme, including warnings against spiritual pride and too much emphasis on verbal testimonials. Also he insisted very strongly that the test of the new birth and the mark of the Christian life was the living of a disciplined, a virtuous, and especially a humble life, clearly rejecting the constant recounting of one's inner religious experience as proof of true Christianity.[45]

But Burkholder accepted revivalism's central, new-birth emphasis. And he wrote: "'The Spirit of God will make the Word of God new in your soul. . . . In so far as Jesus, the true Word of Life, becomes life and light to your soul, in so far will the thoughts and intents of your heart be changed. And if you thus continue in the work of the new birth, your carnal and sinful nature will be brought into death."[46] Such language was similar to Boehm's account of his own conversion. Indeed, in those words of Burkholder was the suggestion of an "entire sanctification" doctrine, a particularly Methodistic emphasis.

Clearly Pietism had deeply influenced Burkholder. One

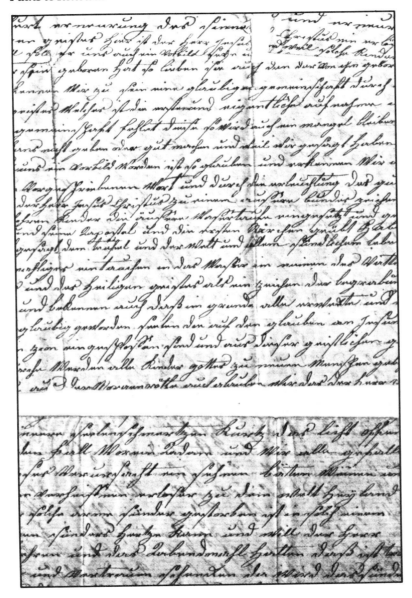

Portion of an Early "River Brethren" confession of faith. (Courtesy Archives of the Brethren in Christ Church)

venerable emphasis of Anabaptists and Mennonites that ran from the sixteenth-century through Heinrich Funck was missing in Burkholder: that Christians must suffer or, as the tradition put it, that they must undergo the "baptism of suffering." The omission was quite in line with the Pietists' celebration of the "sweet Jesus" who warmly embraces each individual lost lamb—in contrast to an Anabaptist emphasis on the "bitter Jesus" who calls his disciples into harsh conflict with the world. The omission was so glaring as to cause Robert Friedmann, author of the classic *Mennonite Piety Through the Centuries*, to be rather critical of Burkholder's work.[47] Friedmann, no friend of Pietism, may have made Pietism and Anabaptist-Mennonitism seem more at odds than they really were.[48] And so he may have failed to see how much Burkholder's work represented a creative fusion of two traditions with much in common. Burkholder's synthesis checked the individualism and overemphasis on personal experience in Pietistic revivalism and preserved the key Mennonite emphasis on a disciplined Christian life as conversion's natural outcome. Yet Friedmann's main point is true: Burkholder, and all those ministers who endorsed his *Address to Youth*, did yield an ancient and key Anabaptist-Mennonite point as they blended Pietism into their version of Mennonite thought.

The same was true of the River Brethren's fusion of Anabaptist and Mennonite outlook with Pietism and revivalism: their Confession made no point at all of the "baptism of suffering." Nor did another piece that fused the two traditions: *A Short Explication of the Written Word of God, Likewise of the Christian Baptism, and the Peaceable Kingdom of Christ*, written by Mennonite Francis Herr, and published at Lancaster in 1790.[49]

Unlike Burkholder, Herr did not quite walk in step with the main body of Mennonites. Sometime between 1780 and 1800, perhaps even before he published his treatise, he left the larger fellowship. He held meetings in his home and more or less began the movement that in the nineteenth century became the Reformed Mennonite Church, whose early strong leader was his son John. Already in Francis Herr there appeared some of the chief Reformed Mennonite characteristics: a kind of fundamentalism with regard to how Scripture had been written; and a determination, remarkably strong even for Mennonites, to achieve a truly pure church through uncompromising discipline.[50] According to Herr the apostles themselves had not been teachers; rather, "the Spirit has broken through them" to establish "the economy of the gospel, as baptism and the Lord's Supper, and the washing of feet, likewise excommunication and forbearing." As did Burkholder, Herr emphasized also that obedience always went with repentance, and that conversion meant to "quit sin and live voluntarily in obedience to the word." Regarding church and world, he taught a thorough dualism, insisting that nonresistant Christians should withdraw totally from voting, holding office, and using courts of law.[51]

Although one part of him sought purity of faith by carrying certain Anabaptist-Mennonite principles to their limits, another part sought assurance more along the path of Pietists and revivalists. Like Martin Boehm and Christian Newcomer, Herr was not satisfied until he had a religious experience that convinced him of his conversion and forgiveness. No doubt such quest for experiential religion was more common among Mennonites than we know; perhaps it even was the norm. In any case, sometime in the early 1770s Herr had joined the Mennonite Church, in which his father preached. But later he had a profound conviction of sin. In the words of a Reformed Mennonite writing much later, "he saw and felt, that, although he was baptized and a member of the church, he was not a member of Christ; that he was yet in his sins, and under condemnation."[52] Herr, then, represented one more attempt to bring the mood and emphases of Pietism and revivalism into an Anabaptist frame.

Francis Herr, like the River Brethren and Martin Kauffman's congregation, ultimately left the main body of the Mennonite church in order to make his fusion of Anabaptist-Mennonitism and Pietism. Many ex-Amish and ex-Mennonites among the United Brethren in fact tried to make the same fusion at first, even if their church as a whole did not; for although United Brethren discipline did not require such points as believers baptism, foot washing, nonswearing of oaths, and pacifism, these points found a place in many heavily ex-Mennonite and ex-Amish United Brethren congregations.[53] Christian Burkholder and all those ministers who endorsed his *Address to Youth* made something of the same fusion within the main body of the Mennonite Church. All illustrate a common quest and a common point: that at the end of the eighteenth century key Mennonites and persons nurtured on Mennonite perceptions of Christian discipline and community saw no necessary contradictions between Anabaptist-Mennonite and Pietistic emphases. Instead, they drew upon either one to correct what they perceived as deficiencies in the other.

In that quest, those who tried to make the fusion lost something of older Anabaptist-Mennonite tradition, however: the emphasis on suffering. That was curious, for they were forming their ideas precisely at a time of crisis that brought Mennonites and other nonresistant peoples some harassment and in a few cases even persecution. The crisis was the American revolution. The era of revolution might have been a time for Mennonites and Amish to again emphasize Christians' confrontation with an evil world, the persecution that results, and "the baptism of suffering." Oddly, that was not quite the result.

9

TESTING MODERN CITIZENSHIP: MENNONITES AND COLONIAL POLITICS

The public face of American Mennonites in the eighteenth century presented a paradox: Mennonites often appeared wealthy, yet refused to protect their wealth by force. Observers who knew little of Mennonite doctrine and practice never failed to notice their wealth and their pacifism. The Reverend Thomas Barton, Church of England missionary at Lancaster, reported in 1760 that "the Country round about Lancaster for several miles is possess'd by the Mennonists, who by their industry and great economy have acquired riches and plenty. They seem to be a simple inoffensive kind of people—with their Doctrine and principles I am not acquainted, but find them in many things to agree with those of the Quakers. They use the same mode of Dress, refuse to put off the Hat, or shew any respect to Superiors; and chuse rather to leave their Properties and Liberty exposed to the first Invader, than bear arms in their Defence."[1]

Different observers saw the paradox in different lights. Some Pennsylvanians resented the sectarians' prosperity because they believed that the rich Quakers and Mennonites were not fulfilling an obligation they owed to their fellow citizens. In some circles it was politically expedient to blame these wealthy sects for any frontier disaster suffered from the French and the Indians. The Mennonites, for their part, declared in 1755 that "it is our fixed principle rather than take up Arms in order to defend our King, our Country or our Selves, to Suffer all that is dear to us to be rend from us, even Life it Self." They meant to say this, they added, not "out of Contempt to Authority, but that herein we act agreeable to what we think is the mind and Will of our Lord Jesus."[2]

German princes had resolved the paradox by imposing special taxes on Mennonites in exchange for military exemption. That pattern harked back to older, feudal patterns in which people lived as subjects, rather than as modern citizens with certain rights.[3] As subjects, people established personal relations with rulers, paying dues in return for protection. Quakers who founded Pennsylvania chose a different pattern. No one in the colony had to do military service. The pattern pointed more toward modern citizenship, albeit in a pacifist version. Dutch Mennonites warned that the policies in Pennsylvania might change. But Mennonites leaving the Palatinate in the 1720s and 1730s mentioned freedom from military service as one of Pennsylvania's attractions.[4]

In the Quaker policy, Mennonites did not necessarily see the distinction between being subjects and being citizens of the more modern kind. Mennonites voted in colonial Pennsylvania and gave political support to the pacifist Quakers. On the other hand they did not identify themselves with the political order to the point of taking full responsibility for it by seeking offices for themselves in the provincial government. Instead of having the outlook of modern citizens, they seem rather to have been trading votes for pacifist privileges, much as in Europe they had traded money, in the forms of special taxes and gifts to protective princes, for those privileges. In any case, in the first fifty years of Pennsylvania's life, war stayed far away. Occasionally the Quakers in the colony's Assembly voted money "for the King's use" in full knowledge that the British would apply it to war and defense. But they did not take upon their own consciences the burden of raising or supplying armies.[5]

By the 1740s, change was on the way. The British begin to require each American colony to recruit and equip soldiers. Previously there had been local militia but only for local emergencies such as Indian raids in the frontier; and the Pennsylvania frontier remained at peace. But now a threat of war with France and Spain raised demands for a new militia act as a gesture of patriotism. Such a bill did not pass when introduced in the Pennsylvania legislature in

1742. Yet it foreshadowed what might come.[6]

As compulsory military service appeared on the horizon, leaders of the Skippack Mennonite congregation wrote to fellow-Mennonites in Holland on May 8, 1742, acknowledging that the Dutch had been right. Mennonites had come to America with insufficient assurances of religious freedom, the Skippackers admitted. Now "there is no guarantee that, if a hostile attack should strike this province, we would not, like all the other provinces, be compelled against our conscience to take up arms and meet the foe with weapons." That would mean "a heavily burdened conscience." The Mennonites had petitioned the Pennsylvania Assembly, but had gotten the reply "that such matter is entirely beyond its authority." Would the Dutch Mennonites please present their case to the authorities in London?[7]

Apparently the 1742 letter went astray. Three years later the Skippack leaders again wrote to Holland. "The flames of war seem to be mounting higher and higher," they reported, and it appeared that "cross and tribulation" might soon "fall to the lot of the nonresistant Christian." Please, would the Dutch intercede with the British government? Meanwhile the Skippackers were determined to publish a German translation of the *Martyrs Mirror.* This was an enormous effort for such a small religious fellowship, but some of the Mennonite leaders had caught a vision of helping their young people become more aware of the example of Anabaptist martyrs. Apparently from what they already knew of Mennonite history, the Skippackers more or less anticipated the worst in conflict with governments. Even as they asked for help they evidently suspected that their Dutch brethren could do nothing for them in London, so they had to prepare for renewed persecution.[8]

This time, however, the Mennonites underestimated the ability of Quakers in the Assembly to maneuver and delay action on a militia bill. In 1747 Benjamin Franklin drafted a plan leading to a wholly voluntary association in place of a militia; and not until 1755 did the Pennsylvania Assembly finally face the need for frontier defense against Indians.[9]

The Quaker success in protecting their own scruples

against military service may well have convinced Mennonites that political action was still the best way to preserve religious liberty. Mennonites had traditionally refused to serve as magistrates. Skippack Mennonites wrote to Holland in 1773 that "we accept no office under the Government because force is used therein." Evidently they meant no offices in the provincial government, not the township or county governments. Many Mennonites served every year as assessors and unarmed constables in Pennsylvania townships. In the 1740s Martin Mylin in Lancaster County and Michael Danner in York County served as county commissioners. A certain Jacob Funk did serve in the Maryland Assembly about 1773-1774, and he had once been a Mennonite. But he was no longer a Mennonite when he was elected.

No Mennonite served in the Pennsylvania Assembly. On the other hand, neither did many other Germans, for the language barrier prevented any more than a handful of them from seeking elected office. In the first half of the eighteenth century only one German served a single term; only two were elected in the 1750s and four others in the 1760s. Mennonites did not seek high office. But, until the revolutionary period produced new political alignments, Mennonites were hardly more isolated from colony-wide political life than were other Germans.[10]

Mennonites certainly voted in the 1750s and 1760s; indeed they did so enough to determine the outcome of many elections in counties where many of them lived. The votes of Mennonites and of other Germans kept Quakers in the Pennsylvania Assembly in those years.

The practice of voting in township and provincial elections probably began even earlier than 1750. From 1706 onward it was not unusual for Mennonites to petition for naturalization, with the request that they be exempted from having to take oaths in court or to bear arms. Apparently they wanted to be naturalized primarily so they could secure their land titles; for in Pennsylvania and other colonies, only British subjects could bequeath land to heirs. But naturalization carried with it the right to vote. In the thirty years from 1700 to 1730 fewer than a hundred Germans (a good

"Peace and War" a stove plate of a type popular among colonial Mennonites at Skippack and elsewhere. (Bucks County Historical Society)

percentage of them Mennonite) became naturalized British subjects in Pennsylvania. Thereafter five times as many did so in a single decade. Between 1740 and 1749 a simplified method of naturalization permitted 852 foreigners to become British subjects. The Mennonite proportion apparently continued to be high, although no exact percentages are available. As a matter of conscience more than half of those naturalized in these years did so by affirmation rather than by oath.[11]

Some Mennonites, like their Quaker neighbors, saw no conflict between fidelity to gospel teaching on the oath and nonresistance, and becoming politically active as citizens. They saw no reason why the state could not exempt conscientious objectors from oath-taking and from military duty. Other Mennonites, most notably Heinrich Funck, the bishop and author who died in 1760, had doubts. Funck chided those in the "nonresistant churches who make an effort to elect officials or magistrates according to their own wishes and ideas" and who "seek these offices themselves and serve in them." He thought that such people wanted to "assure not only those in our own time, but also our children, exemption from the feast of affliction as kept by Jesus." In other words, Funck thought that, by becoming politically active, nonresistant people were exhibiting fear of conflict with the world and fear of following Jesus along the path of suffering.[12]

A Christian state is itself a paradox if one takes seriously the commands to love one's enemies and to do good to those who use one badly. By participating in the free commonwealth on the Delaware, the commonwealth called Pennsylvania, Quakers and Mennonites ignored that contradiction. Like previous peoples who insisted that pacifism and love must apply to practical affairs, earlier Anabaptists and Quakers had previously stood at the margins of nominally Christian political orders. To thus be marginal was probably easier before the modern idea of citizenship, wherein the person is the basic unit of the state rather than merely a personal subject of the ruler; yet even before modern citizenship, those Anabaptists and Quakers suffered much for challenging the idea that force is the basis of social order. Marginality seemed natural also because those earlier Anabaptists and Quakers, like New Testament writers, presumed that no state could ever be really Christian. In words of historian Ernst Crous, "the Anabaptists [had] recognized the state as ordained of God for the maintenance of order by means of the sword in the sub-Christian society of this world. They did not believe, however, that the disciple of Christ was called to perform this coercive function."[13]

What would happen if those responsible for maintaining social order were also disciples of Christ? Early Anabaptists had not resolved this dilemma, for the harsh reality of persecution had made the question moot. But as persecution had ended, there had come new tendencies toward Mennonite inwardness and disinterest in evangelism. These tendencies had given new meaning to the old idea of being the faithful remnant who reject the sword and to the idea that those who bore the sword were "outside the perfection of Christ." As a minority Mennonites had come to terms with the German princes who had welcomed them to their territories. They had agreed not to proselytize. They had consented to pay special taxes for military exemption, and had paid still other taxes and assessments for the military in time of war.[14] Mennonite emigrants from the Palatinate and Zweibrucken came to America with this pattern in their minds. They responded to the demands caused by wars with the French, the Shawnee, and the Delaware as their fathers had responded to exactions brought on by the Rhineland campaigns of Louis XIV.

The problem was, Mennonite thought had never reckoned with the English Whig tradition of self-government. Could a distinction between the nonresistant Christian and the sword-bearing state be clear-cut if the people were in fact the rulers? In the 1750s Pennsylvania's Quakers grappled with the implications of self-government for the peace testimony and raised issues that would challenge Mennonites then and later.

In 1755 the arrival of General Edward Braddock with a thousand British regulars brought long-smoldering issues to a crisis. Braddock's army had orders to force the French to abandon a recently constructed line of forts in western Pennsylvania. With red-coated soldiers marching through the forests to defend Pennsylvania's claim to the upper reaches of the Ohio Valley, the Pennsylvania Assembly could not refuse to vote for a militia bill. After all, the bill was to appropriate money to defend Pennsylvania's own frontier.[15]

At this juncture, in May 1755, several Mennonite ministers and deacons in Lancaster County addressed a petition to the Pennsylvania Assembly. Hans Tschantz, Benjamin Hershey, Christian Wenger, and others asserted their loyalty to the king and pronounced themselves ready to pay "whatever duty, Tax, & c., that the Laws of Great Britain and this province requires." But, they declared, their obligation to their sovereign did not extend to "defending him with

Sword in hand." If the affirmation of allegiance that they had taken upon naturalization had said otherwise, then they were victims of a faulty translation. The Lancaster Mennonites did not mention the militia bill; but obviously they feared that the Assembly would soon pass an act obliging all Pennsylvanians to perform military service.

In their petition Tschantz, Hershey and the other Lancaster churchmen based their understanding of church and state squarely on Romans 13 from which they quoted or paraphrased several verses. Paul's teaching was clear on honoring the king and paying taxes and tolls. But they could not reconcile the express command "to Love our Enemies" with the military obligation they might seem to have accepted by affirming allegiance.[16] The Mennonite petitioners asked the Assembly to modify the pledge taken at naturalization so as to exempt their people from having to defend king and country by force of arms. It was at this point that they said they were prepared "to Suffer all that is dear to us to be rend from us" rather than fight. Yet in fact Mennonites were willing to assist military effort in some other ways.[17]

An army on the march required a long train of wagons to carry baggage, food, and ammunition. The army needed horses, hay, and fodder. When Maryland and Virginia failed to provide enough of such supplies, Benjamin Franklin stepped into the breach. At the end of April, 1755, he rode to Lancaster, got a judge to address the local farmers in German, and distributed a bilingual handbill that called for 150 wagons and teams and 1,500 other horses for the use of Braddock's expedition. By promising (and delivering) high wages for wagoners and high fees for horses leased to the army, Franklin became very popular among the Germans. He explicitly assured them that "no drivers or persons who take care of horses shall be obligated to perform military service or some other duty."[18]

Mennonites were among those who responded to Franklin's appeal; indeed they provided as many as one fifth of the wagons in Braddock's train. According to William Smith, a contemporary pamphlet writer, Mennonite wagoners refused to carry guns or ammunition, but they willingly carried food and other supplies. And some Men-

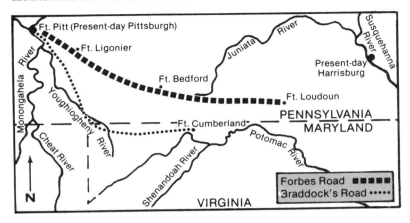

Braddock's and Forbes' roads, over which Mennonite teamsters hauled supplies for the two generals' armies. (Adapted from Ray Allen Billington, *Westward Expansion,* 4th ed.)

nonites who did not travel with the army loaned it horses and provided hay and grain.[19]

Supplying such forage also in later campaigns, Mennonites won praise for "Zeal for his Majesty's service." In 1759, working to organize shipments of oats and rye to General Forbes, Edward Shippen arranged to meet with "the Menists at Landis' "—possibly meaning the Mellinger meetinghouse near Lancaster City where Benjamin Landis was pastor. Shippen reported that the wagoners "were chiefly Menists" and "were very willing to go." Later the same year, Shippen reported spending time "amongst the Menonists treating with them about Waggons & forage." " They Say they have done their share," Shippen reported, yet would "do more," including mentioning Shippen's requests "at their Meetings next Sunday." Mennonites also said they hoped "to be able to persuade one another to set about threshing out their oats and spelts immediately afterwards." Evidently Lancaster Mennonites found nothing incongruous in making announcements at their worship services concerning needs of General Stanwix's army.[20] Being a practical people, not inclined to reflect much about how all sorts of noncombatant activities help to create a war system, they had no scruples against supporting military action in such ways.

In fact, in the panic that spread across Pennsylvania after the first Indian raids in October 1755 some Mennonites gave even more direct support to defense. Petitions were going to the Pennsylvania Assembly demanding that the Assembly organize a militia and appropriate money for defending the frontiers. One such petition from York County asked the Assembly to let the petitioners "shew with what Resolution they [the petitioners] shall endeavor to defend their Lives and Properties, their King and Country." In forwarding several such petitions, the York County justices reported "that the bigest part of its Signers are Menonists, who live about 15 miles westward of York." Conrad Weiser wrote from Tulpehocken on the Berks County frontier: "I believe the people in general up here would fight; I had two or three long beards in my Company, one a Menonist who declared he would live and die with his neighbours [and] had a good gun with him."[21]

Apparently some Mennonites had let themselves get caught up in a popular mood of militarism. To that popular mood the Pennsylvania Assembly also responded. Early in November 1755 the legislators passed a bill to print £60,000 in paper money for defense of the colony, and also levied new taxes on property and on individuals. Two weeks later without making service compulsory they passed a militia bill. While the bills were under debate, twenty prominent Friends submitted a protest against the proposed legislation. Their protest underscores a gap that had developed between many Quakers in the Assembly and the spiritual leaders of their society. It raised the question of paying taxes for war, for it suggested that nonresistants were "raising Sums of Money, and putting them into the Hands of Committees, who may apply them to Purposes inconsistent with the peaceable Testimony we profess." The fact was, the Quakers knew how their tax moneys would be used, so they felt they could no longer slough off the responsibility. Second, the petitioners suggested positive actions that nonresistants could take as alternatives, such as "raising Money to cultivate our Friendship with our Indian Neighbours, and to support such of our Fellow-Subjects who are or may be in Distress."[22]

With the first Indian attacks in 1755, Mennonites as well as some others began a spontaneous program of relief: wagonloads of food and clothing to men, women, and children who had fled from their farms on the frontier, sometimes with Delaware and Shawnee warriors in close pursuit. Some of these refugees fled to Bethlehem and nearby towns in Northampton County. Christopher Sauer the Germantown printer reported in his newspaper that "the day before New Year the Mennonites of Skippack and those living farther up" sent Bethlehem and Nazareth seven wagons full of supplies. Other refugees fled to Tulpehocken in the upper part of Berks County, and a letter from Tulpehocken reported that "Mennonites from the area of Lancaster County have sent several wagonloads of flour, meat, and clothing, &c. for the poor around here." Commented Sauer: "May the Lord have mercy on these poor and wretched inhabitants and awaken some hearts that will follow the Christian and praiseworthy example of the Mennonites of Lancaster County." Valentine Hunsicker of Skippack and Christian Moyer of Franconia, deacons or elders of their respective congregations, directed Mennonite relief from their area. Other help came from Mennonites of Great Swamp, Goshenhoppen, Worcester, and Upper and Lower Saucon.[23]

These first Indian attacks on the exposed frontier settlements led the Pennsylvania Assembly in April 1756 formally to declare war on both the Delaware and Shawnee nations. Thereupon some Quakers, led especially by Israel Pemberton, immediately pursued the alternative of friendship with the Indians rather than war. Along with others Pemberton, who was a politician but sided with the Quakers' spiritual leaders on the war tax issue and resigned from the Assembly, formed a "Friendly Association for Regaining and Preserving Peace with the Indians by Pacific Measures." Since the Indians quite understandably felt cheated of their lands, the Friendly Association proposed to negotiate fairly with them and pay them honest prices, and its members set about raising the necessary money. A few days later

This Andrew Ziegler letter to Israel Pemberton (Oct. 14, 1756) offers Mennonite aid to the Quaker "Friendly Association" efforts for peace with the Indians at the outset of the French and Indian War. (Courtesy Haverford College Library)

Christopher Sauer told Pemberton that he would correspond with "the menonists which are most able and willing to contribute to such a purpose."[24]

Mennonites entered wholeheartedly into the Friendly Association's work. Its positive approach to peacemaking was a new departure for them; never before had they had the opportunity to participate in treaty negotiations. Andrew Ziegler and others from Skippack planned to go to Philadelphia and urge the governor to make peace. Ziegler wrote to Pemberton in October 1756 "that we hat a meeting Do Day about the affairs of the Indians for geatering some money and more of our meetings will do the same." Pemberton's letter books indicate that Ziegler, his brother Michael Ziegler, Jr., and Dielman Kolb were most active in advocating support for the Association among Skippack Mennonites.[25]

Not only Skippackers but Lancaster County Mennonites as well supported these peacemaking efforts. But in 1757 the Delaware and the Shawnee refused to travel to Lancaster to parlay with Pennsylvania's governor. On the other side, angry frontiersmen brought some mangled corpses of the Indians' victims to the treaty commissioners. Such attitudes seem to have diminished Mennonites' enthusiasm. Benjamin Hershey told one of Pemberton's agents that he thought it best to wait for a more successful treaty conference before asking his brethren for the money they had pledged. More than half the Mennonites in Lancaster County were willing to contribute towards the expenses of the treaty, Hershey reported, but others had been persuaded by their neighbors of other faiths to give money to the poor instead.[26]

Nevertheless some Mennonites supported the Friendly Association with generous financial contributions, and even participated in its treaty-making. Isaac Whitelock, a Lancaster Quaker, wrote Pemberton in 1758 that "this week Benjamin Hersey [sic] was at my house and acquainted me that their people had collected" money that Mennonites had promised "for the Indians." The sum was "about Six hundred & Eighty pounds and is to be taken down by the persons appointed, to wit, John Hare and Jacob Myers." These were apparently a New Danville deacon or elder named John Hare (or Herr) and Jacob Myers of Conestoga Township. Herr and Myers were appointed to attend a treaty conference at Easton that turned out to be more successful than the one scheduled at Lancaster in 1757. At Easton, in

242   Land, Piety, Peoplehood

1758, Pennsylvania made peace with the Delawares.[27]

The Friendly Association not only provided Mennonites with an opportunity for active peacemaking; it also brought Mennonites and Quakers together as partners. Mennonites attended Association meetings during the Yearly Meeting of the Society of Friends, and in turn Quaker leaders like Israel Pemberton and Isaac Zane worshiped with Mennonites in Lancaster County.[28] Gradually the Association depended more and more on Mennonite financial support, and as it did, Mennonite influence in it increased. During nine years of the Association's existence Mennonites contibuted a third of the Association's funds; but the proportion was much higher in its later years, the Quaker proportion less. Of £260 on the Association's ledger in 1763, fully £230 had been contributed, the ledger stated, "by Menonists residing in the Counties of Philadelphia and Berks."[29]

Mennonites' concern was perhaps well-being of whites as much as justice for Indians, for Mennonites preferred their money be used to ransom white captives in Indian hands. In June 1760 Pemberton asked the Commissioners for Indian Affairs if they could get information about white settlers held in Indian villages. If the commissioners could persuade the tribes to bring the whites to Pittsburgh, "some small Presents might be given in Proportion to the distance they live from Pittsburgh," as a way "to encourage them [the tribes] therein." "The Trustees of the fund raised by the Menonists will immediately pay to the Commissioners" the price of such presents. In January of 1761 Pemberton informed Benjamin Hershey that several captives had been liberated and others were on the way from Indian villages in the Ohio Valley, thanks to the Mennonite effort.[30]

Ransoming prisoners taken by the Indians may have had an appeal to Mennonites because some of their own people had suffered from Indian raids. More than they realized, Mennonites and Amish were of course part of a white society that was inexorably pushing red people off eastern lands. Most lived in communities not threatened by Indian warriors, but of course some lived in newer communities close enough to the cutting edge of white expansion to be in danger of attack. Indian war parties of the Delaware

Home of Dielman Kolb (1691-1756), Skippack-Salford area minister who helped supervise the translation and printing of the *Martyrs Mirror*, 1745-1748. (Jan Gleysteen collection)

tribe often struck exposed settlements at the foot of the Blue Mountains in upper Berks County and along Swatara Creek in present Lebanon and Dauphin counties. That was the setting of the raid on the home of Amishman Jacob Hochstetler and his family in 1757. Five years later, in 1762, Hochstetler was still trying to get two of his children back. When the Ohio Indians who held his sons came to Philadelphia without them for a treaty with the Pennsylvania authorities, Hochstetler asked for Governor Hamilton's help.[31]

Suffering the heaviest blows from Indians were Mennonites and their neighbors in the Shenandoah Valley of Virginia, where the Mennonite family named Roads met its tragedy. The Williamsburg *Virginia Gazette* reported in 1758 that "the Indians had lately killed and captivated 26 People between Winchester and Augusta Court House [Staunton] and that a large Body of the Inhabitants, to the Number of 300, were removing into Culpeper, and the other Counties on

244 *Land, Piety, Peoplehood*

this side the Blue Ridge." Mennonites were part of this exodus.[32]

In September 1758 some of the refugees had Benjamin Hershey of near Lancaster write to fellow-Mennonites in Holland telling of two hundred families fleeing and fifty persons losing their lives. Their account said, "We were thirty-nine Mennonite families living together in Virginia." One Mennonite family had been murdered and others had fled. Could the Dutch offer some aid? To that letter, signed by Michael Kauffman, Jacob Borner, Samuel Bohm, and Daniel Stauffer, the Dutch soon responded. Fifty English pounds were on the way, they said, which the refugees could obtain through Messrs. Benjamin & Sam Shoemaker of Philadelphia.[33] No doubt the fifty pounds helped, but conditions on the Virginia frontier remained so unsettled that some of the refugees did not return to the Shenandoah Valley for many years. Others must have journeyed back as soon as the immediate threat of war with Indians had passed.

By 1760 the British had defeated the French; and the Indians, deprived of their ally, had decided at least for a time to bury the hatchet. But peace was fragile and illusory. White encroachment on Indian lands or the murder of an Indian by a settler could still put the frontier in flames. Very serious trouble developed in 1763, when a brilliant Indian leader named Pontiac sent war parties against British forts and settlements from the Great Lakes to Pennsylvania, Maryland, and Virginia. Now many more refugees streamed back from frontier settlements than had come even after Braddock's defeat in 1755. Once again Virginia's Shenandoah Valley lay open to raiders. During the summer of 1763 Indians killed isolated farm families in Augusta County. It was in that phase that the family of Mennonite preacher John Roads fell prey to one band led by a renegade white. Other bands struck deep in Pennsylvania. The *Pennsylvania Gazette* reported in July 1763 that "Carlisle was become the Barrier, not a single Inhabitant being beyond it." On both sides of the Susquehanna, the "woods were filled with poor Families, and their Cattle, who make Fires and live like Savages." If Mennonites were benefiting from Indian removal, some of them also risked their lives to harvest crops for some of these refugees, and carried wagonloads of food and clothing to them.[34]

More and more, white settlers killed Indians indiscriminately, including friendly ones. In August 1763, a few miles from Bethlehem, Pennsylvania, some Northampton County settlers massacred a family of Moravian Christian Indians. In September a few miles away others killed and scalped three more of the friendly reds. Then the notorious Paxton Volunteers from Scotch-Irish settlements in present Dauphin County mounted an expedition against the Christian Delawares at Wyalusing on the Upper Susquehanna. They reached the Wyoming Valley only two days after a non-Christian Delaware war party had swept through the valley and left no white settler alive. The Paxtons did not press on to the Christian Indian village, but returned home swearing vengeance. Meanwhile the Delaware war party struck white settlements on the Northampton County frontier, killing and burning extensively. It was then that Ulrich Showalter, a Mennonite, working on the roof of a building in Whitehall Township, saw a dozen warriors crossing the Lehigh River and got to safety in time.[35]

In Lancaster County's Manor Township there was a village of peaceful Conestoga Indians. Without logic and without mercy, some whites turned on them the full fury of settlers' pent-up anger and frustration. Early on the morning of December 14, 1763, a party of frontiersmen entered the village and killed and scalped every man, woman, and child they found. A few of the villagers were away. Mennonite Peter Swarr sheltered one such group and others were out selling brooms. To protect those lucky ones, the authorities lodged them in a Lancaster jail. Then Benjamin Hershey and John Brubaker, both Mennonites, learned that the Paxtons planned to break into the jail and kill the survivors, too. Hershey and Brubaker notified authorities; but the authorities did not act before the Paxtons had carried out their vicious deed. In the end, a Mennonite named Christian Hershey protected the lives of the only Conestoga Indians saved by hiding them in his cellar. There, as later chronicled, "they had to stay all winter until the excitement abated."[36]

The Paxtons became the heroes of Indian-hating frontier people. And perhaps not even all Mennonites condemned them. Abraham Newcomer, a Mennonite gunsmith, testified that the dead Conestogas had threatened to kill and scalp him; a non-Mennonite, Thomas Barton, printed Newcomer's statement in a pamphlet defending the Paxton Volunteers.[37]

A march on Philadelphia by the Paxtons and many of their Scotch-Irish (and some German) supporters brought deep emotions and deep divisions to the surface. Animosity ran high against the Quakers. Critics charged that, instead of defending Pennsylvania, the Quakers and their Friendly Association had lavished presents on Indian murderers. Mennonites, as nonresistants active in the Association, shared the brunt of this popular hostility.

The Pennsylvania government to which frontiersmen brought their complaints was deeply divided. The governor, answerable to the Penn family, was at odds with many of the people's representatives in the Assembly not only over frontier defense but also over taxation. Exasperated assemblymen finally began to call for fundamental change in Pennsylvania's government. Two prominent politicians, Benjamin Franklin and Joseph Galloway, took the lead and asked the British king to take Pennsylvania away from the Penns as proprietors and make it a royal colony.[38]

Although the two politicians themselves were not Quakers, the party backing Franklin and Galloway was the so-called "Quaker Party." As longtime supporters of that faction, Mennonites supported the change, with enough zeal that in 1764 a leader of the opposing Proprietary Party, Samuel Purviance, Jr., expressed alarm when he heard news from Lancaster of Mennonite and Quaker activity against the Penns' rule. (By then William Penn's heirs had long since given up Quakerism.) Purviance suggested that his own party should add a German or two to its ticket to offset Quaker Party influence. And indeed throughout the colony the Proprietary Party managed to draw many Lutheran and Reformed Germans to its side. Commenting specifically about Philadelphia County, the influential Lutheran pastor Henry Melchior Muhlenberg recorded in his diary that "the

English and German Quakers, with the Moravians, Mennonites, [and] Schwenkfelders, formed one party." But "the English of the High Church, the Presbyterian, and the German Lutheran and Reformed joined the other party and prevailed."[39]

A few Mennonites and Quakers differed with their fellows and voted the Proprietary ticket in that 1764 election. In any case they voted. Whatever their political preferences, most Mennonites seemed quite ready to use the franchise to protect their freedom of conscience. They were so politically active at Lancaster that Purviance got worried about "a project laid by the Menonists" to turn a Lancaster County politician out of office in 1765. He proposed spreading rumors of violence at the polls "which will certainly keep great numbers of Menonists at home." And in 1768, when one of Lancaster County's assemblymen decided not to run for reelection, "the head men among the Menonists" held a meeting at the tavern of a man named Matthias Slough, and agreed on a substitute.[40] So however strongly Franconia leader Heinrich Funck deplored the sight of nonresistant people in politics, the Mennonite vote continued to be a factor in Lancaster County and probably to some extent elsewhere.

Mennonite fears of military conscription and the persecution that might result never materialized until the American revolution. In the colonial period Mennonites did not suffer the loss of their property for refusing to take up arms. Instead, Mennonites took up politics and became identified with one faction of Pennsylvania's political spectrum. Ironically, among some neighbors who already resented their refusal to fight, their efforts to protect their liberty of conscience by influencing elections made them all the more obnoxious. In 1760 the pacifist groups, even including the Quakers, composed not more than 25 percent of the population of Pennsylvania.[41] The events of the turbulent years from 1740 to 1770 created new ethnic and religious alliances which made the pacifists into a decided minority with few allies. Politically the developments all but isolated Mennonites and other pacifist peoples and arrayed them against both the Scotch-Irish and many other German voters. That was the background of Mennontes' experiences in the American revolution.

In the later colonial years Maryland and Virginia levied fines on all those, whether conscientious objectors or not, who did not turn out for militia drills. Mennonites paid these fines and suffered no severe repression. Then in 1766 Virginia's assembly, or House of Burgesses, exempted Quakers from fines as well as from militia duty. Soon, in 1769, it received a petition from two men named Jacob Stricklor (or Strickler) and Jacob Coughenor, "on Behalf of themselves, and their Protestant Brethren, of the Sect called Menonists," requesting the same privilege. The Burgesses granted the request. For some reason Strickler and Henry Funk of Virginia repeated the request in 1772, and again, as a 1785 document put it, the Mennonites "were indulged with an exemption." Mennonites in Virginia and Maryland as well as in Pennsylvania could surely agree with what Andrew Ziegler and several other Skippackers wrote to Dutch Mennonites in 1773: " We have never been compelled to bear weapons. With yea and nay we can all testify before our praiseworthy magistrates." For "through God's mercy we enjoy unlimited freedom in both civil and religious affairs."[42]

"Unlimited freedom"—despite the paradox which others perceived between Mennonites' wealth and their pacifism. Mennonites had never really resolved that paradox of their colonial American experience, except to allow their leaders to tell Pennsylvania's rulers that if necessary they would give up their wealth rather than take up arms. Moreover, even as the Skippackers wrote those happy words, the kinds of freedoms Mennonites cherished most were just about to come under sharp question. The American revolution was at hand. And revolutionary patriots, with modern ideas of melding various subgroups into an American peoplehood, would put forward new ideas of citizenship.[43] The patriots would make military service, or at least some equivalent of it, the test of citizenship. Mennonites, already a people in a different way, would be reluctant to go along. That fact, plus Mennonites' past political alignments and their reputation for wealth, induced the patriots to eliminate Mennonites' political influence and to curtail their civil rights.

10

A PEOPLE APART?
MENNONITES IN THE REVOLUTION

In the early stages of the American revolution, some Mennonites ethusiastically supported patriots' efforts to protect colonists' rights. On the other hand, on at least one occasion, if an ardently pro-British Christopher Sauer III is to be believed, some Lancaster Mennonite and Dunker leaders hoped for British victory to "reinstate them in the enjoyment of their former blessings." Sauer said the leaders had even expressed "readiness to assist [the British cause] with their goods and chattels." The great majority of Mennonites were far more neutral. Like most of their German neighbors and many others, they preferred to wait and watch, feeling that events were unfolding over which they had no control.[1]

Those events were not kind to Mennonites and others with a pacifist understanding of following Christ. For these people the American revolution was a wrenching experience. It forced Mennonites to reassess who they were, and whether and how they fit into society about them. In colonial America, as back in Europe, they had assumed that they could be good citizens or at least good subjects[2] without bearing arms. Pennsylvania legislators' refusal to pass a militia bill in 1742 and exemptions from militia duty and fines in other colonies had indicated that in America even lawmakers agreed: there was no conflict between pacifism and citizenship.

But to justify revolution, American patriots felt the need to claim support of all the colonies' people. Indifference or neutrality of any subgroup would weaken their claim. To give substance to the claim, they called for all adult males to gather into local "associations" and pledge to bear arms for

American liberties. The obvious purpose was military, of course, but underlying that purpose more subtly and more profoundly was the goal of bringing Americans together into one cause. More and more the revolutionists spoke the language of a new, American peoplehood. For the moment the test of membership in that peoplehood—the test of new, revolutionary citizenship—was willingness to associate and bear arms. By that test pacifism was no longer compatible with good citizenship.

In colonial times in Pennsylvania, and to a degree in Maryland and Virginia, Mennonites had not only voted but had also helped select candidates and held certain local offices. Now, as part of a power struggle among Pennsylvania's ethnic and religious groups, revolutionists wanted to eliminate the political influence of pacifists, especially of Quakers. Since Mennonites traditionally supported the Quakers, their influence had to be eliminated as well. In all the colonies the patriots tried to flush out neutrals as well as persons who actively supported the British. One method was to pass laws, known as "Test Acts," which demanded oaths or affirmations of allegiance to revolutionary governments. Framers of the law acknowledged that one purpose was to exclude members of pacifist religious sects from politics.[3]

Meanwhile popular opinion turned against the non-associating, non-arming Mennonites—partly on grounds that Mennonites were rich. Associators in Donegal Township of Pennsylvania's Lancaster County complained, for instance, that some non-associators, including some who held back "for Scruple of Conscience," were among "the wealthyest and best seated in the County." Another commentator singled out "the Wealthy Menonists" for his complaint.

County and township committees regularly called for levying heavier fines and taxes on conscientious objectors. A York County mob offered to tar and feather a young Mennonite who became too outspoken. In Lancaster another group of rowdies took men who refused on religious grounds to fight, and paraded them scornfully through the streets.[4] In Maryland also, in Washington County, patriots threatened to pull Menonists and Dunkers out of their houses and make them serve. Patriots in Virginia protested Mennonites' and Quakers' military exemptions.[5]

These experiences gave Mennonites second thoughts about political involvement. Most German settlers were much less enthusiastic about the patriots' cause than were some others, notably the Scotch-Irish; but most church Germans at least drilled with the militia, and thus passed the test of patriotism. Mennonites failed the test. Unlike the French and Indian War, the alternative of giving voluntary relief to war sufferers was not enough to allay suspicion. Ironically, just as patriots were trying to pressure them to become part of the new, revolutionary peoplehood, Mennonites felt more and more alienated. Whether or not the alienation was inevitable, it was a fact. Because of it the revolution induced in Mennonites a mood and strategy of inwardness and withdrawal.

As conflict between American patriots and Great Britain grew heated in 1774 and 1775, Mennonites expressed some support for the patriots' cause, and some bewilderment. The Americans' First Continental Congress, meeting in Philadelphia in September 1774, mixed moderation with forcefulness. Moderately, it agreed to petition British King George III as loyal subjects; more forcefully, it decided to pressure British Parliament by stopping imports of British goods. To stop the imports it called for local "Committees of Observation and Safety."[6] In eastern Pennsylvania several men who were clearly Mennonite, and others who
· may well have been Mennonites, served on these committees. Jacob Wisler of Manor Township, John Brubaker of Earl Township, and John Witmer, Jr., of Lampeter Township were Mennonites elected to the Lancaster County Committee in December 1774. In November 1775 Witmer, Abraham Newcomer of Conestoga Township, and John Brackbill of Strasburg Township were all reelected. Peter Good, a Mennonite miller, was chosen by his Brecknock Township neighbors as a committeeman, first in 1775.[7] But others held back, uncertain. Christopher Schultz of Berks County's Hereford Township noted that "Thousands amongst the Germans" followed the example of the Quakers in not "choosing and sending of Members" to these committees,

EXTRACTS from the VOTES and PROCEEDINGS of the

Committee of Obfervation

for the County of L A N C A S T E R.

At a Meeting of the faid Committee, *held at the* Court-Houfe, *in the Borough of* Lancafter, *on the* 16th *and* 17th *Days of* June, 1775.

J A M E S   B U R D, Efq; in the CHAIR.

On Motion of feveral Members of this Committee, which being fully confidered and fupported.

Refolved, THAT it be recommended, and it is hereby recommended to all the Inhabitants of the County of *Lancafter*, whofe Circumftances will admit of it, and whofe Religious Tenets do not forbid them to enter into ASSOCIATIONS, and take up Arms at this alarming Crifis, in Defence of their Civil and Religious Rights, immediately to provide themfelves with good and fufficient Firelocks, to be approved of by fuch Members of this Committee as refide in the different Townfhips, where fuch Firelocks are furnifhed; and that the Circumftances of the People be alfo judged of and determined by the Committees of their refpective Townfhips.————————Likewife,

Refolved, To recommend it to fuch Perfons, whofe Religious Principles debar them from affociating, taking up, or furnifhing Arms, and who fhall be deemed by the Townfhip Committees of fufficient Ability, to Pay into the Hands of the Committee's Treafurer, the Sum of *Three Pounds Ten Shillings*, to be applied to fuch ufes, as by this Committee fhall be deemed moft advantageous to the Public Intereft.

And, whereas, a large number of the good People of this County, animated with the glorious Caufe is AMERICA, have not only furnifhed themfelves with Arms and other Neceffaries, but have been at a con additional Expence in learning the Military Art.   Officers of

Refolved, That it be further recommended to thofe Perfons, who, from fcruple of Confciencourage or ad to affociating and taking up Arms, to pay to the Committee's Ted in any other ... of Sky, unlefs by the per being lefs than fuch Perfons are affeffed and charged in the Proy affociated ; and that if any fuch have already ed to fuch Public Ufes as the Committee fhall think proper narge them.

Refolved, That the Members of this Committee do Correfpondence for this County, the Names of all fu County of *Lancafter* be divided in the Names of all thofe, who, unmoved by the Cala rder to form B A T T A L I O N S, *viz.* dear and valuable to Freemen, fhall ungene

Lancafter Borough.	Cocalico.	Brecknock.	Paxton.	Conneftogo.	Mountjoy.
Lancafter Townfhip.	Warwick.	Carnarvon.	Upper Paxton.	Martick.	Rapho.
Lampeter.	Heidelberg.	Earl.	Weft Hanover.	Drunmore.	Donnegal.
Manheim.	Elizabeth.	Leacock.	Derry.	Little-Britain.	Hempfield.
[If they choofe	Lebanon.	Sadfbury.	London-Derry.	Colerain.	Manor.
to join the Battalion	Eaft Hanover.	Bart.			
as it now ftands.]	Bethel.	Strafburg.			
		Salifbury.			

The Committee *of* Correfpondence *and* Obfervation, *for the County of* Lancafter,

Earneftly recommend to thofe Inhabitants of this County, who have already fubfcribed for the benevolent purpofe of relieving the diftreffed Poor of the Town of *Bofton*, to be as expeditious as poffible, in paying up their Subfcriptions. Thofe who have not yet fubfcribed, and intend to do it, will, it is hoped, make no further Delay.

Whereas the Committee of Correfpondence and Obfervation, from Reprefentations made to them, have Reafon to imagine that the Divifion already made of the County into Diftricts, for the purpofe of forming Battalions, is not altogether convenient, they think themfelves juftified in admitting of fuch alterations, as may be defired by a Majority of the Officers, as well of the Diftrict, a Townfhip or Townfhips, wifh to detach themfelves from, as of that they may chufe to join.

By Order of the Committee.

WILLIAM BARTON, *Secretary.*

L A N C A S T E R, Printed by FRANCIS BAILEY, in King-Street.

A revolutionary committee's notice concerning conscientious objectors, Lancaster, Pa., June 1775. (Historical Society of Pennsylvania)

but instead "keeping inactive, and watching the Event."[8]

Mennonites and many other Germans looked to Quakers for direction. Quaker leader Isaac Pemberton informed an English Friend that a statement on peace issued by the Philadelphia Friends' Meeting "has been translated into German and dispersed among that people." Thoughtful Germans had wanted Quakers' advice so much, he said, "that the Menonists sent down a special deputation of three of their preachers to the monthly meeting of Gwynned for this purpose." That consultation had led the Quakers to publish and circulate a German translation of their Philadelphia Meeting's peace testimony.[9]

Dramatic fighting between British soldiers and Massachusetts patriots at Lexington and Concord in April 1775 forever altered the situation of conscientious objectors and others who sought to remain neutral. In May patriots in each of the colonies adopted an agreement or Association that obligated everyone who signed it to begin military training to defend his homeland. Patriots were soon drilling in city squares and at rural crossroads.[10]

Mennonites generally refused to join the Association or to learn to be soldiers. A few persons of Mennonite background did turn out. Martin Bowman, an Earl Township farmer and miller, clearly identified in 1775 as a Mennonite, at first did not associate. Then he did, and became Captain Martin Bowman, commander of one of Lancaster County's militia companies. But Bowman was the rare exception. The great majority of Mennonites pleaded religious scruples against bearing arms, and earned local patriots' hostility.[11]

Soon patriots of Rapho and Manheim townships complained to the Lancaster County Committee that persons of such scruple had thrown insults at them. On the other side, the committee heard also "from two of the chief Persons of the Menonists, complaining that Violence and Threats had been used by some People to Members of that Society" for their non-associating stand. The committee dealt with both sides evenhandedly. But that only infuriated some patriots, until an armed mob forced committee members to resign and replaced them with others supposedly less favorable to nonresistants.[12]

Some Mennonites went beyond only refusal to bear arms. For instance late in 1775 John Newcomer, a Mennonite gunsmith in Lancaster County's Lampeter Township, admitted to his county's committee that, yes, he had "refused to enter on the work of making muskets" as the committee was demanding. The committee responded by forbidding him to work at his trade at all. Often other Mennonites and Amish tried to be more cooperative. In July 1776 the same committee exempted another Mennonite gunsmith, Christian Wenger of Leacock Township, from being a soldier precisely because they thought that he was more useful at home, working at his trade. Also, those two "chief persons of the Menonists" assured the committee that except for ways that violated their consciences, "their Members would chearfully co-operate in the Common Cause."[13]

On another occasion some Dunkers, Amish, and Mennonites assured the committee that their members were willing to contribute money "to assist the Common Cause otherwise than by taking up Arms." Christian Rupp and Michael Garber spoke for the Amish, and Benjamin Hershey, Sr., John Herr, Sr., and John Witmer, Sr., represented the Mennonites. And it is clear that in Earl Township, the only locality where such records survive, most Amish and Mennonite conscientious objectors did contribute, giving to a fund whose purposes were vague. The vagueness was probably deliberate. Many nonresistants thought they were giving for nearby poor families or to help refugees from British-occupied Boston; in fact, most of the money went for military expenses.[14]

By summer and autumn of 1775 there were increasingly loud demands for a special tax on those who would not associate. A patriot leader wrote from Hagerstown, Maryland, that some zealots were threatening to go to non-associators' houses "and pull them out by force." Others, he said, "declare they will lay down their Arms" and refuse to muster, if Dunker and Mennonite exemptions continued without penalty. Similar petitions reached the Pennsylvania Assembly.[15]

To that body, in November 1775, Mennonites and Dunkers together sent "a short and sincere Declaration."

A SHORT AND SINCERE

DECLARATION,

TO OUR HONORABLE ASSEMBLY, AND ALL OTHERS IN HIGH OR LOW
STATION OF ADMINISTRATION, AND TO ALL FRIENDS AND IN-
HABITANTS OF THIS COUNTRY, TO WHOSE SIGHT THIS
MAY COME, BE THEY ENGLISH OR GERMANS.

In the first Place we acknowledge us indebted to the most high GOD, who created
Heaven and Earth, the only good Being, to thank him for all his great Goodness
and manifold Mercies and Love through our Saviour JESUS CHRIST, who is come to
save the Souls of Men, having all Power in Heaven and on Earth.

Further we find ourselves indebted to be thankful to our late worthy Assembly,
for their giving so good an Advice in these troublesome Times to all Ranks of People in Pennsylvania, particularly in allowing those, who, by the Doctrine of our Saviour JESUS CHRIST, are persuaded in their Consciences to love their Enemies, and
not to resist Evil, to enjoy the Liberty of their Conscience, for which, as also for all
the good things we enjoyed under their care, we heartily thank that worthy Bo
of Assembly, and all high and low in Office, who have advised to such a peac
Measure, hoping and confiding that they, and all others entrusted with Pow
this hitherto blessed Province, may b   by the same Spirit of Grace,
animated the first Founder of thi   s very weak to give   Proprietor,
Penn, to grant Liberty of Co   ly Dust and Ashes.

great and memorable Day   subject to the higher Powers, and to give in the manner
who   rects us   out   e beareth the Sword not in vain, for he is the Minister of
God, a Revenger to execute Wrath upon him that doeth Evil."

This Testimony we lay down before our worthy Assembly, and all other Persons
in Government, letting them know, that we are thankful, as above mentioned, and
that we are not at Liberty in Conscience to take up Arms to conquer our Enemies,
but rather to pray to God, who has Power in Heaven and on Earth, for US and
THEM.

We also crave the Patience of all the Inhabitants of this Country,—what they
think to see clearer in the Doctrine of the blessed Jesus Christ, we will leave to
them and God, finding ourselves very poor; for Faith is to proceed out of the Word
of God, which is Life and Spirit, and a Power of God, and our Conscience is to be
instructed by the same, therefore we beg for Patience.

Our small Gift, which we have given, we gave to those who have Power over us,
that we may not offend them, as Christ taught us by the Tribute Penny.

We heartily pray that God would govern all Hearts of our Rulers, be they high
or low, to meditate those good Things which will pertain to OUR and THEIR hap-
piness.

———

The above Declaration, written by BENJAMIN HERSHEY, minister of the Menonist
Church, and signed by a number of Elders and Teachers of the Society of Menonists,
and some of the German Baptists, presented to the Honorable House of Assembly
on the 7th day of November, 1775, was most graciously received.

**English version of Mennonite-and-Dunker petition to the Pennsylvania
Assembly, November 1775.** (Courtesy Lancaster Mennonite Historical Society)

Benjamin Hershey, as a Lancaster County Mennonite leader, apparently was its author. The signers said they had welcomed "the Advice to those who do not find Freedom of Conscience to take up arms," namely the admonition "that they ought to be helpful to those who are in Need and distressed Circumstances." They understood the voluntary contributions of nonresistants to be exclusively for the relief of the poor. This request from the state was quite all right, "it being our Principle to feed the hungry and give the Thirsty Drink." On the other hand the petitioning Mennonites and Dunkers said they could not go beyond this, for "we find no Freedom in giving, or doing, or assisting in any Thing by which Men's Lives are destroyed or hurt."[16]

The petition of November 1775 was a humble one, more in the tone of subjects pleading with personal rulers than in the mood of modern citizens demanding rights. The signers even said that if others disagreed with their pacifist interpretation of Jesus' teachings they would not argue, but leave the matter to God, "finding ourselves very poor." On the other hand, those humble Mennonites and Dunkers were indeed asserting a kind of right, an ancient one with biblical precedent in the book of Acts: the right to let faith rather than the state determine Christians' public as well as private behavior.[17] Despite the petition, Pennsylvania's Assembly voted an additional tax on non-associators. About the same time, Maryland's did likewise. Lawmakers clearly thought of the taxes as equivalent to military service.[18]

Consistent with that view, in January 1776 Maryland quit its earlier pattern of exempting conscientious objectors from militia duty and fines. In May Virginia ordered that Mennonites and Quakers be enrolled in the militia and subjected to all ordinary fines and forfeitures if they refused to participate. And North Carolina ruled that all sect members formerly excused as conscientious objectors must either serve or send substitutes.[19]

Early in 1777 Pennsylvania, Maryland, Virginia, and North Carolina each passed stringent militia acts. Under these laws Mennonites and others paid ever heavier fines if they did not drill with their companies or provide substitutes. The fines were in addition to the special tax they paid as "non-associators." Militia officers turned lists of delinquents over to county sheriffs for collecting the penalty money. The laws permitted appeals if an individual believed his fine unjust, and numerous Mennonites appeared before appeal boards. Usually they pleaded for full exemption on grounds of poor health or of having done something that the boards might consider a meritorious public service. (In the latter plea, of course, the embryo of the "alternative" service was beginning to stir.) Or else the Mennonite appellants asked for adjustments in fines because of poverty. They sometimes added that they were "scrupulous of bearing arms"; but since conscientious objection was not allowed as an excuse, they never rested their cases on religious motives.[20]

In Pennsylvania, lists of delinquents kept by militia commanders, along with records of appeals, reveal much about how Mennonites responded to the militia laws. In other states records are less complete, but they corroborate the Pennsylvania evidence. Despite repeated fines, few Mennonites served or even attended the occasional drill. Records of Lancaster County's Earl Township identify 138 Mennonite men of military age; of them, only three served. Of nine Amish, none served. In later communications with Virginia's government, Mennonites of Rockingham and Shenandoah counties claimed they had paid heavy fines for not complying with military orders during the war. And a Shenandoah County military officer complained that several persons on his list, by "Pretending to be in Communion with the Menonists," had not mustered with the militia.[21]

If they did not serve personally, were Mennonites willing to send substitutes? On that issue, their Dunker neighbors came to a clear position, at least by 1780. At an annual meeting of Dunkers held that year at Conestoga, Pennsylvania, delegates were unanimous against the practice and exhorted their members "to hold themselves guiltless and take no part in war or bloodshedding, which might take place if we would pay voluntarily for hiring men." There is no record that Mennonites ever reached such clear consensus. One Lancaster County militiaman said that many Mennonites paid fines because they "Refuse to go or find a Sub-

The revolutionary war Battle of Germantown, Oct. 3, 1777, raged around and on the Germantown Mennonite meetinghouse yard and cemetery; bullet marks are still there. (Art by Ivan Moon)

stitud;" and clearly that was the policy of most. On the other hand, a few appealed for exemption from fines on grounds they had hired and sent others in their places.[22]

Mennonite and Amish appeals for exemptions were common, but usually the petitioners claimed they had served the war effort in other, indirect ways. Very often they had helped in the wagon service. Armies often pressed the teams and wagons of Mennonites and Amish into service, and then the owners went along to protect their property. Sometimes such claims did win exemptions for the owners. Other Mennonites and Amish claimed with some reason but less success that by operating gristmills or pursuing other trades they were contributing to the common cause. Only if connection to the war effort was direct and clear did such reasoning convince officials. Thus they exempted gunsmith Wenger so that he could stay at his trade. In some other cases they allowed conscientious objectors to pay fines by working specified amounts at their trades, such as making shoes or shirts or shoeing horses or providing other direct services for the army.[23]

It is not clear just what Amishmen and Mennonites meant when they pleaded that work such as operating a gristmill contributed to the "common cause" and so should be grounds for exemption. Did they mean that they were consciously contributing to the military effort, or were they saying, more fundamentally, that such constructive contribution to society, rather than the military test, ought to give them a place in the community and serve as credit for good citizenship? Or what did Isaac Kauffman, a Berks County Amish farmer, mean? Once when military persons demanded Kauffman's horse he forthrightly refused, saying: "'You are Rebels and I will not give a horse to such blood spilling persons." Berks County authorities imprisoned Kauffman as a Tory,[24] and indeed he may have had such leanings. Or his words may have revealed a conscience that forbade indirect as well as direct contribution to bloodshed. No doubt such Amishmen and Mennonites were responding with mixed emotions and mixed meanings. They were, after all, just as human as were the patriots. And war seldom makes for pure, unambiguous reasoning.

For many Mennonites, nonresistance meant not only refusing to bear arms but also submitting peaceably to every lawful authority. Mennonite thought offered no theology of revolution. Members of nonresistant groups were reluctant to take any step toward conflict with their legal sovereign George III, even when they agreed that Americans had legitimate complaints. They tended to see the options open to nonresistant Christians as being only neutrality or passive loyalty. And they feared any change in government that might imperil the religious liberty they enjoyed under the king. In fact they had a vested interest in British rule: the "unlimited freedom" which Andrew Ziegler and other Skippackers wrote of, as they described their situation to European friends in 1773.[25] Since Mennonites already felt such "unlimited freedom," to them the patriots' incessant talking of liberty while levying fines on non-associators and pressing wagons into service must have sounded hollow indeed.[26] In a revolutionary society, both faith and recent experience made Mennonites conservative.

Mennonites were not alone in hesitating. Historian Theodore Thayer has written that in the early months of 1776, with rebellion shifting rapidly from mere resistance to a war of independence, many Pennsylvania patriots began to waver. Moderates controlled the Pennsylvania Assembly and still believed in reconciliation with Great Britain. To keep Pennsylvania revolutionary took all the power that more radical colleagues could muster.[27]

In elections held in May 1776 voters once again gave moderates and conservatives a majority in Pennsylvania's Assembly. That vote was not entirely fair, however, for entrenched election rules gave conservative and moderate eastern counties (where most Mennonites lived) more representatives than they deserved, and newer western counties (with more Scotch-Irish people and more radicalism) fewer than their share. After the election, radicals maneuvered to call for a provincial constitutional convention so as to establish a government they thought would speak more for the people. The radicals wanted to set aside Penn's venerable charter and write a new constitution.[28]

Upon learning of the move for a new constitution,

Christian Funk, son of Heinrich Funck and himself a Franconia-area Mennonite bishop, at first feared "that our liberty
might be endangered." Although he wrote his account of
events only after he had come to differ with his fellow-Mennonites, Funk probably expressed well how most Mennonites
felt in 1776. At the time, apprehensive as he was, he decided
to go to a local, Franconia Township meeting that was being
held on the matter, and speak his mind. There he found
"nearly the whole township had assembled," nearly two
thirds in attendance being Mennonite and the rest "church
people." At that point Funk, in a bishop's weighty voice, said
that Mennonites as a "defenceless people" could neither get
involved "in tearing ourselves from the king" nor "institute
or destroy any government."[29]

Mennonite neutrality, whether in Franconia Township
or elsewhere in Pennsylvania, was an obstacle to the revolutionary cause. However much Hershey and other leaders
from Lancaster had adopted the tone of petitioning subjects
in November 1775, Mennonites still used the power of the
vote. By November 1776 Pennsylvania patriots had their new
state constitution, and in that month came the first elections under it. Patriots still feared a large Mennonite vote—
so much that on November 6 a patriot in Philadelphia la-
mented that "there was a large Election in Lancaster Yester-
day" and according to reports "a very great Number of the
German Menonists were there." If that was true, the patriot
continued, "I am ready to pronounce our Convention are
Blown up."[30] Whatever the Mennonite influence, the elections themselves were hardly more fair than under the old
charter, because radicals managed to intimidate many
others from going to the polls and used a test oath or affirmation to keep neutrals away.[31]

The new Pennsylvania constitution exempted
conscientious objectors from having actually to bear arms.
But in the patriots' spirit of forcing all Pennsylvanians into a
revolutionary peoplehood, it demanded some equivalent in
lieu of personal service.[32] The rationale was that every
member of society had a right to protection of life, liberty, and
property, and therefore each had an obligation toward that
protection's expense. The new constitution left no room for

those who held that nonresistance meant having nothing at all to do with instituting or destroying any government, or with contributing to force and bloodshed at all as the basis of social order.

In addition to the new constitution the "Test Acts" represented a clear effort to get all of Pennsylvania's various peoples to join the new revolutionary peoplehood or else be treated as aliens. In 1777 Pennsylvania's Assembly passed a bill "obliging the male white inhabitants of this state to give Assurances of Allegiance." The act declared that allegiance and protection are reciprocal and that "those who will not bear the former are not (nor ought not) to be intitled to the benefits of the latter." Every white male over eighteen was obliged to swear or affirm his loyalty to the free and independent state of Pennsylvania and to renounce the British king. Ostensibly the loyalty statement was to be voluntary: no one could be forced to take the oath or affirmation. But those who did not do so were declared ineligible to vote, hold office, serve on juries, sue for debt, or transfer real estate by deed.[33]

Most Mennonites decided they could not affirm such allegiance. And since the law provided that local authorities could require the loyalty declaration of any suspicious person traveling outside his home county, a few of them recorded their reasons. Wendel Bowman, a Mennonite from Lampeter Township in Lancaster County, was arrested for going to Philadelphia while the British army held the city. He claimed that he was on his way to obtain papers relating to his late father's estate, and had spent only a few hours inside the British lines. The authorities evidently believed him. "I was offered my Liberty on Condition of takeing the Oath," the Lampeter Mennonite later testified, "but I being bred in a religion, whose Principles together, with my Conscience, prohibits my taking an oath of enmity against any party, or individual whatsoever, therefore I must abandon my religion my conscience, and all that is, and Should be dear to me, before I am free to take the oath proposed. . . ." Bowman was ready to forfeit his property or accept imprisonment "if I act in word or deed against the United States." But he could not affirm what the Test Act required.[34]

Henry Funk of Northampton County, a brother of

Christian and formerly a Mennonite preacher, likewise refused, and a justice of the peace jailed him. At the ensuing examination, witnesses agreed that Funk had never said anything against the state. But Funk himself averred that the affirmation was "against my Conscience, because we shall be at Peace with every body and forgive all Men." He offered to pledge "to be true to the State according to the Doctrine of S. Paul Rom. 13, be subject to the higher Powers." This, however, did not satisfy the court.[35]

Mennonite expressions concerning the Test Acts reveal two elements in their thought. First, they saw the law as calling for "an oath of enmity" that ran counter to New Testament commands to love one's enemies. Second, Mennonites understood Paul's teaching in Romans to mean that God had established whatever government existed. Since the days of the Reformation in the sixteenth century, Protestants generally had assigned a positive role to the state, because Reformers had looked upon rulers who were friendly to their cause as agents working to forward God's purposes. By the same token, rulers who opposed Protestantism were thwarting God's designs. Within that Protestant system of thought a theory of revolution could find good soil.

But Mennonites saw the state as outside God's positive purposes. God depended on the church to carry out his positive will, while giving rulers authority to carry out the essentially negative task of restraining the ungodly in their wickedness. So, unlike the patriots with their Test Acts, Mennonites advocated obeying whoever was Caesar at the particular time and place, without asking whether he was good or bad. Christians could expect to suffer for their faith, so a persecuting ruler was no less established by God than was the friendly one who permitted the gospel to be preached. Their contemporaries found reasons, first religious and later secular, for declaring a ruler illegitimate; Mennonites, when pressed, could only apply a very pragmatic test: if the ruler exercised power, then that power came from God. This test was, however, very difficult to apply during revolution. Henry Funk and others like him could "be true to the state" even if the revolutionary party, now in control of

Pennsylvania, represented the state. But since at any time God might permit the king's soldiers to restore British authority, Mennonites such as Funk could not give the revolutionary state their unqualified support.

By not taking the oath or affirmation, Mennonites voluntarily put themselves outside the political process. So long as the Test Acts were in effect, patriots would not have to worry about a large turnout of Mennonites at the polls. Only a handful of Mennonites kept the right to vote by affirming allegiance under the 1777 Test Act.

Clearly those who framed the legislation intended that result. George Bryan, president of the Supreme Executive Council, argued against any effort to modify the law in favor of the nonresistant sects. There was no doubt in Bryan's mind that "no Moravian, Sweinkfelder [sic] or Menonists will be found" among those who "threaten active mischief against the State." But "if many of these people should be found to qualify themselves for enjoying all privileges, they might by appearing at elections disturb the plans layed for the defense of the State." So to relax the law at all, Bryan thought, would be both a political and a military mistake.[36]

But the law had more than those immediate political and military purposes: it was also a law to build the new, revolutionary peoplehood. At least that is the way certain zealots seem to have interpreted it. Even though the 1777 law was quite successful at the immediate goal of preventing certain groups from voting, in 1778 the Pennsylvania Assembly strengthened it by adding new penalties. Now, all those who had neither sworn nor affirmed the pledge of allegiance had to pay double taxes, give up all political rights, and be excluded from certain professions and occupations. The new law gave local authorities wider discretion to put these people in prison, confiscate their property, and banish them.[37] The immediate purpose of the legislation was surely to give authorities a way to deal more forthrightly with suspected Tories whom they could not quite indict for treason.

The law did not induce many Mennonites and Amish to make the pledge; tax lists from all sections of Pennsylvania where they lived record them almost uniformly as persons who had not complied and who therefore had to pay double taxes. In Northampton County, local patriots used it aggressively as a weapon against Mennonite and Moravian communities that they apparently considered to be too much apart from the revolutionary community they were trying to build. Justice Frederick Limbach, an ex-Moravian who apparently held a grudge against his former brethren, ordered all the adult male Mennonites in Northampton County's Upper Saucon and Upper Milford townships, and later Moravian males at Bethlehem and Emmaus, to make the pledge. They refused and he put them in jail. There is no record of particular reasons to suspect their loyalty. As Eve Yoder and Esther Bachman, the wives of imprisoned Mennonites Jacob Yoder and George Bachman, asserted in a petition: they "always beheaved peaceably & quietly and never intermedled in State Affairs But paid their Taxes & Fines, furnished Horses & Teams for the continental Service when ever demanded, and some of them have gone with their Teams as Drivers to carry Provisions to the Army of the united States for which services they have hitherto received no pay."[38]

In June 1778 ten Upper Saucon Mennonites were brought into court in Easton, Pennsylvania. There "they conscientiously scrupled to take" the necessary affirmation. So the court sentenced them to leave the state within thirty days and confiscated all their property. The sheriff sold "even their Beds, Bedings, Linen, Bibles & Books," worth "the amount of about forty thousand Pounds." A sympathetic Moravian noted that "their children's flour was taken out of the sack and even the women's spinning wheels."[39]

At Lancaster, too, in June 1778, a local diarist, Christopher Marshall, recorded that "ten of the Menonists were brought from the back part of this county to this jail, refusing to take the test; committed by Curtis Grubb." Since Grubb, an ironmaster, was a justice of the peace in Lebanon Township of present-day Lebanon County, the Mennonite prisoners probably came from that area. They were still in a Lancaster jail in August when Marshall "spent some time in conversation with some of the Justices and Assemblymen" concerning these "Menonists in prison."[40] Their cases must eventually have been dismissed, for the 1778 Lancaster County Court records tell nothing of such Mennonites' indictment.

In the end the Pennsylvania Assembly sharply reprimanded overzealous local authorities. In December 1778 it softened the law by removing all penalties except double taxation and the loss of the right to vote and hold office.[41] Mennonites continued to pay double taxes and to take no part in political life, but they could go about their daily work without fear of arrest or confiscation of property. In effect lawmakers decided they could tolerate Mennonites and other nonresistants as subjects, even if they could not get them to be citizens by the patriots' definitions.

But by then Mennonites' sense of alienation was strong. In 1778 John Ettwein brought a petition from his fellow Moravians in Bethlehem to the Pennsylvania Assembly. He recorded in his journal that during his stay in Lancaster "four of the leading Mennonites visited me several times and would have liked to have made a petition" for modifications in the Test Act. But, he said, they were most reluctant to address the Assembly as if its members were true representatives of the people. As for representation, Ettwein observed, "we and they had none, because we had been excluded from the election."[42]

However much Mennonites felt alienated and excluded, particularly from politics, they made no great protest against war taxes. It appears that virtually all of them paid the increasingly heavy amounts that the state demanded in order to meet its own war needs and the cost of Continental Congress. At some places in Pennsylvania, neighbors did band together and refuse to pay, but apparently no Mennonite or Amish names are among those indicted for such activity. Records do not identify Mennonites even as delinquent in payments; in many townships, in fact, Mennonites were tax assessors. The tax load on nonresistants, including the special levies for not serving in the militia and double ones for refusing the test oath, were very burdensome. A Quaker observed that he paid more taxes in one year than he had in the previous twenty years taken together.[43] Of course inflation may have been partly to blame.

Mennonites' tax cooperation was quite in contrast to their solid refusal to have anything to do with the militia. In the case of the militia they resisted, even beyond refusal actually to bear arms. In 1777 John Newcomer of Hempfield Township and four other Mennonite constables went to jail because they would not prepare lists of men eligible for military service. Other Mennonites were indicted for the same offense. Jacob Hartman of Lampeter Township faced this charge in November 1779.[44]

Mennonites paid taxes with little resistance largely because they read certain New Testament passages as commanding it. They might have refused, falling back on the scriptural passage that enjoins obedience to God rather than men, but most did not. Their cooperation probably was because they thought (in contrast to the thinking of the Protestant Reformers) that they should not expect any government really to promote God's highest will. With that view, they had no reason to judge whether or not governments or a government's particular policies were furthering God's highest purposes. Another question, however, was not answered so simply by Mennonites' reading of the New Testament: in a revolution, who was really Caesar?

In 1777 Pennsylvania authorities imposed a new levy of £3, 10 s. upon all who would not serve in the militia. They laid the new tax in order to equalize the burden on those who refused to drill (for whatever reason) with those who did drill in militia companies. Of course they also hoped to encourage men to take up arms.

Soon, in the Franconia district, the question of who was Ceasar got mixed with that of paying a special tax in lieu of military service. The way the two questions mixed—with each other and with more personal squabbles—upset the Franconia Mennonite community. The controversy swirled mainly around bishop Christian Funk. At least as Funk recalled thirty years later, other Franconia Mennonite preachers said they and their members could not pay the £3, 10s. tax, for the revolutionary Congress (whom they held responsible) was "rebellious and hostile to the king."[45]

Although he had urged the Franconia Township meeting in 1776 to have nothing to do with instituting or destroying any government, Christian Funk was open to the patriot cause. This, certainly, was the root of his trouble with his fellow Mennonites. Although his brother Henry was imprisoned for refusing to affirm allegiance, Christian Funk was the sort of man who might voluntarily do it, and rumor said that he had. The rumor was untrue, but there were grounds for suspicion. He did not express opposition to Congress. And unlike his fellow ministers, he advised paying the tax—arguing in effect that Congress was now the Caesar who was exercising power.[46]

The events of 1777 greatly disturbed Mennonite congregations in Funk's district. Funk was the bishop in the Franconia, Plains, Salford, Rock Hill, and Swamp congregations in present Montgomery and Bucks counties. At communion time, Funk found many members dissatisfied with him. By his later account he sought out each one to make peace. Twelve persons informed him that their only complaint was "that I had allowed payment of the tax of three pounds ten shillings, and that I had not expressed myself opposed to congress." The wives of two of his fellow preachers, Samuel Bechtel and Abraham Gehman, complained further (and erroneously) that Funk had taken the pledge required by the Test Act. Funk recalled that he was able to satisfy his critics and that the congregations celebrated the Lord's Supper in peace.[47]

Some time thereafter, in his absence according to Funk, "my fellow ministers proposed to the congregation not to pay the tax of three pounds ten shillings; a division however respecting the payment existed in the congregation." Then Andrew Ziegler, the Skippack bishop, told Funk that he (Ziegler) and Christian Moyer "had been in the congregation at Goshenhoppen, and that they had proposed that no person should pay the tax of three pounds ten shillings." To that Funk recalled replying, "'I think we can pay it.'" Funk remembered Ziegler as having been quite outspoken in his opposition. Eventually he and six other preachers visited Funk concerning the issue. By Funk's account he told them that "Caesar had not been considered by the Jews as their legitimate sovereign, and [they] thought they owed him no tribute, and that they had tempted Christ to find a cause against him." He repeated the gospel story about rendering to Caesar what is Caesar's and added: "Were Christ here, he would say, Give unto congress that which belongs to congress, and unto God what is God's." With that, the discussion quickly ended. In Funk's recollection Andrew Ziegler thereupon rose and said, "I would as soon go into war, as to pay the three pounds ten shillings if I were not concerned for my life." Funk said Ziegler then "departed in anger."[48]

Funk recorded those recollections much later, in 1807. His account leaves a picture of a nonresistant patriot surrounded by Mennonite Tories. According to that picture, Funk had the insight to recognize the rebel congress as the de facto Caesar. Events, of course, proved him right. We do not have a careful statement giving Andrew Ziegler's side of the controversy. And even in Funk's recollection there is a puzzle. If the seventy-year-old Ziegler lost his temper and stormed out of the house, what did his parting words mean? Funk put the issue always in terms of recognizing Congress as a legitimate ruler. Did Ziegler mean that rather than pay taxes to rebels he would join the British army, if he were not such a coward? Or did Ziegler imply that to pay a tax as an equivalent to military service was like serving in the army?

Christian Funk's interpretation should be taken cautiously, if at all. To be sure, Mennonites hesitated to acknowledge the new order in Pennsylvania and even longed for the happier days under king and proprietor. But that fact is not enough to explain the controversy over a particular tax imposed by the Pennsylvania Assembly in 1777. Why select this one tax, when all the acts and financial impositions of this usurping body were equally invalid? Surely the explanation must lie in the nature of the tax and not in the fact that it was levied by the Assembly elected under the 1776 Pennsylvania constitution.

Andrew Ziegler's congregations at Skippack, Methacton and Germantown were in a part of Pennsylvania where there were many Quakers. Ziegler had been active in the Friendly Association during the French and Indian War and no doubt had kept up his contacts with Quakers thereafter. In 1775 Mennonite preachers had attended the Quaker Monthly Meeting at Gwynedd in present Montgomery County and urged Friends to translate a Quaker peace statement into German for distribution among Mennonites.[49]

The issue of paying taxes to a revolutionary government disturbed many Quakers, for they, too, believed that they could take no part in setting up or pulling down princes. Quaker historian Arthur Mekeel has pointed out that by 1778 some Friends were arguing that the revolution was the Lord's work and calling for "submission to the powers which rule." They had as precedent the example of Friends in England's Glorious Revolution of 1688, who had affirmed allegiance and paid taxes to the new government of William and Mary. But even Quakers who made that argument said Friends could not pay "levies in lieu of personal military service."[50]

According to Mekeel, the issue of tax payment caused much soul-searching among the Friends. By Mekeel's analysis, Quakers distinguished three categories of taxes. There were taxes assessed for wholly civil purposes. Most Friends believed they could and should pay these, although some objected that to do so would be to recognize a government set up by force. Then there were "mixed taxes," involving both military and civil appropriations; Quakers left the question of paying these to the individual conscience. Finally there were taxes levied wholly for purposes of war. A large majority of Quakers said that their peace testimony did not allow them to pay what were purely war taxes.[51]

Moreover, Quakers agreed almost unanimously that the new tax of £3, 10s. was wholly a war tax, since authorities levied it in lieu of personal military service. Mennonites who looked to the Friends for advice in 1775 and presumably on other occasions would have received that interpretation. It seems very probable that Andrew Ziegler, Christian Moyer, and others who opposed payment of this one specific tax were listening to the Quakers.

The Friends' 1778 Yearly Meeting received requests from several local meetings for a ruling even on taxes for the upkeep of roads and the support of the poor.[52] Some Friends and doubtlessly also some Mennonites objected to paying taxes "more on Account of the Authority that demands the

Taxes than because they are used for War."[53] Those who did were of course making a judgment about which government was truly Caesar.

Some Mennonites evidently agreed with the position of the majority of Quakers—that paying a tax that was expressly a substitute for military service was wrong. But for both Friends and Mennonites, especially for Mennonites, there was a serious complication: a long tradition of paying any and all sums demanded by legitimate government. The problem was a nagging doubt that the blood-spilling rebels had any legitimate claim to authority. Whether many Mennonites and Amish hesitated to pay simply because a tax was a war tax is unclear. In 1775 a Presbyterian minister, preaching at Lancaster in support of defensive warfare, denounced Mennonites because, he said, they paid "a foolish trick on their consciences." The trick was that they refused to pay their taxes and yet "let others come and take their money," even taking pains to put the money where the authorities could "find it handily." According to the minister Jesus had "paid his tax as a peaceable member of the commonwealth." But, "had our Lord been a Mennonist he would have refused to pay tribute to support war."[54]

There was of course fine logic in the minister's statement of what a Mennonite Jesus would have done. Yet as an advocate of just war the Presbyterian divine probably had not thought nearly as long and hard as had the Quakers and Mennonites about how to be nonresistant and yet honor legitimate government, nor had he experienced their practical dilemmas. In any case, laws passed during the American revolution enabled governments to collect militia fines and other military exactions from "Quakers and Menonists" by seizing their property. Under the circumstances, conscientious scruples against paying war taxes could hardly translate into tax resistance or appear as a defense in court records. In the absence of such records, it is impossible to tell how much genuine tax resistance there may have been among Mennonites and Amish. Although Ziegler and Moyer kept most Mennonites in the Franconia district on their side, it is impossible to tell whether, as they accepted the position of the Quaker majority, they represented a consensus of Mennonite thought on the war tax question.

The difference of opinion on the payment of a tax in lieu of military service and on the wider question of allegiance to a government of rebels combined to cause the rift in the Franconia-area Mennonite community. The division was so deep that in 1778 Christian Funk's fellow ministers, temporarily by acting alone, and then more permanently in a meeting with laymen present, ordered him to quit preaching. (Evidently Funk was not present; by his account, he had not been notified.) Thereupon Funk and his supporters began to worship separately. At first the Funkites held their services in the Franconia meetinghouse on alternate Sundays when the regular congregation did not use it, but in time they were locked out. Funk ordained his brother John as a minister, and a son-in-law, John Detweiler, as a deacon. His older brother Henry, the former Northampton County preacher, also joined him.[55]

In 1781 authorities of Northampton County demanded that Henry Funk pay fines for not performing military service. If he were still a recognized minister of the gospel he would have been exempt from such service, but of course some years earlier the Franconia Mennonites had stopped him from preaching. Now a prominent Skippack-area patriot named Daniel Hiester, Jr., rose to Henry Funk's defense. Hiester argued that the Mennonites had read the erstwhile preacher out of their good graces because he had taken the pledge required under the Test Acts, and also because as a miller he had "done a great deal of Business for the publick." Hiester further pointed out that Henry was now preaching for Christian Funk's group, and that Christian was "a remarkably strong Whig" (meaning, of course, a supporter of the revolution). According to the Skippack patriot Christian Funk's followers were the few Mennonites "well affected" toward the patriots' cause.[56]

Hiester's account might seem to support Christian Funk's 1807 explanation of what had divided Franconia Mennonites in 1777. But when Northampton County authorities held hearings on Henry Funk's case, they uncovered rather different evidence. Five Mennonites named Philip Geisinger, Jacob Moyer, John Hiestand, Jacob Weis, and John Schontz testified that the Mennonites had made Henry a preacher about 1770 (it was in 1768) and that he had preached for about three years, but that he had fallen into quarreling with his fellow-Mennonites until they forbade him to preach any more. Under further questioning one witness explained that the quarrels had come because "Mr. Henry Funk was too absolute," and wanted the whole Mennonite "Society to be subject to him." Still another witness, a Mennonite named Jacob Scleip, added that the silencing of Funk as a preacher was "because he was a horse swapper;" and still another cited a specific case in which, he alleged, Funk "did not stick to the truth." Now, the authorities heard, Funk was preaching for his brother Christian's group but did not have authority to baptize.[57]

Such evidence suggests of course that the division surrounding Christian Funk was far more complicated than just the questions surrounding the special war tax. Actually Christian left three different versions of the unhappy events, with rather different explanations. That 1807 account put heavy blame on Andrew Ziegler and Christian Moyer (Funk's uncle), picturing them as sowing division by exploiting the tax question. But a narrative that Funk had composed and printed much earlier in 1785 when events were much fresher, did not turn the case on the tax question at all. By Christian Funk's own 1785 account a certain Jacob Oberholzer had charged before the church that "Christian Funk and his children are very proud and obstinate—if they are spoken to they disregard it." According to the charge, Funk and his family made fun of the sermons preached by the other ministers, and "laugh and ridicule us." 'Besides," Oberholzer continued, "Christian Funk has gone to Peter Cram, John Kindig and Michael Schumacher and advised them to take the affirmation of allegiance." Funk, if his own account was correct, thereupon asked pardon for any error. Told that he had to stand against taking the affirmation of allegiance, he replied: "of that I am clear." The church authorities acting in council nevertheless "suspended me of my functions, and resolved that I should not preach the gospel until I had changed my mind."[58]

In a third narrative, written in 1809, Funk suggested

that the separation happened because he was satisfied with the new government. But that account alluded also to various other charges concerning cheating at Funk's mill and the selling of sheep and a horse. Evidently the business of living in a small rural community caused frictions that needed only a good excuse to come into the open.[59] And evidently the Test Act and tax issues were occasions but not the sole or even the prime reasons for Christian Funk's removal from the ministry and for the first schism among Mennonites in America.

Christian and Henry Funk and their friends are the exceptions that prove the rule. Outsiders such as Hiester, viewing the Mennonite communities, saw only the Funk group as "well affected" towards the American revolution. Christian Funk himself wrote before 1784 that "as far as I know, not only all the congregations, but also all my relatives, excepting three, were of the opinion that congress was composed of rebels, and therefore no government."[60]

With a few exceptions in each region, Mennonites in southeastern Pennsylvania, Maryland, and Virginia were reluctant to give their support to the patriot cause. Many were no doubt genuinely neutral, avoiding any part in questions of state and leaving to God the question of establishing and overthrowing rulers. Others, while remaining true to the biblical teaching on nonresistance, wished in their hearts for return to British rule.

The Amish, too, held back from any involvement. There survives a fragment of a document by an Amishman named Hans Lantz which, according to historian S. Duane Kauffman, "seems to be a well-defined statement of position regarding the American Revolution." Lantz listed Scripture references that taught Christians "to give all just obedience . . . faithfulness, love, honor, and taxes, [and] benevolence," to the king, "and to pray for" him and "live in harmony." He also paraphrased the affirmation of allegiance taken by non-British immigrants to Pennsylvania, and added: "I wish and pray that God will give our King a wise and sensible heart and a willing mind to live cheerfully and faithfully in all commandments and laws of God."[61] Since we cannot be sure of either the document's date or its purpose, Lantz's words are difficult to interpret. But other sources suggest that Amish thought was close to the ideas Lantz expressed.

Amish tradition has long told of seven or more members of the Berks County Amish community being imprisoned and even temporarily sentenced to death at Reading, Pennsylvania. The offense of John Hertzler, Jacob and Stephen Kauffman, Jacob Mast, Christian Schmucker, Christian and Johannes Zug (Zook) was refusal to take up arms against England. Like the case of those Lebanon County Mennonites jailed at Lancaster in 1778, the episode does not appear in surviving court records.[62] However there is official record of that case of the Amishman named Isaac Kauffman, of Bern Township in Berks County, who was indicted and jailed in Reading in 1779 for calling a man a rebel who tried to take his horse for the army. And the names of at least nine Amishmen, seven of them from Bern Township, had "Tory" written next to them on a 1779 tax list. The Amish were seven of twenty-six so designated, or 27 percent of the alleged Tories on the list. If any had committed specific offenses, the list does not record them.[63]

In fact, although the great majority of Amish and Mennonites took a dim view of the revolution, very few violated their peace principles to offer direct assistance to the British. There was that case recounted, perhaps accurately and perhaps not, by Christopher Sauer III of the printing family. According to Sauer, in 1780 a certain Christian Musselman carried a petition from Mennonites and Dunkers in Lancaster County to the British commander in New York City. About to be stopped by a patriot patrol, Musselman destroyed the document which was addressed to the king, and only a summary reached the commander, General Sir Henry Clinton. Sauer reported that those who drew up the petition were Michael Kauffman, Sr., Michael Kauffman, Jr., Philip Shoemaker, and Melchior Brenneman. The Mennonites and Dunkers, he said, not only hoped "to be reinstated in the enjoyment of their former blessings," but were also ready "to assist with their goods and chattels to bring about so desirable an event."[64]

In his pro-British zeal, Sauer may have exaggerated that statement. It is likely that the real point of the Mennonite and Dunker message lay more in another concern Sauer said they expressed: a hope that the British would not construe their sowing grain and planting corn as working to aid the patriots.[65] That concern, at least, was more consistent with the Amish and Mennonite style. For that style was more concerned with the rhythm of God's seasons and with the agricultural calendar than with politics. "Could not leave home," a Lancaster County militia officer once noted on his roster next to the name of a "conscientiously scrupulous" Mennonite, Jacob Hoover, for " 'twas seeding time."[66]

Even if those Mennonites and Dunkers of Lancaster County took the dangerous step of sending a message secretly to the British commander, any offer of assistance they made to the king's soldiers was not for very active help. At most they would hand over flour and meal and pay taxes to the British with better grace than to the patriots. And apparently more Mennonites were ready to give affirmation of allegiance to the loyalist than to the patriot side.

Two loyalist recruiters in western Maryland developed a special affirmation "intended for Menonists, German Baptists, and Quakers, who do not take an Oath or Personally bear Arms." By their own account "Near five Hundred" persons in Pennsylvania, Maryland, and Virginia took either this affirmation or another intended for persons beyond military age. The affirmation for loyalist sympathizers in the peace churches pledged "that I will bear true and faithful Allegiance, to the King of Great Britain, and that I will aid, abet, and assist, his said Majesty, against all enemies and Opposers whatsoever (so far as is consistant [sic], with my religious principles)."[67]

Mennonites and Amish came through the American revolution with their commitment to nonresistance intact. Only a small percentage compromised their faith by taking an active part with either side. Quaker historian Arthur Mekeel has calculated that about 17 percent of the adult male members of the Society of Friends incurred discipline from their meetings for violating Quakers' peace testimony; approximately 13 percent were disowned, that is, put out of the group.[68] There are no records that allow such precise calculation of Mennonites and Amish deviation but certainly the percentage would have been even smaller.

Otherwise, the wartime experiences of the historic peace churches were remarkably alike. Majority opinion among all three groups, Mennonites (and Amish), Friends, and Dunkers, probably favored the old regime. However, each group advocated strict neutrality for its members. One can of course interpret that neutrality as having been more favorable to the British cause than to the patriot, since inaction and peaceful submission were contrary to revolution. Patriots often interpeted it that way, and there is some basis for a pro-Tory reputation that some scholars have helped give the peace churches.[69] Historian Wallace Brown, after a careful study of loyalists in the revolution, wrote in 1975 that "Quakers, Mennonites, Dunkers, and Schwenkfelders were conservative and by simply staying aloof they helped the British...." Yet Brown also added in the same sentence, "but most were genuinely neutral." Such Toryism was not an activist, positive Toryism. Perhaps it should not be called Toryism at all.[70] At least for Mennonites and Amish, the question of which government was in charge was not the central one. The important question was how to remain faithful to their pacifist understanding of the Christian gospel.[71]

In some ways the revolutionary experience broadened the peace stand of Mennonites and Amish (and other pacifists). Prior to 1777 in Pennsylvania, Maryland, and Virginia they had enjoyed exemption from both militia duty and militia fines. But now they had to take stands on whether to provide substitutes, give nonmilitary support to the war effort, and pay special war taxes. These stands were opportunities for expanding their peace testimony. Generally, they refused to send substitutes. Regarding nonmilitary support to the "common cause," Mennonites and others clearly searched for a way to contribute to society in wartime without giving direct aid to military efforts; they made voluntary contributions, and hoped and asked that such contributions might go to war sufferers and other needy people rather than to armies. They did not realize that hope very well; in fact, they seem not to have tried very hard to realize it.

As for paying the equivalent of military service, Mennonites protested, yet acquiesced to the system by which revolutionary lawmakers asked for money as a way of getting pacifists to take part in the war effort.[72] In doing so, the revolution's generation set a precedent. Not until the latter twentieth century would a later generation of Mennonites raise any notable voice to question the system that let them "purchase peace of conscience." Indeed, in the US Civil War Mennonites would widely accept even the sending of substitutes.[73]

Dissatisfaction with the new government and a lingering desire to live under the milder rule of King George III may have motivated, to some degree, some Mennonites to migrate to Ontario, or "Upper Canada," beginning in 1786. Quakers, Mennonites, and Dunkers forfeited many political rights during the war, and taxes continued to be heavy. In 1793 Upper Canada established a Militia Act which exempted conscientious objectors from personal militia duty. The Act specified fines in lieu of such duty, fines which ten or twenty years later would seem to Mennonites quite heavy. But already before that Act, in Pennsylvania there was the idea that Canada might provide a freer climate for pacifists. The *Pennsylvania Gazette* of Philadelphia reported in 1789 that "thirty families of the people called Menonists are about to emigrate from Lancaster County to Niagara, on purpose to avoid the disagreeable consequences of our ridiculous and tyrannical test law."[74]

Actually the motives for migration to Ontario were probably more complex than simply the effects of the Test Act. The first Mennonites to go in 1786 went from Bucks County, Pennsylvania, settling in the Niagara Peninsula on a tract known as "the Twenty" because of its location some twenty miles west of the Niagara River. Very probably what moved them, as Canadian Mennonite historian Frank Epp has speculated, was a mixture of wishing to live under British rule, desire for land, and their being, in Epp's words, "fringe Mennonites." In the 1780s and 1790s other Mennonites went, some of them from Lancaster County. According to historians Marcus Lee Hansen and John B. Brebner, such people had come through the American revolution "under the shadow of disloyalty, subjected to many annoyances because of their non-resistance." Probably they moved also because rising prices for Pennsylvania land were making it difficult to establish sons on farms. In about 1799 the migration swelled, as in that year several more from Bucks County purchased 1,100 more acres in the Twenty. More Pennsylvania Mennonites moved to the Markham area north of Toronto, and also along the Grand River to an area so German that the town was named Berlin—present-day Kitchener.[75]

Whatever mixture of motives for the Ontario trek, the greatest result of the whole revolutionary experience for Mennonites and Amish was to heighten their sense of separation from their neighbors. Rather suddenly, they had found themselves to be a people somewhat apart from the new people the patriots were forming. So they (and apparently Dunkers and Quakers also) emerged from the American revolution to be, more than before, "the quiet in the land."

The political arena, particularly, was not for these newly quieted pacifists, at least not to the degree it had been in colonial times. Under the Test Acts all those who refused the pledge of revolutionary allegiance lost the right to vote, hold office, or serve on juries. In 1783 Virginia repealed all penalties against Quakers and Mennonites. Maryland restored political privileges in 1784 and North Carolina in 1787. Most importantly, Pennsylvania restored them in 1789.[76] Some Mennonites did return to voting. In an 1808 election, Lancaster County candidates on the Federalist ticket are known to have thought it worthwhile to make a special appeal to voters who had scruples against bearing arms.[77] And numerous protests made by some Mennonites from time to time against Mennonite political involvement indicate that many must have been politically active.

Yet the Federalists' appeal probably was not nearly as worthwhile as it would have been before the revolution. Francis Herr in that 1790 writing in which he argued against participating in politics asked: "If we for the gospel and Christ's sake cannot hold any office, how should we be capable to elect others into office?"[78] In other words, Herr assumed that pacifists could not hold office, and upon that premise argued also that they should not vote. And although Herr was apparently too unbending on such matters to suit most Mennonites, there is evidence that quite a few agreed with both his premise and his argument. The efforts of American patriots to form a new national peoplehood had not worked well with Mennonites. Quite a few Mennonites had turned back to being subjects more than citizens. The American revolution had made Mennonites more than ever a people apart.

AFTERWORD

WHO THEN WAS THIS
NEW-WORLD MENNONITE?

"What then is the American, this new man?" a noted immigrant to America, Hector St. John de Crèvecoeur, asked in an essay first published in London in 1782. He answered his own question by telling enthusiastically of a new United States of America where Catholics, Lutherans, Reformed, and Quakers lived and worked side by side. But he was equally enthusiastic about influences that he thought would make Americans become more and more alike, with ethnic differences fading as time passed, and sectarian zeal inevitably giving way to some sort of common creed and faith. Among Americans, he exulted, "the name of Englishman, Frenchman, and European is lost, and in like manner, the strict modes of Christianity as practised in Europe are lost also."[1]

Crèvecoeur wrote as if his remarks applied to all America, but actually if they were accurate at all, they applied mainly to certain regions. The immigrant writer's remarks were "an idealization . . . rooted in the experience of the Middle Colonies," historian Michael Zuckerman has suggested. "The diversity and disestablishment he hailed as generically American were primarily properties of New York, New Jersey, and Pennsylvania," plus the region that stretched from western Maryland and the Shenandoah Valley of Virginia into the southern backcountry.[2] The regions Zuckerman named included almost all of the eighteenth-century North American Mennonite world. And indeed, by the latter eighteenth century the Mennonites and Amish of that world were, to some degree, new persons. They did not necessarily share all of Crèvecoeur's notions, but they could not escape the reality that inspired the essayist's prose. More than an ocean and the passing of seventy-five or eighty years separated Mennonite farmers of Bucks or Lancaster County in Pennsylvania from the harried Swiss refugees who had reached the Netherlands in the first decade of the century.

To begin with, Mennonite farmers in Pennsylvania were comfortably well-off, by both European and American standards. With abundant resources, hard work, and mutual aid they had been able to turn their frequently extensive acreages into some of the most productive farmlands in North America. Even as compared to other German settlers, who had a wide reputation for good farming methods, Mennonites (along with Schwenkfelders) held the best reputation of all.[3] Unlike early Mennonites who had been driven by persecution to scratch a living from limited plots of marginal soils in remote mountain areas of Switzerland or war-ravaged and depopulated sections of the German lands along the Rhine, the Mennonites in America were not subsistence farmers. Already in various places in Europe, Amish and Mennonite farmers had won recognition for being able to transform marginal lands into fertile and productive fields. And as they did so, they produced for a growing market economy.[4]

In America, immigrant Amish and Mennonite farmers quickly became part of a similar pattern. Historians have often assumed that in eighteenth-century America, except in tobacco- or rice-growing regions, farms were either pioneer clearings quite far from markets or, if somewhat more developed, were still largely self-sufficient. But in fact farmers of southeastern Pennsylvania, western Maryland, and the Shenandoah Valley of Virginia were producing for the market and were part of the larger Atlantic economy. Throughout the fifty years before the American revolution, agricultural production developed along commercial-farming lines, especially in areas close to Philadelphia but in other areas as well. Although land values rose faster than estimated value of other kinds of property, farmers were prosperous. As the rural economy prospered, it supported trades and professions that in turn became alternatives to farming and to some extent reduced demand for land and the need to subdivide farms and reduce average farm sizes.[5]

James T. Lemon concluded from his study of Chester and Lancaster counties of eighteenth-century Pennsylvania that this fact of producing for ready markets was very important for Mennonite and Amish life. Producing for the market provided money to buy land, and the ability to purchase and subdivide extensive acreage did much to shape settlement patterns and to create viable, ongoing Mennonite and Amish communities. "Even Mennonites could maintain relatively strong community structure only through the land market;" Lemon concluded, "large tracts were bought for family members and co-religionists."[6] The sense of community rested in part on ability to function in a market economy.

At least in Lemon's view, the Mennonite and Amish peoples' very understanding of community was modified by the impact of the market economy centered in Philadelphia. The clearest evidence of that modification was the manner in which Mennonites wrote their wills. "Most telling," Lemon wrote, was "the degree of insecurity around old age." And "surprisingly this insecurity occurred amongst Mennonites," for they carefully prepared lists "of commodities and money to be supplied to widows."[7] Perhaps in reading the wills, Lemon should not have inferred insecurity or weakness of community so much as simply Swiss-German thoroughness. But truly, individual Mennonites did not seem to write their wills to reflect an assumption that they could look to their religious communities to provide what their widows and children would have needed.

Historian James A. Henretta has questioned some of Lemon's conclusions, arguing that Lemon's own evidence gives a picture of "language and creed" exerting "considerable influence on the whereabouts of people." Rather than showing so much change, the data seemed to Henretta to point to persistence of communal values and to indicate that certain characteristics of culture in southeastern Pennsylvania kept people from becoming fully involved in the market economy. For those eighteenth-century Pennsylvanians, he suggested, "maximizing of profits was less important than meeting household needs and maintaining established social relationships."[8]

Henretta was not writing specifically about Mennonites and Amish; their experience in eighteenth-century America suggests that both he and Lemon were correct. Mennonite and Amish settlers functioned in a society that had, in Lemon's words, brought the "common northwest European qualities of the nuclear family and private control of land" and adapted them on a larger scale to the North American landscape. They accumulated property and apparently regarded land as a commodity under the "unlimited and exclusive control" of the landowner. Mennonites, more than virtually anybody else, seemed "anxious to seek higher yields per acre by more astute [farming] practices." Mennonite landowners seem to have preferred to sell land to one another, rather than to people not of their faith. They practiced mutual aid. And, as historian Martin Brackbill said of the Conestoga Manor area of Lancaster County, Mennonite (and Amish) families seeking new land often chose to settle among others of their faith, even when this meant paying a far higher price than in other, even nearby areas.[9]

Both Amish and Mennonite settlers increased production by expanding the labor force. Invariably this meant purchasing servants, usually newly arrived German or Scotch-Irish redemptioners who would then work for some years in servitude to pay off the debts they had incurred for their passage. Or the settlers hired workers by the year, or for shorter periods. And of course having sizable families meant sons and daughters for labor. Virtually none of the Mennonites and Amish bought slaves, for they opposed slavery on religious grounds—either directly, or because of scruples against conspicuous consumption. (In southeastern Pennsylvania slaveholding was more a matter of conspicuous consumption than of economic necessity,[10] and for Mennonites and Amish conspicuous consumption was also a religious question.) Religious refusal to own slaves did not, however, mean a choice against increasing agricultural production. There were other ways of expanding the work force.

Quite frequently Mennonites received non-Mennonite

indentured servants into their churches, especially German servants. Occasionally they even received some persons of non-Mennonite and non-Swiss, non-Germanic origin. The prominent Mennonite bishop and leader Benjamin Hershey baptized a former servant named Thomas Sullivan, who was born in Ireland. A Scotch-Irishman, Peter Johnson, originally an indentured servant in Berks County, was among the founders of the Trissels Mennonite congregation in northern Rockingham County, Virginia. From time to time a Mennonite daughter married such a man, showing even more strongly that ethnic lines did not define the community as much as did religious ones.[11]

As Crèvecoeur and other contemporaries observed, one characteristic of American society in the latter eighteenth century was that there was not much religious proselytizing.[12] Quite a few Mennonite congregations grew, but the growth did not come from evangelism. Instead, it was apparently a result of natural population increase. Marriages across denominational lines brought some new persons into Mennonite congregations, despite official efforts of Mennonites and other churches to keep marriages within the faith. It is not clear, however, that Mennonites won more than they lost through interfaith unions, since some who had been reared Mennonite united with their partners' churches. In any case, Mennonites fit Crèvecoeur's image of virtually no outright proselytizing. Their pattern may have been due partly to fairly strong ethnic feeling that existed despite the rather frequent intermarriages.

Despite that ethnic feeling, relations among Mennonites and other Pennsylvania-German religious groups, both the Lutheran and Reformed "church" people and the so-called sects such as the Dunkers and the Schwenkfelders, remained friendly. That friendliness owed much to the common language of Pietism. As historian Robert Friedmann has demonstrated, the first contacts between Anabaptists and Pietists in Switzerland in the closing years of the seventeenth century resulted in an outburst of evangelism.[13] In America, early in the eighteenth century, Count Zinzendorf and his Moravians brought another burst of such evangelism, and so did the first generation of Dunkers. But by the

latter eighteenth century Pietism was blurring denominational distinctives to the point of discouraging evangelism
and efforts to proselytize across denominational lines. As
that happened, each religious group came more and more to
be an inherited faith.

Eighteenth-century Mennonites took on much of
Pietism's flavor, absorbing it through hymns, devotional
writings, union-church contacts, and schools that people of
various Pennsylvania-German denominations shared in
common. As a result of Pietism and of their changed circumstances, Mennonites and Amish underwent some crisis of
faith and practice. Some of them resolved the crisis, at least
temporarily and for themselves personally, by accepting the
more individualistic message of emergent American revivalism as it came through the preaching especially of Methodists, United Brethren, and Baptists. Others turned to
humility and to reviving the traditions of their own faiths in
order to renew Mennonite and Amish religious life. Unlike
those who chose American revivalism, those who chose the
latter course sought renewal through stronger religious
community more than through individualism.

During the revolutionary years nonresistance raised a
barrier to full participation in American life, so that by the
early 1780s Mennonites and Amish (and other nonresistant
peoples) found themselves somewhat isolated. To find
themselves treated so much as a people apart was something
of a shock. It probably made them more inclined after the
revolution to be "the quiet in the land" in a system that
allowed them once more to "purchase peace of conscience."
To be sure, after the war they occasionally petitioned for
relief from having to pay fines in order to be exempted from
military drills, and it was several years before all state governments restored the franchise to them. But they rees-
tablished their peace with the political system, and fit back
into it, if perhaps rather more cautiously than before the
revolution. To quite a degree, they once again participated.[14]

In 1795 a Methodist preacher named William Duke offered some insight into the way Americans looked at Mennonites as the century neared its end. In a work commenting
"...on the Present State of Religion in Maryland," Duke

said of Mennonites and Dunkers that they were a problem to society because they had a "scheme of discipline" that was divisive to the social order; it clashed, he said, "with the common methods of government and civil society." Yet the problem was not "that they intend any disturbance or innovation," for they did not. They were "remarkably peaceable and passive," and being so, they were "readily tolerated and excused."[15] Duke had captured a double truth. Mennonite ideas of the believers church, along with nonresistance, close-knit community, and lay leadership, did indeed imply some challenge to the accepted norms of the larger society. Nevertheless Mennonites (and Amish) had found a place within American denominationalism, for Americans found they could tolerate them. In the nation's pluralism and denominationalism there was a niche for these hardworking and successful farmers, craftsmen, and small-scale businessmen, and their families.[16] Even though the events of the revolutionary era had made Mennonites perceive themselves to a degree as a people apart, eighteenth-century America had also made room for them.

KEY TO FOOTNOTES

AMC   Archives of the Mennonite Church, located on the campus of Goshen College, Goshen, Ind.

BCHS   Berks County Historical Society, Reading, Pa.

EPMHL   Eastern Pennsylvania Mennonite Historical Library, at Christopher Dock Mennonite High School, Lansdale, Pa.

HSP   Historical Society of Pennsylvania, Philadelphia, Pa.

LCHS   Lancaster County Historical Society, Lancaster, Pa.

LMHS   Lancaster Mennonite Historical Society, Lancaster, Pa.

ME   *Mennonite Encyclopedia*

MHL   Mennonite Historical Library, Goshen College, Goshen, Ind.

MQR   *The Mennonite Quarterly Review*

PGSPA   Pennsylvania German Society Proceedings and Addresses

PMHB   The Pennsylvania Magazine of History and Biography

NOTES

CHAPTER 1

1. Meroes Claessen te Meer, Paulus Preyers, Heuven Walts, Willem Holter, and Adolf van Dusheyst, from the congregation at Krefeld, to Hendrick Damen and Anthony Gotschalk, servants of the congregation of God in Rotterdam, December 19, 1671, #1248, Papers of the Dutch Mennonites' Commissie voor de Buitenlandsche Nooden (Commission for Foreign Needs) (hereafter cited as CFN), Archives of the Dutch Mennonite Church, Amsterdam Municipal Archives, Amsterdam, The Netherlands. Transcripts, in Dutch and German, of a selection of these documents are in a collection identified as "Dutch Papers" at HSP. The letter is also in Nanne van der Zijpp, "The Dutch Aid the Swiss Mennonites," in Cornelius J. Dyck, ed., *A Legacy of Faith* (Newton, Kan., 1962), 142-43. See also, Valentin Huthwohl and Johann Clements to Hans Vlamingh, January 1, 1672, and Jacob Everling to Hans Vlamingh, January 4, 1672, #1249, Dutch Papers.

2. Congregation at Krefeld to Damen and Gotschalk (note 1).

3. Cornelius J. Dyck, ed., *An Introduction to Mennonite History: A Popular History of the Anabaptists and the Mennonites* (Scottdale, Pa., and Kitchener, Ont., 1981), 36-49; Harold S. Bender, *Conrad Grebel, c. 1498-1526: The Founder of the Swiss Brethren Sometimes Called Anabaptists* (Scottdale, Pa., 1950), 89-136; John L. Ruth, *Conrad Grebel, Son of Zurich* (Scottdale, Pa., and Kitchener, Ont., 1975), 73-106. Ruth based his popular, literary biography of Grebel on Bender's scholarly one. John Howard Yoder, "The Turning Point in the Zwinglian Reformation," *MQR,* 32 (April 1958), 128-40; *ME,* 11, 569-74, Dyck, Bender, and Yoder all make the point that since Zwingli was the one who changed the reform's direction, the Anabaptists did not break with Zwingli, but Zwingli broke from them. Cf. Robert C. Walton, "Was There a Turning Point in the Zwinglian Reformation?" *MQR,* 42 (January 1968), 45-56. See also, James M. Stayer, Werner O. Packull, and Klaus Depperman, "From Monogenesis to Polygenesis: The Historical Discussion of Anabaptist Origins," *MQR,* 49 (April 1975), 83-121. For an anthology on Anabaptist studies in recent years, see James M. Stayer and Werner O. Packull, trans. and eds., *The Anabaptists and Thomas Müntzer* (Dubuque, Iowa, and Toronto, Ont., 1980).

4. Ibid., entire note.

5. Dyck, *Introduction to Mennonite History,* 46-56; Ruth, *Conrad Grebel,* 104-45; Bender, *Conrad Grebel,* 137-62; *ME,* I, 113. For the story of the congregation that emerged out of this first Anabaptist baptism, see Fritz Blanke, *Brothers in Christ: The History of the Oldest Anabaptist Congregation, Zollikon, near Zurich, Switzerland* (Scottdale, Pa., 1961).

6. Dyck, *Introduction to Mennonite History,* 50-56, 62-100; Bender, *Conrad Grebel,* 94, 148-55; Ruth, *Conrad Grebel,* 74.

7. Dyck, *Introduction to Mennonite History,* 71-80; *ME,* II, 851-57.

8. Dyck, *Introduction to Mennonite History,* 101-104; *ME,* III, 777-83.

9. Grebel letter trans. by Walter Rauschenbusch, first published in *The American Journal of Theology,* 9 (January 1905), 91-99, reprinted in Bender, *Conrad Grebel,* 282-87; Ruth, *Conrad Grebel,* 91-96; C. Arnold Snyder, "The Life and Thought of Michael Sattler," manuscript in process for publication by Herald Press (originally, PhD dissertation, McMaster University, 1981), chs. 6, 11.

10. Walter Klaassen, *Anabaptism: Neither Catholic nor Protestant* (Waterloo, Ont., 1981).

11. Snyder, "Life and Thought of Michael Sattler," ch. 9; Dyck, *Introduction to Mennonite History,* 136-45; Harold S. Bender, "The Anabaptist Vision," first published in *Church History,* 13 (March 1944), 3-24, and reprinted in Guy F. Hershberger, ed., *Recovery of the Anabaptist Vision* (Scottdale, Pa., 1957), 29-54. See Hershberger, *Recovery,* for other interpretive works on the rise and meaning of Anabaptism.

12. John H. Yoder, trans. and ed., *The Legacy of Michael Sattler* (Scottdale, Pa., 1973), 27-54; Dyck, *Introduction to Mennonite History,* 56-61; *ME,* IV, 427-34; Myron S. Augsburger, "Michael Sattler, d. 1527: Theologian of the Swiss Brethren Movement," ThD dissertation (1964), Union Theological Seminary.

13. John Horsch, *Mennonites in Europe* (Scottdale, Pa., 1942), 93-114; Dyck, *Introduction to Mennonite History,* 54-55, 63-67, 113-26, 147; *ME,* II, 162 [the "Egg" article]. For hundreds of stories of Anabaptist martyrs, see Thieleman J. van Braght, *The Bloody Theater or Martyrs Mirror of the Defenseless Christians* (Scottdale, Pa., and Kitchener, Ont., 1979).

14. Dyck, *Introduction to Mennonite History,* 105-13, 133; *ME,* III, 577-83; Horsch, *Mennonites in Europe,* 238-39.

15. Dyck, *Introduction to Mennonite History,* 133-35, 150-60; *ME,* I, 102; for the broader economic involvement of the sea-related industries that Mennonites dominated, see Richard W. Unger,

"Dutch Herrings, Technology, and International Trade in the Seventeenth Century," *Journal of Economic History*, 40 (June 1980), 253-79.
    16. Dyck, *Introduction to Mennonite History*, 129-33; *ME*, IV, 330-31, III, 517-19; Horsch, *Mennonites in Europe*, 240-42; Thieleman J. van Braght, *Het Bloedigh Tooneel der Doops-gesinde en Weereloose Christenen* (Dordrecht, 1660). The 1685 edition added *of Martelaers Spiegel (Martyrs Mirror)* after *Tooneel*. The first German edition was translated and published in 1748-1749 at Ephrata, Pa.; the first English edition, Lampeter Square, Pa., 1837. See *ME*, III, 527-28.
    17. *ME*, I, 218-23; Horsch, *Mennonites in Europe*, 328-35.
    18. Dyck, *Introduction to Mennonite History*, 127-29; Horsch, *Mennonites in Europe*, 233-37.
    19. Dyck, *Introduction to Mennonite History*, 129-35; Alfred C. Underwood, *A History of the English Baptists* (London, 1947), 26, 39-45.
    20. *ME*, III, 517-19.
    21. Van der Zijpp, "Dutch Aid the Swiss Mennonites" (note 1), 136-45; Dyck, *Introduction to Mennonite History*, 147; C. Henry Smith, *The Mennonite Immigration to Pennsylvania in the Eighteenth Century* (Norristown, Pa., 1929), 55-57; Delbert L. Gratz, *Bernese Anabaptists and Their American Descendants* (Scottdale, Pa., 1953), 31-37.
    22. Van der Zijpp, "Dutch Aid the Swiss Mennonites," 139-40; *ME*, I, 102-103, II, 344-45.
    23. Van der Zijpp, "Dutch Aid the Swiss Mennonites," 139-40; Horsch, *Mennonites in Europe*, 252-53; *ME*, II, 344-45; On the Polish exiles in Holland, see George H. Williams, *The Polish Brethren* (Missoula, Mont., 1980), 639ff.
    24. Van Braght, *Bloody Theater or Martyrs Mirror* (note 13), 15.
    25. Robert Friedmann, *Mennonite Piety Through the Centuries: Its Genius and Its Literature* (Goshen, Ind., 1949), 159-64, 105-26, 172; J[ohn] C. Wenger, *The Doctrines of the Mennonites* (Scottdale, Pa., 1950), 86-87.
    26. Dyck, *Introduction to Mennonite History*, 147-48; Friedmann, *Mennonite Piety*, 35-36; Horsch, *Mennonites in Europe*, 246-48, 263; Irvin B. Horst, "The Dordrecht Confession of Faith: 350 Years," *Pennsylvania Mennonite Heritage*, 5 (July 1982), 2-8. The Dordrecht Confession was first printed in Dutch as *Confessie ende Vredehandelinghe tot Dordrecht anno 1632* (Haarlem, 1633), in German as *Christliches Glaubensbekenntnus* (Amsterdam, 1664), and in English as *The Christian Confession of the Faith of the harmless Christians, in the Netherlands, known by the name of Mennonists* (Philadelphia, 1727). The English printing of Dordrecht in Philadelphia, accompanied also by a German edition, was the first printing effort by Mennonites in America.
For the complete text of the Dordrecht Confession, see John C. Wenger, *History of the Mennonites of the Franconia Conference* (Scottdale, Pa., 1938), Appendix XII, 435-63. (Wenger used "Dortrecht" as the spelling.) According to a Wenger article in *ME*, II, 92, Swiss Mennonites never accepted Dordrecht, although Swiss-origin Mennonites in the Palatinate did.
    27. *ME*, I, 219-22.
    28. *ME*, I, 98-99, 219-22; Dyck, *Introduction to Mennonite History*, 148-49; Horsch, *Mennonites in Europe*, 262-65.
    29. Martin H. Brackbill, "A Communication," *MQR*, 22 (July 1948), 188-92; Horsch, *Mennonites in Europe*, 262-63; John A. Hostetler, *Amish Society* (Baltimore, 1980), 31-39.
    30. Hostetler, *Amish Society*, 40-46; Dyck, *Introduction to Mennonite History*, 148-49; Horsch, *Mennonites in Europe*, 262-65; *ME*, I, 90-92, 98-99; Milton Gascho, "The Amish Division of 1693-1697 in Switzerland and Alsace," *MQR*, 11 (October 1937), 235-66.
    31. *ME*, I, 105, II, 344-45; van der Zijpp, "Dutch Aid the Swiss Mennonites" (note 1), 136-45.
    32. *ME*, I, 639-40.
    33. *ME*, II, 431-33.
    34. Irvin B. Horst, "Pieter Cornelisz Plockhoy: An Apostle of the Collegiants," *MQR*, 23 (July 1949), 161-85; Leland Harder, "Plockhoy and His Settlement at Zwanendael 1663," *MQR*, 23 (July 1949), 186-99; *Ecclesiastical Records of the State of New York* (Albany, 1901), I, 524; Leland Harder and Marvin Harder, *Plockhoy from Zurik-zee* (Newton, Kan., 1952), 48-71.
    35. Harder and Harder, *Plockhoy*, 63-66.
    36. Berthold Fernow, ed., *Records of New Amsterdam from 1653 to 1674* (New York, 1897), III, 70, IV, 246; *Ecclesiastical Records of the State of New York*, I, 320, 334-35, 348, 386, 485, 505, 513-14, 555.
    37. While Johannes Megapolensis and Samuel Drisius reported to the Classis of Amsterdam, August 5, 1657, that "The people of Gravesend are considered Mennonites," the settlement at Gravesend on Long Island was made by English dissenters led by Lady Deborah Moody and probably did not include Dutch Mennonites; *Ecclesiastical Records of the State of New York*, I, 396. The Reformed Classis congratulated Dominie Nieuwenhuysen, December 9, 1674, that "even from the sect of the Mennonites, at times, one and another are won" through his efforts; ibid., I, 667.
    38. *ME*, IV, 109-10; Horsch, *Mennonites in Europe* (note 13), 266-70; Dyck, *Introduction to Mennonite History* (note 3), 149-50.
    39. William I. Hull, *William Penn and the Dutch Quaker Migration to Pennsylvania* (Swarthmore, Pa., 1935), 191-94, 262-71.
    40. Willem Sewel, *The History of the Rise, Increase, and Progress of the Christian People Called Quakers* (published in many editions, beginning 1725; London, 1811, edition used in this study), II, 357-58, 365 (pagination differs in other editions); Hull, *William Penn*, 88-92, and passim, quotation

from pp. 89-90.

41. Hull, *William Penn*, 196-201, 276-290.

42. Ibid., 239-43; original document is in Streepers mss., HSP.

43. Ibid., 243-54; *Ecclesiastical Records of the State of New York*, I, 906-907, 922, 955-58.

44. Hull, *William Penn*, 209-16; Samuel W. Pennypacker, "The Settlement of Germantown and the Causes Which Led to It," in his *Historical and Biographical Sketches* (Philadelphia, 1883—the article being reprinted from *PMHB*, 4, no. 1 [1880], 1-41, and existing also as separate publications [1899 and 1870]), 15-17; Friedrich Nieper, *Die ersten deutschen Auswanderer von Krefeld nach Pennsylvanien* (Ansbach, 1940), 89-95.

45. Edward Hocker, *Germantown: 1683-1933* (Germantown, Pa., 1933), 10, 16-22. (Many writers on early Germantown have referred to the Krefeld settlers as thirty-three individuals in thirteen families, but thirty-three is probably too low. Hocker observed that these figures are based on the ship lists of freights paid, with children under twelve counted as one-half freights and those less than one year old not counted at all. Hence he concluded that the group was perhaps forty or even fifty persons.) Nieper, *Die ersten deutschen Auswanderer*, 95.

46. Herman Isaacs op den Graeff to Friends in Krefeld, February 12, 1684, in Julius F. Sachse, *Letters Relating to the Settlement of Germantown in Pennsylvania 1683-1684* (Lubeck and Philadelphia, 1903), 31-34.

47. Ibid.; Gary B. Nash, *Quakers and Politics in Pennsylvania, 1681-1726* (Princeton, N.J., 1968), 50-51; Stephanie Grauman Wolf, *Urban Village: Population, Community, and Family Structure in Germantown, Pennsylvania, 1683-1800* (Princeton, N.J., 1976), 104-105; Pastorius quotation is from Wolf.

48. Hull, *William Penn*, 253-54; Hocker, *Germantown*, 24-25.

49. Hull, *William Penn*, 284-92.

50. Pennypacker, *Settlement of Germantown* (note 44), 39-41; Morgan Edwards, *Materials Toward a History of the Baptists in Pennsylvania, Both British and German, Distinguished Into First Day Baptists, Keithian Baptists, Seventh Day Baptists, Tunker Baptists, Mennonist Baptists* (Philadelphia, 1770), I, 96.

51. Rudolphus Varick to Classis of Amsterdam, April 9, 1693, *Ecclesiastical Records of the State of New York*, (note 34), I, 1048-53. Varick, while reporting in 1693, made the trip in June 1690. Hocker, *Germantown*, 26-28. (Iost Harmensen was the Dutch theologian better known as Arminius, proponent of free-will doctrine.)

52. Wenger, *History of the Mennonites of Franconia* (note 26), 87; Hocker, *Germantown*, 28.

53. Nash, *Quakers and Politics*, (note 47), 144-57; Ethyn [?] W. Kirby, *George Keith, 1635-1716* (New York, 1942), 36-37, passim; Jon Butler, "'Gospel Order Improved':The Keithian Schism and the Exercise of Quaker Ministerial Authority," *William and Mary Quarterly*, 31 (October 1974), 431-52; Edward J. Cody, "The Price of Perfection: The Irony of George Keith," *Pennsylvania History*, 39 (January 1972), 1-19.

54. Sewel, *History of the Rise, Increase, and Progress* (note 40), II, 494. Sewel, originally a Dutch Mennonite, published his *History* in 1717 at Amsterdam. See also, Kirby, *George Keith*, 57-58.

55. "An Account of Such as Have Formerly Frequented Friends Meeting and Have Since Followed George Keith and Others," in J. William Frost, ed., *The Keithian Controversy in Early Pennsylvania* (Norwood, Pa., 1980), 371-75. See also, Jon Butler, "Into Pennsylvania's Spiritual Abyss: The Rise and Fall of the Later Keithians, 1693-1703," *PMHB*, 101 (April 1977), 151-170.

56. Hull, *William Penn*, 294-300; Hildegard Binder-Johnson, "The Germantown Protest of 1688 Against Negro Slavery," *PMHB*, 65 (January 1941), 155. For the complete text along with commentary, see: J. William Frost, ed., *The Quaker Doctrine of Anti-Slavery* (Norwood, Pa., 1980), 14-17; Wenger, *History of the Mennonites of Franconia*, Appendix VI, 412-14. See also text material covered by note 34.

57. Ibid., entire note.

58. Ibid.; Thomas E. Drake, *Quakers and Slavery in America* (New Haven, Conn., 1950), 11-14.

59. See J. Herbert Fretz, "The Germantown Anti-Slavery Petition of 1688," *MQR*, 33 (January 1959), 46 n. 12.

60. Butler, "Into Pennsylvania's Spiritual Abyss," 158-61; Julius F. Sachse, *Pietists of Provincial Pennsylvania* (New York, 1970), 66-68; Theodore E. Schmauk, *The Lutheran Church in Pennsylvania, 1638-1800* (Lancaster, Pa., 1902), 74-79, 96-97; Oswald Seidenstricker, "The Hermits of the Wissahickon," *PMHB*, 11 (1887), 440; R. E. E. Harkness, "Early Relations of Baptists and Quakers," *Church History*, 2 (December 1933), 227-42; Davis quotations in Jon Butler, *Power, Authority, and the Origins of American Denominational Order: The English Churches in the Delaware Valley, 1680-1730* (Philadelphia, 1978), 46-48.

61. Jacob Godschalk's narrative of "The beginning or origin of the community of Jesus Christ here at Germantown, who are called Mennonites" was included in a 1773 letter from Andrew Ziegler, et al., to Mennonites in Krefeld. The original manuscript is extant in German and Dutch versions. The Dutch manuscript is in the Schwenkfelder Library, Pennsburg, Pa. This text was the basis for an English translation in Samuel W. Pennypacker, *Hendrick Pannebecker, Surveyor of Lands for the Penns* (Philadelphia, 1894), 46-56. This translation introduced what became a widely copied error: the date 1698 in the original was printed as 1690, suggesting that the Mennonite congregation had begun meeting in Isaac Jacobs van Bebber's house nearly a decade before they actually did. The

German text was first published in 1929 by Christian Neff with the correct date (1698). This led many to believe that a discrepancy existed between the Dutch and German versions on this important point. J. C. Wenger, eminent Mennonite Church historian, has informed the present author that there is not the slightest basis for the often-repeated 1690 date for the beginnings of the Mennonite congregation at Germantown. The original Dutch version clearly reads 1698, as does the German one.

For the text of the 1773 letter in English, see: Wenger, *History of the Mennonites of Franconia* (note 26), Appendix I, 395-404; Harold S. Bender, "The Founding of the Mennonite Church in America at Germantown, 1683-1708," *MQR*, 7 (October 1933), 227-28.

62. Harold S. Bender, "Was William Rittenhouse the First Mennonite Bishop in America?" *MQR*, 7 (January 1933), 42-47.

63. B. C. Roosen, *Geschichte der Mennoniten-Gemeinde zu Hamburg und Altona* (Hamburg, 1886), I, 63; Wenger, *History of the Mennonites of Franconia*, 87-95; Pennypacker, *Settlement of Germantown* (note 44), 53-54.

64. Harold S. Bender, "An Interesting Document on the Early History of Germantown," *MQR*, 5 (October 1931), 284-85; Wenger, *History of the Mennonites of Franconia*, 87-95, Appendix II, 405-406.

65. Bender, "Founding of the Mennonite Church," 227-35; Wenger, *History of the Mennonites of Franconia*, 87-95, Appendix I, 395-404. For a list of members of the Germantown congregation in 1708, see Morgan Edwards, *Materials Toward a History of the Baptists* (note 50), I, 96.

66. Pennypacker, "Settlement of Germantown" (note 44), 47-48; Hocker, *Germantown* (note 45), 32-33.

67. Wenger, *History of the Mennonites of Franconia*, 14-16; Theodore W. Bean, *History of Montgomery County, Pennsylvania* (Philadelphia, 1884), 1020-21; Samuel W. Pennypacker, "Bebber's Township and the Dutch Patrons of Pennsylvania," *PMHB*, 31 (January 1907), 1-18.

68. Bean, *History of Montgomery County*, 1020. For intermarriages among Reformed and Mennonite settlers at Skippack, see Ralph L. Johnson and David H. Bergey, "Genealogical Landmarks and Milestones of the Lower Perkiomen Country," *The Perkiomen Region*, 12 (October 1934), 110-18, 124-31, 137-39, 208-209, and passim. This is a massive compilation from deeds, wills, and church records relating to the pioneer Skippack settlers and their immediate descendants.

69. William J. Hinke, "Records of the Dutch Reformed Congregation at Whitemarsh and Skippack, 1710-1713," *Journal of the Presbyterian Historical Society*, 1 (1909), 110-34.

70. Daniel Kolb Cassel, *A Genealogical History of the Kolb, Kulp, or Culp Family* (Norristown, Pa., 1895), 12-19.

71. Godschalk's account is in the 1773 letter to Krefeld (see note 62), Wenger, *History of the Mennonites of Franconia*, Appendix I, 395-404.

72. Ibid.; on Graeff and the Bowmans, see Martin H. Brackbill, "Origin of the Pequea Settlers (1710)," *MQR*, 45 (April 1971), 84-96.

73. Wenger, *History of the Mennonites of Franconia*, Appendix I, 395-404.

CHAPTER 2

1. A group of 23 Mennonites from the Palatinate landed in Philadelphia in 1754 on the ship *Brothers*. The presence of "Abraham Browbacker, New Lander" on one of the ship's lists indicates that his visit to his former home prompted others to join him in Pennsylvania. Ralph B. Strassburger and William J. Hinke, eds., *Pennsylvania German Pioneers: A Publication of the Original Lists of Arrivals In the Port of Philadelphia From 1727 to 1808* (Norristown, Pa., 1934, republished Baltimore, 1980), I, 612. Family traditions point to others who traveled to Europe to recruit Mennonite settlers, but documentation is rare. On the activities of newlanders, see Albert B. Faust, "Swiss Emigration to the American Colonies in the Eighteenth Century," *American Historical Review*, 22 (October 1916), 32-40.

2. Peter Kolb, Gothard Holl, Hans Burkholder, Johannes Dallem, Ulrich Hackman, Hans Jacob Hiestand, and Johann Georg Becktel to Commissie voor de Buitenlandsche Nooden [Commission for Foreign Needs] (hereafter cited as CFN), May 6, 1727, *2262, Archives of the Dutch Mennonite Church, Amsterdam Municipal Archives, Amsterdam, The Netherlands. Transcripts, in Dutch and German, of a selection of the CFN documents are in a collection identified as "Dutch Papers" at HSP. Research for this chapter came from these transcripts. For a calendar of the CFN papers, see J. G. Hoop de Scheffer, *Inventaris der Archiefstukken* (Amsterdam, 1883), I, 176-463. See also *ME*, I, 105, II, 344-45.

3. This is a recurring refrain in almost all correspondence between the CFN and the Palatinate Mennonites, notably: Hermanus Schijn and Bartolomeus van Leuveningh to Peter Kolb, July 16, 1726, January 21, 1727, April 22, 1727, *2259-2261; Bartolomeus van Leuveningh, Herman te Kate, and Joachim van Anklam to congregations in Ober-Pfalz, May 6, 1732, *2279; Dutch Papers. See also J. G. Hoop de Scheffer, "Mennonite Emigration to Pennsylvania," *PMHB*, 2 (1878), 130-32.

4. Jan Frerichs [Frederickzoon] to H. Schijn, January 6, 1708, *1254, Dutch Papers; Hoop de

Scheffer, "Mennonite Emigration," 124-26; Nanne van der Zijpp, "The Dutch Aid the Swiss Mennonites," in Cornelius J. Dyck, ed., *A Legacy of Faith* (Newton, Kan., 1962), 145-46.

5. J. H. Dubbs, "Samuel Guldin, Pietist and Pioneer," *The Reformed Quarterly Review,* 39 (1892), 309-25; Frerichs to Schijn (note 4).

6. Benedikt Brechbuhl, n.d. 1710, #1262; Peter Kolb, Valentin Hutwol, Barthardt Holl, Tillman Kolb, and Hans Jacob Schnebeli to Hermanus Schijn and Willem van Maurik, January 21, 1710, #1254; Nicholas Moser and Ulrich Holdiger to the Ministers and Elders in Holland, July 22, 1709, #1255; Dutch Papers.

7. Laurens Hendricks to the congregation by the Lamb, July 22, 1709, #1255, Dutch Papers; C. Henry Smith, *The Mennonite Immigration to Pennsylvania in the Eighteenth Century* (Norristown, Pa., 1929), 60-68; van der Zijpp, "Dutch Aid the Swiss Mennonites," 146-49; Faust, "Swiss Emigration" (note 1), 21-23.

8. Benedikt Brechbuhl letters to the CFN, July 18, August 27, September 22 and 26, 1710; January 4, April 4, May 7, June 1, August 12, September 20, 1711; July 2, 1712; November 26, 1714; #1266, 1270, 1275, 1277, 1299, 1324, 1327, 1332, 1347, 1350, 1364, 1371, Dutch Papers. Van der Zijpp, "Dutch Aid the Swiss Mennonites," 148; quotation from Moser and Holdiger to Ministers and Elders (note 6).

9. Benedikt Brechbuhl, Hans Rudolf Nagele, Ulrich Stauffer, Hans Jacob Schnebeli, and Ulrich Meier to Abraham Jacobsz Fries and Hermanus Schijn, February 6, 1714, #1439, Dutch Papers; Hans Jacob Schnebeli, Hans Jacob Histand, Ulrigh Meier, Valentin Christophel, and Hans Rudolf Nagele to Hermanus Schijn, Job Sieuwers, Abraham Jacobs Fries, and Daniel Horneus, March 9, 1715, #1374, Dutch Papers, transcript at LMHS; Smith, *Mennonite Immigration,* 33-34.

10. Hans Stauffer account book, transcript and translation in Schwenkfelder Library, Pennsburg, Pa.; *ME,* IV, 619-20.

11. Hans Jacob Schnebeli to CFN, December 1, 1714, #1371, Dutch Papers; Smith, *Mennonite Immigration,* 36-37.

12. Klaus Wust, *The Virginia Germans* (Charlottesville, Va., 1969), 16-19; Abdel Ross Wentz, *The Beginnings of the German Element in York County, Pennslvania,* PGSPA, 24 (Lancaster, Pa., 1916), 14-15; Vincent H. Todd, ed., *Christoph von Graffenreid's account of the Founding of New Bern* (Raleigh, N.C., 1920), 246-55.

13. Och's appeal is undated, but internal evidence suggests 1715, since it was issued in the name of King George I, whose reign began in 1714, and describes Maryland as a royal province, as it no longer was after late 1715 when Lord Baltimore's proprietary rule resumed. Yet there is no evidence of Mennonite response before 1716. The original document is #2255 among the CFN papers in Amsterdam, and was first published in English translation in J. G. de Hoop Scheffer, "Mennonite Emigration' (note 3), 126-30. Smith, *Mennonite Immigration,* 129-32.

14. #2254, Dutch Papers.

15. Martin H. Brackbill, "New Light on Hans Herr and Martin Kendig," 39 (1935), 79 and 89 n. 9; Joseph C. Burkholder, "Benedict Brechbuhl, Hans Burkholder and the Swiss Mennonite Migration to Lancaster County, Pennsylvania, 31 (1927), 61; both in *Papers Read Before the Lancaster County Historical Society.* Smith, *Mennonite Immigration,* 133.

16. Wust, *Virginia Germans,* 30-32. Henry Z. Jones and Annette K. Burgert, "A New Emigrant List: Bonfeld 1710-1738," *Der Reggeboge/The Rainbow: Quarterly of the Pennsylvania German Society,* 14 (October 1980), 3-20.

17. *ME,* I, 85.

18. Marianne Wokeck, "The Flow and Composition of German Immigration to Philadelphia, 1727-1775," *PMHB,* 105 (July 1981), 149-78; Klaus Wust, "Direct German Immigration to Maryland in the Eighteenth Century," *The Report: A Journal of German-American History,* 37 (1978), 19-28. Two major works on German immigration, written by Annette K. Burgert and by Klaus Wust and scheduled for publication in 1983, will appear too late for this study.

19. Smith, *Mennonite Immigration,* 220; Jones and Burgert, "A New Emigrant List," 3-20.

20. Wokeck, "Flow and Composition," 270; Strassburger and Hinke, *Pennsylvania German Pioneers* (note 1), I, 59-62; Mennonite identification from two lists of departing emigrants, May 10, 1732, #2281, Dutch Papers.

21. Wokeck, "Flow and Composition," 270-71.

22. Martin Lodge, "The Crisis of the Churches in the Middle Colonies, 1720-1750," *PMHB,* 95 (April 1971), 197-98, saw the better planning, organization, and financial support of Mennonite and Schwenkfelder immigration as a major factor in their ability to transfer their institutions to the New World; Peter C. Erb, "Dialogue Under Duress: Schwenkfelder and Mennonite Contact in the Eighteenth Century," *MQR,* 50 (July 1976), 181-99.

23. Van Leuveningh, et al., to congregations in Ober-Pfalz (note 3); CFN to Henrich Kindig and Michel Kriebel, June 12, 1731, #2274; Dirk van Beek to CFN, June 12, 1731, #2274; reports of CFN meetings, May 27, 1727, July 14, 1727, #2262, 2266; Dutch Papers.

24. Mennonite congregation in Amsterdam to Peter Kolb, June 14, 1726, #2259; Hermanus Schijn, et al., to Peter Kolb, January 21, 1727, #2260; van Leuveningh, et al., to congregations in Ober-Pfalz (note 3); Dutch Papers.

25. CFN to Peter Kolb and Fellow Servants (Ministers) in the Palatinate, April 22, 1727, #2261, Dutch Papers.

26. Ibid.; Peter Kolb, et al., to CFN, April 22, 1727, May 6, 1727, #2261-2262; CFN meeting report, May 27, 1727, #2262; Dutch Papers.
27. Albert B. Faust and Gaius M. Brumbaugh, *Lists of Swiss Emigrants in the Eighteenth Century to the American Colonies,* vol. 2, *From the State Archives of Bern and Basel, Switzerland* (Washington, D.C., 1925), 72-73; Strassburger and Hinke, *Pennsylvania German Pioneers* (note 1), I, 10; Smith, *Mennonite Immigration* (note 7), 134-38; On Swiss Mennonite migrations generally, see: Leo Schelbert, "Eighteenth Century Migrations of Swiss Mennonites to America," *MQR,* 42 (July 1968), 163-83, and (October 1968), 285-300; and Delbert Gratz, "Bernese Anabaptists in the Eighteenth Century," *MQR,* 26 (January 1952), 5-21, and (April 1952), 99-122.
28. Strassburger and Hinke, *Pennsylvania German Pioneers,* I, 16; Smith, *Mennonite Immigration,* 136-38; John C. Wenger, *History of the Mennonites of the Franconia Conference* (Scottdale, Pa., 1938), 16-17; William J. Bean, *History of Montgomery County, Pennsylvania* (Philadelphia, 1884), 1020-1021; William J. Hinke, *A History of the Goshenhoppen Reformed Charge, Montgomery County, Pennsylvania* (Lancaster, Pa., 1920), 13-15; William Beery and Judith Beery Garber, *Beery Family History* (Elgin, Ill., 1957), 30-32.
29. Report of CFN meeting (note 23); Peter Kolb, et al., to CFN, April 22, 1727, May 20, 1727, #2261, 2263, Dutch Papers; Strassburger and Hinke, *Pennsylvania German Pioneers,* I, 12-13; Smith, *Mennonite Immigration,* 181-82; Hinke, *History of the Goshenhoppen Reformed Charge,* 13-15; Charles R. Roberts, "Germanic Immigrants Named in Early Pennsylvania Ship Lists," *PGSPA,* 39 (Norristown, Pa., 1930), 10-11.
30. A letter of recommendation for the departing Martins by Nicholas Stumpf, January 22, 1731, #2271; Dutch Papers.
31. A "church letter" for the Martins sent by Heinrich Kindig and Michel Kreibel to CFN, May 9, 1731, #2272; a similar "church letter" for the Horsch family sent by Heinrich Kindig and Michel Kreibel to CFN, May 9, 1731, #2273, Dutch Papers.
32. Van Beek to CFN (note 23); Strassburger and Hinke, *Pennsylvania German Pioneers,* I, 47-57; Annette K. Burgert, "Some Pennsylvania Pioneers From Hassboch and B :Uohl in the Palatinate," *Der Reggeboge/The Rainbow: Quarterly of the Pennsylvania German Society,* 12 (April 1978), 15-18.
33. Van Leuveningh, et al., to congregations in Ober-Pfalz (note 3); Namelists (Naamlysts), May 10, 1732, #2281; Heinrich Kindig and Michel Kreibel to CFN, May 10, 1732, #2280; Dutch Papers.
34. Strassburger and Hinke, *Pennsylvania German Pioneers,* I, 59-65, 79-83; Smith, *Mennonite Immigration* (note 7), 195-98; Roberts, "Germanic Immigrants" (note 30), 10-11; Charles D. Spotts, *The People of Bowmansville* (Lancaster, Pa., 1970), 3-6.
35. Peter Kolb, et al., to CFN July 11, 1726, #2260, noted the limited supply of land, high rents, increases in the head tax, as well as the threat of war; Mennonite congregation at Amsterdam to Peter Kolb, et al., July 16, 1726 (date uncertain; date on document differs with date in Hoop de Scheffer [note 2]), #2259; Dutch Papers. Smith, *Mennonite Immigration,* 204.
36. Hans Burkholder to Bartolomeus van Leuveningh, February 27, 1742, #1489, Dutch Papers; Smith, *Mennonite Immigration,* 205.
37. Johann Runckel to CFN, June 13, 1711, #1334, Dutch Papers; Smith, *Mennonite Immigration,* 71-72; Hendricks to the congregation by the Lamb (note 7).
38. CFN to Hans Burkholder, March 6, 1744, #2286, Dutch Papers. For an overview of Amish emigration, see J. Virgil Miller, "Amish-Mennonites in Northern Alsace and the Palatinate in the Eighteenth Century and Their Connections With Immigrants to Pennsylvania," *MQR,* 50 (October 1976), 272-80.
39. Strassburger and Hinke, *Pennsylvania German Pioneers,* I, 162-63; *Colonial Records,* IV, 171-74. On the Detweiler settlement at Northkill, see Joseph F. Beiler, "Our Fatherland in America: The Detweiler Family," *The Diary,* 6 (October 1974), 240. On Hans Sieber and the Sieber-Beiler land grant, including a plan of the tract, see Joseph F. Beiler, "Our Fatherland in America: The Sieber Family," *The Diary,* 7 (November 1975), 262-63. Families with familiar Amish surnames like Stutzman, Kurtz, Reichenbach, Schlabach, and Hochstetler immigrated as early as 1727, but these individuals have not been positively identified as Amish. Many surnames found among Amish and Mennonite communities were also found among Reformed and, to a lesser extent, Lutheran and Catholic immigrants. Grant M. Stoltzfus, *History of the First Amish Mennonite Communities in America* (Harrisonburg, Va., 1958), 34-35. For a discussion of the question of first Amish arrivals, see John A. Hostetler, *Amish Society* (Baltimore, 1980), 55-56.
40. Strassburger and Hinke, *Pennsylvania German Pioneers,* I, 188-94; Joseph F. Beiler, "Our Fatherland in America: The Zimmerman Family," *The Diary,* 10 (August 1978), 252; Stoltzfus, *History of the First Amish Mennonite Communities,* 36-37, 46-47. For the Kauffman diary, see S. Duane Kauffman, "Miscellaneous Amish Historical Documents," *Pennsylvania Mennonite Heritage,* 2 (July 1978), 12-14 and S. Duane Kauffman, *Christian Kauffman: His Descendants and His People* (Baltimore, 1980), 227. Kauffman reproduces a transcription of the diary, the original apparently not extant. An original transcription is in the William Merwine File, HSP.
41. Burkholder to van Leuveningh (note 37); Stoltzfus, *History of the First Amish Mennonite Communities,* 38-39; Strassburger and Hinke, *Pennsylvania German Pioneers,* I, 204-207, 328-29; Joseph F. Beiler, "Our Fatherland in America: The Zook-Zug Family," *The Diary,* 10 (June 1978), 189; Joseph F. Beiler, "Our Fatherland in America: The Kurtzes," *The Diary,* 9 (December 1977), 262;

Joseph F. Beiler, "Our Fatherland in America: The Koenig-King Family," *The Diary*, 8 (September 1976), 191; Joseph F. Beiler, "Our Fatherland in America: The Hertzler-Hartzler Family," *The Diary*, 7 (June 1975), 143-44 and (July 1975), 165-68.

42. Earl Township and Lebanon Township Tax Lists, LCHS; Joseph F. Beiler, "Abraham Drachsel," *The Diary*, 9 (March 1977), 69-72; James E. Landing, "Amish Settlement in North America: A Geographical Brief," *Bulletin of the Illinois Geographic Society*, 12 (December 1970), 65-69.

43. Congregation in Hamburg to the congregation by the Sun in Amsterdam, March 11, 1707, ☛2244; David Rutgers, Jr. to CFN, November 24, 1707, ☛2245; Adrian van Alkmaar to the congregations by the Lamb and the Tower, April 8, 1709, ☛2248; Dutch Papers. On the identity of these emigrants, see: John Tribekko and George Ruperti, *List of Germans from the Palatinate Who Came to England in 1709* (Baltimore, 1965), 5-10; Hoop de Scheffer, "Mennonite Emigration" (note 3), 122-23; Walter Allen Knittle, *Early Eighteenth Century Palatinate Emigration* (Baltimore, 1965), 47-66.

44. William I. Hull, *William Penn and the Dutch Quaker Migration to Pennsylvania* (Swarthmore, Pa., 1935), 386-390.

45. Jacob Telner to the congregation by the Lamb, August 6, 1709, ☛2250; Martin Kendig, et al., to CFN, June 24, 1710, ☛2253; Dutch Papers. They sailed on the *Maria Hope*. For a narrative of the voyage, see William J. Hinke, "Diary of the Rev. Samuel Guldin, Relating to His Journey to Pennsylvania, June to September, 1710," *Journal of Presbyterian History*, 21 (March 1930), 28-41, and (June 1930), 64-73. Martin H. Brackbill, "Origin of the Pequea Settlers (1710)," *MQR*, 45 (January 1971), 84-95.

46. Strassburger and Hinke, *Pennsylvania German Pioneers*, I, 328-29; "Skippack Alms Book, 1738-1954," transcribed and trans. by Raymond E. Hollenbach, typescript (1968), copy in Menno Simons Historical Library, Eastern Mennonite College, Harrisonburg, Va.

47. Strassburger and Hinke, *Pennsylvania German Pioneers*, I, 759; Pequea-Conestoga Amish Alms Book, in possession of Joseph F. Beiler, Gordonsville, Pa.

48. Harold S. Bender, "A Swiss Mennonite Document of 1754 Bearing on the Background of the Origin of the Brethren in Christ Church," *MQR*, 34 (October 1960), 308-309. See also: Ira D. Landis, "Origins of the Brethren in Christ Church and Its Later Divisions," *MQR*, 34 (October 1960), 297-99; Faust and Brumbaugh, *Lists of Swiss Emigrants* (note 27), II, 29-31, 61.

49. Bender, "Swiss Mennonite Document," 308-309; Bowmansville congregation Alms Book, LMHS; Strassburger and Hinke, *Pennsylvania German Pioneers*, I, 626-36.

50. Bowmansville congregation Alms Book, LMHS; Strassburger and Hinke, *Pennsylvania German Pioneers*, I, 731-32.

51. "Petition of the Subscribers Members of the Menonist Church," December 10, 1785, Religious Petitions, Archives Division, Virginia State Library, Richmond, Va., and reproduced in Richard K. MacMaster, et al., *Conscience in Crisis: Mennonites and Other Peace Churches in America, 1739-1789, Interpretation and Documents* (Scottdale, Pa., and Kitchener, Ont., 1979), 333-34.

52. CFN to Kolb, et al. (note 25).

CHAPTER 3

1. William J. Hinke, "Diary of the Rev. Samuel Guldin, Relating to His Journey to Pennsylvania, June to September, 1710," *Journal of Presbyterian History*, 21 (June 1930), 70; James T. Lemon, *The Best Poor Man's Country: A Geographical Study of Early Southeastern Pennsylvania* (Baltimore, 1972), 65.

2. *Pennsylvania Archives*, second series, vol. 19, 622-24; Martin H. Brackbill, "New Light on Hans Herr and Martin Kendig," *Papers Read Before the Lancaster County Historical Society*, 39 (1935), 81-83. See also: Joseph C. Burkholder, "Benedict Brechbuhl, Hans Burkholder, and the Swiss Mennonite Migration to Lancaster County, Pennsylvania," *Papers Read Before the Lancaster County Historical Society*, 31 (1927), 57-62; Martin H. Brackbill, "Origin of the Pequea Settlers (1710)," *MQR*, 45 (January 1971), 84-95.

3. James Steel to Martin Milin and Christian Heer, 27 1st month, 1731; James Steel to Martin Kundig and Hans Heer, 20 xbr (December) 1732; fols. 17 and 47, James Steel Letterbook, 1730-1741; Logan Papers, HSP. Thomas Sergeant, *View of the Land Laws of Pennsylvania* (Philadelphia, 1838), 36-41; Lemon, *Best Poor Man's Country*, 54-56.

4. Lemon, *Best Poor Man's Country*, 56.

5. Martin H. Brackbill, "The Manor of Conestoga in the Colonial Period," *Papers of the Lancaster County Historical Society*, 42 (1938), 22-26; Sergeant, *View of Land Laws*, 195-97.

6. Lemon, *Best Poor Man's Country*, 80.

7. Brackbill, "Manor of Conestoga," 25-26; Lemon, *Best Poor Man's Country*, 82.

8. Brackbill, "New Light on Hans Herr and Martin Kendig" (note 2), 83; C. Henry Smith, *The Mennonite Immigration to Pennsylvania in the Eighteenth Century*, (Norristown, Pa., 1927), 173;

Burkholder, "Benedict Brechbuhl" (note 2), 59-62; Henry Z. Jones, Jr., and Annette K. Burgert, "A New Emigrant List: Bonfeld, 1710-1738," *Der Reggeboge/The Rainbow, Quarterly of the Pennsylvania German Society*, 14 (October 1980), 13-17.

9. Rev. William Wappeler, S. J., to Rev. Father Provincial of Lower Rhine Province, August 5, 1742, 574J, Maryland Province Archives, Georgetown University Library, Washington, D.C.; Rev. Jedidiah Andrews to Rev. Thomas Prince, October 14, 1730, as quoted in William J. Hinke, *History of the Goshenhoppen Reformed Charge*, PGSPA, 27 (Lancaster, Pa., 1920), 37-38.

10. Andrews to Prince, as quoted in Hinke, *History of the Goshenhoppen Reformed Charge*, 38.

11. Joseph F. Beiler, "Our Fatherland in America: Shiplists," *The Diary*, 4 (July 1972), 138-40; 4 (August 1972), 159-60; 4 (September 1972), 178-80; 5 (April 1973), 80; 5 (May 1973), 99-100. Grant M. Stoltzfus, *History of the First Amish Mennonite Communities in America* (Harrisonburg, Va., 1958), 46-50, 59. See also, John Umble, "Memoirs of an Amish Bishop," *MQR*, 22 (April 1948), 102-103.

12. Joseph F. Beiler, "The Amish in the Pequea Valley Before 1800," *The Diary*, 6 (July 1974), 162-64; Joseph F. Beiler, "The Rupp, Schowalter, and Schenk Families," *The Diary*,10 (February 1978), 30; Lemon, *Best Poor Man's Country* (note 1), 67.

13. Beiler, "Amish in the Pequea Valley," 16; Bern Township Tax Lists, BCHS. For maps of early Amish land grants, see *The Diary*, 4 (July 1972), 139; 4 (September 1972), 179.

14. Joseph F. Beiler, "Christian Beiler Landgrants," *The Diary*, 7 (May 1975), 119-20; Joseph F. Beiler, "Bishop Jacob Hertzler," *The Diary*, 7 (July 1975), 165-68; Joseph F. Beiler, "The Speicher Family," *The Diary*, 7 (August 1975), 190-92; Ralph B. Strassburger and William J. Hinke, eds. *Pennsylvania German Pioneers: A Publication of the Original Lists of Arrivals In the Port of Philadelphia From 1727 to 1808* (Norristown, Pa., 1934, republished Baltimore, 1980), I, 188, 327, 396.

15. Joseph F. Beiler, "The Detweiler Family," *The Diary*, 6 (October 1974), 239-40; Joseph F. Beiler, "Shiplists," *The Diary*, 4 (September 1972), 180; Stoltzfus, *History of the First Amish Mennonite Communities*, 46-47.

16. C-156, A-236, Lancaster County Deeds, courthouse at Lancaster, Pa.; Earl Township Tax Lists, LCHS; Joseph F. Beiler, "Jacob Kurtz," *The Diary*, 9 (November 1977), 262; Beiler, "Rupp, Schowalter, and Schenk Families," 28-32; Strassburger and Hinke, *Pennsylvania German Pioneers*, I, 365-66; Portia Showalter Everett, *History of the Showalter Family* (n.p., 1964), 26-31.

17. *Pennsylvania Archives*, second series, vol. 19, 597, 639, 642, 700, 724, 746; C-322, C-327, Lancaster County Deeds, courthouse at Lancaster, Pa.; Ira D. Landis, "Hans Groffs Aplenty," *Mennonite Research Journal*, 14 (July 1973), 27-29; Frank R. Diffenderffer, *The Three Earls* (New Holland, Pa., 1876), 22-26.

18. C-322, C-327, Lancaster County Deeds, courthouse at Lancaster, Pa.; Landis, "Hans Groffs Aplenty," 27-29; Martin G. Weaver, *Mennonites of Lancaster Conference* (Scottdale, Pa., 1931), 121-122.

19. *Pennsylvania Archives*, third series, vol. 1, 64-65; Weaver, *Mennonites of Lancaster Conference*, 122-24; Donald F. Durnbaugh, ed., *The Brethren in Colonial America: A Source Book on the Transplantation and Development of the Church of the Brethren in the Eighteenth Century* (Elgin, Ill., 1967), 66. The German "*Graf*" translates as "earl," and various sources suggest that Graeff therefore also gave his name to Earl Township.

20. Diffenderffer, *Three Earls*, 26; Weaver, *Mennonites of Lancaster Conference*, 122-23.

21. Strassburger and Hinke, *Pennsylvania German Pioneers*, I, 14; Samuel S. Wenger, *The Wenger Book* (Lancaster, Pa., 1976), 162-63.

22. Brackbill, "Manor of Conestoga" (note 5), 25-28.

23. Conestoga Township Tax List, 1757.

24. Earl Township Tax Lists, 1750, 1756, 1758; LCHS.

25. Ibid.; Lemon, *Best Poor Man's Country* (note 1), 90-91.

26. Brecknock Township Tax List, 1756, LCHS; Lemon, *Best Poor Man's Country*, 90.

27. Earl Township Tax List, 1780, LCHS.

28. Ibid.; Amish and Mennonite identification from "A List of the Non Associaters that has Subscribed and the Sums Annexed & their Religion in Earl Township Lanctr. County," Peter Force Collection, Library of Congress, Washington, D.C., reproduced in Richard K. MacMaster, et al., *Conscience in Crisis: Mennonites and Other Peace Churches in America, 1739-1789, Interpretation and Documents* (Scottdale, Pa., and Kitchener, Ont., 1979), 250-55.

29. Earl Township Tax List, 1780, LCHS.

30. Ibid.; Amish and Mennonite identification from "A List of the Non Associaters," MacMaster, *Conscience in Crisis*, 250-55 (see note 28).

31. B-141, Lancaster County Wills, courthouse at Lancaster, Pa.; Brackbill, "Manor of Conestoga" (note 5), 38.

32. Lemon, *Best Poor Man's Country* (note 1), 156-57.

33. Ibid., 154.

34. B-141, B-125, Lancaster County Wills, courthouse at Lancaster, Pa.

35. B-118, B-102, B-74, Lancaster County Wills, courthouse at Lancaster, Pa.

36. A1-68, A1-83, A1-84, A1-117, A1-185, A1-190, A1-196, B-74, B-80, B-89, B-102, B-118, B-141, Lancaster County Wills, courthouse at Lancaster, Pa.

37. Ibid.

38. James T. Lemon, "Early Americans and their Social Environment," *Journal of Historical Geography*, 6 (April 1980), 120-21.

39. Earl Township Tax List, 1756, LCHS. On Mennonite participation in a market economy, see: Lemon, *Best Poor Man's Country* (note 1), 204-10; James T. Lemon, "The Weakness of Place and Community in Early Pennsylvania," in James R. Gibson, ed., *European Settlement and Development in North America* (Toronto, 1978), 190-207.

40. John C. Wenger, *History of the Mennonites of the Franconia Conference* (Scottdale, Pa., 1938), 17-20; Henry J. Buck, *History of Montgomery County, Pennsylvania* (Philadelphia, 1884), 134, 1020-21, 1132-33.

41. James Y. Heckler, *The History of Harleysville and Lower Salford Township* (first published at Harleysville, Pa., 1886, reprinted at Schwenksville, Pa., 1958, without pagination), passim. Heckler summarized deeds relating to land sales within Lower Salford Township; for comparative figures from Lancaster County, see Lemon, *Best Poor Man's Country*, 67, 87.

42. James Y. Heckler, *The History of Franconia Township* (first published at Harleysville, Pa., 1901, republished at Allentown, Pa., 1960), 19-20; Lemon, "Early Americans and their Social Environment," 120.

43. Buck, *History of Montgomery County*, 134, 1019-1021.

44. Perkiomen and Skippack Township Tax List, 1756, HSP.

45. Ibid.

46. Jacob Clemens Record and Account Book, 1749-1782, with translation by Raymond E. Hollenbach, microfilmed copy at Menno Simons Historical Library, Eastern Mennonite College, Harrisonburg, Va., entries for November 26, 1750; October 16, 1751; October 5, 1752; and September 26, 1753. "Record of Indentures, 1771-1773," *PGSPA*, 16 (1907), 16, 26, 46, 144, 146, 149-50, and passim.
Lists of servants and masters are unusual in the records, but a 1750 Earl Township, Lancaster County tax list indicated eight servants in the township with five Mennonites and one Amishman among their owners, and a 1769 one lists thirty-three servants with ten Mennonites among the owners. The 1769 list also indicates "Freemen with Parents" (i.e., taxable young males living at home) and "Freemen" (i.e., those living with employers); there were fourteen living with parents, six of them Mennonite and two Amish, while in the second category there were twenty, seven of the twenty living in homes known to have been Mennonite. Typical entries are: "William Hamilton at Martin Hoover"; "Peter Burkholder at Christian Burkholder"; and "John Kilpatrick at Christian Carpenter." According to the two lists, a much higher percentage of Mennonites than of the township's whole population had servants. This is also true of hired men, that is, of those "Freemen." As for slaves, there were sixteen in Earl Township in 1769, and among the dozen owners, nine had English or Welsh surnames, and three had German.

47. Jacob Latchar (Latschaw), a Mennonite, was taxed for a Negro in the 1779 and 1780 assessments of Colebrookdale Township in Berks County, as was also Henry Gable who was possibly a Mennonite; see original lists at BCHS, or *Pennsylvania Archives*, 3rd series, XVIII, 215, 343. Samuel W. Pennypacker, "Pennypacker's Mills," *Bulletin of the Historical Society of Montgomery County, Pennsylvania*, 22 (Fall 1980), 222; John Woolman, *A Journal of the Life, Gospel Labors, and Christian Experiences of...John Woolman* (first published at Philadelphia, 1774, and variously reproduced, sometimes as :The Journal of John Woolman, e. g., by The Citadel Press, Secaucus, N.J., 1972), pp. 72-73 of the 1972 edition; Alan Tully, "Patterns of Slaveholding in Colonial Pennsylvania: Chester and Lancaster Counties 1729-1758," *Journal of Social History*, 6 (Spring 1973), 284-305; "John Hunt's Diary," :Proceedings of the New Jersey Historical Society, 53 (January 1935), 28-29.

48. See note 44; Duane E. Ball, "Dynamics of Population and Wealth in Eighteenth Century Chester County, Pennsylvania," *Journal of Interdisciplinary History*, 6 (Spring 1976), 629-31.

49. See note 44.

50. Ibid.

51. James Steel to Michael Zeigler, 8th 1st mo. 1734/5; James Steel to Henry Pannebaker, undated, follows 5 4th mo. 1733; fols. 93 and 273, James Steel Letter Book, 1730-1741, Logan Papers, HSP.

52. Lemon, *Best Poor Man's Country* (note 1), 86.

53. Heckler, *History of Harleysville and Lower Salford Township* (note 41), 92, 97, 205, and passim, as paginated in MHL copy; Theodore W. Bean, *History of Montgomery County, Pennsylvania* (Philadelphia, 1884), 946-47, 1020-21.

54. Heckler, *History of Franconia Township* (note 42), 11-14.

55. Lemon, *Best Poor Man's Country*, 91, 108.

56. Heckler, *History of Harleysville and Lower Salford Township*, 58-59, 62-63, 102-113, 141-42, as paginated in MHL copy.

57. H-2, 567; H-14, 190, 193; Philadelphia County Deeds, Municipal Archives, Philadelphia, Pa.; Gertrude M. Ziegler, *The Ziegler Family and Related Families in Pennsylvania* (Zelienople, Pa., 1978), 83-85.

58. Ibid., 104-105, as paginated in MHL copy; Amy Histand Gehman and Mary Latshaw Bower, *History of the Hereford Mennonite Congregation at Bally, Pennsylvania* (Bally, Pa., 1936), 6-7.

59. Edward Hocker, *Germantown: 1683-1933* (Philadelphia, 1933), 54-59; "Concerning the Land Investigation Between the Evangelical Lutheran, the Reformed and the Mennonists in Neugoschenhoppen 1796," Archives of St. Paul's Evangelical Lutheran Church, Red Hill, Pa.; "Title to

the New Goshenhoppen Church Land, January 29, 1796," and "Deed of the New Goshenhoppen Church, Montgomery County, Pa., February 23, 1796," in William J. Hinke, comp., "Reformed Church Documents, 1790-1809," Archives of the Evangelical and Reformed Historical Society, Lancaster Theological Seminary, Lancaster, Pa.; William J. Hinke, *A History of the Goshenhoppen Reformed Charge, Montgomery County, Pennsylvania, 1727-1819,* PGSPA, 27 (Lancaster, Pa., 1920), 114-16.
  60. Hereford Township Tax Lists, BCHS; Edward H. Quinter and Rev. Charles L. Allwein, *Most Blessed Sacrament Church, Bally, Pennsylvania* (Bally, Pa., 1976), 33-43.
  61. Gehman and Bower, *History of the Hereford Mennonite Congregation* 8-12.
  62. Hereford Township Tax Lists, 1767, 1779.
  63. Ibid., for 1768.
  64. New Hanover Township Tax Lists, 1769, 1772, microfilm, Archives Division, Pennsylvania State Historical and Museum Commission, Harrisburg, Pa.
  65. Lemon, *Best Poor Man's Country* (note 1), 20-22, 63-64, 173, 186-93, 216-17, quotation on 224; *Die Germantauner Zeitung,* 24 July 1787.
  66. From an anonymous sermon, the speaker identified only as "an old brother," Box 51, John F. Funk Papers, AMC.
  67. Morgan Edwards, *Materials Toward a History of the Baptists in Pennsylvania, Both British and German, Distinguished Into First Day Baptists, Keithian Baptists, Seventh Day Baptists, Tunker Baptists, Mennonist Baptists* (Philadelphia, 1770), I, 95.

CHAPTER 4

  1. James T. Lemon, *The Best Poor Man's Country: A Geographical Study of Early Southeastern Pennsylvania* (Baltimore and London, 1972), 51, 71-83; John C. Wenger, *History of the Mennonites of the Franconia Conference* (Scottdale, Pa., 1938), 400.
  2. Lemon, *Best Poor Man's Country,* 69; John F. Wayland, *The German Element of the Shenandoah Valley* (Bridgewater, Va., 1964), 60-63. On the importance of land prices, see: Frederick Jackson Turner, *The Frontier in American History* (New York, 1920), 100-101; Carl Bridenbaugh, *Myths and Realities: Societies of the Colonial South* (Baton Rouge, 1954), 120-30; Robert W. Ramsey, *Carolina Cradle: Settlement of the Northwest Carolina Frontier 1747-1762* (Chapel Hill, N.C., 1964), 15-21.
  3. Wayland, *German Element,* 60-63.
  4. Lemon, *Best Poor Man's Country,* 59; Robert D. Mitchell, *Commercialism and Frontier: Perspectives on the Early Shenandoah Valley* (Charlottesville, 1977), 33.
  5. Martin H. Brackbill, "The Manor of Conestoga in the Colonial Period," *Papers of the Lancaster County Historical Society,* 42 (January 1938), 18-23, 28-32; Abdel Ross Wentz, "The Beginnings of the German Element in York County, Pennsylvania," PGSPA, 24 (Lancaster, Pa., 1916), 12-21.
  6. Klaus Wust, *The Virginia Germans* (Charlottesville, 1969), 29-32.
  7. Ann Stricker Milbourne, ed., "Colony West of the Blue Ridge Proposed by Jacob Stauber and Others," *Virginia Magazine of History and Biography,* 35 (July* 1927), 175-90, and 36 (January 1928), 58-70; William P. Palmer, ed., *Calendar of Virginia State Papers* (Richmond, 1875), I, 217-20; H. R. McIlwaine, ed., *Executive Journals of the Council of Colonial Virginia 1680-1754* (Richmond, 1927), IV, 223-24; Mitchell, *Commercialism and Frontier,* 26-28.
  8. Wust, *Virginia Germans,* 30-31.
  9. Palmer, *Calendar of Virginia,* I, 217-20; Klaus Wust, "Jacob Stover and His 147 Germans in London in 1731," *Rockingham Recorder,* 3 (April 1979), 20-23.
  10. Klaus Wust, *Saint Adventures on the Virginia Frontier* (Edinburg, Va., 1977), 41.
  11. Wust, *Virginia Germans,* 36.
  12. William J. Hinke and Charles E. Kemper, eds., "Moravian Diaries of Travel Through Virginia," *Virginia Magazine of History and Biography,* 11 (January 1904), 229.
  13. H. Frank Eshleman, *Historic Background and Annals of the Swiss and German Pioneer Settlers of Southeastern Pennsylvania* (Lancaster, Pa., 1917), 325; Harry A. Brunk, *History of the Mennonites in Virginia 1727-1900* (i.e., Vol. I; Harrisonburg, Va., 1959), 17-22, 26, 32-35.
  14. Brunk, *History of Mennonites in Virginia,* I, 34-35.
  15. Lemon, *Best Poor Man's Country* (note 1), 59; Thomas Sergeant, *View of the Land Laws of Pennsylvania* (Philadelphia, 1838), 45.
  16. Wentz, "Beginnings of the German Element" (note 5), 56-57, 114-17.
  17. *Minutes of the Provincial Council of Pennsylvania,* commonly called, and hereafter cited as *Colonial Records,* IV, 75; *Pennsylvania Archives,* second series, Vol. VII, 215-16. Some scholars have questioned whether Michael Danner, Sr., was really a Mennonite since in 1770 a Michael Danner was a member of the Dunkers' Conestoga congregation at Ephrata, Pa. However, a warrant of April 13, 1772 (York County, Pa., Deed AA-12-287) named Michael Danner, Sr., as trustee "for the Menonist

Congregation" in York County's Manheim Township, and I know of no church land ever being deeded to a trustee who was not of the congregation's faith. Moreover, the Dunker evidence does not designate "Sr." after the name of its Michael Danner, and Ephrata is quite distant from York County township in question. I conclude that Michael Danner, Sr., in York County, was a Mennonite.

18. *Colonial Records,* IV, 69.

19. Ibid.; Wentz, "Beginnings of the German Element," 57-58.

20. Wentz, "Beginnings of the German Element," 86-88; Lida Bowman Meckley, "The Mennonites of York County, Pennsylvania," typewritten paper (1939), copy at LMHS; William J. Hinke and Charles E. Kemper, eds., "Moravian Diaries of Travel Through Virginia," *Virginia Magazine of History and Biography,* 11 (April 1904), 372.

21. Hinke and Kemper, "Moravian Diaries" (April 1904), 372; Frederick County Debt Book (1753), fol. 48, Maryland Hall of Records, Annapolis, Md.; Morgan Edwards, "Materials Towards a History of the Baptists in the Province of Maryland" (1772), mircofilm, fol. 11, Southern Baptist Historical Commission, Nashville, Tenn.

22. Abram W. Sangrey, *Martin Boehm* (Ephrata, Pa., 1976), 6-8.

23. I-125, I-195, I-501, Augusta County Wills, courthouse at Staunton, Va.; Joseph A. Waddell, *Annals of Augusta County, Virginia* (Harrisonburg, Va., 1979), 78.

24. C-115, C-145, Shenandoah County Wills, courthouse at Woodstock, Va.; 4-84, Frederick County Wills, courthouse at Winchester, Va.; William Beery and Judith Beery Garber, *Beery Family History* (Elgin, Ill., 1957), 42-43.

25. Lemon, *Best Poor Man's Country* (note 1), 67-69, 82, 87-88, 92-94.

26. Joseph F. Beiler, "The Amish in the Pequea Valley Before 1800," *The Diary,* 6 (July 1974), 162-64.

27. Harvey Hostetler, *Descendants of Jacob Hochstetler* (Elgin, Ill., 1912), 29ff.

28. Bern Township Tax Lists, 1767, 1784, BCHS; Grant M. Stoltzfus, *History of the First Amish Mennonite Communities in America* (Harrisonburg, Va., 1958), 46-47.

29. Lebanon and Bethel Township Tax Lists, LCHS; Joseph F. Beiler, "Abraham Drachsel," *The Diary,* 9 (March 1977), 69-72; Joseph F. Beiler, "The Kanagy Family," *The Diary,* 7 (May 1975), 117-20.

30. Caernarvon Township Tax Lists, LCHS; M-269, Lancaster County Deeds, courthouse at Lancaster, Pa.; Stoltzfus, *History of the First Amish Mennonite Communities,* 60-61, 68-70.

31. A-180, A-182, A-183, A-186, A-188, A-190, A-193, A-195, B-312, B-317, Northampton County Deeds, courthouse at Easton, Pa.; P-400, Philadelphia County Wills, courthouse at Philadelphia, Pa.; John Baer Stoudt, *The Life and Times of Colonel John Siegfried* (Northampton, Pa., 1914), 31-32.

32. Brecknock Township and Earl Township Tax Lists, 1756-1789, LCHS.

33. Antrim Township and Letterkenny Township Tax Lists, courthouse at Carlisle, Pa.

34. Frederick County Debt Books, 1753-1773, Maryland Hall of Records, Annapolis, Md.; Edwards, "Materials" (note 21); James O. Lehman, "The Mennonites of Maryland During the Revolutionary War," *MQR,* 50 (July 1976), 200-29; "Proceedings of the Committee of Observation for Elizabeth Town District (Washington County)," *Maryland Historical Magazine,* 12 (December 1917), 341-42.

35. Washington County Direct Tax Assessment, 1783, Maryland Hall of Records, Annapolis, Md.; Richard K. MacMaster, et al., *Conscience in Crisis: Mennonites and Other Peace Churches in America, 1739-1789, Interpretation and Documents* (Scottdale, Pa., and Kitchener, Ont., 1979), 353, note 109.

36. Washington County Direct Tax Assessment, 1783.

37. Ibid.; Roy M. Showalter, *Fragmentary Glimpses of the History of the Mennonites of the Beaver Creek District, Washington County, Maryland* (Maugansville, Md., 1960), 3-13.

38. Washington County Direct Tax Assessment, 1783; MacMaster, *Conscience in Crisis,* 353, note 109 (and for documents concerning Henry Newcomer's involvement in Tory plotting, pp. 492-97); Henry G. Spayth, *History of the Church of the United Brethren in Christ* (Circleville, Ohio, 1851), 37; Herbert C. Bell, *History of Leitersburg District, Washington County, Maryland* (Leitersburg, Md., 1898), 25-26, 136-39. On the Rohrers, see B-64, B-145, Washington County Deeds, courthouse at Hagerstown, Md.; and on Samuel Bechtel, see Washington and Franklin County Mennonite Historical Committee, *A Record of Mennonite Bishops, Ministers, and Deacons That Served and Are Serving in the Washington County, Maryland, and Franklin County, Pennsylvania, Conference Area* (Hagerstown, Md., 1968), 8-9.

39. Lemon, *Best Poor Man's Country* (note 1), 73-74, 82.

40. Ibid., 73-83.

41. Charles D. Spotts, *The People of Bowmansville* (Lancaster, Pa., 1970), 5-7.

42. Brecknock and Earl Township Tax Lists, LCHS.

43. Ibid.; Bowmansville congregation Alms Book, LMHS; MacMaster, *Conscience in Crisis,* 296; Franklin Ellis and Samuel Evans, *History of Lancaster County, Pennsylvania* (Philadelphia, 1883), 674.

44. Ibid., entire note.

45. Beery and Garber, *Beery Family History* (note 24), 7; Manchester and Hellam Township Tax Lists, York County Historical Society, York, Pa.

46. "Petition of the Subscribers Members of the Menonist Church," December 10, 1785, Religious Petitions, Archives Division, Virginia State Library, Richmond, Va., and reproduced in Richard

K. MacMaster, et al., *Conscience in Crisis: Mennonites and Other Peace Churches in America, 1739-1789, Interpretation and Documents* (Scottdale, Pa., and Kitchener, Ont., 1979), 333-34.

47. D-362, D-465, Lancaster County Deeds, courthouse at Lancaster, Pa.; 8-287, 10-90, 12-525, Frederick County Deeds, courthouse at Winchester, Va.

48. H-447, N-175, Northern Neck Patents, Virginia State Library, Richmond, Va.; 4-157, Frederick County Wills, courthouse at Winchester, Va.; B-427, G-446, Shenandoah County Wills, courthouse at Woodstock, Va.; Robert Lee Evans, *History of the Descendants of Jacob Gochenour* (Boyce, Va., 1977), 1-3.

49. Q-30, Q-33, Q-346, S-8, Lancaster County Deeds, courthouse at Lancaster, Pa.; D-21, Shenandoah County Wills, C-275, Shenandoah County Deeds, courthouse at Woodstock, Va.

50. BB-7, Lancaster County Deeds, courthouse at Lancaster, Pa.; 11-329, 13-371, 15-20, Frederick County Deeds, courthouse at Winchester, Va.; A-387, B-328, B-516, C-407, C-421, C-458, Shenandoah County Deeds, B-33 Shenandoah County Wills, courthouse at Woodstock, Va.; Henry Kagy, *The Kagy Family* (Harrisburg, Pa., 1898), 248.

51. Ibid., entire note; "Petition" cited in note 46; 19-331, 19-340, 19-387, 20-319, Augusta County Deeds, courthouse at Staunton, Va.; Brunk, *History of Mennonites in Virginia* (note 13), I, 48-54.

52. Rockingham County Tax Lists, 1785-1788, transcripts, Harrisonburg-Rockingham County Historical Society, Harrisonburg, Va.

53. George M. Smith, "Family and Commercial Farms of Virginia's Lower Valley in 1786: A Preliminary Analysis of the Commission Survey Books, *Hite et al.* v. *Fairfax et al.*," unpublished paper, Shenandoah Valley Historical Institute, James Madison University, Harrisonburg, Va., pp. 8-12; Smith has analyzed two manuscript volumes in the Clark-Hite Papers, Filson Club Library, Louisville, Ky. Samuel Kercheval, *A History of the Valley of Virginia* (Strasburg, Va., 1925), 151.

54. Smith, "Family and Commercial Farms," Appendix, pp. 1-4, 8-11, 17-20, 26-27.

55. Brunk, *History of Mennonites in Virginia,* I, 112, 430-31; Gaius Marcus Brumbaugh, *Genealogy of the Brumbaugh Families* (New York, 1913), 263-71; Oren Frederic Morton, *A History of Rockbridge County, Virginia* (Staunton, Va., 1920), 88-89; John W. Wayland, *A History of Shenandoah County, Virginia* (Strasburg, Va., 1969), 423-24, 583-84; Wust, *Virginia Germans* (note 6), 95-96; Charles F. Kauffman, *A Genealogy and History of the Kauffman-Coffman Families* (Scottdale, Pa., 1940), 287-90; Clement L. Martzloff, ed., "Rev. Paul Henkel's Journal," *Ohio Archeological and Historical Society Publications,* 23 (April 1914), 171.

56. Brunk, *History of Mennonites in Virginia,* I, 430-31.

CHAPTER 5

1. Christopher Schultz, as trans. and quoted in Dietmar Rothermund, *The Layman's Progress: Religious and Political Experience in Colonial Pennsylvania 1740-1770* (Philadelphia, 1961), 62.

2. Rothermund, *Layman's Progress,* ch. 3, esp. 54-55, 143; Russell E. Richey, ed., *Denominationalism* (Nashville, 1977); Laura L. Becker, "Diversity and Its Significance in an Eighteenth Century Town," in Michael Zuckerman, ed., *Friend and Neighbors: Group Life in America's First Plural Society* (Philadelphia, 1982), 208, 215.

3. Joseph E. Illick, *Colonial Pennsylvania: A History* (New York, 1976), 244; David Hawke, *In the Midst of a Revolution* (Philadelphia, 1961), 65; David Hawke, *The Colonial Experience* (New York, 1966), 364-66; Peter Brock, *Pacifism in the United States: From the Colonial Era to the First World War* (Princeton, 1968), 159, 191; quotation from Rebecca Brooks Gruver, *An American History* (New York, 1981), 66.

4. Martin H. Schrag, "The Impact of Pietism Upon Early American Mennonites," in F. Ernest Stoeffler, ed., *Continental Pietism and Early American Christianity* (Grand Rapids, Mich., 1976), 76; J[ohn] C. Wenger, "The Mennonites Establishing Themselves in Pennsylvania," *Mennonite Life,* 2 (July 1947), 28.

5. James T. Lemon, *The Best Poor Man's Country: A Geographical Study of Early Southeastern Pennsylvania* (Baltimore and London, 1972), 7-8; Samuel W. Pennypacker, *Heinrick Pannebecker, Surveyor of Land for the Penns* (Philadelphia, 1894), 55-56; for the 1773 letter, see John C. Wenger, *History of the Mennonites of the Franconia Conference* (Scottdale, Pa., 1938), Appendix I, 395-404.

6. Andrew Ziegler to Israel Pemberton, October 14, 1756, Papers of the Friendly Association, Quaker Collection, Haverford College Library, Haverford, Pa.; *Pennsylvania Gazette,* February 15, 1770; February 22, 1785 petition, manuscript, LCHS.

7. John R. Weinlick, "Moravianism in the American Colonies," in Stoeffler, *Continental Pietism.*

8. *ME,* II, 28-29; Dietmar Rothermund, "Mennonites and Moravians," *MQR,* 32 (January 1958), 73.

9. Levin Theodore Reichel, *The Early History of the Church of the United Brethren (Unitas Fratrum), Commonly Called Moravian* (Nazareth, Pa., 1888), 91-99; John Joseph Stoudt, "Count Zinzendorf and the Pennsylvania Congregation of God in the Spirit: The First American Oecumenical Movement," *Church History,* 9 (September 1940), 371-73.

10. Ibid., entire note; Martin Grove Brumbaugh, *A History of the German Baptist Brethren in Europe and America* (Mount Morris, Ill., 1899), 475; Reichel, *Early History,* 81, 103; Franz Rink and Frederick S. Weiser, "Genealogical Data From the Registers of the Moravian Congregation in the Oley Valley, Berks County, Pennsylvania," *Der Reggeboge/The Rainbow: Quarterly of the Pennsylvania German Society,* 14 (January 1980), 8; Philip C. Coll, *Annals of the Oley Valley* (Reading, 1926), 15ff.; Stoudt, "Count Zinzendorf," 377.

11. Harold S. Bender, *Two Centuries of American Mennonite Literature: A Bibliography of Mennonitica Americana 1727-1928* (Goshen, Ind., 1929, 1; Wenger, *History of the Mennonites of Franconia* (note 5), 316; *Ausbund* (Germantown, Pa., 1742); Robert Friedmann, *Mennonite Piety Through the Centuries: Its Genius and Its Literature* (Goshen, Ind., 1949), 231-32; *Die Ernsthafte Christenpflicht* (Ephrata, Pa., 1745); *Güldene Aepffel in Silbern Schalen* (Ephrata, Pa., 1745).

12. *ME,* III, 527-28; Wenger, *History of the Mennonites of Franconia,* 318-22. Some unbound pages of the *Martyrs Mirror* were still at Ephrata at the time of the revolutionary war, and six soldiers hauled them away in two wagons, probably to use as wadding in their guns!

13. Letter printed in Wenger, *History of the Mennonites of Franconia,* 319; Heinrich Funck, *Ein Spiegel der Tauffe, mit Geist mit Wasser und mit Blut* (Germantown, Pa., 1744), published in English as Henry Funk, *A Mirror of Baptism, with the Spirit, with Water, and with Blood* (Mountain Valley, Va., 1851).

14. John L. Ruth, *'Twas Seeding Time: A Mennonite View of the American Revolution* (Scottdale, Pa., and Kitchener, Ont., 1976), 12-13; Friedmann, *Mennonite Piety,* 231-34; Funk, *A Mirror of Baptism.*

15. Ibid.; Heinrich Funck, *Eine Restitution, Oder eine Erklärung einiger Haupt-puncten des Gesetzes* (Philadelphia, 1763), published in English as Henry Funk, *Restitution, or an Explanation of Several Principal Points of the Law* (Elkhart, Ind., 1915), 9-10.

16. Donald F. Durnbaugh, "Relationships of the Brethren with the Mennonites and Quakers, 1708-1865," *Church History,* 35 (March 1966), 36-39; Donald F. Durnbaugh, comp. and trans., *European Origins of the Brethren: A Source Book on the Beginnings of the Church of the Brethren in the Early Eighteenth Century* (Elgin, Ill., 1958), 340; Donald F. Durnbaugh, "Brethren Beginnings: The Origins of the Church of the Brethren in Early Eighteenth Century Europe," PhD dissertation, University of Pennsylvania (1960).

17. Durnbaugh, "Relationships," 40.

18. Donald F. Durnbaugh, ed., *The Brethren in Colonial America: A Source Book on the Transplantation and Development of the Church of the Brethren in the Eighteenth Century* (Elgin, Ill., 1967), 65-73.

19. Brumbaugh, *History of the German Baptist Brethren* (note 10), 298-310.

20. Charles S. Keyser, *The Keyser Family* (Philadelphia, 1889), 31ff.; Durnbaugh, *Brethren in Colonial America* 175, 209-16.

21. Lida Bowman Meckley, "The Mennonites of York County, Pennsylvania," typewritten paper (1939), copy at LMHS, 93-98; William Beery and Judith Beery Garber, *Beery Family History* (Elgin, Ill., 1957), 31, 39; John A. Brillhart, *Pictorial History of the Brillharts of America* (Scottdale, Pa., 1926), 19. Regarding whether or not Danner was a Dunker or a Mennonite, see note 17 of Ch. 4.

22. Kenneth G. Hamilton, ed., *The Bethlehem Diary, 1742-1744* (Bethlehem, Pa., 1971), I, 92; William J. Hinke, ed., "Diary of Lischy's and Rauch's Journey Among the Reformed Congregations in Pennsylvania," *Reformed Church Review,* 11 (April 1907), 77-82, 89; Rothermund, "Mennonites and Moravians" (note 8), 71, 73; Don Yoder, "Brother Hantsch Visits the Mennonites: A Moravian Diary of 1748," *The Pennsylvania Dutchman,* 3 (November 1, 1951), 1, 5-6.

23. Funk, *Restitution* (note 15), 9-12.

24. Winthrop S. Hudson, *Religion in America* (New York, 1965), 81.

25. Theron F. Schlabach, "Mennonites, Revivalism, Modernity," *Church History,* 48 (December 1979), 402; Lemon, *Best Poor Man's Country* (note 5), 22, 42-64, 98-117.

26. Laura L. Becker, "Diversity and Its Significance in an Eighteenth Century Town," in Michael Zuckerman, ed., *Friend and Neighbors: Group Life in America's First Plural Society* (Philadelphia, 1982), 208; Stephanie Grauman Wolf, *Urban Village: Population, Community, and Family Structure in Germantown, Pennsylvania. 1683-1800* (Princeton, 1980), 151-52, 209-10, 217.

27. *Pennsylvania Gazette,* December 20, 1759, January 17, 1760; William Travis, *History of the Germantown Academy* (Philadelphia, 1882), 8-12; Joseph Jackson, *A History of the Germantown Academy* (Philadelphia, 1910), 34, 63, 71, 261-65; Wolf, *Urban Village,* 239; Concord School Trustees Minute Book, cited in Harry and Margaret Tinckom, *Historic Germantown* (Philadelphia, 1955), 17.

28. Henry Melchoir Muhlenberg, *The Journals of Henry Melchoir Muhlenberg, in Three Volumes,* trans. and ed. by Theodore G. Tappert and John W. Doberstein (Philadelphia, 1942), I, 211; James Y. Heckler, *The History of Harleysville and Lower Salford Township* (first published at Harleysville, Pa., 1886; reprinted at Schwenksville, Pa., 1958, without pagination), 6, 205-207, as paginated in MHL copy; H-319, Lancaster County Deeds, courthouse at Lancaster, Pa.; cf. Jane Evans Best, "Three Bears of Earl Township, Lancaster County," *Pennsylvania Mennonite Heritage,* 4 (October

1981), 14. On the 1775 title, see S1-399, Lancaster County Deeds, courthouse at Lancaster, Pa. A plot of the tract was printed in *The Diary*, 10 (January 1978), 13.

29. William J. Hinke, *A History of the Goshenhoppen Reformed Charge, Montgomery County, Pennsylvania, 1727-1819*, PGSPA, 27 (Lancaster, Pa., 1920), 119. Wirtz was sympathetic to the Moravians and later served as pastor of both Reformed and Presbyterian congregations: Charles H. Glatfelter, *Pastors and People: German Lutheran and Reformed Churches in the Pennsylvania Field, 1717-1793*, vol. 2, *The History* (Breinigsville, Pa., 1981), 95, passim; David R. Johnson, "Christian Strenge, Fraktur Artist," *Der Reggeboge/The Rainbow, Quarterly of the Pennsylvania German Society*, 13 (July 1979), 1-13; Martin G. Weaver, *Mennonites of Lancaster Conference* (Scottdale, Pa., 1931), 206-207. On other non-Mennonite teachers, see Frederick S. Weiser, "The Place of Fraktur Among the Mennonites: An Introduction to the Fraktur Collection of the Lancaster Mennonite Historical Society," *Pennsylvania Mennonite Heritage*, 4 (January 1981), 6-9.

30. Frederick S. Weiser, "IAE SD: The Story of Johann Adam Eyer (1755-1837), Schoolmaster and Fraktur Artist," in Frederick S. Weiser, ed., *Ebbes fer Alle-Ebber, Ebbes fer Dich* (Breinigsville, Pa., 1980), 439-42, 472, 481-506. (IAE SD stands for "Johann Adam Eyer, Schuldiener".)

31. On Dock's reputation, his Mennonitism and his chronology, see especially Gerald C. Studer, *Christopher Dock: Colonial Schoolmaster* (Scottdale, Pa., 1967), 24-26, 59-62, 17-19, 121-22. See also, Martin G. Brumbaugh, *The Life and Works of Christopher Dock* (Philadelphia, 1908), 12-14. (In the absence of clear church membership lists, it is impossible to confirm absolutely that Dock ever formally joined a Mennonite congregation. Yet, except for his surname, there is as much or more reason to assume his membership as there is to assume that of many other persons of the time, persons whose Mennonite membership has not been questioned. And regarding the name "Dock," there were many families now presumed to have been Mennonite in the eighteenth century whose surnames are not present-day "Mennonite" names.) "Skippack Alms Book, 1738-1954," transcribed and trans. by Raymond E. Hollenbach, typescript (1968), copy in Menno Simons Historical Library, Eastern Mennonite College, Harrisonburg, Va., pp. 65-68; deed to Salford meetinghouse property, March 25, 1763, as quoted in Wenger, *History of the Mennonites in Franconia* (note 5), 133; Christoph Dock, *Eine Einfältige und Gründlich Abgefasste Schulordnung . . .* (Germantown, Pa., 1770), printed in facsimile and in English translation in Brumbaugh, pp. 27-156, quotation from p. 131.

32. Christopher Sauer [II], "Publisher's Preface" (to Dock's *Schulordnung*) and letter of Christopher Sauer I to Dielman Kolb, August 3, 1750, reproduced in Brumbaugh, *Life and Works of Christopher Dock*, (in facsimile on pp. 29-35 and in English, pp. 91-97); [Christopher Dock], "Hundert nötige Sitten-Regeln für Kinder," from *Geistliches Magazien* No. 40, reproduced in Brumbaugh (in facsimile on pp. 167-182 and in English, pp. 202-224). For an interesting discussion of Dock's rules, see Wolf, *Urban Village* (note 26), 305-06.

33. Dock, *Eine. . .Schulordnung*; Sauer to Kolb (see note 32), quotation from p. 96 in Brumbaugh's translation.

34. Frederick G. Livingood, *Eighteeth Century Reformed Church Schools*, PGSPA, 38 (Norristown, Pa., 1930), 228-30; Charles L. Maurer, *Early Lutheran Education in Pennsylvania*, PGSPA, 40 (Philadelphia, 1932), 166-67; *ME*, I, 6-7.

35. Undated copy, possibly in the handwriting of Isaac Kolb, Jr., Andreas Kolb Papers, EPMHL; Brumbaugh, *Life and Works of Christopher Dock*, 241-48.

36. B-125 (1755), Lancaster County Wills, courthouse at Lancaster, Pa.; Travis, *History of Germantown Academy* (note 27), 12-13; Tinckom, *Historic Germantown* (note 27), 17.

37. Worcester Township Deed, Henry Rittenhouse to Peter Keyser, et al., October 6, 1739, in I-13, fol. 119, Philadelphia County Deeds, courthouse at Philadelphia, Pa. The majority of these *Vorschriften* are in the Schwenkfelder Library, Pennsburg, Pa.; see also: Studer, *Christopher Dock* (note 31), 179-97, 387-403; Brumbaugh, *Life and Works of Christopher Dock* (note 31), 249; Weiser, "Place of Fraktur" (note 29), 4; I-C, fol. 1357 (1772), Lancaster County Wills, courthouse at Lancaster, Pa.; *Pennsylvania Gazette*, February 15, 1770.

38. See ch. 6.

39. Schlabach, "Mennonites, Revivalism, Modernity" (note 29), 398-415; John B. Frantz, "The Awakening of Religion Among the German Settlers in the Middle Colonies," *William and Mary Quarterly*, 33 (April 1976), 267-80; Sem Sutter, "Mennonites and the Pennsylvania German Revival," *MQR*, 50 (January 1976), 37-57.

CHAPTER 6

1. Frederick S. Weiser and Howell J. Heaney, comps., *The Pennsylvania German Fraktur of the Free Library of Philadelphia: An Illustrated Catalogue*, vol. 2 (Breinigsville, Pa., 1976), plate 948. For a good, quick introduction to *Fraktur* art and its relation esp. to Mennonites, see: Don Yoder, et al., *Pennsylvania German Fraktur and Color Drawings* (printed in Lititz, Pa., 1969); Don Yoder, "Fraktur in Mennonite Culture," *MQR*, 48 (July 1974), 305-42; Henry S. Borneman, *Pennsylvania*

German Illuminated Manuscripts: A Classification of Fraktur-Schriften and An Inquiry into Their History and Art (New York, 1973); Donald A. Shelley, The Fraktur-Writings or Illuminated Manuscripts of the Pennsylvania Germans (printed in Allentown, Pa., 1961).

2. Yoder, "Fraktur," 310-15; Weiser and Heaney, plate 237; Yoder, Pennsylvania German Fraktur, plate 55.

3. Yoder, Pennsylvania German Fraktur, plate 55; Yoder, "Fraktur," 310-13; John Howard Yoder, trans. and ed., The Schleitheim Confession (Scottdale, Pa., and Kitchener, Ont., 1977), 11-12; John H. Yoder, trans. and ed., The Legacy of Michael Sattler (Scottdale, Pa., 1973), 27-54. For an excellent study of the relation of Schleitheim's principles to Franconia Mennonites, see: Beulah S. Hostetler, "Franconia Mennonite Conference and American Protestant Movements, 1840-1940," PhD dissertation, University of Pennsylvania (1977); also an article based on her dissertation—Beulah S. Hostetler, "The Charter as a Basis for Resisting the Impact of American Protestant Movements," MQR. 52 (April 1978), 127-40.

4. Weiser and Heaney, plate 237; Yoder, Pennsylvania German Fraktur, plate 55.

5. Frederick S. Weiser, "The Place of Fraktur Among the Mennonites: An Introduction to the Fraktur Collection of the Lancaster Mennonite Historical Society," Pennsylvania Mennonite Heritage, 4 (January 1981), 6. This Fraktur, signed "From me, Jacob Botz Schoolmaster, March 8, 1775," is illustrated and translated on the front and back cover of the periodical. For a succinct comparision of Anabaptism and Pietism, see: Robert Friedmann, Mennonite Piety Through the Centuries: Its Genius and Its Literature (Goshen, Ind., 1949), 11-12.

6. Ada Kadelbach, "Hymns Written by American Mennonites, '" MQR. 48(July 1974), 343.

7. Dietmar Rothermund, The Layman's Progress: Religious and Political Experience in Colonial Pennsylvania 1740-1770 (Philadelphia, 1961), 62. For a compendium on Pietism in colonial America, esp. in the German churches and sects, see: F. Ernest Stoeffler, ed., Continental Pietism and Early American Christianity (Grand Rapids, Mich., 1976).

8. See ch. 1; ME. II, 634.

9. Die Ernsthaffte Christenflicht (Ephrata, Pa., 1745), 16-32; Friedmann, Mennonite Piety. 189-95.

10. Bowmansville congregation, Lancaster Conference, LMHS; Franconia and Skippack congregations, Franconia Conference, EPMHL; Northkill Amish congregation, Catherine Miller, Grantsville, Md.; Pequea Amish congregation, Joseph F. Beiler, Gordonville, Pa. On the Franconia and Skippack books, see also: John C. Wenger, "The Alms Book of the Franconia Mennonite Church, 1767-1936," MQR. 10 (July 1936), 161-72; and Wenger, "The Alms Book of the Skippack Mennonite Church, 1738-1936," MQR. 10 (April 1936), 138-48.

11. Hans Tschantz Sermon Note Book, portions trans. Noah G. Good, located at LMHS. Measuring about 5 in. by 12 in., this small, cowhide-covered book has entries dated between 1743 and 1765 in the hand of Hans Tschantz, a Mennonite church leader in Lancaster County. The same handwriting of a Hans Schantz signed the 1755 petition to the Pennsylvania General Assembly, MQR. 33 (April 1959), 143-51.

12. "The Skippack Alms Book, 1738-1954," transcribed and trans. by Raymond E. Hollenbach, typescript (1968), copy at Menno Simons Historical Library, Eastern Mennonite College, Harrisonburg, Va.

13. Ibid.; see also: "The Franconia Alms Book," transcribed and trans. by Raymond E. Hollenbach, typescript (1968), same location. Regarding Mennonite serving publicly as overseers of the poor, see for instance: James Y. Heckler, The History of Harleysville and Lower Salford Township (first published at Harleysville, Pa., 1886; reprinted at Schwenksville, Pa., 1958, without pagination), 117-18, 214-22, as paginated in MHL copy.

14. Frederick B. Tolles, "Quietism Versus Enthusiasm: The Philadelphia Quakers and the Great Awakening," PMHB. 69 (January 1945), 26-49; Frederick B. Tolles, Meetinghouse and Countinghouse: The Quaker Merchants of Colonial Philadelphia, 1682-1763 (Chapel Hill, 1948); Jack D. Marietta, "Ecclesiastical Discipline in the Society of Friends," PhD dissertation, Stanford University (1968), 155ff.; Jack D. Marietta, "Wealth, War and Religion: The Perfecting of Quaker Asceticism. 1740-1783," Church History. 43 (June 1974), 230-41; Kenneth L. Carroll, "A Look at the 'Quaker Revival of 1756,' " Church History, 65 (Autumn 1976), 63-80; Howard W. Kriebel, The Schwenkfelders in Pennsylvania. PGSPA. 13 (Norristown, Pa., 1904), 57-64.

15. Martin E. Lodge, "The Crisis of the Churches in the Middle Colonies, 1720-1750," PMHB. 95 (April 1971), 197-98.

16. For some esp. helpful histories of Pietism, see: Dale W. Brown, Understanding Pietism (Grand Rapids, Mich., 1978); James Bemesderfer, Pietism and Its Influence on the Evangelical United Brethren (Annville, Pa., 1966), chs. 1-3; and F. Ernest Stoeffler, The Rise of Evangelical Pietism (Leiden, Netherlands, 1971). Stoeffler, Continental Pietism (note 6), 18ff., 60, 64, 67.

17. Ibid., all sources.

18. John R. Weinlick, "Moravianism in the American Colonies," and Donald F. Durnbaugh, "The Brethren in Early American Church Life," both in Stoeffler, Continental Pietism.

19. See histories of Pietism cited in note 16, and esp. Friedmann, Mennonite Piety (note 4), 11-12.

20. Friedmann, "Gelassenheit," ME. II, 448; Friedmann, Mennonite Piety. 12, 76; Brown, Understanding Pietism. 19-20.

21. "Church Record St. Paul's Lutheran Church, Upper Hanover Township, Montgomery County, Pa.," comp. by Raymond E. Hollenbach and Annette K. Burgert, typescript (1971), 81, copy in author's possession.

22. Morgan Edwards, *Materials Toward a History of the Baptists in Pennsylvania, Both British and German, Distinguished Into First Day Baptists, Keithian Baptists, Seventh Day Baptists, Tunker Baptists, Mennonist Baptists* (Philadelphia, 1770), I, 69. By contrasting Edwards' general statements about Mennonites with his extensive data on the origin, progress, ministry (including biographical sketches), and membership of each Dunker congregation, one may well conclude that Edwards probably obtained what he recorded about Mennonites from Christopher Sauer II or some other well-informed Dunker. Edwards was a great collector of facts, which almost always prove to be quite accurate. It is very unlikely that he would have eliminated the name of a single preacher or congregation or any other small detail about Mennonite church life, had he gotten such detailed information directly from the Mennonites themselves.

23. *ME*, IV, 179; Friedmann, *Mennonite Piety*.

24. [Gerrit Roosen], *Christliches Gemüths-gespräch* (Ephrata, Pa., 1769).

25. E.g., John Shank (1791) "Original Inventory," and Samuel Byers (1790), same, at York County's courthouse, York, Pa.; C-51 (Henry Coghnaur, 1789), E-200 (Jacob Stickley, 1798), D-512 (Benjamin Layman, 1788), and D-88 (Tobias Miley, 1784), Shenandoah County Inventories, at courthouse, Woodstock, Va.; 1-125 (Martin Kauffman, 1749), 4-370 (Henry Coffman, 1771), and 1-12 (Abraham Strickler, 1746), Augusta County Inventories, at courthouse, Staunton, Va.

26. Martin G. Brumbaugh, *The Life and Works of Christopher Dock* (Philadelphia, 1908), 144-46.

27. Ibid., [Gerrit Roosen], *Conversation on Saving Faith for the Young* (Scottdale, Pa., 1941), 120-23.

28. Brumbaugh, *Life and Works*, 102, 131-37.

29. Gerald C. Studer, *Christopher Dock: Colonial Schoolmaster* (Scottdale, Pa., 1967), 359-71; Yoder, "Fraktur," (note 1), 316-17; Kadelbach, "Hymns," (note 6), 343-45.

30. *Ausbund* (Germantown, Pa., 1742); *ME*, II, 879-80; Martin E. Ressler, "Ein Unpartheyisches Gesang-Buch," *Pennsylvania Mennonite Heritage*, 2 (October 1979), 13-19.

31. *Ein Unpartheyisches Gesangbuch* (Lancaster, Pa., 1804).

32. *ME*, II, 880.

33. *Die Kleine Geistliche Harfe der Kinder Zions* (Germantown, Pa., 1803); *ME*, II, 880. The two hymns are *Ausbund* #134 and *Kleine Geistliche* #423, and *Ausbund* #61 and *Kleine Geistliche* #129.

34. John C. Wenger, *History of the Mennonites of the Franconia Conference* (Scottdale, Pa., 1938), 400-401.

35. Friedmann, *Mennonite Piety* (note 4), 141-43; *Die Ernsthafte Christenflicht* (Ephrata, Pa., 1745); *ME*, I, 161.

36. *ME*, IV, 698; Adam Krehbiel to Peter Weber, May 25, 1773, Johannes Neff to Johannes Weber, August 20, 1786, 1-536, Weber Collection, AMC; Gerhard Tersteegen to Abraham Wagner, May 15, 1753, VOC-T1, Schwenkfelder Library, Pennsburg, Pa.; Gerhard Tersteegen, *Geistliches Blumengärtlein inniger Seelen* (Frankfurt and Leipzig, 1727, and then in America, Germantown, Pa., 1747); C-51 (Henry Coghnaur, 1789), E-200 (Jacob Stickley, 1798), D-512 (Benjamin Layman, 1788), and D-88 (Tobias Miley, 1784), Shenandoah County Inventories, at courthouse, Woodstock, Va.; 1-125 (Martin Kauffman, 1749), 4-370 (Henry Coffman, 1771), and 1-12 (Abraham Strickler, 1746), Augusta County Inventories, at courthouse, Staunton, Va.

37. Andrew S. Birkey, *Practitioner of Physick: Dr. Abraham Wagner* (Pennsburg, Pa., 1954), 54-59, 75-76.

38. Charles H. Glatfelder, *Pastors and People: German Lutheran and Reformed Churches in the Pennsylvania Field, 1717-1793*, vol. 2, *The History* (Breinigsville, Pa., 1981), 283-84. Estate inventories of Mennonite preachers in Lancaster and York Counties, Pa.; Washington County, Md.; Augusta and Shenandoah Counties, Va.; located at the courthouses of the respective counties.

39. Heinrich Funck, *Ein Spiegel der Tauffe, mit Geist mit Wasser und mit Blut* (Germantown, Pa., 1744), published in English as Henry Funk, *A Mirror of Baptism, with the Spirit, with Water and with Blood* (Mountain Valley, Va., 1851); Heinrich Funck, *Eine Restitution, Oder eine Erklärung einiger Haupt-puncten des Gesetzes* (Philadelphia, 1763), published in English as Henry Funk, *Restitution, or an Explanation of Several Principal Points of the Law* (Elkhart, Ind., 1915).

40. John L. Ruth, *'Twas Seeding Time: A Mennonite View of the American Revolution* (Scottdale, Pa., and Kitchener, Ont., 1976), 12-13.

41. E1-34, Intestate Records, Lancaster County Wills, courthouse at Lancaster, Pa.

42. Funk, *A Mirror of Baptism*; Funk, *Restitution*.

43. Hans Tschantz Sermon Note Book (note 11).

44. Ibid.

45. Ibid.

46. Ibid.

47. Ibid.

48. Hostetler, "Franconia Mennonite Conference and American Protestant Movements" (note 3); Hostetler, "Charter as a Basis" (note 3), 127-40. Sermon as quoted in John F. Funk, *The Mennonite Church and Her Accusers* (Elkhart, Ind., 1878), 58. The minister was either one Christian Holdeman

of Upper Salford Township or Christian Funk, a bishop and son of Heinrich Funck.
   49. Box 51, John F. Funk Papers, AMC.
   50. Ibid.
   51. Ibid.
   52. Joseph C. Leichty, "Humility: The Foundation of Mennonite Religious Outlook in the 1860s," *MQR*, 54 (January 1980), 27-30.
   53. Ruth, *Twas Seeding Time* (note 40), 12-13.
   54. Funk, *A Mirror of Baptism* (note 39), 12, 79-111; Friedmann, *Mennonite Piety* (note 4), 231-32. For the interpretation of Funck (or Funk) and the comparison with Christian Burkholder given here and in the section that follows I am quite indebted to conversations with Theron F. Schlabach, editor of the Mennonite Experience in America series; indeed, Schlabach furnished some of the language of the text.
   55. Funk, *Restitution* (note 39).
   56. Ibid., 388-93.
   57. Ibid., 223-24, 226.
   58. Ibid., 269.
   59. Ibid., 270-71.
   60. Theron F. Schlabach, "Mennonites, Revivalism, Modernity," *Church History*, 48 (December 1979), 411-15; Leichty, "Humility" (note 52), 5-31.
   61. Christian Burkholder, *Nützliche und Erbauliche Anrede an die Jugend* (Ephrata, Pa., 1804), published in English as *Useful and Edifying Address to the Young*, in *Christian Conversation on Saving Faith, for the Young*, in *Questions and Answers* (Lancaster, Pa., 1857). Burkholder actually wrote the book in 1792.
   62. Friedmann, *Mennonite Piety* (note 4), 241-42.
   63. Schlabach, "Mennonites, Revivalism, Modernity," 411-15.
   64. See chs. 9—10.

CHAPTER 7

   1. Theodore G. Tappert, "The Influence of Pietism in Colonial American Lutheranism," in F. Ernest Stoeffler, ed., *Continental Pietism and Early American Christianity* (Grand Rapids, Mich., 1976), 24; Charles H. Glatfelter, *Pastors and People: German Lutheran and Reformed Churches in the Pennsylvania Field, 1717-1793*, vol. 2, *The History* (Breinigsville, Pa., 1981), 161-69.
   2. Maurice A. Mook, "An Early Amish Colony in Chester County, Pennsylvania," *Mennonite Historical Bulletin*, 16 (July 1955), 1-3.
   3. Martin G. Weaver, *Mennonites of Lancaster Conference* (Scottdale, Pa., 1931), 43-44, 78, 176.
   4. Ibid., 109, 199.
   5. Ibid., 151-53; P-14, P-51, Lancaster County Deeds, at courthouse, Lancaster, Pa.
   6. Henry Melchoir Muhlenberg, *The Journals of Henry Melchoir Muhlenberg, in Three Volumes*, trans. and ed. by Theodore G. Tappert and John W. Doberstein (Philadelphia, 1942), I, 84; Muhlenberg also (III, 181) mentioned a Lutheran elder whose parents had helped to "establish the burial place near the Mennonite Meeting House, and therefore had burial rights there."
   7. "Concerning the Land Investigation Between the Evangelical Lutheran, the Reformed and the Mennonists in Neugoschenhoppen 1796," Archives of St. Paul's Evangelical Lutheran Church, Red Hill, Pa.; "Title to the New Goshenhoppen Church Land, January 29, 1796," and "Deed of the New Goshenhoppen Church, Montgomery County, Pa., February 23, 1796," in William J. Hinke, comp., "Reformed Church Documents, 1790-1809," Archives of the Evangelical and Reformed Historical Society, Lancaster Theological Seminary, Lancaster, Pa.; William J. Hinke, *A History of the Goshenhoppen Reformed Charge, Montgomery County, Pennsylvania, 1727-1819*, PGSPA, 27 (Lancaster, Pa., 1920), 114-16; Amy Histand Gehman and Mary Latshaw Bower, *History of the Hereford Mennonite Congregation at Bally, Pennsylvania* (Bally, Pa., 1936), 7, copies at EPMHL, and BCHS.
   8. 63-750, 46-265, Berks County Deeds, at courthouse, Reading, Pa; Gehman and Bower, 5-7; Edward H. Quinter and Charles L. Allwein, *Most Blessed Sacrament Church, Bally, Pennsylvania* (Bally, Pa., 1976), 34, 40. On the question of whether Mennonites helped the Catholics for pay: "Lower Berks Mennonites," *Reading Eagle*, April 28, 1895, in A. S. Jones Scrapbook, I-219, BCHS, says: "They cooperated with them in building the Catholic Church, hauling building material and giving aid otherwise without charging a cent." But Quinter and Allwein stated that "they were, no doubt, paid a fair wage."
   9. Lida Bowman Meckley, "The Mennonites of York County, Pennsylvania," typewritten paper (1939), copy at LMHS; *Lutherans in Berks County: Two Centuries of Continuous Organized Church Life, 1723-1923* (Kutztown and Reading, Pa., copyright by H. S. Kidd, 1923), 158-59.
   10. E-15, fol. 570, Northhampton County Deeds, at courthouse, Easton, Pa.

11. J[ohn] C. Wenger, *The Mennonite Church in America* (Scottdale, Pa., 1966), 75. Concerning the surviving benches, see Joyce Clemmer Munro, *Franconia Mennonites: The Eighteenth Century Settlement* (Souderton, Pa., 1976), 5.

12. Ibid., 75; Munro, 5-6. The Hereford table still exists, in the Bally Mennonite Meetinghouse, Bally, Pa.

13. Munro, 5-6; Weaver, *Mennonites of Lancaster* (note 3), 199.

14. Weaver, *Mennonites of Lancaster*, 153.

15. Stony Brook Subscription Paper, LMHS.

16. *Dictionary of American Biography*, II, 404-405.

17. Thomas Hughes, *A Journal (1778-1789)* (Cambridge, 1947), 88-89.

18. Ibid.

19. Ibid.

20. Christian Burkholder, *Nützliche und Erbauliche Anrede an die Jugend* (Ephrata, Pa., 1804), published in English as *Useful and Edifying Address to the Young*, in *Christian Spiritual Conversation on Saving Faith, for the Young, in Questions and Answers* (Lancaster, Pa., 1857), 244-45. Burkholder actually wrote the book in 1792.

21. John C. Wenger, *History of the Mennonites of the Franconia Conference* (Scottdale, Pa., 1938), 400.

22. Tappert, (note 1), 24.

23. *ME*, III, 510; Wenger, *History of the Mennonites of Franconia*, 34.

24. *ME*, IV, 72-73.

25. John B. Frantz, "The Awakening of Religion Among the German Settlers in the Middle Colonies," *William and Mary Quarterly*, 33 (April 1976), 267-80; Sem C. Sutter, "Mennonites and the Pennsylvania German Revival," *MQR*, 50 (January 1976), 37-57.

26. John F. Funk, *The Mennonite Church and Her Accusers* (Elkhart, Ind., 1878), 50-53.

27. Hans Tschantz Sermon Note Book, portions trans. by Noah Good, located at LMHS (see note 11 of ch. 6).

28. *ME*, I, 723-24.

29. *ME*, I, 200-201, 220-21.

30. Christian Funk, *A Mirror for All Mankind* (Norristown, Pa., 1814), 10-15.

31. Ibid.

32. Ibid.

33. Wenger, *History of the Mennonites of Franconia* (note 22), 401.

34. Funk, *A Mirror for All Mankind*, 10; Wenger, *History of the Mennonites of Franconia*, 31-32; Tschantz Sermon Note Book (note 27).

35. Tschantz Sermon Note Book.

36. Ibid.; Funk, *Mennonite Church* (note 26), 41, 51-52.

37. Earl Kauffman, "Anabaptist Influence on United Methodism in Central Pennsylvania," *Mennonite Historical Bulletin*, 38 (July 1977), 4-5.

38. Wenger, *History of the Mennonites of Franconia*, 401.

39. Morgan Edwards, *Materials Toward a History of the Baptists in Pennsylvania, Both British and German, Distinguished Into First Day Baptists, Keithian Baptists, Seventh Day Baptists, Tunker Baptists, Mennonist Baptists* (Philadelphia, 1770), I, 95; Tschantz Sermon Note Book.

40. Edwards, *Materials*, I, 95; Earl Township Tax Assessment, 1769, LCHS.

41. Regarding the generalization that virtually every congregation's ministers were well-off financially, the evidence is too extensive to cite; it exists in the tax lists and in other sources used in this book. Theron F. Schlabach, "Mennonites, Revivalism, Modernity," *Church History*, 48 (December 1979), 398-415.

42. Stephanie Grauman Wolf, *Urban Village: Population, Community, and Family Structure in Germantown, Pennsylvania, 1683-1900:R* (Princeton, N.J., 1976), 229-32.

43. Ibid., 214-16; Laura L. Becker, "Diversity and Its Significance in an Eighteenth-Century Pennsylvania Town," in Michael Zuckerman, ed., *Friends and Neighbors: Group Life in America's First Plural Society* (Philadelphia, 1982), 199; Charles S. Keyser, *The Keyser Family* (Philadelphia, 1889), 37-38, 139; A. J. Fretz, *A Brief History of Bishop Henry Funck and Other Funk Pioneers* (Elkhart, Ind., 1899), 629-34; Richard MacMaster, "Goshenhoppen Profiles: Ethnic Congregations in Eastern Pennsylvania," unpublished paper read at meeting of the American Society of Church History, December 27, 1982, Washington, D.C.; Harry and Margaret Tinkcom, *Historic Germantown: From the Founding to the Early Part of the Nineteenth Century . . .* (Philadelphia, 1955), 17.

44. See Ch. 3, material covered by notes 51 and 52, and Ch. 9, material covered by notes 24-30.

45. Richard K. MacMaster, et al., *Conscience in Crisis: Mennonites and Other Peace Churches in America, 1739-1789, Interpretation and Documents* (Scottdale, Pa., and Kitchener, Ont., 1979), 52, 173-74, 196-97, 200-01, 206-10; these pages include printing of various relevant primary documents.

46. Martin Boehm, trans. and quoted in Henry G. Spayth, *History of the Church of the United Brethren in Christ* (Circleville, Ohio, 1851), 28.

47. Spayth, 28-29.

48. *ME*, I, 348. I infer the pattern described from various sources, principally Funk, *A Mirror for All Mankind* (note 30); correspondence in Andreas Kolb Papers, EPMHL; and Wenger, *History of the Mennonites of Franconia* (note 22), 411. Edwards, *Materials* (see note 39), I, 95.

49. Wenger, *History of the Mennonites of Franconia*, 41; Perkiomen, Skippack, and Lower Salford Township tax lists, 1772, Archives Division, Pennsylvania State Historical and Museum Commission, Harrisburg, Pa.

50. Funk, *A Mirror for All Mankind*, 14; Franklin Ellis and Samuel Evans, *History of Lancaster County, Pennsylvania, with Biographical Sketiches* ... (Philadelphia, 1883), 339; account of Hammer Creek congregation, on pp. 5-6 of a notebook in Deacon Jonas W. Bucher Collection, LMHS.

51. October 1781 document in MacMaster, *Conscience in Crisis*, 338-39.

52. Wenger, *History of the Mennonites of Franconia*, 402-404; Funk, *A Mirror for All Mankind*, 10-11.

53. H[arold] S. Bender, "A Swiss Mennonite Document of 1754 ..." *MQR*, 34 (October 1960), 308; *ME*, II, 21-22, 178-81.

54. "Skippack Alms Book, 1738-1954," transcribed and trans. by Raymond E. Hollenbach, typescript (1968), copy at Menno Simons Historical Library, Eastern Mennonite College, Harrisonburg, Va.

55. Schlabach, "Mennonites, Revivalism, Modernity" (note 41), 398-415.

56. Ibid., 405-407; Richard K. MacMaster, "Neither Whig Nor Tory: The Peace Churches in the American Revolution," *Fides et Historia*, 9 (Spring 1977), 8-24.

CHAPTER 8

1. See, e.g., William W. Sweet, *Religion in Colonial America* (New York, 1942), 271-318; Perry Miller and Alan Heimert, comps., *The Great Awakening* (Indianapolis, 1967); Charles H. Maxson, *The Great Awakening in the Middle Colonies* (Gloucester, Mass., 1958); Edwin S. Gaustad, *The Great Awakening in New England* (Gloucester, Mass., 1965).

2. James Hastings Nichols, *Corporate Worship in the Reformed Tradition* (Philadelphia, 1968), 108.

3. James Tanis, "Reformed Pietism in Colonial America," in F. Ernest Stoeffler, ed., *Continental Pietism and Early American Christianity* (Grand Rapids, Mich., 1976), 72.

4. Martin Schrag, "The Impact of Pietism Upon Early American Mennonites," in Stoeffler, *Continental Pietism*, 83.

5. Ibid., 85-86.

6. Martin Lodge, "The Crisis of the Churches in the Middle Colonies, 1720-1750," *PMHB*, 95 (April 1971), 195-220.

7. Ibid., 219.

8. John B. Frantz, "The Awakening of Religion Among the German Settlers in the Middle Colonies," *William and Mary Quarterly*, 33 (April 1976), 266-88.

9. Sem C. Sutter, "Mennonites and the Pennsylvania German Revival," *MQR*, 50 (January 1976), 37-57; Schrag, "Impact of Pietism," 74-122.

10. Isaac Neidig, "A Biography of John Neidig," Archives Division, United Theological Seminary Library, Dayton, Ohio.

11. Christian Burkholder, *Nützliche und Erbauliche Anrede an die Jugend* (Ephrata, Pa., 1804), published in English as *Useful and Edifying Address to the Young*, in *Christian Spiritual Conversation on Saving Faith, for the Young, in Questions and Answers* (Lancaster, Pa., 1857), 221-24. Burkholder actually wrote the book in 1792.

12. Schrag, "Impact of Pietism," 105.

13. Henry G. Spayth, *History of the Church of the United Brethren in Christ* (Circleville, Ohio, 1851), 32.

14. Wesley M. Gewehr, *The Great Awakening in Virginia, 1740-1790* (Gloucester, Mass., 1965), 108-109.

15. Spayth, *History of the United Brethren*, 28-30.

16. Ibid., 31.

17. Kenneth E. Rowe, "Martin Boehm and the Methodists," *Methodist History*, 8 (July 1970), 49-53. Rowe reproduces the text of a statement signed by Boehm on April 12, 1811, published first in *The Methodist Magazine*, 6 (1823), 210-11; Rowe however doubted that the text was an absolutely faithful quotation.

18. Henry Boehm, *Reminiscences: Historical and Biographical* (New York, 1866), 225.

19. Rowe, "Martin Boehm," 52.

20. Tanis, "Reformed Pietism" (note 2), 70; J. Steven O'Malley, *Pilgramage of Faith: The Legacy of the Otterbeins* (Metuchen, N.J., 1973), 166-84.

21. A. W. Drury, *History of the Church of the United Brethren in Christ* (Dayton, Ohio, 1924), 107; Rowe, "Martin Boehm," 52, and *The Methodist Magazine* (see note 17).

22. Boehm's account as reproduced in: Spayth, *History of the United Brethren* (note 13); Rowe, "Martin Boehm"; and *The Methodist Magazine*, 6 (1823), 210-11.

23. A. W. Drury, *The Life of the Rev. Philip William Otterbein* (Dayton, Ohio, 1913), 117-22, 133, 140-41; Spayth, *History of the United Brethren*, 41-42; Sutter, "Mennonites and the Pennsylvania Revivial" (note 9), 42.

24. Lancaster ministers' document as reproduced in John F. Funk, *The Mennnite Church and Her Accusers* (Elkhart, Ind., 1878), 44-45.

25. John Hildt, ed., *The Life and Journal of the Rev'd Christian Newcomer* (Hagerstown, Md., 1834), 3-7; "Records of Saltenreich's Reformed Church," 24, typescript, Evangelical and Reformed Historical Society, Lancaster Theological Seminary, Lancaster, Pa.; Phares Brubaker Gibble, *History of the East Pennsylvania Conference of the Church of the United Brethren in Christ* (Dayton, Ohio, 1951), 23-27.

26. Hildt, *Life and Journal of Christian Newcomer*, 39.

27. Ibid., 5-7, 9, 12-13.

28. Ibid., 22-23, 31, 45, and passim; September 15, 1800, entry, Henry Boehm Journals, 1800-1839, microfilm, United Methodist Church Commission on Archives and History, Drew University Library, Madison, N.J.

29. Hildt, *Life and Journal of Christian Newcomer*, 26, 28, 32, 35, 39-40, 55, and passim.

30. Ibid., 62.

31. Sanford G. Shelter, *Two Centuries of Growth and Struggle* (Scottdale, Pa., 1963), 97.

32. Barton Sensenig, *The Sensineys of America* (Philadelphia, 1943), 16-17, 32-35, 142-43; Gibble, *History of the East Pennsylvania Conference* (note 25), 50-55.

33. Gibble, *History of the East Pennsylvania Conference* (note 25), 40-44, 243-44, 300, 309-11, 340-43; Martin G. Weaver, *Mennonites of Lancaster Conference* (Scottdale, Pa., 1931), 230-31; Roy Showalter, *Fragmentary Glimpses of the Mennonites of the Beaver Creek District, Washington County, Maryland* (Maugansville, Md., 1960); J. Maurice Henry, *History of the Church of the Brethren in Maryland* (Elgin, Ill., 1936), 169-72. The Mt. Lena Mennonite congregation acquired the former Church of the Brethren property in 1966.

34. Robert B. Semple, *A History of the Rise and Progress of the Baptists in Virginia* (Richmond, Va., 1810), 183-87.

35. Ibid., 187-89.

36. Garnett Ryland, *The Baptists of Virginia, 1699-1926* (Richmond, Va., 1955), 56.

37. Boehm's own account of his experiences, given in the form of answers to questions asked by his son Henry in 1811 less than a year before he died on March 23, 1812, was printed first in *The Methodist Magazine*, 6 (1823), 210-12. It was published for the first time from the original manuscript in Rowe, "Martin Boehm" (note 17). Rowe doubted that the *Methodist Magazine* text was an absolutely faithful quotation. For the Mennonite document, see Funk, *Mennonite Church and Her Accusers* (note 24), 41-56.

38. Richard K. MacMaster, et al., *Conscience in Crisis: Mennonites and Other Peace Churches in America, 1739-1789. Interpretation and Documents* (Scottdale, Pa., 1979), 482-92; John Ffirth, *The Experience and Gospel Labors of the Rev. Benjamin Abbott* (Harrisonburg, Va., 1820), 101-105.

39. Document in Funk, *Mennonite Church and Her Accusers*, 41-56.

40. Ibid., 43-45.

41. Schrag, "Impact of Pietism" (note 4), 93-121; Carlton O. Wittlinger, *Quest for Piety and Obedience: The Story of the Brethren in Christ* (Nappanee, Ind., 1978), 551-54; Martin H. Schrag, *The First Brethren in Christ Confession of Faith* (Grantham, Pa., 1974).

42. This is the central theme of Wittlinger, *Quest for Piety and Obedience*.

43. Donegal Township Tax Returns, 1777-1779, LCHS; Schrag, *First Brethren in Christ Confession of Faith* , 14-15; Martin H. Schrag, "Influences Contributing to an Early River Brethren Confession of Faith," *MQR*, 38 (October 1964), 351-52; Martin H. Schrag, "The Brethren in Christ Attitude Toward the 'World'," PhD dissertation, Temple University (1967), 37-54, 104, copies in Messiah College Library, Grantham, Pa. and MHL.

44. Wittlinger, *Quest for Piety and Obedience*, 2-12, 20, 24, 41-44, 551-54; Schrag, "Impact of Pietism," 114; Harold S. Bender, "An Amish Church Discipline of 1779," *MQR*, 11 (April 1937), 163-68.

45. Boehm, quoted in Spayth, *History of the United Brethren* (note 13), 30; Burkholder, *Useful and Edifying Address to the Young* (note 11), 183-84, 188-89, 221-24.

46. Burkholder, *Useful and Edifying Address to the Young*, 221-24.

47. Robert Friedmann, *Mennonite Piety Through the Centuries: Its Genius and Its Literature* (Goshen, Ind., 1949), 11-12, 241-42.

48. Although he did recognize points that Pietism and Anabaptism both emphasized: ibid., 12.

49. For the Brethren in Christ confession, see note 41. Francis Herr, *A Short Explication of the Written Word of God* (Lancaster, Pa., 1790); Herr wrote his pamphlet, published in English and German editions, as a statement against positions taken by the Society of Friends, and drew a response in Benjamin Mason, *Light Rising Out of Obscurity* (Philadelphia, 1790) with neither of the polemics giving any clue to the background or context of the controversy.

50. See esp.: [John Herr], *Life of John Herr* (n.p., n.d., from external evidence published 1827); and Daniel Musser, *The Reformed Mennonite Church, Its Rise and Progress, With Its Principles and Doctrines* (Lancaster, Pa., 1873).

51. Herr, *Short Explication*, 25, 28-33, 39-43.

52. Musser, *Reformed Mennonite Church*, 296.

53. Sutter, "Mennonites and the Pennsylvania German Revival" (note 9), 49-50; A. W. Drury, *Disciplines of the United Brethren in Christ. 1814-1841* (Dayton, Ohio, 1895), 3; Earl H. Kauffman, "Anabaptist Influence on United Methodism in Central Pennsylvania," *Mennonite Historical Bulletin,* 38 (July 1977), 4-5. On how quickly U.B.s, even some with Mennonite background, moved away from Mennonite-style pacifism, see Theron F. Schlabach, "Mennonites, Revivalism, Modernity," *Church History,* 48 (December 1979), 413-14.

CHAPTER 9

1. William Stevens Perry, ed., *Historical Collections Relating to the American Colonial Church* (New York, 1878), II, 315.
2. Guy F. Hershberger, "A Newly Discovered Mennonite Petition of 1755," *MQR,* 33 (April 1959), 143-51.
3. See Shumel N. Eisenstadt, *Modernization: Protest and Change* (Englewood Cliffs, 1966), 14; Theron F. Schlabach, "Mennonites, Revivalism, Modernity," *Church History,* 48 (December 1979), 400.
4. See ch. 1.
5. Schlabach, "Mennonites, Revivalism, Modernity," 404-405; Hermann Wellenreuther, "The Political Dilemma of the Quakers in Pennsylvania 1681-1748," *PMHB,* 94 (April 1970), 158.
6. John Shy, "A New Look at Colonial Militia," *William and Mary Quarterly,* 20 (January 1963), 181.
7. Elizabeth Horsch Bender, "A Pennsylvania Letter of 1745 to Mennonite Leaders in Holland," *Mennonite Historical Bulletin,* 32 (October 1971), 4-5.
8. Ibid.
9. Jack D. Marietta, "Conscience, the Quaker Community, and the French and Indian War," *PMHB,* 95 (January 1971), 4-5.
10. John C. Wenger, *History of the Mennonites of the Franconia Conference* (Scottdale, Pa., 1938), Appendix I, 400; Alan Tully, "Englishmen and Germans: National Group Contact in Colonial Pennsylvania, 1700-1755," *Pennsylvania History,* 45 (July 1978), 254; Charles H. Glatfelter, *Pastors and People: German Lutheran and Reformed Churches in the Pennsylvania Field, 1717-1793,* vol.2, *The History* (Breinigsville, Pa., 1981), 334.
11. Richard K. MacMaster, et al., *Conscience in Crisis: Mennonites and Other Peace Churches in America 1739-1789, Interpretation and Documents* (Scottdale, Pa., and Kitchener, Ont., 1979), 67.
12. Heinrich Funck, *Eine Restitution, Oder eine Erklärung einiger Haupt-puncten des Gesetzes* (Philadelphia, 1763), published in English as Henry Funk, *Restitution, or an Explanation of Several Principal Points of the Law* (Elkhart, Ind., 1915), 270.
13. Ernst Crous, "Nonresistance," *ME,* III, 898.
14. See ch. 1.
15. Lee McCardell, *Ill-Starred General* (Pittsburgh, 1958), 135-42.
16. Hershberger, "A Newly Discovered Mennonite Petition" (note 2).
17. Ibid.
18. *Pennsylvanische Berichte,* May 16, 1755; Lewis Burd Walker, ed., *The Burd Papers: The Settlement of the Waggoners' Accounts Relating to General Braddock's Expedition* (Philadelphia, 1899); Dietmar Rothermund, *The Layman's Progress: Religious and Political Experience in Colonial Pennsylvania 1740-1770* (Philadelphia, 1961), 87, 171.
19. Walker, *The Burd Papers* ; Arthur Graeff, *The Relations Between the Pennsylvania Germans and the British Authorities 1750-1776* (Norristown, Pa., 1939), 87-88.
20. Sylvester K. Stevens and Donald H. Kent, eds., *The Papers of Colonel Henry Bouquet* (Harrisburg, 1940), VI, 146, 168-71.
21. *Minutes of the Provincial Council of Pennsylvania,* commonly called, and hereafter cited as *Colonial Records,* VI, 659-60; *Pennsylvania Archives,* first series, vol. II, 514-15.
22. *Pennsylvania Archives,* eighth series, vol. V, 4101-4103; Jack D. Marietta, "Wealth, War, and Religion: The Perfecting of Quaker Asceticism," *Church History,* 43 (June 1974), 230-41.
23. *Pennsylvanische Berichte,* December 16, 1755, January 16, 1756; H. M. M. Richards, *The Pennsylvania Germans in the French and Indian War, PGSPA,* 15 (Lancaster, Pa., 1906), 199-202.
24. Christopher Sauer to Israel Pemberton, 4 mo. 25, 1756, Papers of the Friendly Association, Quaker Collection, Haverford College, Haverford, Pa.; Milton Ream, "Philadelphia Friends and the Indians," in John M. Moore, ed., *Friends in the Delaware Valley* (Haverford, Pa., 1981), 203-205.
25. Pemberton letters, passim; see esp. Andrew Ziegler to Israel Pemberton, October 14, 1756; Papers of the Friendly Association.
26. Isaac Whitelock to Israel Pemberton, 11 7th mo 1757, Papers of the Friendly Association.
27. Isaac Whitelock to Israel Pemberton, 24th 8th mo 1758, Papers of the Friendly Association.
28. Israel Pemberton to Benjamin Hershey, 14th 1 mo 1761, Papers of the Friendly Association.

29. Friendly Association Account Book, HSP.

30. Israel Pemberton to Commissioners, 7th day, 6th month, 1760 (draft), Pemberton Papers, HSP; Israel Pemberton to Benjamin Hershey (note 28).

31. *Pennsylvania Journal and General Advertizer*, October 6, 1757; *Pennsylvania Gazette*, October 6, 1757; *Pennsylvanische Berichte*, October 15, 1757; *Pennsylvania Archives*, first series, IV, 99.

32. *Pennsylvania Gazette*, July 27, 1758.

33. Documents in H. Frank Eshleman, *Authentic Background and Annals of the Swiss and German Pioneer Settlers of Southeastern Pennsylvania* (Lancaster, Pa., 1917), 325-26.

34. *Pennsylvania Gazette*, July 28, 1763, August 4, 1763.

35. Timothy Green to John Elder, October 5, 1763, John Elder Papers, Dauphin County Historical Society, Harrisburg, Pa.; *Pennsylvania Gazette*, October 20, 1763, November 3, 1763; John Baer Stoudt, *The Life and Times of Colonel John Siegfried* (Northampton, Pa., 1914), 14-18.

36. Edward Shippen to Joseph Shippen, January 5, 1764, Shippen Papers, American Philosophical Society, Philadelphia, Pa.; *Colonial Records* (note 21), IX, 107-108; Hubertis M. Cummings, "The Paxton Killings," *Journal of Presbyterian History*, 44 (December 1966), 241-42; C. H. Martin, "Two Delaware Indians Who Lived on the Farm of Christian Hershey," *Papers Read Before the Lancaster County Historical Society*, 34 (October 1930), 217-20.

37. John R. Dunbar, ed., *The Paxton Papers* (The Hague, 1957), 282; David Sloan, "A Time of Sifting and Winnowing: The Paxton Riots and Quaker Non-Violence in Pennsylvania," *Quaker History*, 66 (Spring 1977), 3-22.

38. James H. Hutson, "The Campaign to Make Pennsylvania a Royal Province, 1764-1770," *PMHB*, 94 (October 1970), 429-54.

39. Samuel Purviance, Jr., to James Burd, September 10, 1764, Shippen Papers, HSP; William J. Mann, *Life and Times of Henry Melchior Muhlenberg* (Philadelphia, 1887), 397-98.

40. Samuel Purviance, Jr., to James Burd, September 20, 1765; Edward Shippen to James Burd, September 16, 1768; William Atlee to James Burd, September 20, 1768; Shippen Papers, HSP.

41. Jack D. Marietta, "A Note on Quaker Membership," *Quaker History*, 54 (Spring 1970), 40-43.

42. John Pendleton Kennedy, ed., *Journals of the House of Burgesses of Virginia* (Richmond, 1906), XI, 256, 267, and XII, 266, 280; in the 1769 document the name was "Jacob Stricklor," and in the 1772 one it was "Jacob Strickley"—presumably referring to the same person, with the surname normally spelled "Strickley," although the 1772 document might have referred to a "Jacob Stickley" instead. Wenger, *History of the Mennonites of Franconia* (note 10), Appendix I, 400.

43. Schlabach, "Mennonites, Revivalism, Modernity" (note 3), 407.

CHAPTER 10

1. Evidence of support for patriots comes from the Association of the Freemen and Inhabitants of the County of Lancaster, May 1, 1775, Curtis Grubb Papers, HSP; the quotations are from a memo Christopher Sauer III prepared for Major Oliver DeLancey, Jr., September 1, 1780, Sir Henry Clinton Papers, William L. Clements Library, University of Michigan, Ann Arbor, Mich., memo published in Richard K. MacMaster, et al., *Conscience in Crisis: Mennonites and Other Peace Churches in America, 1739-1789, Interpretation and Documents* (Scottdale, Pa., and Kitchener, Ont., 1979), 481-82; the final statement has support in Christopher Schultz to Edward Burd, January 10, 1775, Schwenkfelder Library, Pennsburg, Pa.

2. See ch. 9, material covered by note 3.

3. See, for example, a May 25, 1778, letter from Pennsylvania Assembly's Vice-President Bryan, *Pennsylvania Archives*, second series, III, 169-70.

4. Peter Force Collection, Library of Congress, Washington, D.C.; *Pennsylvania Archives*, first series, VIII, 328-29; both documents published in MacMaster, *Conscience in Crisis*, 246-47, 348-49. *Memoirs of the Life of John Adlum* (Chicago, 1968), 7-10; Abraham Reincke Beck, ed., "Extracts from the Brethren's Congegation and House Diaries of the Moravian Church at Lititz, Pennsylvania," *Penn-Germania*, 1 (November/December 1912), 491.

5. Jacob Stull to Samuel Beall, Jr., August 5, 1775, Force Collection; Dunmore (Shenandoah) County Committee Petition, July 23, 1776, Legislative Petitions, Archives Division, Virginia State Library, Richmond, Va.

6. MacMaster, *Conscience in Crisis*, 213-17.

7. *Pennsylvania Archives*, second series, XIII, 283-86, 294; see also, MacMaster, *Conscience in Crisis*, 217-19.

8. Schultz to Biddle, January 12, 1775, Schwenkfelder Library, Pennsburg, Pa.

9. Israel Pemberton to John Fothergill, February 15, 1775, Pemberton Papers, HSP.

10. Theodore Thayer, *Pennsylvania Politics and the Growth of Democracy, 1740-1776* (Harrisburg, 1953), 166.

11. MacMaster, *Conscience in Crisis*, 295-97; see two lists of Lancaster non-associators in the Force Collection (note 4), lists published in *Conscience in Crisis*, 250-55.

12. MacMaster, *Conscience in Crisis*, 234; quotation from a June 3, 1775 letter from Edwd. Shippen, et al. to the Lancaster County Committee, Yeates Family Correspondence, HSP, letter published in *Conscience in Crisis*, 237-41.

13. Regarding Newcomer, see fol. 78, Lancaster County Committee Minute Book, Force Collection; regarding Wenger, see fol. 126, the same minute book; regarding the two "chief persons" of the Mennonites, see that June 3, 1775, letter (note 12). See also MacMaster, *Conscience in Crisis*, 298-300.

14. MacMaster, *Conscience in Crisis*, 221; July 1, 1775, meeting, Lancaster County Committee Minute Book, fol. 45, Force Collection; quotation from an appeal to Congress, "Form of subscription for the Menonists &c" which was either presented or drafted at the meeting, Yeates Family Correspondence, HSP; both documents published in *Conscience in Crisis*, 245-46.

15. August 5, 1775, letter, J. Stull to Saml. Beall Junr., Force Collection, published in MacMaster, *Conscience in Crisis*, 270-271; regarding petitions to the Pa. Assembly, see: *Pennsylvania Archives*, eighth series, VIII, 7473-7490, 7505-7507; and *Conscience in Crisis*, 260-66. See also: *Conscience in Crisis*, 221-23; John A. Neuenschwanger, *The Middle Colonies and the Coming of the American Revolution* (Port Washington, N.Y., 1974), 179.

16. "A short and sincere Declaration": printed first as a broadside, in English and German, by Henry Miller of Philadelphia, published in John C. Wenger, *History of the Mennonites of the Franconia Conference* (Scottdale, Pa., 1938), Appendix IV, 409-10, and in MacMaster, *Conscience in Crisis*, 266-67.

17. Ibid.; Theron F. Schlabach, "Mennonites, Revivalism, Modernity," *Church History*, 48 (December 1979), 406; Acts 5: 29.

18. *Pennsylvania Archives*, eighth series, VIII, 7473-7490, 7505-7507; MacMaster, *Conscience in Crisis*, 222-24; Neuenschwanger, *Middle Colonies*, 179; *Pennsylvania Gazette* (Philadelphia), December 6, 1775; *Proceedings of the Conventions of the Province of Maryland, Held at the City of Annapolis in 1774, 1775 and 1776* (Baltimore, 1836), 74.

19. *Proceedings of the Conventions of Maryland*, 74-75; *Virginia Statutes at Large*, IX, 139; *Colonial and State Records of North Carolina*, X, 200.

20. MacMaster, *Conscience in Crisis*, 282-83, 324-26.

21. Regarding Pennsylvania Amish and Mennonites, see the two lists of Lancaster non-associators (note 11), and MacMaster, *Conscience in Crisis*, 295-97; regarding Virginia Mennonites: on communications with the government, see two petitions dated November 2, 1784 and December 10, 1785, Religious Petitions, Virginia State Library, Richmond, Va., documents published in *Conscience in Crisis*, 332-34; on the military officer's complaint, see "A List of Alexander Machir's Company in the Strasb[ur]g District [Shenandoah County]," Twyman Williams Papers, Virginia State Library.

22. Donald F. Durnbaugh, ed., *The Brethren in Colonial America: A Source Book on the Transplantation and Development of the Church of the Brethren in the Eighteenth Century* (Elgin, Ill., 1967), 353-54; MacMaster, *Conscience in Crisis*, 297; "Appeal Docket for Lancaster County, 1777-1779," Records of the Office of the Comptroller General, Military Accounts, Box 23, Record Group 4, Archives Division, Pennsylvania State Historical and Museum Commission, Harrisburg, Pa.

23. MacMaster, *Conscience in Crisis*, 297-300. For one example of Mennonite involvement in the wagon service, see *Pennsylvania Archives*, second series, III, 375-77, document also published in *Conscience in Crisis*, 346-47.

24. Clemency File, Records of the Supreme Executive Council, Pennsylvania State Historical and Museum Commission, Harrisburg, Pa., documents published in MacMaster, *Conscience in Crisis*, 474-77.

25. 1773 Skippack letter in Wenger, *History of the Mennonites of Franconia* (note 16), Appendix I, 395-404.

26. John L. Ruth, *'Twas Seeding Time: A Mennonite View of the American Revolution* (Scottdale, Pa., and Kitchener, Ont., 1976), is, overall, an eloquent statement on this point.

27. Thayer, *Pennsylvania Politics* (note 10), 177.

28. Ibid., 179; Owen S. Ireland, "The Ethnic-Religious Dimension of Pennsylvania Politics, 1778-1779," *William and Mary Quarterly*, 30 (July 1973), 423-48; Dietmar Rothermund, "The German Problem of Colonial Pennsylvania," *PMHB*, 84 (January 1960), 9-10; Thayer, *Pennsylvania Politics*, 103-104; Wayne L. Bockleman and Owen S. Ireland, "The Internal Revolution in Pennsylvania: An Ethnic-Religious Interpretation," *Pennsylvania History*, 41 (April 1974), 125-60.

29. Christian Funk, *A Mirror for All Mankind* (Norristown, Pa., 1814), 7-8.

30. E. Wickersham to James Burd, November 6, 1776, Burd Papers, HSP.

31. Thayer, *Pennsylvania Politics*, 196.

32. *Journals of the House of Representatives of Pennsylvania, 1776-1781* (Philadelphia, 1782), I, 66.

33. *Pennsylvania Statutes at Large*, IX, 110-13. Similar legislation passed in Virginia, *Virginia Statutes at Large*, IX, 281-82, X, 194.

34. Clemency File, Records of the Supreme Executive Council, Pennsylvania State Historical and Museum Commission, Harrisburg, Pa., document published in MacMaster, *Conscience in Crisis* (note 1), 421-23.

35. Ibid., entire note, 414-15.

36. George Bryan to John Thorne, May 25, 1778, *Pennsylvania Archives*, second series, III, 169-70, letter also published in MacMaster, *Conscience in Crisis*, 429-30.

37. *Pennsylvania Statutes at Large*, IX, 238-45.

38. MacMaster, *Conscience in Crisis*, 397-402; Yoder/Bachman petition, Clemency File, Records of the Supreme Executive Council, Pennsylvania State Historical and Museum Commission, Harrisburg, Pa., document published in *Conscience in Crisis*, 441-42.

39. Ibid., entire note; Kenneth G. Hamilton, *John Ettwein and the Moravian Church During the Revolutionary Period* (Bethlehem, Pa., 1940), 296; MacMaster, *Conscience in Crisis*, 439.

40. June 2 and August 6, 1778, entries, Christopher Marshall Diary, HSP; MacMaster, *Conscience in Crisis*, 398-99.

41. *Pennsylvania Packet & General Advertiser*, December 9, 1778; MacMaster, *Conscience in Crisis*, 405, 438-39, 447.

42. Hamilton, *John Ettwein*, 290-91; MacMaster, *Conscience in Crisis*, 426.

43. See government documents, September 1780 through January 1781, regarding the conspiracy to obstruct the collection of taxes; Records of the Supreme Executive Council and Records of the Supreme Court, Pennsylvania State Historical and Museum Commission, Harrisburg, Pa.; documents published in MacMaster, *Conscience in Crisis*, 384-88. "A Sentimental Journal of 21 Days" by "Three Serjeants of The 23rd Regiment," Sir Henry Clinton Papers (note 1), document published in *Conscience in Crisis*, 502-504.

44. MacMaster, *Conscience in Crisis*, 288.

45. Funk, *A Mirror for All Mankind* (note 29), 10. Funk wrote this account in 1807.

46. Ibid., 10-15.

47. Ibid., 12-13.

48. Ibid., 13-15; for an article that makes a great deal of Funk's patriotism, based on his advice to give to Congress that which belonged to Congress, see Edward Shannon, "Christian Funk, the Mennonite Patriot," *Daughters of the American Revolution Magazine*, 115 (March 1981), 212-14, 279.

49. Pemberton to Fothergill (note 9).

50. Arthur J. Mekeel, *The Relation of the Quakers to the American Revolution* (Washington, D.C., 1979), 191-92.

51. Ibid., 192.

52. Ibid.

53. Moses Brown to Anthony Benezet, 2nd 10th mo 1780, reproduced in George Brookes, *Friend Anthony Benezet* (Philadelphia, 1937), 429-35.

54. John Carmichael, *A Self-Defensive War Lawful* (Philadelphia, 1775), 17-18.

55. Wenger, *History of the Mennonites of Franconia* (note 17), 345-51; *ME*, II, 424.

56. *Pennsylvania Archives*, second series, III, 461-63, document also published in MacMaster, *Conscience in Crisis* (note 1), 335-36.

57. Robert Levers to The Honorable William Moore Esquire, October 31, 1781, Military Affairs (1779-1782), Northampton County, Pennsylvania State Historical and Museum Commission, Harrisburg, Pa., letter published in MacMaster, *Conscience in Crisis*, 338-39.

58. All three accounts (1785, 1807, 1809) are in Funk, *A Mirror for All Mankind* (note 29). 1785 quotations on 25-27.

59. Ibid., 32-34.

60. Ibid., 30.

61. S. Duane Kauffman, "Miscellaneous Amish Mennonite Documents," *Pennsylvania Mennonite Heritage*, 2 (July 1979), 16; cf. "Huguenot-Dunkard-Mennonite Discipline," *Pennsylvania German*, 3 (April 1902), 91, which attributes this document to John Jacob Kauffman and dates it 1760.

62. Mrs. Wm. [Donna Schmucker] DeCosta, *The Schmucker Family: 1752-1974* (Chicago, 1974), 6-7; C. Z. Mast, "Imprisonment of the Amish in the Revolutionary War," *Mennonite Historical Bulletin*, 13 (January 1952), 6-7. Regarding authenticity, see: John R. Smucker, *Jonas Smucker: Ancestors and Descendants* (n.p., 1975), 124; MacMaster, *Conscience in Crisis*, 519, note 19.

63. Regarding Kauffman, see Clemency File, Records of the Supreme Executive Council, Pennsylvania State Historical and Museum Commission, Harrisburg, Pa., documents published in MacMaster, *Conscience in Crisis*, 474-77. Bern Township tax list of 1779, BCHS; see also *Conscience in Crisis*, 466.

64. Sauer memo prepared for Major DeLancey (note 1).

65. Ibid.

66. Ruth, *'Twas Seeding Time* (note 26), 152, 206-209. The final sentence is borrowed almost verbatim from 152.

67. Sir Guy Carleton Papers, Colonial Williamsburg Foundation, Research Archives, Williamsburg, Va., documents published in MacMaster, *Conscience in Crisis*, 498-500.

68. Mekeel, *Relation of Quakers* (note 50), 326.

69. Richard A. Overfield, "A Patriot Dilemma: The Treatment of Passive Loyalists and Neutrals in Revolutionary Maryland," *Maryland Historical Magazine*, 68 (Summer 1973), 140-59; Richard A. Overfield, "The Loyalists of Maryland During the American Revolution," PhD dissertation, University of Maryland (1968); Mekeel, *Relation of Quakers* ; Henry J. Young, "The Treatment of the Loyalists in

Pennsylvania." PhD dissertation, John Hopkins University (1955); Robert McCluer Calhoon, *The Loyalists in Revolutionary America 1760-1781* (New York, 1973).

70. Wallace Brown, "Loyalists and Non-Participants," in John Parker and Carol Urness, eds., *The American Revolution: A Heritage of Change* (Minneapolis, 1975), 126-27; Richard K. MacMaster, "Neither Whig Nor Tory: The Peace Churches in the American Revolution," *Fides et Historia*, 9 (Spring 1977), 8-24.

71. Ruth, *'Twas Seeding Time*, passim, esp. 205-10.

72. See the two Virginia Mennonite petitons cited in note 21, and MacMaster, *Conscience in Crisis*, 531-36.

73. Peter Brock, *Pacifism in the United States: From the Colonial Era to the First World War* (Princeton, 1968), 335, 390-91, 409; Guy F. Hershberger, "Mennonites in the Civil War," *MQR*, 18 (July 1944), 131-44.

74. Frank H. Epp, *Mennonites in Canada, 1786-1920: A History of a Separate People* (Toronto, 1974), 56, 93-97, 100-103; *Pennsylvania Gazette*, (Philadelphia), February 4, 1789, document printed in MacMaster, *Conscience in Crisis*, 449.

75. Epp, *Mennonites in Canada*, 56-57; L. J. Burkholder, *A Brief History of the Mennonites in Ontario* . . . (Markham, Ont., 1935), 29-35; Marcus Lee Hansen and John Bartlet Brebner, *The Mingling of the Canadian and American Peoples* (New Haven, 1940), 83-86.

76. MacMaster, *Conscience in Crisis*, 529; *Virginia Statutes at Large*, XI, 252-53.

77. Alan Kreider, "Lancaster County Politics, 1799-1810," *Journal of the Lancaster County Historical Society*, 67 (Winter 1963), 35.

78. Francis Herr, *A Short Explication of the Written Word of God* (Lancaster, Pa., 1790), 40.

AFTERWORD

1. Hector St. John de Crèvecoeur, *Letters from an American Farmer*, (London and New York, 1912), 43, 48-51.

2. Michael Zuckerman, ed., *Friends and Neighbors: Group Life in America's First Plural Society* (Philadelphia, 1982), 15.

3. James T. Lemon, *The Best Poor Man's Country: A Geographical Study of Early Southeastern Pennsylvania* (Baltimore and London, 1972), 188-91.

4. ME, II, 303-04, 309-11, and IV, 111; Jean Séguy, "Religion and Agricultural Success: . . . French Anabaptists from the Seventeenth to the Nineteenth Centuries," *MQR*, 47 (July 1973), 181-205, 221-24; Cornelius J. Dyck, ed., *An Introduction to Mennonite History: A Popular History of the Anabaptists and the Mennonites* (Scottdale, Pa., and Kitchener, Ont., 2nd. ed., 1981), 50, 150.

5. Lemon, *Best Poor Man's Country*, 179-183; Duane E. Ball and Gary M. Walton, "Agricultural Productivity Changes in Eighteenth-Century Pennsylvania," *Journal of Economic History*, 36 (March 1976), 102-17; Jackson T. Main, *The Social Structure of Revolutionary America* (Princeton, N. J., 1965), 7-8; Robert D. Mitchell, *Commercialism and Frontier: Perspectives on the Early Shenandoah Valley* (Charlottesville, Va., 1977), 4-8. (According to Mitchell, "commercial tendencies were present from the beginning of permanent settlement and were the most dynamic element in the emerging pioneer economy. . . . The earliest phase of development included local commercialism within the context of unspecialized general farming and a brisk land market. . . . As population increased and spread out and as links with external market centers were consolidated, the proportion of farm products used for subsistence declined.") On the importance of alternate occupations, see Duane E. Ball, Dynamics of Population and Wealth in Eighteenth-Century Chester County, Pennsylvania," *Journal of Interdisciplinary History*, 6 (Spring, 1976), 621-44; James A. Henretta, *The Evolution of American Society, 1700-1815: An Interdisciplinary Analysis* (Lexington, Mass., 1973), 107.

6. James T. Lemon, "Early Americans and Their Social Environment," *Journal of Historical Geography*, 6 (April 1960), 120.

7. James T. Lemon, "The Weakness of Place and Community in Early Pennsylvania," in James R. Gibson, ed., *European Settlement and Development in North America* (Toronto, 1978), 200-03; Lemon, "Early Americans," 121.

8. James A. Henretta, "Families and Farms: Mentalité in Pre-Industrial America," *William and Mary Quarterly*, 35 (January 1978), 4, 15-16; Lemon, *Best Poor Man's Country* (note 3), 221.

9. Lemon, "Early Americans," 116-17; Lemon, *Best Poor Man's Country* (note 3), 216, 81-82, 71; Martin H. Brackbill, "The Manor of Conestoga in the Colonial Period," *Papers of the Lancaster County Historical Society*, 42 (1938), 26.

10. Alan Tully, "Patterns of Slaveholding in Colonial Pennsylvania: Chester and Lancaster Counties, 1729-1758," *Journal of Social History*, 6 (Spring 1973), 284-305.

11. Johann Georg Schroeder, "Exorcism—1789," *Der Reggeboge/The Rainbow: Quarterly of the Pennsylvania German Society*, 9 (Summer 1975), 9; Sanford Shetler, *Two Centuries of Struggle and Growth: A history of Allegheny Mennonite Conference* (Scottdale, Pa., 1963), 97.

12. Crèvecoeur, *Letters* (note 1), 48-51.

13. Robert Friedmann, *Mennonite Piety Through the Centuries: Its Genius and Its Literature* (Goshen, Ind., 1949), 35-36.

14. Richard K. MacMaster with Samuel L. Horst and Robert F. Ulle, *Conscience in Crisis: Mennonites and Other Peace Churches in America, 1739-1789. Interpretations and Documents* (Scottdale, Pa., and Kitchener, Ont., 1979), 332-33, 535; Kenneth W. Keller, *Rural Politics and the Collapse of Pennsylvania Federalism* (Philadelphia: The American Philosophical Society, 1982); Alan Kreider, "Lancaster County Politics: 1799-1810," *Journal of the Lancaster County Historical Society,* 67 (Winter 1963), 35; Theron F. Schlabach, "Mennonites, Revivalism, Modernity 1683-1850," *Church History,* 48 (Dec 1979), 408-09.

15. William Duke, *Observations on the Present State of Religion in Maryland* (Baltimore, 1795), 33.

16. See Edwin Scott Gaustad, *Dissent in American Religion* (Chicago, 1973), 130-41, esp. 133-34.

BIBLIOGRAPHICAL ESSAY

I. PRIMARY SOURCES IN EUROPE

European sources for eighteenth-century Mennonite emigration to North America are extensive.the papers of Dutch Mennonites' Commission for Foreign Needs in the Municipal Archives at Amsterdam, covering the many years from 1671 to 1810, form the principal collection on which any study of this subject must rely. For a variety of reasons Mennonites and Amish from various places in Europe, especially in regions along the Rhine River, looked to the Commission for assistance. To help them emigrate the Commission frequently provided organization, financial aid, and influence with governmental authorities. Therefore Commission officials corresponded extensively with Mennonite pastors and others in the Palatinate, in various German states, and in America. About the 1880s a Dutch Mennonite minister and scholar, Jacob G. de Hoop Scheffer, organized the Commission's papers and included them in *Inventaris der Archiefstukken* (Amsterdam, 1883), I, 176-463. Others have retained his numbering system for transcripts or translations of portions of the larger collection in their possession. A microfilm copy of the collection is in Bethel College Library, North Newton, Kansas, and transcripts of many of the important items used for this study are in the so-called "Dutch Papers" in the Historical Society of Pennsylvania in Philadelphia.

In places such as Krefeld, Hamburg, and the Palatinate, other American Mennonite correspondence has surfaced in church and family archives. An important 1773 letter, written by ministers at Skippack and reporting on the state of the Mennonite Church in North America (including some remarks about the Amish), is an example. A Dutch manuscript of this letter is in the Schwenkfelder Library, Pennsburg, Pa.; an English translation made from the Dutch is available in, among other locations, an appendix to John C. Wenger, *History of the Mennonites of the Franconia Conference* (Telford, Pa.: Franconia Mennonite Historical Society, 1937). Until recently no version of the letter in its original German was known to exist, but Nelson P. Springer of the Mennonite Historical Library at Goshen College, Goshen, Ind., has discovered a copy extant in the Mennonitische Forschungsstelle in the Palatinate at the Weierhof, near Marnheim, Germany; a transcript of the German text and a translation from it into English by Elizabeth Horsch Bender are now in the hands of the editor of *The Mennonite Quarterly Review*. Also in the Mennonitische Forschungsstelle is the Peter Weber

Collection, consisting of papers (including considerable correspondence from Mennonites in America) that are especially useful for documenting the progress of Pietism among Mennonites. A descriptive calendar of this collection appears in the *Mennonite Historical Bulletin*, 43 (April, July 1982), 1-4, 5-8.

A source for names of Mennonite ministers is the *Naamlyst van de Professoren en Predikanten der Doopsgezinden*, an irregular series running at least from 1757 to 1829 giving names of Mennonite leaders in the Netherlands; in the 1770s and 1780s the lists included information on some North American congregations and leaders. A file of these pamphlets, or typescript facsimiles, can be found in various Mennonite libraries, including the Menno Simons Historical Library at Eastern Mennonite College, Harrisonburg, Va. Finally, in her *Eighteenth Century Emigrants from German-Speaking Lands to North America—Volume I: The Northern Kraichgau* (Breinigsville, Pa., 1983), Annette Kunselman Burgert included considerable information and translation of contemporary documents related to Mennonite emigration from that Kraichgau region.

II. Primary Sources in America

A. Private Collections

American Mennonite sources are surprisingly limited. Miss Catherine Miller, Grantsville, Md., owns a Northkill Amish alms book from Berks County, Pa., covering years beginning in 1768, and Joseph F. Beiler, Gordonsville, Pa., has a similar book from the Conestoga-Pequea Amish congregation, covering years beginning in 1774. The Lancaster Mennonite Historical Society, Lancaster, Pa., vigorously collects genealogical and historical materials of Mennonites in its region, yet virtually its only eighteenth-century materials are an alms book and related papers (1754-1790) of the Bowmansville Mennonite congregation, Bowmansville, Pa., plus a sermon notebook of Lancaster County bishop Hans Tschantz (d. 1776). Congregational alms books from Skippack (1738-1917) and from Franconia (1742-1930), farther east in Pennsylvania, are in another vigorously administered regional Mennonite archive, the Eastern Pennsylvania Mennonite Historical Library at Christopher Dock High School, Lansdale, Pa.; microfilm and typed transcripts are available at the Menno Simons Historical Library just mentioned, in the Archives of the Mennonite Church mentioned above, and elsewhere. Accounts of contributions and expenditures of the Germantown congregation, and records of communicants and of the poor fund, were once complete for 1770-1790. In the 1880s they were in the hands of Daniel Kolb Cassel, but unfortunately, they are now only partially extant, in quotations in Cassel's *History of the Mennonites* . . . (Philadelphia: the author, 1887), and in transcripts in the John F. Funk Papers, Archives of the Mennonite Church.

Although Amish and Mennonite settlers from Pennsylvania to North Carolina were economically active, only a few accounts or ledgers of their farms and businesses have survived. The Lancaster County Historical Society, Lancaster, Pa., has some receipts from Martin Mylin (d. 1749), Mennonite leader and county commissioner, and an account book with some entries by a Mennonite deacon named Jacob Hartman (d. 1790). The Eastern Pennsylvania Mennonite Historical Library, mentioned above, has a more substantial collection of account books, weaving pattern books, and other business records dating from the mid-eighteenth century in its Godschalk-Godschalk, Jacob Wismer, and Isaac Kolb collections. The Kolb papers include letters written by a Mennonite schoolmaster in Northampton County and others relating to troubles in the Germantown congregation in the 1790s; the Wismer and Godschalk collections have been translated by Raymond E. Hollenbach, and made available on microfilm. Account books of a Mennonite family named Stauffer, of the Bally-Boyertown area, are in the Schwenkfelder Library, Pennsburg, Pa., some of them only in transcript form. The Stauffer papers include records kept in Alzey in the Palatinate and a partial journal of the family's migration to Pennsylvania in 1709. Account books of a Clemens family are available, as translated by Hollenbach, in Alan G. Keyser, ed., *The Account Book of the Clemens Family of Lower Salford Township, Montgomery County, Pennsylvania, 1749-1857* (Breinigsville, Pa.: The Pennsylvania German Society, 1975). Amish family papers, including a diary kept on board the *Charming Nancy* in 1737, were published by S. Duane Kauffman in "Miscellaneous Amish Mennonite Documents," *Pennsylvania Mennonite Heritage*, 2 (July 1979), 12-16, using transcripts at the Historical Society of Pennsylvania, Philadelphia, as his source. Frederick S. Weiser has published the roll book of a schoolmaster who taught in Mennonite congregations, the original manuscript being in a collection of the Goshenhoppen Historians, Salford, Pa.; it appears on pp. 481-506 of Weisner's "IESD: The Story of Johann Adam Eyer, Schoolmaster and Fraktur Artist," a chapter in Albert F. Buffington et al., *Ebbes fer Alle—Ebber Ebbes fer Dich: Something for Everyone, Something for You* ... (Breinigsville, Pa.: The Pennsylvania German Society, 1980), 435-506. And papers of Mennonite Bachmans and Kageys who lived in Virginia's Shenandoah County at the time of the American revolution may be found in the Henry Kagey Papers at Duke University, Durham, N.C.

B. Public Records
State. A major source for the Mennonite experience in America must be public records. A substantial body of eighteenth-century Pennsylvania records are most accessible in the series of *Colonial*

Records and the nine series of *Pennsylvania Archives*, published under the auspices of the Commonwealth of Pennsylvania beginning in 1838. Records of the Provincial Council and the Assembly and related correspondence and records of the Supreme Executive Council and other revolutionary war committees are included in these published volumes. The third series of the *Pennsylvania Archives* printed tax returns for each county in the state between 1768 and 1785 in some cases, but primarily between 1779 and 1781. Revolutionary War muster rolls were published in the second series, together with records of many county Committees of Safety.

A series published by the state of Maryland since 1883, *Archives of Maryland*, includes many comparable records. The Virginia State Library has published *Journals of the House of Burgesses of Virginia 1619-1776* (Richmond, Va., 1905-1915) and the *Calendar of Virginia State Papers and Other Manuscripts* (Richmond, Va., 1875-1894). Considerable material on early North Carolina is available in *Colonial Records of North Carolina* (Raleigh, N.C., 1886-1890). Some Mennonite material can be gleaned from each of these published sources, but the Pennsylvania records yield by far the most.

Valuable unpublished material for Mennonite history exists in national and especially state archives. In the Library of Congress, Washington, D. C., is a very extensive set of materials on the American revolution, the Peter Force Collection; although gathered in the 1830s for possible publication in *American Archives*, much of the collection remains unprinted. The Archives Division of the Pennsylvania Historical and Museum Commission in Harrisburg, Pennsylvania, offered rich deposits for this study. The records of the Council of Safety and those of the Supreme Executive Council, notably the Clemency File (all in Record Group 27), included much unpublished material on Mennonites in the American revolution, as did the records of the Pennsylvania Supreme Court and the records of the Courts of Oyer and Terminer (Record Group 33). The Minute Books and General Assembly File (Record Group 7) had fewer items. The Records of the Office of Comptroller General (Record Group 4) included Forfeited Estates Accounts and Militia Fine Exonerations which were of limited value, and the Military Accounts, Associators, and Militia, in Record Group 4, which aided this study far more. The usefulness of these collections has been greatly increased by the publication of Gerald R. Brunk, Mary Jean Kraybill, and James O. Lehman, *A Guide to Select Revolutionary War Records: Pertaining to Mennonites and Other Pacifist Groups in Southeastern Pennsylvania* (Harrisonburg, Va.: Eastern Mennonite College Department of History, 1974).

County. Tax assessments, deeds, wills, and other documents in county courthouses reveal much about the life of Amish and Mennonite settlers. The records of Chester County, Pennsylvania, in the courthouse at West Chester, are complete from the first settlement in 1683. Tax lists are relatively complete from the 1750s for Lancaster County, Pa., including present Dauphin and Lebanon counties, and are readily accessible on microfilm in the Lancaster County Historical Society, Lancaster, Pa., and in the Archives Division of the Pennsylvania Historical and Museum Commission, Harrisburg, Pa. A comparable record is extant for Berks County, with tax lists from 1754 on deposit in the Berks County Historical Society, Reading, Pa., and available on microfilm there and in the Archives Division just mentioned. The York County Historical Society, York, Pa., has complete tax lists from the 1750s onward and has also made them available on microfilm. Tax lists for Philadelphia County, including present Montgomery County, are complete only from 1780, in the Municipal Archives, City Hall, Philadelphia, Pa. Earlier tax assessments for some townships are in the Historical Society of Pennsylvania, also in Philadelphia, Pa. Records of Cumberland County, including tax records from the 1750s, are in complete form in the courthouse at Carlisle, Pa.

Maryland records have been centralized at the Hall of Records in Annapolis. Debt books in the Land Office records, particularly those from 1753 to 1773, are a convenient source for study of Mennonite settlement, as is detailed information on landowners in Washington County, where Mennonites generally located, to be found in records of a state tax assessment in 1783. Deeds and wills in the Washington County Court House in Hagerstown supplement this information. A statement of the number and name of the tenants on the Manor of Conococheague on the Potomac in present Washington County and the value of their improvements, included in a Maryland Loyalist's claim in England for compensation after the revolution, exists in photostat in the Western Maryland Room of the Washington County Public Library in Hagerstown, Md.

In Virginia, tax records from 1782 onward for the counties where Mennonites lived are readily accessible in the Archives Division of the Virginia State Library, Richmond, Va. The records of Augusta County, which included Rockingham and substantial parts of present-day Shenandoah and Page counties, are complete and well indexed in the Augusta County Court House at Staunton. Records of Rockingham County were seriously damaged in 1864, but those that remain are now in the courthouse at Harrisonburg. The Shenandoah County Court House, Woodstock, Va., has complete records for its county from 1772. The Frederick County Court House in Winchester is the depository for information dating from settlement of the oldest county in the Lower Shenandoah Valley. George M. Smith has compiled records of surveys made in 1786 by Jonathan Clark in Shenandoah and Frederick counties for use in the lawsuit of *Hite* v. *Fairfax*. Now in the Clark-Hite Papers, Filson Club Library, Louisville, Ky., these surveys include detailed information on land use, household size, and sizes and uses of buildings. *Wills, etc.; the problem of identification.* Public records offer information on the regions where Mennonites and Amish lived, but seldom identify members of any religious communion. In very few localities can one identify Mennonites and Amish with certainty. A document compiled in Earl Township for the Lancaster County Committee of Safety, now in the Peter Force Collection described above, does identify persons of military age in 1775 by religion. A similar record of "Menonists and Dunkers" exists for Washington County, Md., extant in the Papers of the Elizabeth Town District of the Frederick County Committee of Safety, Maryland Historical Society, at Baltimore. A petition from "members of the Menonist Church" in 1785, in the Archives Division of the Virginia State Library, Richmond, Va., identified many Virginia Mennonites. All three were published in *Conscience in Crisis: Mennonites and Other Peace Churches in America, 1739-1789, Interpretations and Documents* (Scottdale, Pa., and Kitchener, Ont.: Herald Press, 1979), whose writer-editors were Richard K. MacMaster, with Samuel L. Horst and Robert F. Ulle.

In the absence of official church records, some Amish and Mennonite individuals can be identified from sources such as deeds for meetinghouse properties, congregational alms books, and specific provisions made in wills; for example, the sources contain bequests to the poor of Mennonite congregations or requirements that appraisers of the estate be members of the congregation in question. Such provisions were more frequent in the wills of Mennonites and other so-called sectarian peoples than in those of "church" peoples. The records of Lancaster, Montgomery (Philadelphia), and York counties in Pennsylvania, and of Shenandoah and Augusta counties in Virginia provide many examples.

III. SECONDARY WORKS

A. Immigration, Settlement, and the Founding of Congregations

The Dutch scholar de Hoop Scheffer, organizer of the papers of the Commission on Foreign Needs, was the first historian to use materials in the Mennonite Church Archives in Amsterdam extensively for the history of Mennonite immigration to North America. Under the title "Mennonite Emigration to Pennsylvania," Samuel W. Pennypacker translated an article by Scheffer and published it in the *Pennsylvania Magazine of History and Biography,* 2 (1878), 117-138. In *Historical and Biographical Sketches* (Philadelphia, 1883) and in an earlier work on local history, *Phoenixville and Its Vicinity from the Settlement to 1871* (Philadelphia, 1872), Governor Pennypacker included considerable material on Mennonites in Germantown and elsewhere in southeastern Pennsylvania. Also, having discovered and translated the 1773 letter from Andrew Ziegler and other Skippack Mennonites to their brethren in Krefeld, Pennypacker published that document in *Hendrick Pannebecker, Surveyor of Lands for the Penns* (Philadelphia, 1894). Daniel Kolb Cassel's *History of the Mennonites* . . . (Philadelphia: the author, 1887) is useful chiefly for source material included in this study. Cassel also published genealogies of Pennsylvania Mennonite families. C. Henry Smith published several books important to this study, especially *The Mennonite Immigration to Pennsylvania in the Eighteenth Century* (Norristown, Pa.: The Pennsylvania German Society, 1929). Flawed only by a tendency common among Mennonite historians to assume too easily that certain surnames on ship lists identified their bearers as Amish or Mennonite, that book made good use of Dutch Mennonite and other European sources. Henry Frank Eshleman, *Historic Background and Annals of the Swiss and German Pioneer Settlers of Southeastern Pennsylvania* (Lancaster, Pa.: n. p., 1917; reprinted, Baltimore: Genealogical Publishing Company, 1969) included English translations of some letters to the Dutch Mennonite Commission for Foreign Needs and other primary materials on immigration. Marianne Wokeck, "The Flow and Composition of German Immigration to Philadelphia, 1727-1755," *Pennsylvania Magazine of History and Biography*, 105 (July 1981), 249-278, has helped to put Mennonite immigration in context.

Important both for the European background and for Germantown's beginnings are: Harold S. Bender, "Founding of the Mennonite Church in America at Germantown, 1683-1708," *Mennonite Quarterly Review*, 7 (October 1933), 227-250; William I. Hull, *William Penn and the Dutch Quaker Migration to Pennsylvania* (Swarthmore, Pa.: Swarthmore College, 1935); and Friedrich Nieper, *Die ersten deutschen Auswanderer von Krefeld nach Pennsylvanien* (Ansbach: C. Brügel & Sohn, 1940). Jon Butler's *Power, Authority, and the Origins of the American Denominational Order: the English Churches in the Delaware Valley* (Philadelphia: The American Philosophical Society, 1978) and his earlier article, "Into Pennsylvania's Spiritual Abyss: The Rise and Fall of the Later Keithians, 1693-1703," *Pennsylvania Magazine of History and Biography*, 101 (1977), 151-170, provided a context for Mennonite beginnings at Germantown. J. William Frost, *The Keithian Controversy in Early Pennsylvania* (Norwood, Pa.: Norwood Editions, 1980), made this link explicit.

Significant details about Amish settlers can be found in Grant M. Stoltzfus, *History of the First Amish Mennonite Communities in America* (Harrisonburg, Va.: Eastern Mennonite College, 1958), a limited-edition work extant in various Mennonite research libraries and elsewhere; but the most recent scholarship on Amish beginnings in Europe and America is synthesized in John A. Hostetler, *Amish Society* (Baltimore: The Johns Hopkins University Press,

1980). Joseph F. Beiler, an Amish historian living at Gordonville, Pa., has published numerous valuable articles on Amish settlements in eighteenth-century America in the Amish periodical *The Diary*, published at Gordonville.

Klaus Wust, *The Virginia Germans* (Charlottesville, Va.,: The University Press of Virginia, 1969), is an outstanding survey of German settlers in western Virginia based on extensive research. Two much older works, Samuel Kercheval, *A History of the Valley of Virginia* (Winchester, Va.: S. H. Davis, 1833; Strasburg, Va.: Shenandoah Publishing House, 1925) and John W. Wayland, *The German Element of the Shenandoah Valley of Virginia* (Charlottesville: The Michie Co., 1907), are still valuable also for the contexts of Mennonite settlement and early life in Virginia.

B. Religious Histories

Harold S. Bender, *Two Centuries of American Mennonite Literature: A Bibliography* (Goshen, Indiana: Mennonite Historical Society, 1929), is a most excellent guide to published source materials of certain kinds. A very comprehensive listing of published sources by and about Mennonites throughout the world is a two-volume work, Nelson P. Springer and A. J. Klassen, compilers, *Mennonite Bibliography, 1631-1961* (Scottdale, Pa., and Kitchener, Ont.: Herald Press, 1977). And of course a standard source is *The Mennonite Encyclopedia: A Comprehensive Reference Work on the Anabaptist-Mennonite Movement* (Hillsboro, Kan., Newton, Kan., and Scottdale, Pa.: Mennonite Brethren Publishing House, Mennonite Publication Office, and Mennonite Publishing House, 4 vols., 1955-1959).

The historiography of the Mennonite experience in North America began with the publication of Morgan Edwards, *Materials Towards a History of the Baptists in Pennsylvania both British and German, Distinguished into Firstday Baptists, Keithian Baptists, Seventh day Baptists, Tuncker Baptists, Mennonist Baptists* (Philadelphia: printed by Joseph Crukshank and Isaac Collins, 1770). Edwards also compiled, but never published, "Material Towards a History of the Baptists in the Province of Maryland," and "Materials Towards a History of the Baptists in the Province of Virginia," which also contain sections on the "Menonist-Baptists"; the original manuscripts are in Crozer Seminary Library, Chester, Pa., and a microfilm edition is available in various research libraries and from the Historical Commission of the Southern Baptist Convention, Nashville, Tennessee. Edwards learned far less about the Mennonites than he did about the "Tuncker Baptists" (present Church of the Brethren), but he did include a congregational list of 1708 from Germantown and other valuable information. Robert Proud, *The History of Pennsylvania* (Philadelphia: Zachariah Poulson, 1798), and William M. Mervine, ed., *History of the Province of Pennsylvania by Samuel Smith* (Philadelphia: The Colonial Society of Pennsylvania, 1913), represent other eighteenth-century comments on Mennonite origins, immigration, and settlement.

John C. Wenger, *History of the Mennonites of the Franconia Conference* (Telford, Pa.: Franconia Mennonite Historical Association, 1937), is an example of a denominational conference history written by a professional and making excellent use of primary sources; a forthcoming book by John L. Ruth will also offer well-researched, extensive detail on Franconia Mennonites. Martin G. Weaver, *Mennonites of Lancaster Conference* (Scottdale, Pa.: Mennonite Publishing House, 1931), is primarily concerned with districts, congregations, and preachers, but provides much information not available elsewhere. Harry A. Brunk, *History of Mennonites in Virginia, 1727-1900* (Staunton, Va.: McClure Press, 1959; Vol. I of 2 vols.), is a very valuable work on Mennonite settlement and development outside of Pennsylvania. A well-written history of Mennonites in Canada, often providing background and context as well as interpretations relevant to the present study, is Frank H. Epp, *Mennonites in Canada, 1786-1920: The History of a Separate People* (Toronto: Macmillan of Canada, 1974; Vol. I of a multivolume series).

Theron F. Schlabach, "Mennonites, Revivalism, Modernity— 1638-1850," *Church History*, 48 (December 1979), 398-415, is an interpretive essay on the Mennonite's moving toward greater modernity in some areas of life and persistence in traditional values in others. Several works which focus on later times, yet provide insights for understanding eighteenth-century Mennonites and Amish are: Joseph Liechty, "Humility, The Foundation of the Mennonite Religious Outlook in the 1860s," *The Mennonite Quarterly Review*, 54 (January 1980), 5-31; a dissertation by Sandra F. Cronk, "Gelassenheit: The Rites of the Redemptive Process in Old Order Amish and Old Order Mennonite Communities" (PhD dissertation, University of Chicago, 1977), and an article by her with the same title in *The Mennonite Quarterly Review*, 60 (January 1981), 5-44; Beulah Hostetler, "Franconia Mennonite Conference and American Protestant Movements, 1840-1940" (PhD dissertation, University of Pennsylvania, 1977); and Rodney J. Sawatsky, "History and Ideology: American Mennonite Identity Definition Through History" (PhD dissertation, Princeton University, 1977). A classic work on Mennonite literature and thought from the sixteenth to the nineteenth century, including material on Mennonites in America, is Robert Friedmann, *Mennonite Piety Through the Centuries* (Goshen, Indiana: Mennonite Historical Society, 1949), which strongly argues that Pietistic influence did much to move Mennonites away from the faith of sixteenth-century Swiss Anabaptists.

A new kind of religious history is represented in J. William Frost's work entitled *The Quaker Family in Colonial America: A Portrait of the Society of Friends* (New York: St. Martin's Press, 1973), and in the work of Jack Marietta, most notably his "Ecclesiastical Discipline in the Society of Friends" (PhD dissertation, Stanford University, 1968), and two of his articles, "Conscience, the Quaker Community, and the French and Indian War," *Pennsylvania Magazine of History and Biography* 95 (January 1971), 3-27, and his "Wealth, War and Religion: The Perfecting of Quaker Asceticism, 1740-1783," *Church History*, 43 (June 1974), 230-41. Relevant to this study as writings on a related pacifist group, these works are also models of how religious history ought to be researched and written. Martin E. Lodge, "The Crisis of the Churches in the Middle Colonies, 1720-1750," *Pennsylvania Magazine of History and Biography*, 95 (1971), 192-210, and John B. Frantz, "The Awakening of Religion among the German Settlers in the Middle Colonies," *William and Mary Quarterly*, 33 (April 1976), 266-288, are helpful on the Great Awakening; Sem C. Sutter, "Mennonites and the Pennsylvania German Revival," *The Mennonite Quarterly Review*, 50 (January 1976), 37-57, relates the colonial Great Awakening directly to Mennonites. Dietmar Rothermund, *The Layman's Progress: Religious and Political Experience in Colonial Pennsylvania, 1740-1770* (Philadelphia, Pa.: University of Pennsylvania Press, 1961), makes masterful use of literary sources and offers insightful interpretation. The present writer is in deep debt to F. Ernest Stoeffler, ed., *Continental Pietism and Early American Christianity* (Grand Rapids, Mich.: William B. Eerdmans Publishing Company, 1976)—especially to Martin Schrag's excellent essay, "The Impact of Pietism Upon Early American Mennonites." A valuable parallel source is Charles H. Glatfelter, *Pastors and People: German Lutheran and Reformed Churches in the Pennsylvania Field* (Breinigsville, Pa.: The Pennsylvania German Society, 1981).

Significant for understanding Mennonites as well as Dunkers in early America are Donald F. Durnbaugh's works in Church of the Brethren history, notably *European Origins of the Brethren* (Elgin, Illinois: The Brethren Press, 1958), his sourcebook *The Brethren in Colonial America* (Elgin, Illinois: The Brethren Press, 1967), and "Relationships of the Brethren with Mennonites and Quakers," *Church History*, 35 (March 1966), 35-59. Dietmar Rothermund, "Mennonites, Moravians, and Salvation in Colonial America," *The Mennonite Quarterly Review*, 32 (January 1958), 70-73, deals with the neglected area of Mennonite-Moravian relationships. Kenneth G. Hamilton, *John Ettwein and the Moravian Church During the Revolutionary Period* (Bethlehem, Pa.: Moravian Historical Society, 1940), sheds much light on these relations in a time of stress for both denominations.

C. Recent Regional Studies:
Geography, Economics, Ethnicity, Demography, etc.

Guiding the research and writing of this book have been con-
cepts and methodology developed in several recent studies. Gary
Nash's *Quakers and Politics in America, 1681-1727* (Princeton,
N.J.: Princeton University Press, 1968) opened new vistas on early
Pennsylvania society. James T. Lemon and Gary Nash, "The Dis-
tribution of Wealth in Eighteenth Century America: A Century of
Change in Chester County, Pennsylvania, 1693-1802," *Journal of
Social History*, 2 (1968), 1-24, demonstrated what could be done
with local records. Expanding on the same kind of material, James
T. Lemon published *The Best Poor Man's Country: A Geographical
Study of Early Southeastern Pennsylvania* (Baltimore, Md.: The
Johns Hopkins Press, 1972)—a book invaluable to Mennonite his-
tory and one whose methods and data especially underlie
substantial sections of the present work. In "Families and Farms:
Mentalitè in Pre-Industrial America," *William and Mary Quarterly*,
35 (January 1978), 3-32, James A. Henretta challenged some of
Lemon's conclusions but did not set them aside. An article by
Duane E. Ball, "Dynamics of Population and Wealth in Eighteenth
Century Chester County, Pennsylvania," *Journal of Interdisciplinary History*, 6 (1976), 621-644, offered closely related perspectives. Stephanie Grauman Wolf's excellent *Urban Village: Population, Community, and Family Structure in Germantown, Pennsylvania* (Princeton, N.J.: Princeton University Press, 1976) is a work
which influenced this book far more than the number of footnote
references suggests. That is true also of Robert D. Mitchell's *Commercialism and Frontier: Perspectives on the Early Shenandoah
Valley* (Charlottesville, Va.: University Press of Virginia, 1977). Two
especially significant essays are included in James R. Gibson, ed.,
European Settlement and Development in North America (Toronto: University of Toronto Press, 1978): one by Mitchell entitled
"The Formation of Early American Cultural Regions," and one by
Lemon, "The Weakness of Place and Community in Early Pennsylvania."

The ethnic and religious diversity of the Middle Colonies provided the context of the Mennonite experience in eighteenth-
century America. This diversity received special attention in Alan
Tully, *William Penn's Legacy: Politics and Social Structure in Pro-
vincial Pennsylvania, 1726-1755* (Baltimore, Md.: The Johns
Hopkins University Press, 1978); in an article by Tully, "Englishmen
and Germans: National Group Contact in Colonial Pennsylvania,
1700-1755," *Pennsylvania History*, 45 (July 1978), 237-256; and in
Michael Zuckerman, ed., *Friends and Neighbors: Group Life in
America's First Plural Society* (Philadelphia: Temple University
Press, 1982). Laura L. Becker, "Diversity and Its Significance in an
Eighteenth-Century Pennsylvania Town," is a particularly valuable

chapter of *Friends and Neighbors*. A very helpful survey of the literature on the region is Douglas Greenberg, "The Middle Colonies in Recent American Historiography," *William and Mary Quarterly*, 36 (July 1979), 396-427. Among articles on specialized topics useful to this study are: Duane E. Ball and Gary M. Walton, "Agricultural Productivity Changes in Eighteenth-Century Pennsylvania," *Journal of Economic History*, 36 (March 1976), 102-117; Alan Tully, "Literacy Levels and Educational Development in Rural Pennsylvania 1729-1755," *Pennsylvania History*, 39 (October 1972), 301-312; and Tully, "Patterns of Slaveholding in Colonial Pennsylvania: Chester and Lancaster Counties, 1729-1758," *Journal of Social History*, 6 (Spring 1973), 284-305.

D. Church-State Relations,
and Mennonites and Other Pacifists in Wartime

Substantial literature exists on the relations of the nonresistant sects with the state. A Harvard College honors thesis by Wilbur J. Bender in 1926, "Pacifism Among the Mennonites, Amish Mennonites, and Schwenkfelders of Pennsylvania to 1783," was published in *The Mennonite Quarterly Review*, 1 (July, October 1927), 23-40, 21-48, and reprinted as *Nonresistance in Colonial Pennsylvania* (Scottdale, Pa.: Mennonite Publishing House, 1934). Guy F. Hershberger, *Nonresistance and the State: The Pennsylvania Quaker Experiment in Politics, 1682-1756* (Scottdale, Pa.: Mennonite Publishing House, 1936), and his "Pacifism and the State in Colonial Pennsylvania," *Church History*, 8 (March 1939), 54-74 still provide valuable insight. Robert L. D. Davidson, *War Comes to Quaker Pennsylvania, 1682-1756* (New York: Columbia University Press, 1957) and Ralph L. Ketcham, "Conscience, War, and Politics in Colonial Pennsylvania," *William and Mary Quarterly*, 20 (October 1963), 412-439, are also useful, but lack the interpretive skill shown by Jack D. Marietta in his two articles mentioned above. Marietta accepted a thesis concerning the nature and changes of the Quaker peace testimony and the political effects, a thesis to be found in Hermann Wellenreuther, "The Political Dilemma of the Quakers in Pennsylvania 1681-1748," *Pennsylvania Magazine of History and Biography*, 94 (April 1970), 135-172, and developed more fully by Wellenreuther in *Glaube und Politik in Pennsylvania 1681-1776: Die Wandlungen der Obrigkeitsdoktrin und des "Peace Testimony" der Quaker* (Köln: Böhlau Verlag, 1972). Other significant articles on peace-church related aspects of church and state issues include: Walter Klaassen, "Mennonites and War Taxes," *Pennsylvania Mennonite Heritage*, 1 (April 1978) 17-23; James O. Lehman, "The Mennonites of Maryland During the Revolutionary War," *The Mennonite Quarterly Review*, 50 (July 1976), 200-229; Roger E. Sappington, "North Carolina and the Non-Resistant Sects During the American War of Independence,"

Quaker History, 60 (Spring 1971), 29-47; Glenn Weaver, "Mennonites During the French and Indian War," *Mennonite Historical Bulletin*, 16 (April 1955), 2-3; and John C. Wenger, "Franconia Mennonites and Military Service," *The Mennonite Quarterly Review*, 10 (October 1936), 222-245. An overview can be found in Peter Brock, *Pacifism in the United States: From the Colonial Era to the First World War* (Princeton, N.J. : Princeton University Press, 1968), and in Richard K. MacMaster et al., *Conscience in Crisis*, mentioned above.

Wayne L. Bockleman and Owen S. Ireland, "The Internal Revolution in Pennsylvania: An Ethnic-Religious Interpretation," *Pennsylvania History*, 41 (April 1974), 125-160, and Ireland, "The Ethnic-Religious Dimension of Pennsylvania Politics, 1778-1779," *William and Mary Quarterly*, 30 (July 1973), 423-448, have revised older views of the American revolution and provided clearer understanding of the Mennonite experience. For the context of Mennonite political involvement in colonial Pennsylvania, James H. Hutson's studies are helpful and interpretive, namely his "Benjamin Franklin and Pennsylvania Politics, 1751-1755: A Reappraisal," *Pennsylvania Magazine of History and Biography*, 93 (July 1969), 303-371; "The Campaign to Make Pennsylvania a Royal Province," *Pennsylvania Magazine of History and Biography*, 94, 95 (October 1970, January 1971), 427-463, 28-49; and *Pennsylvania Politics, 1746-1770* (Princeton, N.J.: Princeton University Press, 1972). Kenneth W. Keller, *Rural Politics and the Collapse of Pennsylvania Federalism* (Philadelphia: The American Philosophical Society, 1982), carried the ethnic-religious dimension in Pennsylvania politics to 1800, and into the century to be covered by Volume II of the *Mennonite Experience in America* series.

INDEX

329

THE AUTHOR

Richard K. MacMaster is executive director of the Shenandoah Valley Historical Institute, located at James Madison University, and is engaged in a two-year study of "Cultural Pluralism in the Shenandoah Valley of Virginia, 1730-1810" funded by The National Endowment for the Humanities.

He has taught American history and American religious history as an associate professor at James Madison University since 1976. He has also taught at Eastern Mennonite College and Western Carolina University. He did his undergraduate work at Fordham University, earning an A.B. in 1958 and an M.A. in history in 1962. He received his doctorate in history from Georgetown University in 1968.

He is coauthor with Samuel L. Horst and Robert F. Ulle of *Conscience in Crisis: Mennonites and Other Peace Churches in America. 1739-1789* (Herald Press, 1979). He is author of *The Five George Masons* (Charlottesville: University of Virginia Press, 1975).

He lives in Bridgewater, Virginia, with his wife, Eve Bowers MacMaster and their three children.